ATM and Cell Relay Service for Corporate Environments

Daniel Minoli
DVI Communications, Inc.
and
New York University

Michael Vitella
Bell Communications Research, Inc.

McGraw-Hill, Inc.

New York   San Francisco   Washington, D.C.   Auckland   Bogotá
Caracas   Lisbon   London   Madrid   Mexico City   Milan
Montreal   New Delhi   San Juan   Singapore
Sydney   Tokyo   Toronto

Library of Congress Cataloging-in-Publication Data

Minoli, Daniel, date.
  ATM and cell relay service for corporate environments / Daniel
Minoli, Michael Vitella.
      p.   cm.—(McGraw-Hill series on computer communications)
  Includes index.
  ISBN 0-07-042591-4
  1. Asynchronous transfer mode. 2. Broadband communication
systems. 3. Local area networks (Computer networks). 4. Integrated
services digital networks. I. Vitella, Michael. II. Title.
III. Series.
TK5105.M557   1994
621.382—dc20   94-10290
                                                              CIP

1 2 3 4 5 6 7 8 9 0   DOC/DOC   9 0 9 8 7 6 5 4

ISBN 0-07-042591-4

*The sponsoring editor for this book was Marjorie Spencer, the editing
supervisor was Stephen M. Smith, and the production supervisor was
Donald F. Schmidt. It was set in Century Schoolbook by Inkwell
Publishing Services.*

Printed and bound by R. R. Donnelley & Sons Company.

Portions copyright © 1993 The ATM Forum.

For Gino, Angela,
Anna,
Emmanuelle, Emile, and Gabrielle

And for Debbie, Kevin, and Christopher

Contents

Preface

Asynchronous transfer mode (ATM) is a high-bandwidth, low-delay switching and multiplexing technology now becoming available to the corporate telecom planner. It can be utilized for enterprise networks that use completely private or completely public communication facilities, or are hybrid. ATM is the technology of choice for evolving B-ISDN public networks as well as next-generation LANs. Cell relay service is one of the key services enabled by ATM. ATM supports speeds of 155 Mbits/s and 622 Mbits/s now, and will go as high as 10 Gbits/s in the future. As an option, ATM will operate at DS3 (45 Mbits/s) and lower speeds.

Cell relay service supports a variety of new applications such as desk-to-desk video conferencing, multimedia conferencing, multimedia messaging, distance learning, imaging tasks (including computer-aided design and manufacturing), animation, and cooperative work (for example, joint-document editing).

ATM is now rapidly being put into place to allow high-speed, seamless interconnection of LANs and WANs. Cell relay is one of two "fastpacket" technologies that have been introduced recently. A variety of vendors is now readying end-user products for market introduction and many products are already on the market for a year or so. A number of carriers either already provide services or are poised to do so in the future.

This book aims at explaining the technology and ensuing benefits to the user community, particularly students, network managers, equipment developers, communication software developers, information providers, and sophisticated end users.

After defining cell relay concepts and positioning cell relay service applicability in enterprise networks (Chap. 1), the text proceeds to examine the underlying ATM apparatus (Chap. 2), followed by a discussion of adaptation aspects (Chap. 3). The need for signaling is covered in Chap. 4. Cell relay service itself is discussed next (Chaps. 5 and 6). In addition to cell relay service, ATM can support other fastpacket services, as discussed in Chap. 7. Support of basic multimedia (voice and $n \times 64$ kbits/s video) is discussed next (Chap. 8). Chapter 9 discusses

ATM LANs. Cell relay management issues are discussed in Chap. 10. Commercial equipment and service availability are covered in Chap. 11, and user migration strategies from the current technology base are examined in Chap. 12.

Acknowledgments

The following Bellcore colleagues are warmly thanked for their moral support of this undertaking: A. R. Tedesco, S. M. Walters, J. J. Amoss, H. J. Fowler, D. Rouse, L. S. Newman, and J. E. Holcomb. The following individuals are also thanked: Dick Vigilante, New York University; Lance Lindstrom, DataPro Research Corporation; Tony Rizzo, *Network Computing* magazine; Joanne Dressendofer, IMEDIA; Mark Laubach, HP Laboratories; Anne Ferris, The ATM Forum; Al Tumolillo, Probe Research Corporation; and Ben Occhiogrosso, DVI Communications, Inc. Special thanks to Bellcore for the moral encouragement to proceed with this book.

This book does not reflect *any* policy, position, or posture of Bell Communications Research, Inc., or the Regional Bell Operating Companies. The writing of this book was the independent effort of the authors, and all ideas expressed are strictly those of the authors. Data pertaining to the public switched network are based on publicly available information. References to vendor products, services, and equipment are intended solely as examples of the *state of the art* of a given technology, and have not been verified by the vendors. Any such references are not intended and should not be construed as recommendations or endorsements of any product, service, or equipment.

Daniel Minoli
Michael Vitella

1

ATM and
Cell Relay Service—
An Overview

1.1 Introduction

1.1.1 Background

Asynchronous transfer mode (ATM), as the term is used in current parlance, refers to a high-bandwidth, low-delay switching and multiplexing technology that is now becoming available for both public and private networks. ATM principles and ATM-based platforms form the foundation for the delivery of a variety of high-speed digital communication services aimed at corporate users of high-speed data,[1] LAN interconnection,[2] imaging,[3] and multimedia[4] applications. Residential applications, such as video distribution, videotelephony, and other information-based services, are also planned. ATM is the technology of choice for evolving broadband integrated services digital network (B-ISDN) public networks, for next-generation LANs, and for high-speed seamless interconnection of LANs and WANs. ATM supports transmission speeds of 155 Mbits/s and 622 Mbits/s, and will be able to support speeds as high as 10 Gbits/s in the future. Networks operating at these speeds have been called gigabit networks.* As an option, ATM will operate at the DS3 (45 Mbits/s) rate; some proponents are also looking at operating at the DS1 (1.544 Mbits/s) rate. While ATM in the strict

---

*Some high-end scientific applications (e.g., visualization at high voxel density) already require terabit networks.

sense is simply a Data Link Layer protocol, ATM and its many support-ing standards, specifications, and agreements constitute a platform supporting the integrated delivery of a variety of switched high-speed digital services.

Cell relay service (CRS)* is one of the key new services enabled by ATM. CRS can be utilized for enterprise networks that use completely private communication facilities, use completely public communication facilities, or use a hybrid arrangement. It can support a variety of evolving corporate applications, such as desk-to-desk videoconferencing of remote parties, access to remote multimedia video servers (for exam-ple, for network-based client/server video systems), multimedia confer-encing, multimedia messaging, distance learning, business imaging (including CAD/CAM), animation, and cooperative work (for example, joint document editing). CRS is one of three "fastpacket"† technologies that have entered the scene in the 1990s [the other two are frame relay service and Switched Multimegabit Data Service (SMDS)]. A generic ATM platform supports all of these fastpacket services (namely, it can support cell relay service, frame relay service, and SMDS), as well as circuit emulation service.

1993 saw the culmination of nine years of ATM standards-making efforts. Work started in 1984 and experienced an acceleration in the late 1980s and early 1990s. With the ITU-TS (International Telecom-munications Union Telecommunication Standardization) standards and the ATM Forum implementers' agreements, both of which were finalized in 1993,‡ the technology is ready for introduction in the corporate environment. In particular, a user-network interface (UNI§) specification that supports switched cell relay service as well as the critical point-to-multipoint connectivity, important for new applications, has been finalized (multiservice UNIs are also contem-plated). In 1993, the ATM Forum also published a broadband inter-carrier interface (B-ICI§) specification; this specification is equally critical for wide-area network (WAN) inter-LATA service. At press time, a variety of vendors were readying end-user products for 1994 market introduction; some prototype products have been on the mar-

---

*In this book, the term *cell relay* is used synonymously with cell relay service. The term *ATM* used by itself refers to the underlying technology, platform, and principles. *B-ISDN* refers to the overall blueprint for the evolution of public networks. *ATM protocol* refers to the Data Link Layer protocol (ITU-T I.361).

†Some also use the term *fast packet*.

‡Phase 2 follow-up standards work is now underway.

§In this book concepts are introduced in an iterative manner: A concept may be introduced and briefly discussed, then treated in greater detail later. In this specific instance, Fig. 1.1, which is provided later, shows the physical positioning of the UNI and B-ICI in a typical ATM network.

ket since the early 1990s. A number of carriers either already provide services or are poised to do so in the immediate future.

A key aspect of B-ISDN in general and ATM in particular is the support of a wide range of data, video, and voice applications in the same public network. An important element of service integration is the provision of a range of services using a limited number of connection types and multipurpose user-network interfaces. ATM supports both nonswitched permanent virtual connections (PVCs) and switched virtual connections (SVCs). In a PVC service, virtual connections between endpoints in a customer's network are established at service subscription time through a provisioning process; these connections or paths can be changed via a subsequent provisioning process or via a customer network management (CNM) application. In SVC, the virtual connections are established as needed (that is, in real time) through a signaling capability. ATM supports services requiring both circuit-mode and packet-mode information transfer capabilities. ATM can be used to support both connection-oriented (e.g., frame relay service) and connectionless services (e.g., SMDS).[5,6]

1.1.2 Course of investigation: applying ATM to enterprise networks

This book is aimed at corporate practitioners who may be interested in determining how they can deploy ATM and cell relay technology in their networks at an early time and reap the benefits. The purpose of this first chapter is to provide an overview of key ATM/cell relay service concepts. These concepts will be revisited in more depth in the chapters that follow. The book has four major segments: (1) platform technology applicable to all B-ISDN services, (2) cell relay service, (3) interworking and support of basic multimedia, and (4) use of ATM in corporate enterprise networks. Table 1.1 provides a roadmap of this investigation.

The text is not a research monograph on open technical issues related to ATM, such as traffic descriptors, ingress/egress traffic policing, object-oriented signaling, etc. A literature search undertaken in the spring of 1993 showed that about 5000 papers and trade articles have been written on ATM in the previous nine years, including Refs. 7 through 15. The purpose of this book, therefore, is to stick to the facts and avoid unnecessary hype. There are a few books already available, but these tend to focus on protocol issues. This text aims at a balance between standards, platforms, interworking, and, most important, deployment issues.

In summary, a network supporting cell relay service accepts user data units (called cells) formatted according to a certain layout and sends these data units in a connection-oriented manner (i.e., via a fixed

TABLE 1.1 Areas of Investigation in This Text

1. ATM and cell relay service: an overview

2. ATM platform aspects and ATM proper

3. ATM Adaptation Layer

4. Signaling

5. Cell relay service—a formal definition

6. Cell relay service—traffic and performance issues

7. Support of fastpacket services and CPE

8. ATM interworking: support of basic multimedia

9. Third-generation LANs

10. Network management

11. Typical user equipment and public carrier service availability

12. How to migrate a pre-ATM enterprise network to CRS

established path), with sequentiality of delivery, to a remote recipient (or recipients). Every so often a cell may be dropped by the network to deal with network congestion; however, this is a very rare event. The user needs a signaling mechanism in order to tell the network what he or she needs. The signaling mechanism consists of a Data Link Layer capability (where the Data Link Layer has been partitioned into four sublayers) and an application-level call-control layer. ATM switches and other network elements supporting cell relay service can also support other fastpacket services. If the user wishes to use ATM to achieve a circuit-emulated service, certain adaptation protocols in the user equipment will be required. Other adaptation protocols in the user equipment are also needed to obtain fastpacket services over an ATM platform. ATM supports certain operations and maintenance procedures that enable both the user and the provider to monitor the "health" of the network. Figure 1.1 is a physical view of an ATM network.

A glossary of some of the key ATM and related concepts, based on a variety of ATM standards and documents, is given in Table 1.2 (pp. 6–9).

1.1.3 Early corporate applications of ATM

Table 1.3 depicts some of the proposed applications for ATM/cell relay service.

1.2 Basic ATM Concepts

1.2.1 ATM protocol model: an overview

ATM's functionality corresponds to the Physical Layer and *part* of the Data Link Layer of the Open Systems Interconnection Reference Model

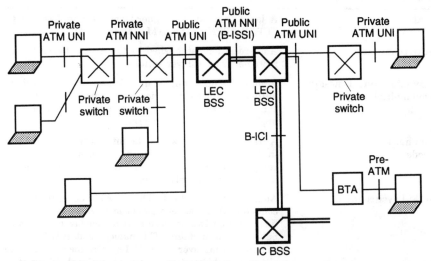

Figure 1.1 A physical view of an ATM/CRS private/public network. BSS = broadband switching system (B-ISDN switch); BTA = broadband terminal adapter; B-ISSI = broadband interswitching system interface; BICI = broadband intercarrier interface; LEC = local exchange carrier; IC = interexchange carrier.

(OSIRM). This protocol functionality must be implemented in appropriate user equipment (for example, routers, hubs, and multiplexers) and in appropriate network elements (for example, switches and service multiplexers). A *cell* is a block of information of short fixed length (53 octets) that is composed of an "overhead" section and a payload section (5 of the 53 octets are for overhead and 48 are for user information), as shown in Fig. 1.2. Effectively, the cell corresponds to the Data Link Layer frame that is taken as the atomic building block of the cell relay service. The term *cell relay* is used because ATM transports user cells reliably and expeditiously across the network to their destination. ATM is a transfer mode in which the information is organized into cells; it is asynchronous in the sense that the recurrence of cells containing information from an individual user is not necessarily periodic.

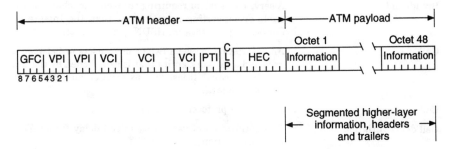

Figure 1.2 ATM cell layout.

TABLE 1.2 Glossary of Key ATM Terms

AAL	A layer that adapts higher-layer user protocols (e.g., TCP/IP, APPN) to the ATM protocol (layer).
AAL connection	An association established by the AAL between two or more next higher layer entities.
Asynchronous time-division multiplexing	A multiplexing technique in which a transmission capability is organized in a priori unassigned time slots. The time slots are assigned to cells upon request of each application's instantaneous real need.
Asynchronous transfer mode	A transfer mode in which the information is organized into cells. It is asynchronous in the sense that the recurrence of cells containing information from an individual user is not necessarily periodic.
ATM Layer connection	An association established by the ATM Layer to support communication between two or more ATM service users (i.e., between two or more next higher layer entities or between two or more ATM management entities). The communication over an ATM Layer connection may be either it is bidirectional or unidirectional. When it is bidirectional, two VCCs are used. When it is unidirectional, only one VCC is used.
ATM Layer link	A section of an ATM Layer connection between two adjacent active ATM Layer entities (ATM entities).
ATM link	A virtual path link (VPL) or a virtual channel link (VCL).
ATM peer-to-peer connection	A virtual channel connection (VCC) or a virtual path connection (VPC).
ATM traffic descriptor	A generic list of traffic parameters that can be used to capture the intrinsic traffic characteristics of a requested ATM connection.
ATM user-user connection	An association established by the ATM Layer to support communication between two or more ATM service users [i.e., between two or more next-higher-layer entities or between two or more ATM management (ATMM) entities]. The communication over an ATM Layer connection may be either bidirectional or unidirectional. When it is bidirectional, two VCCs are used. When it is unidirectional, only one VCC is used.
Broadband	A service or system requiring transmission channels capable of supporting rates greater than the Integrated Service Digital Network (ISDN) primary rate.
Call	An association between two or more users or between a user and a network entity that is established by the use of network capabilities. This association may have zero or more connections.
Cell	ATM Layer protocol data unit.
Cell delay variation	A quantification of variability in cell delay for an ATM Layer connection.
Cell header	ATM Layer protocol control information.

TABLE 1.2 Glossary of Key ATM Terms (*Continued*)

Cell loss ratio	The ratio of the number of cells "lost" by the network (i.e., cells transmitted into the network but not received at the egress of the network) to the number of cells transmitted to the network.
Cell transfer delay	The transit delay of an ATM cell successfully passed between two designated boundaries.
Connection	The concatenation of ATM Layer links in order to provide an end-to-end information transfer capability to access points.
Connection admission control (CAC)	The procedure used to decide if a request for an ATM connection can be accepted based on the attributes of both the requested connection and the existing connections.
Connection endpoint (CE)	A terminator at one end of a layer connection within a SAP.
Connection endpoint identifier (CEI)	Identifier of a CE that can be used to identify the connection at a SAP.
Corresponding entities	Peer entities with a lower-layer connection among them.
Header	Protocol control information located at the beginning of a protocol data unit.
Layer connection	A capability that enables two remote peers at the same layer to exchange information.
Layer entity	An active element within a layer.
Layer function	A part of the activity of the layer entities.
Layer service	A capability of a layer and the layers beneath it that is provided to the upper-layer entities at the boundary between the layer and the next higher layer.
Layer user data	Data transferred between corresponding entities on behalf of the upper-layer or layer management entities for which they are providing services.
Multipoint access	User access in which more than one terminal equipment (TE) is supported by a single network termination.
Multipoint-to-multipoint connection	A collection of associated ATM VC or VP links and their associated endpoint nodes, with the following properties: (1) All N nodes in the connection, called endpoints, serve as root nodes in a point-to-multipoint connection to all of the $(N - 1)$ remaining endpoints. (2) Each of the endpoints on the connection can send information directly to any other endpoint [the receiving endpoint cannot distinguish which of the endpoints is sending information without additional (e.g., higher-layer) information].
Multipoint-to-point connection	A multipoint-to-point connection where the bandwidth from the root node to the leaf nodes is zero, and the return bandwidth from the leaf node to the root node is nonzero.
Network node interface (NNI)	The interface between two network nodes.

TABLE 1.2 Glossary of Key ATM Terms (*Continued*)

Operation and maintenance (OAM) cell	A cell that contains ATM Layer Management (LM) information. It does not form part of the upper-layer information transfer.
Peer entities	Entities within the same layer.
Physical Layer (PHY) connection	An association established by the PHY between two or more ATM, entities. A PHY connection consists of the concatenation of PHY links in order to provide an end-to-end transfer capability to PHY SAPs.
Point-to-multipoint connection	A collection of associated ATM VC or VP links, with associated endpoint nodes, with the following properties: (1) One ATM link, called the root link, serves as the root in a simple tree topology. When the root node sends information, all of the remaining nodes on the connection, called Leaf Nodes, receive copies of the information. (2) Each of the leaf nodes on the connection can send information directly to the root node. The root node cannot distinguish which leaf is sending information without additional (higher-layer) information. (3) The leaf nodes cannot communicate with one another directly with this connection type.
Point-to-point connection	A connection with only two endpoints.
Primitive	An abstract, implementation-independent interaction between a layer service user and a layer service provider or between a layer and the Management Plane.
Protocol	A set of rules and formats (semantic and syntactic) that determines the communication behavior of layer entities in the performance of the layer functions.
Protocol control information (PCI)	Information exchanged between corresponding entities, using a lower-layer connection, to coordinate their joint operation.
Protocol data unit (PDU)	A unit of data specified in a layer protocol and consisting of protocol control information and layer user data.
Relaying	A function of a layer by means of which a layer entity receives data from a corresponding entity and transmits them to another corresponding entity.
Service access point (SAP)	The point at which an entity of a layer provides services to its layer management entity or to an entity of the next higher layer.
Service data unit (SDU)	A unit of interface information whose identity is preserved from one end of a layer connection to the other.
Source traffic descriptor	A set of traffic parameters belonging to the ATM traffic descriptor used during the connection setup to capture the intrinsic traffic characteristics of the connection requested by the source.
Structured data transfer	The transfer of AAL user information supported by the CBR AAL when the AAL user data transferred by the AAL are organized into data blocks with a fixed length corresponding to an integral number of octets.

TABLE 1.2   Glossary of Key ATM Terms (*Continued*)

Sublayer	A logical subdivision of a layer.
Switched connection	A connection established via signaling.
Symmetric connection	A connection with the same bandwidth value specified for both directions.
Traffic parameter	A parameter for specifying a particular traffic aspect of a connection.
Trailer	Protocol control information located at the end of a PDU.
Transit delay	The time difference between the instant at which the first bit of a PDU crosses one designated boundary and the instant at which the last bit of the same PDU crosses a second designated boundary.
Unstructured data transfer	The transfer of AAL user information supported by the CBR AAL when the AAL user data transferred by the AAL are not organized into data blocks.
Virtual channel (VC)	A communication channel that provides for the sequential unidirectional transport of ATM cells.
Virtual channel connection (VCC)	A concatenation of VCLs that extends between the points where the ATM service users access the ATM Layer. The points at which the ATM cell payload is passed to or received from the user of the ATM Layer (i.e., a higher layer or ATM management entity) for processing signify the endpoints of a VCC. VCCs are unidirectional.
Virtual channel link (VCL)	A means of unidirectional transport of ATM cells between the point where a VCI value is assigned and the point where that value is translated or removed.
Virtual path (VP)	A unidirectional logical association or bundle of VCs.
Virtual path connection (VPC)	A concatenation of VPLs between virtual path terminators (VPTs). VPCs are unidirectional.
Virtual path link (VPL)	A means of unidirectional transport of ATM cells between the point where a VPI value is assigned and the point where that value is translated or removed.

The ATM architecture utilizes a logical protocol model to describe the functionality it supports. The ATM logical model is composed of a User Plane, a Control Plane, and a Management Plane. The *User Plane*, with its layered structure, supports user information transfer. Above the Physical Layer, the ATM Layer provides information transfer for all applications the user may contemplate; the ATM Adaptation Layer (AAL), along with associated services and protocols, provides service-dependent functions to the layer above the AAL. In approximate terms, the AAL supplies the balance of the Data Link Layer not included in the ATM Layer. The AAL supports error checking, multiplexing, segmentation, and reassembly. It is generally implemented in user equipment but may occasionally be implemented in the network at an interworking

TABLE 1.3 Possible early applications of ATM in real environments (partial list)

Application	Advantages of ATM use	Associated true-to-life business issues
WAN interconnection of existing enterprise network	High bandwidth; switched service	Unknown cost; geographic availability; equipment availability
WAN interconnection of existing LAN, especially FDDI (fiber distributed data interface) LANs	High bandwidth; switched service	Unknown cost; geographic availability
WAN interconnection of mainframe and supercomputer channel[16]	High bandwidth; only service that supports required throughput (200 Mbits/s); switched service	Unknown cost; geographic availability; equipment availability
WAN interconnection of ATM-based LANs	High bandwidth; switched service; multipoint connectivity	New application, not widely deployed; unproven business need; unknown cost; geographic availability
Support of distributed multimedia	High bandwidth; switched service; multipoint connectivity	New application, not widely deployed; unproven business need; unknown cost; geographic availability
Support of statewide distance learning with two-way video	High bandwidth; switched service; multipoint connectivity	New application, not widely deployed; unproven market; other solutions exist; unknown cost; geographic availability
Support of videoconferencing (including desktop video)	High bandwidth; switched service; multipoint connectivity	Not widely deployed; unproven market; other solutions exist, particularly at lower end (e.g., 384-kbits/s H.200 video); unknown cost; geographic availability
Residential distribution of video (video dial tone)	High bandwidth; switched service; multipoint connectivity	Unproven market; other solutions exist, particularly CATV; expensive for this market; needs MPEG II (Motion Picture Expert Group) hardware; geographic availability

(i.e., protocol conversion) point. The *Control Plane* also has a layered architecture and supports the call control and connection functions. The *Control Plane* uses AAL capabilities as seen in Fig. 1.3; the layer above the AAL in the Control Plane provides call control and connection control. It deals with the signaling necessary to set up, supervise, and release connections. The *Management Plane* provides network supervi-

User Equipment   Network Switch

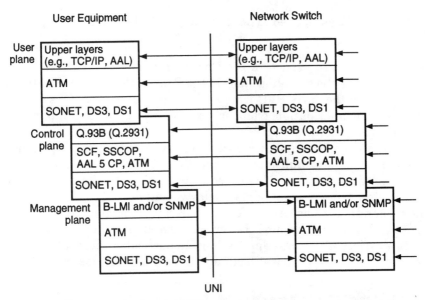

UNI

Figure 1.3 Planes constituting the ATM protocol model.

sion functions. It provides two types of functions: Layer Management and Plane Management. Plane Management performs management functions related to the system as a whole and provides coordination among all planes. Layer Management performs management functions relating to resources and parameters residing in its protocol entities. See Fig. 1.3. (The various protocols identified in this figure will be discussed at length later.)

As noted in this description, four User Plane protocol layers are needed to undertake communication in an ATM-based environment:

1. A layer below the ATM Layer, corresponding to the Physical Layer. The function of the Physical Layer is to manage the actual medium-dependent transmission. Synchronous Optical Network (SONET) is the technology of choice for speeds greater than 45 Mbits/s.

2. The ATM Layer (equating approximately, for comparison, to the upper part of a LAN's medium access control layer), which has been found to meet specified objectives of throughput, scalability, interworking, and consistency with international standards. The function of the ATM layer is to provide efficient multiplexing and switching, using cell relay mechanisms.

3. The layer above the ATM Layer, that is, the AAL. The function of the AAL is to insulate the upper layers of the user's application protocols [e.g., TCP/IP (Transmission Control Protocol/Internet Protocol)] from the details of the ATM mechanism.

4. Upper layers, as needed. These include TCP/IP, IBM APPN, OSI TP, etc.

Several layers are needed in the Control Plane. Early PVC service users do not need the signaling stack in the Control Plane (this situation is analogous to the early PVC frame relay environment). SVC service needs both an information transfer protocol stack and a companion signaling protocol stack.

ATM is intended to support a variety of user needs, including high-speed data, video, and multimedia applications. These applications have varying quality of service (QOS) requirements. For example, video-based services have stringent delay, delay variation, and cell loss goals, while other applications have different QOS requirements. Carriers are proposing to support a number of service classes in order to tailor cell relay to a variety of business applications. In particular, there have been proposals to support a "guaranteed" and a "best efforts" class.

1.2.2 Classes of ATM applications

Two main service categories for ATM have been identified (from the network point of view): (1) interactive broadband services and (2) distributive broadband services. See Table 1.4.[6]

1.2.3 Virtual connections

Just as in traditional packet switching or frame relay, information in ATM is sent between two points not over a dedicated, physically owned facility, but over a shared facility composed of virtual channels.* Each user is assured that, although other users or other channels belonging to the same user may be present, the user's data can be reliably, rapidly, and securely transmitted over the network in a manner consistent with the subscribed quality of service. The user's data is associated with a specified virtual channel. ATM's "sharing" is not the same as a random access technique used in LANs, where there are no guarantees as to how long it can take for a data block to be transmitted: in ATM, cells coming from the user at a stipulated (subscription) rate are, with a very high probability and with low delay, "guaranteed" delivery at the other end, almost as if the user had a dedicated line between the two points. Of course, the user does not, in fact, have such a dedicated (and expensive) end-to-end facility, but it will seem that way to users and applications on the network. Cell relay service allows for a dynamic transfer rate, specified on a per-call basis. Transfer capacity is assigned by negotiation and is based

---

*The access lines are "owned" by the user, but the WAN facilities are shared.

TABLE 1.4   Broadband Services Supported by ATM/Cell Relay

Interactive services	*Conversational services* provide the means for bidirectional communication with real-time, end-to-end information transfer between users or between users and servers. Information flow may be bidirectional symmetric or bidirectional asymmetric. Examples: high-speed data transmission, image transmission, videotelephony, and videoconferencing. *Messaging services* provide user-to-user communication between individual users via storage units with store-and-forward, mailbox, and/or message handling (e.g., information editing, processing, and conversion) functions. Examples: message handling services and mail services for moving pictures (films), store-and-forward image and audio information. *Retrieval services* allow users to retrieve information stored in information repositories (information is sent to the user on demand only). The time at which an information sequence is to start is under the control of the user. Examples: film, high-resolution images, information on CD-ROMs, and audio information.
Distributive services	Distribution services without user individual presentation control provide a continuous flow of information that is distributed from a central source to an unlimited number of authorized receivers connected to the network. The user can access this flow of information without having to determine at which instant the distribution of a string of information will be started. The user cannot control the start and order of the presentation of the broadcast information, so that depending on the point in time of the user's access, the information will not be presented from its beginning. Examples: broadcast of television and audio programs. *Distribution services with user individual presentation control* provide information distribution from a central source to a large number of users. Information is rendered as a sequence of information entities with cyclical repetition. The user has individual access to the cyclically distributed information, and can control the start and order of presentation. Example: broadcast videography.

on the source requirements and the available network capacity. Cell sequence integrity on a virtual channel connection is preserved by ATM.

Cells are identified and switched by means of the label in the header, as seen in Fig. 1.2. In ATM, a *virtual channel* (VC) is used to describe unidirectional transport of ATM cells associated by a common unique identifier value, called the *virtual channel identifier* (VCI). Even though a channel is unidirectional, the channel identifiers are assigned bidirectionally. The bandwidth in the return direction may be assigned symmetrically, or asymmetrically, or it could be zero. A *virtual path* (VP) is used to describe unidirectional transport of ATM cells belonging to virtual channels that are associated by a common identifier value, called the *virtual path identifier* (VPI). See Fig. 1.4.

VPIs are viewed by some as a mechanism for hierarchical addressing. In theory, the VPI/VCI address space allows up to 16 million virtual connections over a single interface; however, most vendors are building equipment supporting (a minimum of) 4096 channels on the user's interface. Note that these labels are only locally significant (at a given interface). They may undergo remapping in the network; however, there is an end-to-end identification of the user's stream so that data can flow reliably. Also note that on the network trunk side more than 4096 channels per interface are supported.

Figure 1.5 illustrates how the VPI/VCI field is used in an ATM WAN. Figure 1.6 depicts the relationship of VPs and VCs as they might be utilized in an enterprise network.

1.3 ATM Protocols:
An Introductory Overview

Figure 1.7 depicts the cell relay protocol environment, which is a particularization of the more general B-ISDN protocol model described earlier. The user's equipment must implement these protocols, as must the network elements to which the user connects.* Some of the key functions of each layer are described next.

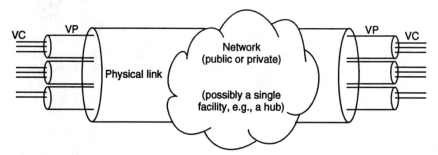

Figure 1.4 Relationship of VCs and VPs.

---

*In the network (as well as in the user's equipment), two pieces of equipment may implement the stack. For example, the channel service unit may implement the network-bound Physical Layer, while the ATM router may implement the network-bound ATM Layer. [A special Physical Layer protocol (see Chap. 7) may be implemented between the channel service unit and the router.]

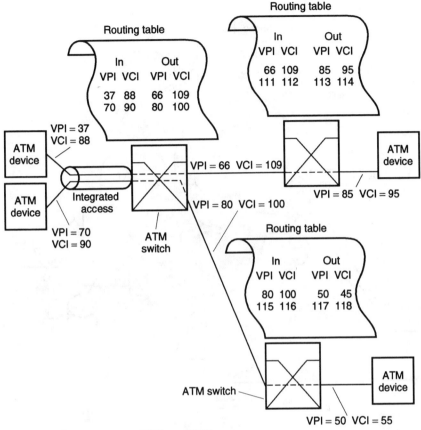

Figure 1.5 Illustrative use of VPIs and VCIs.

1.3.1 Physical Layer functions

The Physical Layer consists of two *logical* sublayers: the Physical Medium–Dependent (PMD) Sublayer and the Transmission Convergence (TC) Sublayer. The PMD includes only physical medium–dependent functions. It provides bit transmission capability, including bit transfer, bit alignment, line coding, and electrical-optical conversion. The Transmission Convergence Sublayer performs the functions required to transform a flow of cells into a flow of information (i.e., bits) that can be transmitted and received over a physical medium. Transmission Convergence functions include (1) transmission frame generation and recovery, (2) transmission frame adaptation, (3) cell delineation, (4) header error control (HEC) sequence generation and cell header verification, and (5) cell rate decoupling.

The transmission frame adaptation function performs the actions that are necessary to structure the cell flow according to the payload struc-

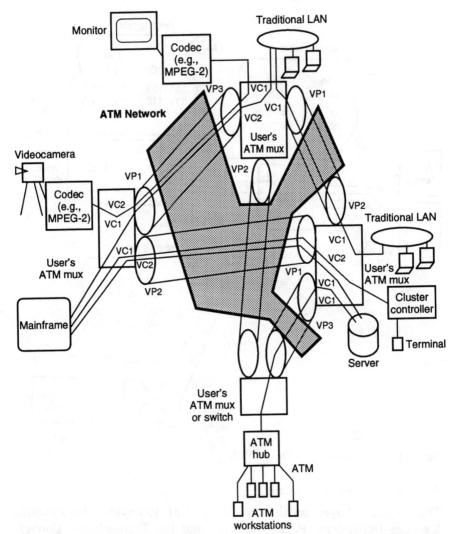

Figure 1.6 Example of use of VPs and VCs in an enterprise network (broadband switches not shown for simplicity). [*Note:* VPs and VCs can be preprovisioned (PVCs) or on-demand (SVC with signaling).]

ture of the transmission frame (transmit direction) and to extract this cell flow out of the transmission frame (receive direction). In the United States, the transmission frame requires SONET envelopes above 45 Mbits/s. Cell delineation prepares the cell flow in order to enable the receiving side to recover cell boundaries. In the transmit direction, the payload of the ATM cell is scrambled. In the receive direction, cell boundaries are identified and confirmed, and the cell flow is descrambled. The HEC mechanism covers the entire cell header, which is available to this layer by the time the cell is passed down to it. The code

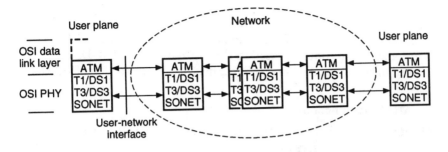

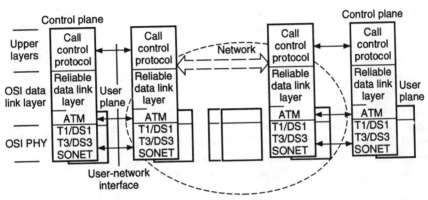

Figure 1.7 CRS environment, protocol view. Top: User Plane (information flow). Bottom: Control Plane (signaling).

used for this function is capable of either single-bit correction or multiple-bit error detection. The transmitting side computes the HEC field value. Cell rate decoupling includes insertion and suppression of idle cells, in order to adapt the rate of valid ATM cells to the payload capacity of the transmission system.

The service data units crossing the boundary between the ATM Layer and the Physical Layer constitute a flow of valid cells. The ATM Layer is unique, that is, independent of the underlying Physical Layer. The data flow inserted in the transmission system payload is physical medium–independent; the Physical Layer merges the ATM cell flow with the appropriate information for cell delineation, according to the cell delineation mechanism.

The transfer capacity at the UNI is 155.52 Mbits/s, with a cell-fill capacity of 149.76 Mbits/s because of Physical Layer framing overhead. Since the ATM cell has 5 octets of overhead, the 48-octet information field equates to a maximum of 135.631 Mbits/s of actual user information.[*] A second UNI interface is defined at 622.08 Mbits/s, with a service

*Some argue that only about 85 percent of this capacity is available to the user because of QOS and magnetic cell flow issues.

bit rate of approximately 600 Mbits/s. Access at these rates requires a fiber-based loop. Other UNIs at the DS3 rate and perhaps at the DS1 rate are also being contemplated in the United States. The DS1 UNI is discussed in the context of an electrical interface (T1); so is the DS3 UNI.

1.3.2 ATM Layer functions

ATM supports a flexible transfer capability common to all services, including connectionless services (if these are provided). The transport functions of the ATM Layer are independent of the Physical Layer implementation. As noted, connection identifiers are assigned to each link of a connection when required and are released when no longer needed. The label in each ATM cell is used to explicitly identify the VC to which the cells belong. The label consists of two parts: the VCI and the VPI. A VCI identifies a particular VC link for a given virtual path connection (refer to Fig. 1.6). A specific value of VCI is assigned each time a VC is switched in the network. With this in mind, a VC can be defined as a unidirectional capability for the transport of ATM cells between two consecutive ATM entities where the VCI value is translated. A VC link is originated or terminated by the assignment or removal of the VCI value.

The functions of ATM include the following

Cell multiplexing and demultiplexing. In the transmit direction, the cell multiplexing function combines cells from individual VPs and VCs into a noncontinuous composite cell flow. In the receive direction, the cell demultiplexing function directs individual cells from a noncontinuous composite cell flow to the appropriate VP or VC.

Virtual path identifier and virtual channel identifier translation. This function occurs at ATM switching points and/or cross-connect nodes. The value of the VPI and/or VCI field of each incoming ATM cell is mapped into a new VPI and/or VCI value (this mapping function could be null).

Cell header generation/extraction. These functions apply at points where the ATM Layer is terminated (e.g., user's equipment). The header error control field is used for error management of the header. In the transmit direction, the cell header generation function receives cell payload information from a higher layer and generates an appropriate ATM cell header except for the HEC sequence (which is considered a Physical Layer function). In the receive direction, the cell header extraction function removes the ATM cell header and passes the cell information field to a higher layer.

For the UNI, as can be seen in Fig. 1.2, 24 bits are available for cell routing: 8 bits for the VPI and 16 bits for the VCI. Three bits are available for payload type identification; this is used to provide an indication of whether the cell payload contains user information or network information. In user information cells, the payload consists of user information and, optionally, service adaptation function information. In network information cells, the payload does not form part of the user's information transfer. The header error control field consists of 8 bits.

The initial thinking was that if the cell loss priority (CLP) is set by the user (CLP value is 1), the cell is subject to discard, depending on the network (congestion) conditions. If the CLP is not set (CLP value is 0), the cell has higher priority. More recent thinking proposes not making use of this bit on the part of the user (i.e., it must always be set to 0 by the user).

ATM is discussed further in Chap. 2.

1.3.3 ATM Adaptation Layer

Additional functionality on top of the ATM Layer (i.e., in the ATM Adaptation Layer) may have to be provided by the user (or interworking) equipment to accommodate various services. The ATM Adaptation Layer enhances the services provided by the ATM Layer to support the functions required by the next higher layer. The AAL function is typically implemented in the user's equipment, and the protocol fields it requires are nested within the cells' payload.

The AAL performs functions required by the User, Control, and Management Planes and supports the mapping between the ATM Layer and the next higher layer. Note that a different instance of the AAL functionality is required in each plane. The AAL supports multiple protocols to fit the needs of the different users; hence, it is service-dependent (namely, the functions performed in the AAL depend upon the higher-layer requirements). The AAL isolates the higher layers from the specific characteristics of the ATM Layer by mapping the higher-layer protocol data units into the information field of the ATM cell and vice versa. The AAL entities exchange information with the peer AAL entities to support the AAL functions.

The AAL functions are organized in two logical sublayers, the Convergence Sublayer (CS) and the Segmentation and Reassembly Sublayer (SAR). The function of the CS is to provide the AAL service to the layer above it; this sublayer is service-dependent. The functions of the SAR are (1) segmentation of higher-layer information into a size suitable for the information field of an ATM cell and (2) reassembly of the contents of ATM cell information fields into higher layer information.

Connections in an ATM network support both circuit-mode and packet-mode (connection-oriented and connectionless) services of a single medium and/or mixed media and multimedia. ATM supports two types of traffic: constant bit rate (CBR) and variable bit rate (VBR). CBR transfer rate parameters for on-demand services are negotiated at call setup time. (Changes to traffic rates during the call may eventually be negotiated through the signaling mechanism; however, initial deployments will not support renegotiation of bit rates.) CBR transfer rate parameters for permanent services are agreed upon with the carrier from which the user obtains service. This service would be used, for example, to transmit real-time video. VBR services are described by a number of traffic-related parameters (minimum capacity, maximum capacity, burst length, etc.). VBR supports packet like traffic (e.g., variable-rate video, LAN interconnection, etc.). The AAL protocols are used to support these different connection types.

In order to minimize the number of AAL protocols, however, a service classification is defined based on the following three parameters: (1) the timing relation between source and destination (required or not required), (2) the bit rate (constant or variable, already discussed), and (3) the connection mode (connection-oriented or connectionless). Other parameters, such as assurance of the communication, are treated as quality of service parameters, and therefore do not lead to different service classes for the AAL. The five classes of application are

Class A: Timing required, bit rate constant, connection-oriented

Class B: Timing required, bit rate variable, connection-oriented

Class C: Timing not required, bit rate variable, connection-oriented

Class D: Timing not required, bit rate variable, connectionless

Class X: Unrestricted (bit rate variable, connection-oriented or connectionless)

Class A service is an on-demand, connection oriented, constant-bit-rate ATM transport service. It has end-to-end timing requirements. This service requires stringent cell loss, cell delay, and cell delay, variation performance. The user chooses the desired bandwidth and the appropriate QOS during the signaling phase of an SVC call to establish a Class A connection (in the PVC case, this is prenegotiated). This service can provide the equivalent of a traditional dedicated line and may be used for videoconferencing, multimedia, etc.

Class B service is not currently defined by formal agreements. Eventually it may be used for (unbuffered) compressed video.

Class C service is an on-demand, connection-oriented, variable-bit-rate ATM transport service. It has no end-to-end timing requirements. The user chooses the desired bandwidth and QOS during the signaling phase of an SVC call to establish the connection.

Class D service is a connectionless service. It has no end-to-end timing requirements. The user supplies independent data units that are delivered by the network to the destination specified in the data unit. SMDS is an example of a Class D service.

Class X service is an on-demand, connection-oriented ATM transport service where the AAL, traffic type (VBR or CBR), and timing requirements are user-defined (i.e., transparent to the network). The user chooses only the desired bandwidth and QOS during the signaling phase of an SVC call to establish a Class X connection (in the PVC case, this is prenegotiated).

Three AAL protocols have been defined in support of these User Plane applications: AAL Type 1, AAL Type 3/4, and AAL Type 5. Type 1 supports Class A, Type 3/4 supports Class D, and Type 5 supports Class X. It appears that the computer communication community (e.g., LAN and multiplexing equipment) will use AAL Type 5. Additionally, the ATM service likely to be available first (and the one supported by evolving computer equipment vendors) is Class X (that is, cell relay service).

Note that two stacks must be implemented in the user's equipment in order to obtain VCs on demand (i.e., SVC service) from the network. With this capability, the user can set up and take down multiple connections at will. The Control Plane needs its own AAL; there has been agreement to use AAL 5 in the Control Plane. Initially only PVC service will be available in the United States. In this mode, the Control Plane stack is not required, and the desired connections are established at service initiation time and remain active for the duration of the service contract. Also note that AAL functions (SAR and CS) must be provided by the user equipment (except in the case where the network provides interworking functions). Additionally, the user equipment must be able to assemble and disassemble cells (i.e., run the ATM protocol).

AAL is discussed further in Chap. 3. Signaling is discussed in Chap. 4.

1.4 Multiservice ATM Platforms

SMDS and frame relay PVC are currently available fastpacket services. SMDS is a high-performance, packet-switched public data service being deployed by the Regional Bell Operating Companies (RBOCs), GTE, and SNET in the United States. SMDS is also being deployed in Europe. Frame relay PVC is a public data service that is widely available today and is expected to be deployed by all RBOCs and most interexchange carriers by the end of 1994. Frame relay SVC should be available in the 1994–1995 time frame. ATM is a switching and multiplexing technology that is being embraced worldwide by a wide spectrum of carriers and suppliers. This new technology can switch and transport voice, data, and video at very high speeds in a local or wide area. What is the relationship of SMDS and frame relay to ATM?

SMDS and frame relay are carrier services, whereas ATM is a technology, as indicated at the beginning of this chapter. ATM will be used by carriers to provide SMDS, frame relay, and other services, including cell relay service (a fastpacket service based on the native ATM bearer service capabilities). Customers who deploy SMDS or frame relay now will be able to take advantage of the benefits of ATM technology without changing the services they use as carriers upgrade their networks to ATM. The customer's investment in SMDS or frame relay equipment and applications is thus preserved.[17]

SMDS is based on well-defined specifications and provides switched, LAN-like transport across a wide area.[1] SMDS service features include a large maximum packet size, an addressing structure that enables data transfer among all SMDS customers, the ability to send the same SMDS packet to several destinations by specifying one address (group addressing), address screening, and strict quality of service values. As ATM technology is deployed within public carrier networks, SMDS service features will not change. The current SMDS interface between the customer and the network uses an access protocol based on the IEEE 802.6 standard. As ATM technology is deployed, this existing SMDS interface will be maintained. The published requirements for ATM switching and transmission technology specify that the existing well-defined SMDS communications interface with the customer must be supported by ATM. When a carrier introduces ATM-based switching systems, customers need not see any effect on their SMDS service. Any technology conversion will be made within the carrier networks. Thus, customers reap the benefits of the latest technology development, while maintaining a consistency and continuity in the service they already employ. Because ATM and IEEE 802.6 technology are both cell based and have the same size cells, such conversion will be facilitated.[17]

In addition, with the introduction of ATM, SMDS can be combined with other services over a new ATM multiservice communications interface. In this case, the communications interface between the customer and the network is based on ATM protocols for all the services on the multiservice interface, including SMDS and frame relay service. This combination was foreseen in the development of ATM standards. In fact, AAL 3/4 (the ATM Adaptation Layer for SMDS) was specifically designed by ITU–T to carry connectionless services like SMDS. Figure 1.8 depicts the typical platform configuration for carrier-provided ATM-based services.

With its large capacity and multiservice capability, ATM provides SMDS with a faster and more scalable technology platform whose cost can be shared among multiple services. SMDS, along with frame relay PVC, is encouraging the use of high-speed, wide-area public networking in the United States. SMDS and frame relay provide ATM

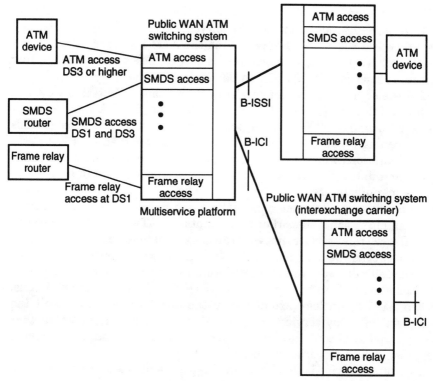

Figure 1.8 Multiservice broadband switching system. B-ISSI = broadband interswitching system interface; B-ICI = broadband interexchange carrier interface.

with significant revenue-producing services that will justify its deployment and allow users and carriers to benefit from the multiservice technology platform.

Frame relay PVC will be a key low-cost, low-overhead broadband data service available in public networks for at least the rest of this decade. The service is currently provided via both frame and ATM switching platforms; ATM simply provides a faster, more scalable platform, as discussed, for SMDS.[18] It appears that frame relay PVC access rates will probably not be extended beyond DS3 (currently, the standards and the deployed services only cover speeds up to 2.048 Mbits/s). This presents the PVC-oriented customer with the possibility of needing to interwork emerging cell relay PVC service with frame relay PVC service. If a user requires PVC service at access speeds of DS3 and above (for example, to aggregate traffic), it is likely that the user will use the ATM cell relay PVC service. This is because customer premises equipment with high-speed wide-area interfaces (e.g., routers) will use ATM technology, thus making cell relay PVC a good choice. As new applications are developed that require these speeds, it is likely that cell relay

PVC service will need to interwork with the users' large installed base of lower-speed wide-area networks for years to come. To meet this need to interwork, the Frame Relay Forum, the ATM Forum, and standards bodies are working on specifications to assure the smooth interworking of these services (ITU-T I.555, in particular).

For the same reasons that carriers are choosing ATM technology (i.e., speed and flexibility), workstation, computer, hub, and LAN manufacturers are turning to ATM for their next-generation networking needs. This is happening because current networks based on Ethernet, FDDI, etc., have limitations when handling the multimedia communications (video, voice, and data) that will flow among future workstations in a network. These manufacturers see global multimedia communications among devices as essential. To meet these networking needs, future workstations and computers will transport user information in ATM cells. Public carriers will offer cell relay service that will transport ATM cells across metropolitan area networks (MANs), across WANs, and internationally as networks evolve. Cell relay service is targeted initially toward high-end users with multimedia needs to transport video, voice, and data across their WANs. When ATM technology extends from the desktop and throughout the network, cell relay service will join SMDS and frame relay as another service that data communications managers can use to support evolving high-bandwidth corporate applications.

Cell relay service is described in Chaps. 5 and 6. Additional aspects of fastpacket are covered in Chap. 7.

1.5 Commercial Availability of ATM Equipment and Network Services

As with any other service, at least three parties are needed to make this technology a commercial reality (if any of these three parties fails to support the service, the service will not see any measurable commercial deployment): (1) carriers must deploy the service, (2) equipment manufacturers must bring user products to the market,[*] and (3) users must be willing to incorporate the service in their networks. (Some observers add two more forces: agencies supporting R&D and standardization, and the trade press to "educate" the end users.) The early phases of ATM research, including all of the work already accomplished in standards organizations (that is, the topics treated in Chaps. 2 through 10 of this book), cover the first item. The industry activity discussed briefly below and in Chap. 11 covers the second item. The user analysis that will follow (not covered

---

[*]In order for item 1 to occur, some vendors must bring out network products; this point refers to user products (see ISDN switches versus availability of cost-effective terminal adapters).

in this book), where users assess applicability, cost, support of embedded base, and manageability, all of it in situ, in their own environment (rather than in a multicolor brochure), covers the third item.

The paragraphs to follow describe industry activities that show encouraging signs of the acceptance of cell relay as a commercially viable networking technology. However, as with all new technologies, there are a number of potential hurdles and roadblocks that can delay or deter its success. History has shown that in spite of industry standards, interoperability problems can exist if different manufacturers implement subsets (or supersets) of the required networking features. Networking hardware may preceed the availability of software applications designed to exploit the networking power of ATM, and this may slow user acceptance of cell relay. In addition, advances in existing technologies (e.g., the emergence of "fast" Ethernet) may extend the life cycle of existing products and slow the acceptance of new technologies. These challenges must be met to make ATM cell relay a long-term commercial success.

Vendors are in the process of bringing products to the market. By 1994 there already were several vendors of ATM hubs and a dozen vendors of ATM workstation plug-ins. Some equipment vendors are building stand-alone premises switches; others are adding switching capabilities to their hubs and at the same time are developing ATM adapter cards for workstations to allow them to connect to the hub. Some are also working on bridge-router cards for ATM hubs that enable Ethernet LANs to connect to ATM. About three dozen vendors had announced firm equipment plans by publication time. Over 320 companies have joined the ATM Forum, which is an organization whose goal is to expedite and facilitate the introduction of ATM-based services. PC/workstation cards are expected to become available for about $1000 per port, although the initial cost was in the $2800–5000 range.

Carriers are deploying broadband switching systems (BSSs) based on ATM technology to support a variety of services. As noted earlier, ATM is designed to be a multi-service platform. For example, frame relay and SMDS will be early services supported on these platforms; another early service is cell relay service, which allows users to connect their ATM equipment using the native ATM bearer service.

Early entrants, including Adaptive, AT&T Network Systems, Cabletron, Digital Equipment Corporation, Fore Systems, Fujitsu, GDC, Hughes, Newbridge, Stratacom, Sun, SynOptics, and Wellfleet, were demonstrating ready or near-ready products for a variety of user networking needs in 1994. The first products were targeted to the local connectivity environment, but WAN products are also expected soon. Additionally, about a dozen vendors have working carrier-grade switching products.

Hubs and switches to support the bandwidth-intensive applications listed earlier, such as video, are becoming available. Typical premises switches now support 8 to 16 155-Mbits/s ports over shielded twisted pair or multimode fibers [lower speeds (45 or 100 Mbits/s) are also supported]. Some systems can grow to 100 ports. Typical backplane throughput ranges from 1 or 2 Gbits/s, up to 10 Gbits/s. A number of these products support not only PVC but also SVC; some also support multipoint SVC service. Products already on the market (e.g., from Hughes LAN, Synoptics, Newbridge, Adaptive, Fore Systems, etc.) are priced as low as $1500 per port. Some of the hubs also act as multiprotocol routers, either (1) accepting ATM devices internally for WAN interconnection over SMDS and frame relay networks, (2) accepting ATM devices internally for WAN interconnection over a cell relay network, or (3) accepting traditional devices internally for WAN interconnection over a cell relay network (these are stand-alone ATM multiprotocol routers).

One major push now is in the network management arena. Users need the capability to integrate the support of ATM products into the overall enterprise network, specifically the corporate management system. Some typical features recently introduced include automatic reconfiguration of virtual connections in case of failure, loopback support, performance and configuration management, and Simple Network Management Protocol (SNMP) functionality [with private management information base (MIB) extensions].

Interface cards for high-end workstations (e.g., SPARCstation) are also appearing (e.g., Synoptics, Adaptive, etc.). These typically support 45 Mbits/s (DS3) on twisted-pair cable and 100 or 155 Mbits/s on multimode fiber, consistent with the ATM Forum specification. Some even support prototype 155-Mbits/s connectivity on shielded twisted pair. These boards are already available for as little as $1250.

Specifically for WAN cell relay service, Sprint has already demonstrated a prototype service operating at the DS3 rate. A three-phase approach has been announced publicly by the company. Phase 1 (1993) entails frame relay interconnectivity with local exchange carriers, Phase 2 (1993–1994) supports PVC cell relay service at the DS3 rate, and Phase 3 (1994–1995) enhances the Cell Relay Service to 155 Mbits/s. AT&T, Wiltel, BellSouth, NYNEX, and Pacific Bell have also announced deployment plans for ATM platforms and for cell relay service. There is strong support for the introduction of cell relay service at the local level. Now users can expect public cell relay service in a number of key metropolitan areas.

In addition to the international and domestic standards, additional details and clarifications are needed to enable the deployment of the technology. To this end, in 1992, Bellcore completed generic requirements that suppliers need in order to start building ATM equipment that will enable the BOCs to offer PVC cell relay services. Work on generic requirements for ATM equipment that provides SVC cell relay was completed at Bellcore in 1994. In particular, Bellcore has already published (preliminary) requirements to define nationally consistent cell relay PVC exchange and cell relay PVC exchange access services, including

"Cell Relay PVC Exchange Service," 1993 [CR PVC exchange service is a public cell relay intra-LATA service offering from local exchange carriers (LECs)]

"Cell Relay PVC Exchange Access CRS (XA-CRS)," 1993 [a PVC XA-CRS is provided by an LEC to an interexchange carrier (IC) in support of the IC's inter-LATA cell relay PVC offering]

"Cell Relay SVC Exchange Service," 1993

The Framework Advisories, Technical Advisories, and Technical Requirements can be used by (1) LECs interested in providing nationally consistent cell relay PVC exchange service to their customers, (2) suppliers of ATM equipment in the local customer environment (e.g., ATM LANs, ATM routers, ATM DSUs, ATM switches), and (3) suppliers of ATM equipment in LEC networks.

The development of nationally consistent LEC cell relay (as well as an exchange access cell relay) service is critical to provide a consistent set of service features and service operations for customers who will want to use the service on a national basis. The following phases of nationally consistent service have been advanced. It is possible that LECs may be offering "pre-nationally consistent" cell relay PVC to meet customers' near-term demand for the service in the late 1993–early 1994 period. These carriers are expected to support a nationally consistent cell relay PVC exchange service at some point thereafter.

- Phase 1.0: Nationally consistent cell relay PVC exchange service based on a core set of service features by the fourth quarter of 1994. The core set is proposed to be a subset of the preliminary generic requirements published by Bellcore in 1993.

- Phase 2.0: Nationally consistent cell relay PVC exchange service based on generic requirements published by Bellcore in 1994 by the second quarter of 1995. Phase 2.0 builds on the capabilities of Phase 1.0 and supports expanded capabilities in some areas, such as traffic management, congestion management, and customer network management.

- Phase 3.0: This will see the initial support of a cell relay SVC exchange service in mid to late 1995 based on generic requirements expected to be published in 1994.

Figure 1.9 depicts the set of Bellcore generic requirements in support of ATM, SMDS, cell relay, and frame relay.[17] These are just some of the key documents that form the foundation for ATM. Standards bodies such as the ITU-T and ANSI (American National Standards Institute) T1S1, and industry bodies such as the ATM Forum and the Frame Relay Forum also publish related documents.

1.6   Typical Examples of Cell Relay Usage in an Enterprise Context

1.6.1   Front-end and back-end usages

Cell relay/ATM is being contemplated at the local-area network level as well as the wide-area network level. Several approaches have been followed by vendors:

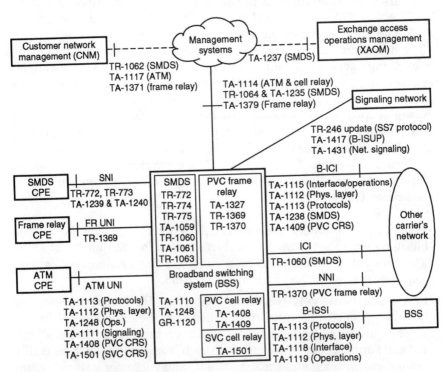

Figure 1.9   ATM, SMDS, cell relay, and PVC frame relay generic requirements.

1. TR-NWT-00246, Bellcore Specification of Signaling System 7, B-ISUP, Issue 2, December 1993.
2. TR-TSV-000772, Generic System Requirements in Support of SMDS, May 1991.
3. TR-TSV-000773, SMDS Requirements, Objectives, and Interfaces, Revision 1, December 1993.
4. TR-TSV-000774, SMDS Operations Technology Network Element Generic Requirements, Issue 1, March 1992, Supp. 1, March 1993.
5. TR-TSV-000775, Usage Measurement Generic Requirements In Support of Billing for Switched Multi-Megabit Data Service, Issue 1, June 1991.
6. TA-NWT-001248, Generic Operations Requirements for Broadband Switching Systems, Issue 2, October 1993.
7. TA-TSV-001059, Generic Requirements for SMDS Networking, Bellcore, Issue 2, August 1992.
8. TR-TSV-001060, Switched Multi-Megabit Data Service Generic Requirements for Exchange Access and Intercompany Serving Arrangements, Issue 1, December 1991, and Revision 1, August 1992; Revision 2, March 1993.
9. TA-TSV-001061, Operations Technology Network Element Generic Requirements in Support of Inter-Switch and Exchange Access SMDS, Issue 1, May 1991.
10. TR-TSV-001062, Generic Requirements for SMDS Customer Network Management Services, Bellcore, Issue 1, March 1992.
11. TR-TSV-001063, Operations Technology Network Element Generic Requirements in Support of Exchange Access SMDS and Intercompany Serving Arrangements, Issue 1, March 1992; Revision 1, March 1993.
12. TR-TSV-001064, SMDS Phase 1 Operations Information Model, December 1993.
13. TA-NWT-001110, Broadband ISDN Switching System Generic Requirements, Issue 2, July 1993.
14. TA-NWT-001111, User to Network Access Signaling Requirements, July 1993.
15. TR-NWT-001112, Broadband ISDN User to Network Interface and Network Node Interface Physical Layer Generic Criteria, July 1993.
16. TA-NWT-001113, Asynchronous Transfer Mode (ATM) and ATM Adaptation Layer (AAL) Protocols Generic Requirements, Issue 2, July 1993.
17. TA-NWT-001114, Generic Requirements for Operations Interfaces Using OSI Tools: Broadband ISDN Operations, Issue 2, October 1993.
18. TA-NWT-001115, Broadband InterCarrier Interface (B-ICI) Requirements, September 1993.
19. TA-NWT-001117, ATM Customer Network Management (CNM), September 1993.
20. TA-TSV-001118, Broadband InterSwitching System Interface (B-ISSI) and Network Generic Requirements, July 1993.
21. TA-NWT-001119, B-ISSI Operations, December 1993.
22. GR-1120-CORE, Guide to Generic Requirements for Usage Information to Support Billing for ATM Broadband Networking, Issue 1, December 1993.
23. TA-NWT-001235, Exchange Access SMDS Operations Interface Model, April 1993.
24. TA-TSV-001237, A Framework for High Level Generic Requirements for SMDS Exchange Access Operations Management Services, July 1993.
25. TA-TSV-001238, SMDS 155 Mbps ATM B-ICI, December 1992.
26. TA-TSV-001239, Low Speed SMDS Access via Data Exchange Interface (DXI), June 1993.
27. TA-TSV-001240, Frame-Based Access to SMDS via SRI, June 1993.
28. TA-NWT-001248, B-ISDN Network Operations Criteria, Issue 2, October 1993.
29. FA-NWT-001327, Frame Relay NE Operations Functional Requirements, Bellcore, Issue 1, December 1992.
30. TR-TSV-001369, Frame Relay (PVC) Exchange Service Definition, May 1993.
31. TR-TSV-001370, Exchange Access Frame Relay (PVC) Service Definition, May 1993.
32. TA-TSV-001371, Frame Relay (PVC) Customer Network Management Service, September 1993.
33. TA-NWT-001379, Frame Relay Network Operations Using OSI, July 1993.
34. TA-TSV-001408, Generic Requirements for Exchange PVC Cell Relay Service, Issue 1, August 1993.
35. TA-TSV-001409, Generic Requirements, Issue 1, November 1993.
36. TA-NWT-001417, B-ISUP Generic Requirements, Issue 1, February 1994.
37. TA-NWT-001431, CCS Network Signaling Specification Supporting B-ISDN Generic Requirements, Issue 1, May 1994.
38. TA-NWT-001501, Generic Requirements for Exchange SVC Cell Relay Service, December 1993.

Figure 1.9 *(Continued)*

1. Use of ATM technology between traditional local or remote LAN hubs; Fig. 1.10 shows a case of interconnection of remote hubs. (The LAN hubs are implicit in the figure.)

2. Introduction of ATM cards on traditional routers for access to a public cell relay service (see Fig. 1.11).

3. Introduction of ATM-based LAN hubs, extending ATM all the way to the desktop, for front-end applications (see Fig. 1.12).

4. Development of private-enterprise ATM switches to support generic corporate networking.

5. Development of carrier-grade multiservice ATM switches (also known as broadband switching systems) to support services such as cell relay service, frame relay service, and SMDS.

6. Development of related equipment (for example, Fig. 1.13 depicts usage in a channel extension environment).

Some industry proponents expect to see Fortune 1000 users passing the majority of their LAN-to-WAN traffic through premises-based ATM switches by 1997. Approximately 50 percent of the ATM traffic in these companies is expected to be in support of LAN interconnection, for LANs serving traditional business applications, and for traditional enterprise data applications, such as mainframe channel extension; the other 50 percent of the traffic is expected to be split fairly evenly among application supporting real-time video, imaging, real-time voice, and multimedia.

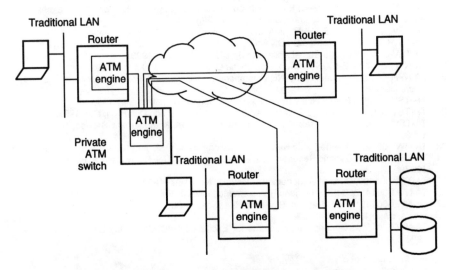

Figure 1.10 Private ATM technology to interconnect dispersed LAN hubs. ATM engine = the logic implementing ATM, control, and, optionally, user plane protocols.

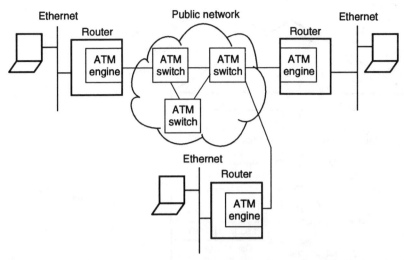

Figure 1.11 Routers used in conjunction with a public cell relay service. ATM engine = the logic implementing ATM, control, and, optionally, user plane protocols.

Figure 1.14 depicts a typical "full-blown" ATM/cell relay arrangement for both WAN and LAN applications. This supports ATM to the desktop for such applications as desk-to-desk videoconferencing and multimedia. Figure 1.15 depicts an example of the protocol machinery across a router/public switch arrangement that is expected to be a common deployment scenario in client/server environments. Figure 1.16 depicts an example in

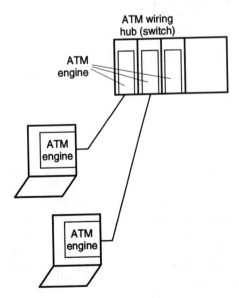

Figure 1.12 ATM to the desktop.

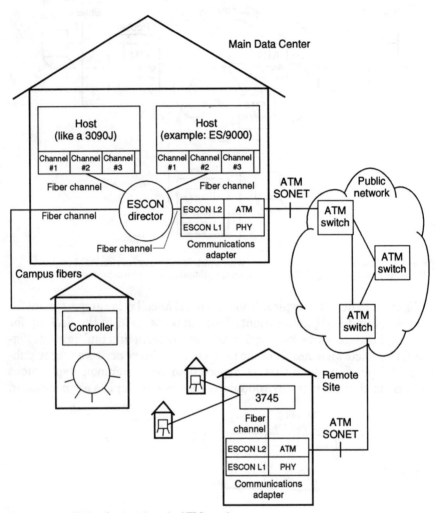

Figure 1.13 Channel extension via ATM services.

a videoconferencing application, also from a protocol point of view. Figure 1.15 shows an example in a corporate network supporting business imaging.

Figure 1.18 depicts a more complete enterprisewise use of cell relay service, while employing a public WAN CRS network. For this example, ATM-ready workstations and devices connected to an ATM-based hub with ATM WAN router capabilities (the router could also be a separate device) can get direct access to the ATM WAN. Some of the hub and router vendors are taking this path to the market. The figure also shows that traditional LAN users can employ an ATM-ready router to obtain the benefit of cell relay WAN services without having to replace their

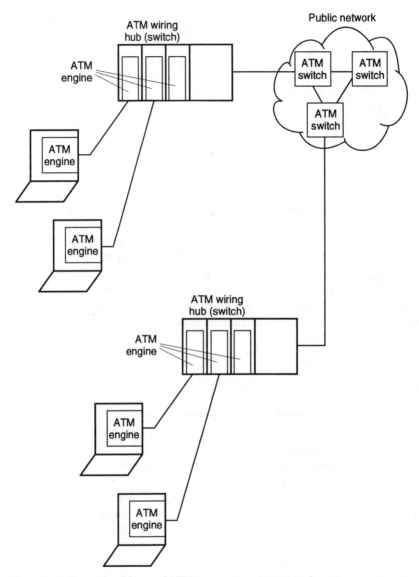

Figure 1.14 Example of usage of ATM in an enterprise network.

desktops or in-house wiring. It also depicts another route to the market, followed by some of the more sophisticated multiplexer manufacturers: The multiplexer can connect traditional data devices, mainframe channels, and video to a cell relay WAN network by supporting ATM on the trunk side. Some of these multiplexers also support traditional LANs on the house side over a frame relay interface. (*Note:* Carrier-deployed ATM "service nodes" in close proximity of the user location but on the

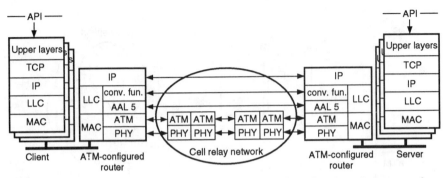

Figure 1.15 Typical corporate application from a protocol-stack point of view. conv.fun. = convergence function.

network side of the interface support these same services plus LAN emulation service.)

Figure 1.19 depicts some user applications of cell relay service in the case where the user wants to develop a private ATM/cell relay service WAN. Note the need to (1)install privately managed switches, (2) use dedicated high-speed WAN lines, and (3) backhaul remote locations to a remote switching site. Public cell relay service may prove less demanding in terms of users' responsibility. Hybrid arrangements are also possible.

1.6.2 Client/server issues

The client/server architecture being put in place in many organizations is truly distributed in the sense that the corporate user has access to data regardless of where the data are located, be they on a system in another campus, another city, another state, or another continent. Client/server applications require extensive interchange of data blocks, often entailing multiple transactions. Low end-to-end delay is critical in making client/server computing possible.[19]

Applications requiring large transfers (e.g., 50–100 kbits) are not unusual in these environments, particularly for imaging video, and

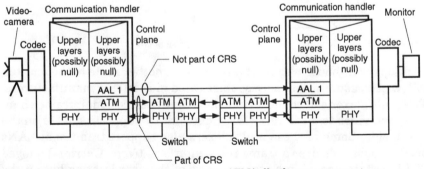

Figure 1.16 Example of video application over ATM/cell relay arrangement.

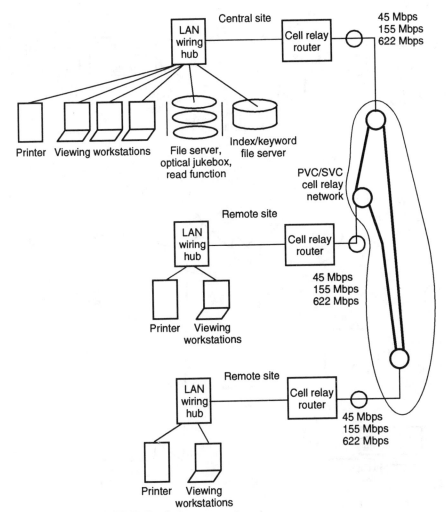

Figure 1.17 Use of ATM/cell relay to support imaging.

multimedia applications (the last two applications also have stringent delay sensitivities). A 100-MByte data unit across the application programming interface (API) running on a remotely located LAN-resident server is segmented into approximately 60 Ethernet frames. Each Ethernet frame is then segmented into approximately 30 cells by an ATM-configured router for delivery over a public cell relay network.

Some wish to clarify the implications of the interplay between the network(or private ATM switch) performance in terms of cell loss/mutilation, response time, latency, and the end-to-end error correction protocols (e.g., included in TCP). For example, if one of the 29 cells that

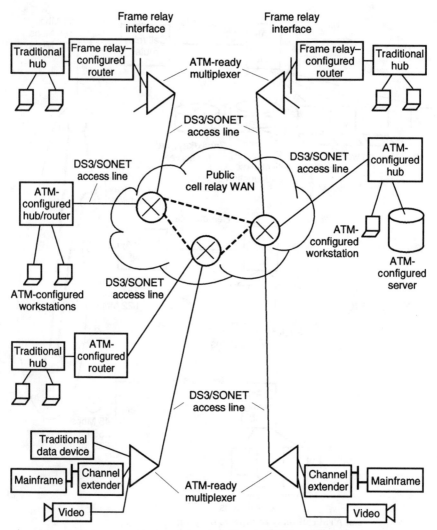

Figure 1.18 CRS to support enterprise networking in WAN applications.

made up a frame is lost, the entire frame (30 cells) needs to be retransmitted by TCP. Under heavy user load as well as coterminous ATM switch overload (whether public or private), the combination of client/server architecture and ATM communication could result in degradation, saturation, or instability. A number of simulation-based studies have shown that, when properly engineered, the network should behave as expected.

Chapter 9 covers ATM-based LANs, while Chaps. 11 and 12 cover other details pertaining to the deployment of ATM in users' environments.

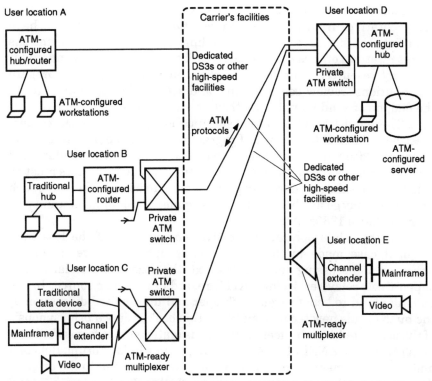

Figure 1.19 CRS to support enterprise networking in WAN applications (private network).

1.7 The Value of Standards

It is a well-known fact that standards benefit not only an industry but an entire economy. Many industries would not have arisen (e.g., the VCR industry, the CD audio industry, television, radio, etc.) if it were not for standards. Standards make a level playing field, fostering competition; this is in contrast to vendor proprietary approaches, where only those vendors have access to a market or have disproportionate control of it. However, for a standard to be effective, it must be widely available, without restrictions on promulgation, discussion, commentary, proliferation, distribution, and duplication. In our opinion, a standard is not an open standard if it is restricted, copyrighted, or patented, if it represents someone's intellectual property, or if it is "owned" by someone (sounds mighty close to a proprietary system to us!) because all of these factors frustrate the exact purpose for which the standard aims to exist (or has a reason to exist). There is much discussion at large about "free trade," "free movement of information," and "lack of censorship."

Standards are developed by industry consensus. This means that representatives from many companies, typically several dozen, have input into the standard. These proceedings can go on for years, and the representatives of these companies travel to many meetings and invest company resources back home to work on technical issues, prepare contributions, review contributions, and act as editors, chairs, etc. In the end, no one individual or institution should be able to claim ownership. There must be a free flow of specification information. Developers must be able to obtain copies. Programmers must be able to use the material. Documentaries must be able to write down the standard and comment on how they implemented various aspects. Educators must be able to discuss the standard and promulgate it to users. Otherwise, such a standard may go nowhere, as many examples of voluminous standards from the (late) 1980s illustrate.

Given this philosophical imperative, and in spite of the less than eloquent case made in these terse paragraphs, we have taken the approach of discussing here, in this text, the dozens of standards that support cell relay service and ATM, regardless of their source. In the end, all stand to benefit from such oper and uninhibited discussion at the birth of this new technology. Since this book is only a brief synopsis of the estimated 15 cubic feet of standards material that forms the basis for ATM (ITU-T, ANSI T1S1, ATM Forum, Frame Relay Forum, Bellcore, and other documents), the reader is constantly referred to the original documents for the full-scale detail. In particular, developers, who stand to benefit commercially from their efforts, should definitely refer to the original documentation for the necessary level of detail. The purpose of this book is strictly pedagogical and for the end user. Each of the more than 100 documents alluded to earlier can be obtained from the original source for $100 or less.

References

1. D. Minoli, *Enterprise Networking—Fractional T1 to SONET, Frame Relay to BISDN*, Artech House, Norwood, Mass., 1993.
2. D. Minoli, *1st, 2nd, and Next Generation LANs*, McGraw-Hill, New York, 1994.
3. D. Minoli, *Imaging in Corporate Environments: Technology and Communication*, McGraw-Hill, New York, 1994.
4. D. Minoli and B. Keinath, *Distributed Multimedia: Through Broadband Communication Services*, Artech House, Norwood, Mass., 1994.
5. D. Minoli et al., *ATM Layer Bearer Service/Cell Relay Service Extended Stage 1 Description for Public Service Offerings*, T1S1.5/93-021, February 1993.

6. T1S1.5/93-52, *Broadband Aspects of ISDN Baseline Document, T1S1 Technical Subcommittee*, August 1990, Chief Editor: Erwin Fandrich.

7. D. Minoli, "The New Wide Area Technologies: SMDS and B-ISDN," *Network Computing*, pp. 88ff., August 1991.

8. D. Minoli, "Understanding ATM—Part 1," *Network Computing*, pp. 128ff., Oct. 15, 1992.

9. D. Minoli, "Understanding ATM—Part 2," *Network Computing*, pp. 156ff., Nov. 15, 1992.

10. D. Minoli, "Third-Generation LANs," *UNIX Expo 92 Proceedings*, Bruno Blemheim Inc., Fort Lee, N.J., 1992.

11. D. Minoli, "Third Generation LANs," *Proceedings of Texpro 1993*, Pacific Bell, San Francisco, April 1993.

12. D. Minoli, "Cell Relay and ATM," WAN Insert to *Network Computing* and *Communications Week*, pp. 22 ff., August 1993.

13. D. Minoli, "Wide Area Networking for Multimedia?", WAN Insert to *Network Computing* and *Communications Week*, pp. 60ff., August 1993.

14. D. Minoli, "Broadband Integrated Services Digital Network," Datapro Communications Series: *Broadband Networking*, Report #2890, April 1992.

15. D. Minoli, "ATM and Cell Relay Concepts," Datapro Communications Series: *Broadband Networking*, Report #2880, April 1992.

16. J. T. Johnson, "Applications Catch Up to ATM," *Data Communications*, pp. 41–42, July 1993.

17. F. Gratzer and S. Walters, "ATM and Fast Packet Services—Perfect Together," *Bellcore DIGEST*, vol. 10 (6), pp. 3ff., 1993.

18. D. Minoli, "Designing Scalable Networks," *Network World Collaboration*, pp. 17ff., January 10, 1994.

19. D. Minoli, *Analyzing Outsourcing: Reengineering Information and Communication Systems*, McGraw-Hill, New York, 1995.

2

Asynchronous Transfer Mode

As noted in Chap. 1, ATM is a new transport and switching technology that can be used in a variety of telecommunications and computing environments. ATM is a cell-based technology, designed to support user applications requiring high-bandwidth, high-performance transport and switching. This chapter provides a summary description of the peer-to-peer ATM protocol at the user-network interface in support of cell relay service and other ATM capabilities. It describes functionality in the User Plane, thereby enabling a PVC service. The addition of Control Plane support enables the user to obtain an SVC service; the operation of the ATM Layer in the Control Plane is nearly identical to that of the User Plane (the Control Plane functionality is discussed in Chap. 4). Some aspects of the underlying transport mechanism are also briefly covered at the end of the chapter.

A description of general aspects of the access interface(s) between the user and the network is followed by a description of the protocol across such an interface. The protocols and related requirements are associated with two functional OSIRM layers: the Data Link Layer and the Physical Layer. Figure 2.1 depicts this peer-to-peer protocol view of the service. Figure 2.2 depicts communication through a set of network peers. As described in ITU-T Recommendation X.210, *Open Systems Interconnection, Layer Service Definition Conventions*,[1] the service defined at the Data Link Layer also relies on the capabilities of the Physical Layer. This view of cell relay service in general and of the ATM protocol in particular establishes requirements on what an entity in the ATM Layer (whether the entity is in the network or in the user's equipment),

42   Chapter Two

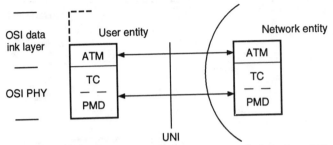

Figure 2.1 Peer entities across the user-network interface. TC = Transmission Convergence Sublayer; PMD = Physical Medium–Dependent Sublayer.

defined in ITU-T Recommendation I.361, *B-ISDN ATM Layer Specification*,[2] and in T1S1.5/92-410, *Broadband ISDN—ATM Layer Functionality and Specification*,[3] expects the remote peer entity to support. The physical aspects of the UNI supporting cell relay service are based on the B-ISDN UNI defined in ITU-T Recommendation I.432, *B-ISDN User-Network Interface—Physical Layer Specification*[4] and on the ATM Forum's *UNI Specification*[5] for public UNIs. This discussion only provides an overview; the reader interested in additional details should consult Refs. 6 and 7.

This chapter only covers the interface between user equipment and a public network; intra-CPE interfaces (for example, for ATM-based LANs), although similar in many respects to the interface between the CPE and the network, are not addressed. Table 2.1 depicts some of the key ITU-T standards in support of ATM in general and the peer-to-peer cell relay protocol in particular.

2.1   Access Interface

This section defines the concept of access interface. This is accomplished by defining an access reference configuration, functional entities (groups), and logical reference points.

An *access reference configuration* for B-ISDN is defined in ITU-T Recommendation I.413, *B-ISDN User-Network Interface*.[8] This configu-

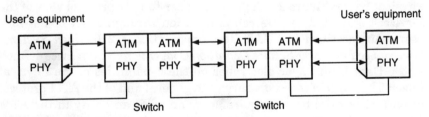

Figure 2.2   Cascaded ATM entities.

TABLE 2.1   Key ITU-T Standards in Support of ATM

F.811	B-ISDN Connection-Oriented Bearer Service
F.812	B-ISDN Connectionless Bearer Service
I.113	B-ISDN Vocabulary of Terms
I.121R	Broadband Aspects of ISDN [Basic Principles and Evolution]
I.150	B-ISDN ATM Functional Characteristics
I.211	B-ISDN Service Aspects
I.311	B-ISDN General Network Aspects
I.321	B-ISDN Protocol Reference Model and Its Applications
I.327	B-ISDN Functional Architecture Aspects
I.356	Quality of Service Configuration and Principles
I.361	B-ISDN ATM Layer Specification
I.362	B-ISDN AAL Functional Description
I.363	B-ISDN AAL Specification
I.371	Traffic Control and Resource Management
I.374	Network Capabilities to Support Multimedia
I.413	B-ISDN UNI
I.432	B-ISDN UNI Physical
I.555	Interworking with Frame Relay
I.555	Interworking with ISDN
I.610	B-ISDN OAM Principles
I.cls	Support for Connectionless Data Service on B-ISDN
Q.93B (now Q.2931)	B-ISDN Call Control
Q.SAAL 1 and 2 (now Q.2110 and Q.2130)	Signaling AALs [Q.2110, Service-Specific Connection-Oriented Protocol (SSCOP); Q.2130, Service-Specific Coordination Function (SSCF)]

ration forms the basis for the definition of access interfaces supporting cell relay service.

Functional entities are logical abstractions of functions typically found in network equipment and in users' equipment, also known as customer premises equipment (CPE). Public network switch-termination functions are modeled by the broadband line terminator/exchange terminator (B-LT/ET) functional group. The CPE is modeled by the broadband network termination 2 (B-NT2) functional group; NT2 functions include concentration, switching, and resource management. Broadband network termination 1 (B-NT1) functions support line termination, line maintenance, and performance monitoring. The broadband terminal

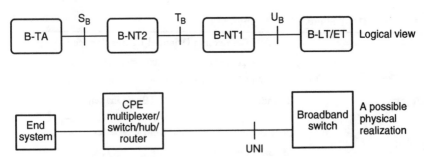

Figure 2.3 B-ISDN access reference configurations. B-TA = broadband terminal adapter.

equipment, such as a workstation, is modeled by the broadband terminal equipment (B-TE) functional group.

Logical reference points are defined between B-ISDN functional entities. *TB* is the logical reference point between a B-NT2 and a B-NT1. UB is the logical reference point between a B-NT1 and a B-LT/ET. In this description, the UNI is associated with the UB reference point. See Fig. 2.3.

Note: This description only covers the case where there is a single B-NT2 (however, several B-TEs may be connected to the B-NT2). The case where the B-NT2 is null and there are several B-TEs connected to a single UNI is not addressed in the initial view of ATM services in the United States.

2.2 ATM-Level Protocol

2.2.1 Overview

UNI protocols define the way in which users communicate with the public network for the purpose of accessing the service provided by the network. Figure 2.4 illustrates the B-ISDN Protocol Reference Model, which is the basis for the protocols that operate across the UNI (this is another common way to represent the protocol model of Fig. 1.3). The B-ISDN Protocol Reference Model is described in ITU-T Recommendation I.121. This model is made up of three planes, already discussed in Chap. 1: the User Plane, the Control Plane, and the Management Plane. Table 2.2 provides a summary of the functions supported by each plane.

The UNI specified at this level includes the functions associated with the User Plane at the Physical Layer and the ATM Layer. The Physical Layer provides access to the physical medium for the transport of ATM cells. It includes methods for mapping cells to the physical medium (i.e., the Transport Convergence Sublayer) and methods dependent on the physical medium (i.e., the Physical Medium–Dependent Sublayer). The ATM layer provides for the transport of cells between end-user locations. An ATM cell contains a header that contains control information, iden-

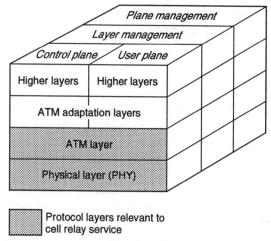

Protocol layers relevant to
cell relay service

Figure 2.4 B-ISDN protocol reference model.

tifies the type of cell, and contains routing information that identifies a logical channel (i.e., a VPC or a VCC) over which the cell is to be forwarded.

The interactions of each protocol layer with other layers and with its own layer management are described in terms of primitives. Primitives describe abstractly the logical exchange of information and control

TABLE 2.2 Functions of Various Planes of the Protocol Model

User Plane	Provides for the transfer of end-user information. It consists of the Physical Layer and the ATM Layer. The model also includes ATM Adaptation Layers and higher layers necessary for each end-user application. (Because these layers are specific to each application, they are not part of the cell relay service described here and in Chap. 5.)
Control Plane	Provides for the transfer of information to support connection establishment and control functions necessary for providing switched services. The Control Plane shares the ATM and Physical Layer with the User Plane. Also, it contains AAL procedures and higher-layer signaling protocols. The Control Plane is discussed in Chap. 5.
Management Plane	Provides for operations and management functions and the capability to exchange information between the User and the Control Planes. The Management Plane is made up of the *Layer Management* (for layer-specific management functions such as detection of failures and protocol abnormalities) and the *Plane Management* (for management and coordination functions related to the complete system). The Management Plane is discussed in Chap. 10.

through a service access point, while not imposing any constraint on the implementation. Figures 2.5, 2.6, and 2.7 depict some aspects of this protocol machinery.

2.2.2 ATM Layer

The ATM Layer provides for the transport of fixed-size cells between end-user locations. It is implemented in users' equipment (workstations, routers, private switches, etc.) and in network equipment. ATM cells from end users are forwarded across virtual connections through the public network. These connections are provided at subscription time or in real time via signaling (as described in Chap. 4). The ATM Layer also provides multiplexing functions to allow the establishment of multiple connections across a single UNI.

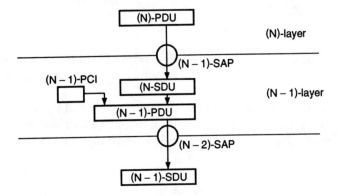

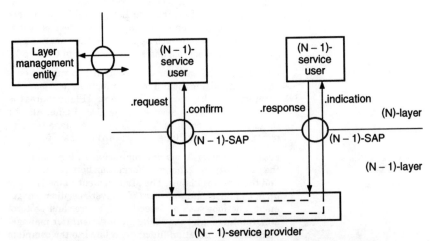

Figure 2.5 SAPs (top) and primitives (bottom). SAP = service access point; PDU = protocol data unit; SDU = service data unit; PCI = protocol control information.

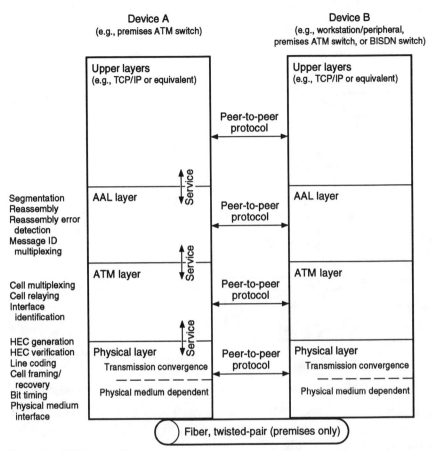

Figure 2.6 ATM protocols.

Service provided to the upper layer.   The ATM-Layer service is based on fixed-size ATM service data units which consist of 48 octets. It provides for the transparent transfer of ATM SDUs between communicating peer upper-layer entities. To accomplish this, the ATM Layer generates a 53-octet ATM cell by prepending a 5-octet header to the ATM SDU. The header contains routing and protocol control information. The interaction between the ATM Layer and its service users is implemented by the primitives shown in Table 2.3.

Service expected from the lower layer.   The ATM Layer expects the Physical Layer to support the transparent transport of ATM cells between peer ATM entities. The exchange of information between the ATM Layer and the Physical Layer is implemented by the primitives shown in Table 2.4. The PHY-SDU parameter in these primitives contains the 53-octet cell to be transmitted between peer ATM entities.

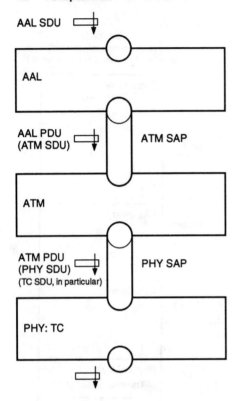

Figure 2.7 Pertinent ATM SAPs.

ATM cell format.   The ATM cell format used across the UNI is shown in Fig. 2.8 (which is another way of looking at Fig. 1.2). Table 2.5 describes the meaning of the fields.

End-to-end operations administration and maintenance capabilities need to be supported. For VPs, operation functions are supported via specially marked ATM cells, which are transmitted over VCs with specific VCI values* (these are known as F4 flows). For VCs, operation functions are supported via cells marked with an appropriate codepoint in the Payload Type Indicator field (these are known as F5 flows). The functions supported are shown in Table 2.6. Figure 2.9 illustrates the difference between these two OAM flows.   see table 2.7 (F5)

Table 2.7 provides the encoding for the PTI field. Code point 100_B (B = binary) indicates a segment OAM F4 cell flow used to monitor the status of a segment within the virtual connection. Code point 101_B indicates an end-to-end OAM F5 cell flow used to monitor the status of a connection end to end. Code point 110_B is reserved for future traffic control and resource management procedures.

*VCI is 4 for end-to-end operations and 3 for segment information.

TABLE 2.3 ATM Layer Primitives

ATM-DATA.request (ATM_SDU, Submitted_Loss_Priority, Congestion_Indication, SDU_Type)	Used to request transmission of an ATM SDU across a VPC or VCC to a peer entity
ATM-DATA.indication (ATM_SDU, Received_Loss_Priority, Congestion_Indication, SDU_Type)	Used by the ATM Layer to indicate to the service user the arrival of an ATM cell

Description of parameters:

ATM_SDU: The 48 octets of information to be transferred by the ATM Layer between peer communicating upper-layer entities.

Submitted_Loss_Priority: The relative importance of the ATM_SDU contained in this primitive. Two values are possible. A value of "high" indicates that the resulting ATM cell has higher (or equivalent) loss priority than a cell with a value of "low." A high value may be translated to a cell loss priority value of 0 in the cell header. Similarly, a low value may be translated to a CLP value of 1 in the cell header.

Congestion_Indication: This parameter indicates whether this cell has passed through one or more network nodes experiencing congestion. It has two values: True or False.

SDU_Type: This parameter indicates the type of SDU to be transferred between peer upper layer entities. It can take only two values, 0 and 1, and its use is as determined by the higher layer. For example, AAL Type 5 sets SDU_Type to 1 to indicate the last cell of a frame. In other words, this field is currently used by the AAL Type 5 Common Part protocol to distinguish between cells that contain the last segment of an AAL Type 5 Common Part PDU and those that do not. AAL Type 1 and AAL Type 3/4 always set the bit to 0.

Received_Loss_Priority: This parameter indicates the CLP field marking of the received ATM_PDU. Two values are possible. A value of "high" indicates that the received ATM cell has higher (or equivalent) loss priority than a cell with a value of "low." A high value may be translated to a cell loss priority value of 0 in the cell header. Similarly, a low value may be translated to a CLP value of 1 in the cell header.

ATM Layer procedures. This section summarizes the functions performed by ATM layer entities.

ATM sending procedures. These procedures are performed by an ATM entity to send ATM cells to a peer ATM entity. The procedures are organized according to the categories of functions performed by the ATM Layer.

ATM layer connections. As described earlier, the ATM service is provided by means of virtual connections. For the PVC cell relay service, connections are established at subscription time. For SVC service,

TABLE 2.4 Physical Layer Primitives

PHY-DATA.request (PHY_SDU)	Requests the Physical Layer to transport an ATM cell between peer ATM entities over an existing connection.
PHY-DATA.indication (PHY_SDU)	Indicates to the ATM Layer that an ATM cell has been received over an existing connection.

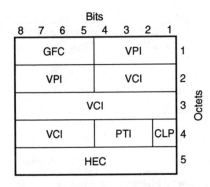

Figure 2.8 ATM cell format.

connections are established by a signaling mechanism. As will be seen in Chap. 4, about one dozen parameters need to be specified to describe a connection (for example, called party, bandwidth, quality of service, etc.).

Cell rate decoupling. A sending ATM entity must add unassigned cells to the assigned cell stream to be transmitted, so that a continuous cell stream matching the line rate of the UNI is provided to the Physical Layer. This is necessary in order for the Physical Layer to perform adequate cell delineation functions. Unassigned cells are empty cells which have the first 4 octets of the cell header encoded as depicted in Fig. 2.10. Unassigned cells do not carry information. Therefore, they must be extracted at the receiving ATM entity and not passed to the upper layer.

Loss priority indication. Traffic management functions may use tagging as a way to control traffic entering the network across the UNI. The network may choose to tag cells that violate a traffic descriptor for the connection by setting the CLP bit to 1. If cell discarding is necessary, these cells would be discarded first. Some traffic management procedures are discussed in Chap. 6.

ATM receiving procedures. This section describes the procedures an ATM entity executes when receiving an ATM cell to ensure its proper processing. These procedures include the provision for sequenced processing of ATM cells which arrive across a virtual connection.

Sequenced ATM processing. ATM cells received across a virtual connection must be processed in sequence to ensure adequate service to the higher layers.

Cell validation procedures. The cell validation procedures determine whether a received cell is an unassigned cell and detect invalid header patterns. These procedures also detect cells received with inactive VPI/VCI values (e.g., VPI/VCI values which identify inactive connections). Unassigned cells and cells found to be in error are discarded.

TABLE 2.5   ATM Cell Fields

Generic Flow Control (GFC)	The 4-bit GFC field has only local significance and may be used to provide standardized local functions at the customer site (e.g., passive bus support); the field is ignored and may be overwritten by the public network.
Virtual Path Identifier/Virtual Channel Identifier	The 24-bit VPI/VCI field indicates the virtual connection over which a cell is to be forwarded. The number of connections needed across the UNI is less than 2^{24}, therefore, only some bits of the VPI and VCI subfields are used. Those bits are called *allocated bits*, and all other bits in the VPI/VCI field are set to 0. A VPI value of 0 is not available for user-to-user virtual path identification. Similarly, a VCI value of 0 is not available for user-to-user virtual channel identification.
Payload Type Indicator (PTI)	The 3-bit PTI field indicates whether the cell contains user information or layer management information. Code points 000 to 011 indicate user information; these PTI values identify two types of end-user information and whether the cell has experienced congestion (the two types of information are used by the end-user application). For user data, the public network does not change the SDU_Type indicated by the PTI field. The public network can, however, change the PTI value from Congestion_Experienced = False to Congestion_Experienced = True. Code points 100 to 111 identify different types of operations flows. See Table 2.7.
Cell Loss Priority	This 1-bit field allows the user to indicate the relative cell loss priority of the cell. The network may attempt to provide a higher cell loss priority (or equivalent) for cells marked with high priority than for cells marked with low priority. The current view is to only let the user set CLP to the value 0.
Header Error Control	The 8-bit HEC field is used by the Physical Layer to detect transmission errors in the cell header and in some cases for cell delineation.

Cell discrimination based on PTI value.   A receiving ATM Layer entity processes cells according to the type of payload they contain as indicated by the value in the PTI field. User cells (PTI values 000–100) are forwarded across the appropriate virtual channel. If neces-

TABLE 2.6 Layer Management Functions Included in Cell Relay Service

Fault management functions	Alarm surveillance: AIS (alarm indication signal)
	Alarm surveillance: FERF (far-end receive failure; now known as remote defect indicator)
	Connectivity verification: cell loopback continuity check
Performance management functions	Forward monitoring Backward reporting Monitoring/reporting
Activation/deactivation	Performance monitoring Continuity check

sary, PTI values may be modified to indicate whether the cell experienced congestion.

Layer Management cells (PTI values of 101–111) are used to provide various operations flows to support functions like performance monitoring and trouble sectionalization. CPE supporting the UNI is not required to support these operations flows. However, network equipment must support them so that it can interface with end-user equipment supporting these functions. (This topic is revisited in Chap. 10.)

2.2.3 Layer Management

There are two types of interactions between the ATM entity and the ATM Management entity. One interaction is for the exchange of local information between these two entities. The primitives are shown in Table 2.8 (the parameters are not shown for simplicity). The other interaction is for peer-to-peer communication between ATM Management entities. The primitives for this interaction are shown in Table 2.9. For more details, refer to Ref. 2, 5, or 6. (This topic is revisited in Chap. 10.)

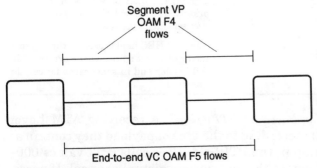

Figure 2.9 OAM F4 and F5 flows.

TABLE 2.7 PTI Code Points

PTI code point	Meaning
000	User data—SDU_Type 0, no congestion experienced
001	User data—SDU_Type 1, no congestion experienced
010	User data—SDU_Type 0, congestion experienced
011	User data—SDU_Type 1, congestion experienced
100	Segment OAM F5 flow cell
101	End-to-end OAM F5 flow cell
110	Reserved for future traffic control and resource management functions
111	Reserved for future use

2.2.4 Physical Layer

Although the emphasis of this chapter is on the ATM Layer, a brief discussion of the underlying Physical Layer is also provided. Figure 2.11 depicts some of the key Physical Layer protocols supported.

As noted, the Physical Layer is made up of two sublayers: the Transmission Convergence Sublayer and the Physical Medium–Dependent Sublayer. The TC Sublayer "maps" the cell stream to the underlying framing mechanism of the physical transmission facility and generates the required protocol control information for the Physical Layer (e.g., SONET overhead octets). It also generates the HEC. The PMD Sublayer deals with the electrical or optical aspects of the physical interface (e.g., timing, power, jitter).

The UNI providing the service's access interface includes the physical characteristics of facilities that provide actual realizations of the U_B reference point. In practical terms, this access interface specifies the means and characteristics of the connection mechanism between CPE supporting cell relay service and a LEC's switch providing the same service. UNIs are specified by characteristics such as physical and electromagnetic/optical characteristics, channel structures and access

←	4 octets		→	
GFC	VPI	VCI	PTI	CLP
AAAA	0s	0s	XXX	0

A: This bit is available for use by appropriate ATM layer function.
X: This bit is a don't care bit.

Figure 2.10 First four octets of cell header for unassigned cells.

TABLE 2.8   ATM Management Primitives for Local Communication

ATMM-MONITOR.indication	Issued by an ATM Layer Management entity to deliver the content of an ATM_PDU received by the ATM entity, to facilitate an OAM function
ATMM-ASSIGN.request	Issued by an ATM Layer Management entity to request the establishment of an ATM link
ATMM-ASSIGN.confirm	Issued by an ATM Layer Management entity to confirm the establishment of an ATM link
ATMM-REMOVE.request	Issued by an ATM Layer Management entity to request the release of an ATM link
ATMM-REMOVE.confirm	Issued by an ATM Layer Management entity to confirm the release of an ATM link
ATMM-ERROR.indication	Issued by an ATM Layer Management entity to indicate an error and invoke appropriate management actions
ATMM-PARAMETER-CHANGE.request	Issued by an ATM Layer Management entity to request a change in a parameter of the ATM link

capabilities, user-network protocols, maintenance and operations characteristics, performance characteristics, and service characteristics.

The physical access channel for ATM-based fastpacket services such as cell relay service supports one of the following access rates: 622.080 Mbits/s (future); 155.520 Mbits/s; 44.736 Mbits/s; 1.544 Mbits/s (perhaps in the future). The corresponding channel signal formats are STS-12c (Synchronous Transport Signal Level 12, concatenated), STS-3c, DS3 (Digital Signal Level 3), and DS1.

Physical-Layer mappings.   The mapping of cells onto the DS1, DS3, and SONET STS-3c has also been defined.[9] Some key aspects of how cells are inserted over the underlying framing mechanism are discussed below.

TABLE 2.9   ATM Management Peer-to-Peer Primitives

ATMM-DATA.request (ATM_SDU, Submitted_Loss_Priority, PHY_CEI(s))	Issued by an ATM Layer Management entity to request transfer of a management ATM_SDU
ATMM-DATA.indication (ATM_SDU, Received_Loss_Priority, PHY_CEI, Congestion_Indication)	Issued to an ATM Layer Management entity to indicate the arrival of a management ATM_SDU

Note: CEI is the connection endpoint identifier.

Adaptation
layer

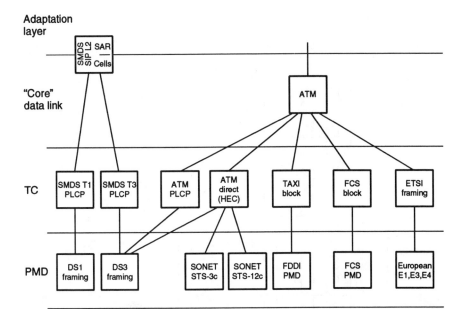

Figure 2.11 Key Physical Layer protocols supported. PLCP = Physical Layer convergence procedure; FCS = fiber channel standard; FDDI = fiber distributed data interface; ETSI = European Telecommunications Standards Institute.

The challenge at the receiving end is to extract the cell from the underlying frame, that is, to establish cell boundaries.

Mapping of ATM cells into 1544-kbit/s DS1 frame. Frame format. The multiframe structure for the 24-frame multiframe as described in ITU-T Recommendation G.704 is used. The ATM cell is mapped into bits 2 to 193 (i.e., time slots 1 to 24 described in Recommendation G.704) of the 1544-kbit/s[*] frame, with the octet structure of the cell aligned with the octet structure of the frame (however, the start of the cell can be at any octet in the DS1 payload; (see Fig. 2.12).

Cell rate adaption. The cell rate adaption to the payload capacity of the frames is performed by the insertion of idle cells, as described in ITU-T Recommendation I.432, when valid cells are not available from the ATM Layer.

Header error control generation. The Header Error Control value is generated and inserted in the specific field in compliance with ITU-T Recommendation I.432.

Scrambling of the ATM cell payload (optional). As an option, the ATM cell payload (48 bytes) can be scrambled before it is mapped into the 1544-kbit/s signal. In the reverse operation, following termination

*As of press time, however, standards for the delivery of ATM over a DS1 access were still being investigated.

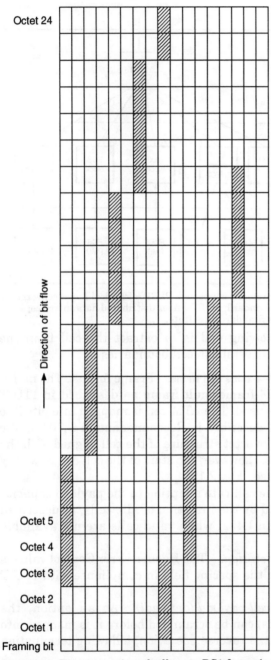

Figure 2.12 Direct mapping of cells onto DS1 frame (example).

of the 1544-kbit/s signal, the ATM cell payload is descrambled before being passed to the ATM Layer. The self-synchronizing scrambler with the generator polynomial $x^{43} + 1$ is used.

Cell delineation. Cell delineation is performed using the header error control mechanism as defined in ITU-T Recommendation I.432. This direct mapping approach means that the algorithm parses 5 octets on the fly until a 5-octet boundary is found through the HEC procedure. Once the header boundary is found, the rest of the cell boundary is established by counting 48 additional octets.

Cell header verification and extraction. The cell header verification is performed in compliance with ITU-T Recommendation I.432. Only valid cells are passed to the ATM Layer.

Mapping of ATM cells into 44,736-kbit/s DS3 frame

Frame format. The multiframe format at 44,736 kbits/s, as described in ITU-T Recommendation G.704, is used.

Two mappings are available:

1. Physical Layer Convergence Protocol (PLCP)–based mapping of ATM cells, derived from SMDS principles

2. A direct (HEC-based) mapping, established in 1993

This discussion focuses on PLCP, since the direct mapping is similar to the DS1 mapping.

The ATM PLCP defines a mapping of ATM cells onto existing 44,736-kbit/s facilities. The DS3 PLCP consists of a 125–µs frame within a standard 44,736-kbit/s payload. Note that there is no fixed relationship between the PLCP frame and the 44,736-kbit/s frame; i.e., the PLCP can begin anywhere inside the 44,736-kbit/s payload. The PLCP frame, Fig. 2.13, consists of 12 rows of ATM cells, each preceded by 4 octets of overhead. Nibble stuffing is required after the twelfth cell to fill the 125-µs PLCP frame. Although the PLCP is not aligned with the 44,736-kbit/s framing bits, the octets in the PLCP frame are nibble-aligned with the 44,736-kbit/s payload envelope. Nibbles begin after the control bits (F, X, P, C, or M) of the 44,736-kbit/s frame. The stuff bits are never used in the 44,736-kbits/s, i.e., the payload is always inserted. The reader interested in a detailed explanation of the DS3 framing format may refer to Ref.10 or other material. Octets in the PLCP frame are described in the following sections.

Cell rate adaption. The cell rate adaption to the payload capacity of the PLCP frame is performed by the insertion of idle cells, as described in ITU-T Recommendation I.432, when no valid cells are available from the ATM Layer.

PLCP (1 octet)	Framing (1 octet)	POI (1 octet)	POH (1 octet)	PLCP payload (53 octets)	
A1	A2	P11	Z6	First ATM cell	
A1	A2	P10	Z5	Second ATM cell	
A1	A2	P09	Z4	Third ATM cell	
A1	A2	P08	Z3		
A1	A2	P07	Z2		
A1	A2	P06	Z1		
A1	A2	P05	X		
A1	A2	P04	B1		
A1	A2	P03	G1		
A1	A2	P02	X		(13 or 14 nibbles)
A1	A2	P01	X	Eleventh ATM cell	
A1	A2	P00	C1	Twelfth ATM cell	Trailer

Figure 2.13 PLCP frame. POI = path overhead indicator; POH = path overhead; BIP-8 = bit interleaved parity-8; X = unassigned (receiver to ignore). [*Note:* Order and transmission of all PLCP bits and octets are from left to right and top to bottom. This figure shows the most significant bit (MSB) on the left and the least significant bit (LSB) on the right.]

Header error control generation.   The HEC generation is based on the algorithm described in ITU-T Recommendation I.432.

Cell delineation.   Since the cells are in predetermined locations within the PLCP, framing on the 44,736-kbit/s signal and then on the PLCP is sufficient to delineate cells.

Cell header verification and extraction.   The cell header verification is consistent with ITU-T Recommendation I.432. Only valid cells are passed to the ATM Layer.

PLCP overhead utilization.   The following PLCP overhead bytes/nibbles are activated across the UNI:

- A1: Frame alignment
- A2: Frame alignment
- B1: PLCP path error monitoring
- C1: Cycle/stuff counter
- G1: PLCP path status
- Px: Path overhead identifier
- Zx: Growth octets
- Trailer nibbles

Frame alignment (A1, A2).   The PLCP framing octets use the same framing pattern: A1 = 11110110, A2 = 00101000.

PLCP path error monitoring (B1).   The BIP-8 field supports path error monitoring, and is calculated over a 12 × 54 octet structure consisting of the POH field and the associated ATM cells (648 octets) of the *previous* PLCP frame.

Cycle/stuff counter (C1). The cycle/stuff counter provides a nibble-stuffing opportunity cycle and length indicator for the PLCP frame. A stuffing opportunity occurs every third frame of a three-frame (375-μs) stuffing cycle. The value of the C1 code is used as an indication of the phase of the 375 μs stuffing opportunity cycle, as follows:

C1 code	Frame phase of cycle	Trailer length
11111111	1	13
00000000	2	14
01100110	3 (no stuff)	13
10011001	3 (stuff)	14

Notice that a trailer containing 13 nibbles is used in the first frame of the 375 ms stuffing opportunity cycle. A trailer of 14 nibbles is used in the second frame. The third frame provides a nibble-stuffing opportunity. A trailer containing 14 nibbles is used in the third frame if a stuff occurs. If it does not, the trailer will contain 13 nibbles.

PLCP path status (G1). The PLCP path status is allocated to convey the received PLCP status and performance to the transmitting far end. This octet permits the status of the full receive/transmit PLCP path to be monitored at either end of the path.

Path overhead identifier (P00–P11). The path overhead identifier (POI) indexes the adjacent path overhead (POH) octet of the PLCP.

Growth octets. These are reserved for future use. The receiver ignores the values contained in these fields.

Trailer nibbles. The content of each of the 13 or 14 trailer nibbles is 1100.

Other Mappings.   Other mappings have been defined. Direct mappings for E1, DS2, and STS-3c are available.[4]

References

1. ITU-T Recommendation X.210, *Open Systems Interconnection, Layer Service Definition Convention,* Geneva, Switzerland, 1989.
2. ITU-T Recommendation I.361, *B-ISDN ATM Layer Specification*, Geneva, Switzerland, June 1992.
3. T1S1.5/92-410, *Broadband ISDN—ATM Layer Functionality and Specification,"* August 1992.
4. ITU-T Recommendation I.432, *B-ISDN User-Network Interface—Physical Layer Specification*, Geneva, Switzerland, June 1992.

5. ATM Forum, *ATM User-Network Interface Specification*, Version 3.0, August, 1993.

6. Bellcore, *Asynchronous Transfer Mode (ATM) and ATM Adaptation Layer (AAL) Protocols Generic Requirements*, TA-NWT-001113, Issue 2, July 1993.

7. ANSI T1.ATM-1993, *Broadband ISDN—ATM Layer Functionality and Specification*, New York.

8. ITU-T Recommendation I.413, *B-ISDN User-Network Interface*, Geneva, Switzerland, 1991.

9. ITU Draft Recommendation G.804, *ATM Cell Mapping into Plesiochronous Digital Hierarchy*, Geneva, Switzerland, February 1993.

10. D. Minoli, *Enterprise Networking—Fractional T1 to SONET, Frame Relay to BISDN*, Artech House, Norwood, Mass., 1993.

3

ATM Adaptation Layer

3.1 Introduction

As discussed in the previous two chapters, the Protocol Reference Model applicable to both the User Plane and the Control Plane (see Fig. 3.1) is divided into three protocol layers: the *Physical Layer*, the *ATM Layer,* and the *AAL and Service-Specific Layers.*

- The Physical Layer provides the ATM Layer with access to the physical transmission medium. Its functions include transmission of bits across the physical medium, timing recovery, line coding, cell delineation, cell scrambling and descrambling, and generation and checking of the header error control.

- The ATM Layer provides for the transport of ATM cells between the endpoints of a virtual connection. It is the basis for native cell relay service as well as other services. ATM cells are delivered across the network in the same sequence they are received from the CPE.

- The AAL maps the upper-layer data into cells for transport across the network. The Service-Specific Layers perform application-dependent processing and functions.

This chapter focuses on AAL protocols. As noted, the AAL performs the functions necessary to adapt the capabilities provided by the ATM Layer to the needs of higher-layer applications using CRS or other ATM-based services.[1-4] AALs are typically implemented in end user equipment, as shown, for example, in Fig. 1.16, but can also (occasionally) be found in the network, as seen later. The functions of the AAL include segmentation and reassembly of the higher-layer data units and mapping them into the

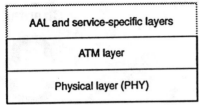

Figure 3.1 Protocol reference model.

fixed-length payload of the ATM cells. Effectively, AAL protocols allow a user with some preexisting application, say using TCP/IP, to get the benefits of ATM. To date, three AAL protocol types have been standardized: AAL Type 1 for circuit emulation (or CBR) services, and AAL Type 3/4 and AAL Type 5 for VBR services. A number of service-specific parts have also been standardized. For many years "AAL" meant segmentation/reassembly and error detection only. With the recent inclusion of service-specific functions into the AAL, the functionality has been significantly increased. Two examples of service-specific parts are briefly discussed at the end of this chapter. In AAL Type 1, 1 octet of the cell payload is reserved for control; the remaining 47 octets are utilized for user information. AAL Type 3/4 reserves 4 octets of each cell payload for control use. AAL Type 5 provides all 48 octets of each cell (except for the last cell of a higher-layer packet; see Sec. 3.5.2) for user information.

Note: In this discussion, the term *user* is employed consistent with protocol parlance, unless noted otherwise. Namely, it represents the (protocol) entity just above the AAL Layer; it does not refer to the ultimate user of the (corporate) network. Such a corporate user would access ATM through the top of the protocol stack, e.g., via an application such as E-mail over TCP/IP over ATM.

Recall, for positioning, as we proceed, that AAL provides the balance of capabilities to "fill out" part, but not all, of the Data Link Layer in the OSIRM. Typically the stack {AAL, ATM, PHY} runs just under the Logical Link Control of a traditional LAN, or directly under TCP/IP in an ATM-based LAN or ATM-based WAN.

The novice reader may choose to skip this chapter on first reading; alternatively, the reader may read the first few sections to understand what the AAL aims at doing, without concentrating on how it does it.

3.2 AAL Model

Architecturally, the AAL is a layer between the ATM Layer and the "service layer" (the service layer is shown in Fig. 3.5). The purpose of the ATM Adaptation Layer is to provide the necessary functions to support the service layer that are not provided by the ATM Layer. The functions provided by the AAL depend upon the service. VBR users may require such functions as PDU delimitation, bit error detection and correction, and cell loss detection. CBR users typically require source clock frequency recovery and detection and possible replacement of lost cells.

Figure 3.2 depicts the positioning of the AAL in the context of the corporate user equipment. AAL capabilities can also be used at an interworking point in the carrier's network, as shown in Fig. 3.3 (this topic is reexamined in Chap. 7). Figure 3.4 shows a classification of services that has been used for specifying ATM Adaptation Layers for different services.

Five AAL protocol types to support the following services are covered in this chapter:

- CBR service using the AAL 1 protocol
- VBR service using the AAL 3/4 Common Part protocol
- VBR service using the AAL 5 Common Part protocol
- Frame relay service (the Frame Relay Service-Specific AAL protocol, which utilizes the AAL 5 Common Part protocol)
- UNI signaling service (the UNI Signaling AAL protocol, which utilizes the AAL 5 Common Part protocol)

The AAL for VBR services consists of two parts: a Common Part (CP) and a Service-Specific Part (SSP). The SSP is used to provide those additional capabilities, beyond those provided by the CP, that are necessary to support the user of the AAL. For some applications the SSP may be "null"; in these cases, the user of the AAL utilizes the AAL Common Part (AALCP) directly. For all AAL types, the AAL receives information from the ATM Layer in the form of 48-octet ATM service data units (ATM_SDU). The AAL passes information to the ATM Layer in the form of a 48-octet ATM_SDU. Figure 3.5 depicts some of the more common protocol arrangements.

Section 3.3 discusses the AAL description for Class 1 (e.g., circuit emulation services), and Sec. 3.4 discusses the AAL description for Class

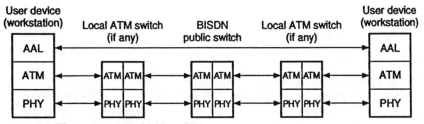

Figure 3.2 The positioning of AAL in CPE.

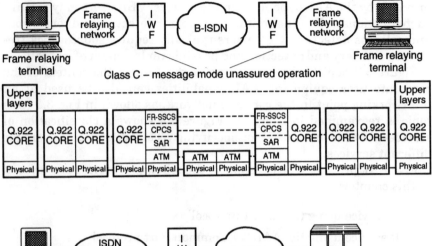

Figure 3.3 Use of AAL protocols at interworking points.

3/4 (e.g., connectionless data services, such as SMDS). Maximum commonality between Class 4 and Class 3 (e.g., connection-oriented data services) AALs has been sought, and people now refer to this AAL as AAL 3/4. The AAL specification for Class 2 services (e.g., variable-bit-rate video services) may occur at a future date. Section 3.5 describes AAL 5, Sec. 3.6 covers the Frame Relay Service-Specific AAL, and Sec. 3.7 briefly covers the signaling AAL.

3.3 AAL Type 1

3.3.1 Overview

One of the services possible with an ATM platform is emulation of a dedicated line (typically at 1.544 or 45 Mbits/s). This type of service is also known as Class A or CBR service. To support CBR services, an adaptation layer is required in the user's equipment for the necessary

Attributes	Class 1	Class 2	Class 3	Class 4
Timing between source and destination	Related		Nonrelated	
Bit rate	Constant	Variable		
Connection mode	Connection-oriented			Connection-less

Figure 3.4 Classification of services for AAL specification. Examples of services: Class 1, circuit emulation; Class 2, variable bit rate video; Class 3, connection-oriented data; Class 4, support of connectionless data transfer; Class X, unrestricted.

functions that cannot be provided by the ATM cell header. Some characteristics and functions that may be needed for an efficient and reliable transport of CBR services are identified below.

Ideally, CBR services carried over an ATM-based network should appear to the corporate user as equivalent to CBR services provided by the circuit switched or dedicated network. Some characteristics of these CBR services are

1. Maintenance of timing information
2. Reliable transmission with negligible reframes
3. Path performance monitoring capability

CBR services with the above characteristics can be provided by assigning the following functions for the CBR Adaptation Layer:

1. Lost cell detection
2. Synchronization
3. Performance monitoring

(These functions may not be required by all the CBR services.)

Therefore, the CBR AAL performs the functions necessary to match the service provided by the ATM Layer to the CBR services required by its service user. It provides for the transfer of AAL_SDUs carrying information of an AAL user supporting constant-bit-rate services. This layer is service-specific, with the main goal of supporting services that

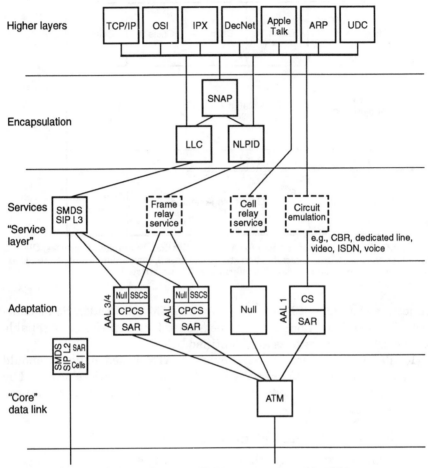

Figure 3.5 Support of user applications. CPCS = common part CS; SSCS = service-specific CS; LLC = logical link control; SNAP = Subnetwork Access Protocol; NLPID = Network Layer Protocol ID.

have specific delay, jitter, and timing requirements, such as circuit emulation. It provides timing recovery, synchronization, and indication of lost information.

The AAL 1 functions are grouped into Segmentation and Reassembly Sublayer functions and Convergence Sublayer functions. The existing agreements in ITU-T Recommendation I.363 and the ANSI CBR AAL Standard[3] provide two basic modes of operation for the CBR AAL:

- Unstructured data transfer (UDT)
- Structured data transfer (SDT)

When the UDT mode is operational, the AAL protocol assumes that the incoming data from the AAL user are a *bit stream* with an associated bit clock. When the SDT mode is operational, the AAL protocol assumes that the incoming information is *octet blocks* of a fixed length (such as an $n \times 64$ kbit/s channel with 8-kHz integrity) with an associated clock. While the SDT mode of operation has not been completely specified in the standards, a substantial enough body of agreements exists to assume that by the end of 1994 a complete SDT mechanism will be defined.

3.3.2 CBR AAL services

AAL Type 1 services and functions. The CBR AAL functions are grouped into two sublayers, the SAR Sublayer and the Convergence Sublayer. The SAR is responsible for the transport and bit error detection (and possibly correction) of CS protocol control information. The CS performs a set of service-related functions. It blocks and deblocks AAL_SDUs, counting the blocks, modulo 8, as it generates or receives them. Also, it maintains bit count integrity, generates timing information (if required), recovers timing, generates and recovers data structure information (if required), and detects and generates indications to the AAL management (AALM) entity of error conditions or signal loss. The CS may receive reference clock information from the AALM entity which is responsible for managing the AAL resources and parameters used by the AAL entity. The services provided by AAL Type 1 to the AAL user are

- Transfer of service data units with a constant source bit rate and the delivery of them with the same bit rate
- Transfer of timing information between the source and the destination
- Transfer of structure information between the source and the destination
- Indication of lost or errored information that is not recovered by AAL Type 1, if needed

Specifically, the functions are:

1. Segmentation and reassembly of user information
2. Handling of cell delay variation
3. Handling of cell payload assembly delay
4. Handling of lost and misinserted cells
5. Source clock recovery at the receiver
6. Recovery of the source data structure at the receiver

7. Monitoring of AAL-PCI for bit errors

8. Handling of AAL-PCI bit errors

9. Monitoring of the user information field for bit errors and possible corrective actions

SAR functions.   The SAR functions are

- Mapping between the CS_PDU and the SAR_PDU (the SAR Sublayer at the transmitting end accepts a 47-octet block of data from the CS and then prepends a 1-octet SAR_PDU header to each block to form the SAR_PDU).

- Indicating the existence of a CS function (the SAR can indicate the existence of a CS function; the use of the indication mechanism is optional).

- Sequence numbering (for each SAR_PDU payload, the SAR sublayer receives a sequence number value from the CS).

- Error protection (the sequence number and the CSI bits are protected).

A buffer is used to handle cell delay variation. When cells are lost, it may be necessary to insert an appropriate number of dummy SAR_PDUs. Figure 3.6 depicts the AAL Type 1 frame layout.

Convergence Sublayer functions.   The functions of the CS are

- Handling of cell delay variation for delivery of AAL_SDUs to the AAL user at a constant bit rate (the CS layer may need a clock derived at the S_B or T_B interface to support this function).

- Processing the sequence count to detect cell loss and misinsertion.

- Providing the mechanism for timing information transfer for AAL users requiring recovery of source clock frequency at the destination end.

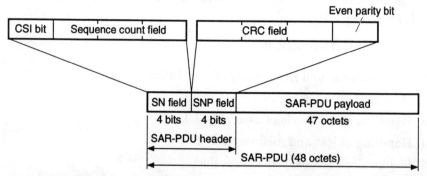

Figure 3.6 AAL Type 1 frame layout. SN = sequence number; SNP = sequence number protection; CSI = Convergence Sublayer indication.

- Providing the transfer of Structure information between source and destination for some AAL users.

- Supporting forward error correction (particularly for video)

For those AAL users that require transfer of structured data [e.g., 8-kHz structured data for circuit-mode bearer services for 64-kbit/s-based ISDN (see Chap. 8)], the Structure parameter is used. This parameter can be used when the user data stream to be transferred to the peer AAL entity is organized into groups of bits. The length of the structured block is fixed for each instance of the AAL service. The length is an integer multiple of 8 bits. An example of the use of this parameter is to support circuit-mode services of the 64-kbit/s-based ISDN. The two values of the Structure parameter are

Start. This value is used when the DATA is the first part of a structured block, which can be composed of consecutive data segments.

Continuation. This value is used when the value Start is not applicable.

The use of the Structure parameter depends on the type of AAL service provided; its use is agreed upon prior to or at the connection establishment between the AAL user and the AAL.

I.363 notes that "for certain applications such as speech, some SAR functions may not be needed." For example, I.363 provides the following guidance for CS for voice-band signal transport [which is a specific example of CBR service (see Chap. 8)]:

- *Handling of AAL user information.* The length of the AAL_SDU (i.e., the information provided to the AAL by the upper-layer protocols) is 1 octet (for comparison, the SAR_PDU is 47 octets).

- *Handling of cell delay variation.* A buffer of appropriate size is used to support this function.

- *Handling of lost and misinserted cells.* The detection of lost and inserted cells, if needed, may be provided by processing the sequence count values. The monitoring of the buffer fill level can also provide an indication of lost and misinserted cells. Detected misinserted cells are discarded.

P and non-P formats. The 47-octet SAR_PDU payload used by CS has two formats called non-P and P formats, as seen in Fig. 3.7. These are used to support transfer of information with Structure.

Note that in the non-P format, the entire CS_PDU is filled with user information.

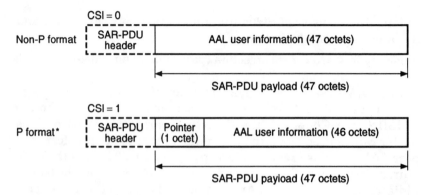

* Used when the SAR-PDU SN = 0, 2, 4, or 6

Figure 3.7 Non-P and P formats.

Partially filled cells. I.363 notes that SAR_PDU payload may be filled only partially with user data in order to reduce the cell payload assembly delay. In this case, the number of leading octets utilized for user information in each SAR_PDU payload is a constant that is determined by the allowable cell payload assembly delay. The remainder of the SAR_PDU payload consists of dummy octets.

Clocking issues. Besides the UDT/SDT issues discussed earlier, the other basic CBR service attribute that determines the AAL functionality required to support a service is the status of the CBR service clock:[5]

- Synchronous
- Asynchronous

Since the service clock is assumed to be frequency-locked to a network clock in the synchronous case, its recovery is done directly with a clock available from the network. For an asynchronous service clock, the AAL provides a method for recovering the source clock at the receiver. Two methods are available, the synchronous residual time stamp (SRTS) method and the adaptive clock method. The SRTS method is used to recover clocks with tight tolerance and jitter requirements, such as DS1 or DS3 clocks. The adaptive clock recovery method has not been described in enough detail to determine what types of service clocks are supported [presumably less accurate clocks with looser low-frequency jitter (i.e., wander) specifications] or what, if any, added agreements are needed. However, since adaptive clock recovery is common in user equipment, this method is assumed to be available.

The support of DS1 and DS3 CBR service

- Uses the entire 47-octet information payload available with the basic CBR AAL protocol.

- Uses the UDT mode of operation.

- Uses the SRTS method of timing recovery, if the service clock is asynchronous.

- Maintains bit count integrity by inserting the appropriate alarm indication signal for the service supported as a DS1 and DS3 error control measure.

3.3.3 CBR AAL mechanism

The CBR AAL provides its service over preestablished AAL connections. The establishment and initialization of an AAL connection is performed through the AALM. The transfer capacity of each connection and other connection characteristics are negotiated prior to or at connection establishment (the CBR AAL is not directly involved in the negotiation process, which may be performed by management or signaling). The AAL receives from its service user a constant-rate bit stream with a clock. It provides to its service user this constant-rate bit stream with the same clock. The CBR service clock can be either synchronous or asynchronous relative to the network clock. The CBR service is called synchronous if its service clock is frequency-locked to the network clock. Otherwise, the CBR service is called asynchronous.

The service provided by the AAL consists of its own capability plus the capability of the ATM Layer and the Physical Layer. This service is provided to the AAL user (e.g., an entity in an upper layer or in the Management Plane). The service definition is based on a set of service primitives that describe in an abstract manner the logical exchange of information and control. Functions performed by the CBR AAL entities are shown in Table 3.1.

The logical exchange of information between the AAL and the AAL user is represented by two primitives, as shown in Table 3.2.

Service expected from the ATM Layer. The AAL expects the ATM Layer to provide for the transparent and sequential transfer of AAL data units, each of length 48 octets, between communicating AAL entities over an ATM Layer connection, at a negotiated bandwidth and QOS. The ATM Layer transfers the information in the order in which it was delivered to the ATM Layer and provides no retransmission of lost or corrupted information.

TABLE 3.1   Functions Performed by CBR AAL

Detection and reporting of lost SAR_PDUs	Detects discontinuity in the sequence count values of the SAR_PDUs and senses buffer underflow and overflow conditions.
Detection and correction of SAR_PDU header error	Detects bit errors in the SAR_PDU header and possibly corrects a 1-bit error.
Bit count integrity	Generates dummy information units to replace lost AAL_SDUs to be passed to the AAL user in an AAL-DATA.indication.
Residual time stamp (RTS) generation	Encodes source service clock timing information for transport to the receiving AAL entity.*
Source clock recovery	Recovers the CBR service source clock.
Blocking	Maps AAL_SDUs into the payload of a CS_PDU.
Deblocking	Reconstructs the AAL_SDU from the received SAR_PDUs and generates the AAL-DATA. indication primitive.
Structure pointer generation and extraction	Encodes in a 1-octet structure pointer field at the sending AAL entity the information about periodic octet-based block structures present in AAL-DATA.request primitives. The receiving AAL entity extracts the structure pointer received in the CS_PDU header field to verify locally generated block structure.

*Refer to Ref. 3 for a description of the time stamp mechanism.

Interactions between the SAR and the Convergence Sublayer.   The logical exchange of information between the SAR and the Convergence Sublayer is represented by the primitives of Table 3.3.

Interacting with the Management Plane.   The AALM entities in the Management Plane perform the management functions specific to the AAL. Also, the AALM entities, in conjunction with the Plane Management, provide coordination of the local interactions between the User Plane and the Control Plane across the layers.

The AAL entities provide the AALM entities with the information required for error processing or abnormal condition handling, such as indication of lost or misdelivered SAR_PDUs and indication of errored SAR_PDU headers.

TABLE 3.2 Primitives for CBR AAL

AAL-DATA.request (AAL_SDU, Structure)	This primitive is issued by an AAL user entity to request the transfer of an AAL_SDU to its peer entity over an existing AAL connection. The time interval between two consecutive AAL-DATA.request primitives is constant and a function of the specific AAL service provided to the AAL user.
AAL-DATA.indication (AAL_SDU, Structure, Status)	This primitive is issued to an AAL user entity to notify the arrival of an AAL_SDU over an existing AAL connection. In the absence of error, the AAL_SDU is the same as the AAL_SDU sent by the peer AAL user entity in the corresponding AAL-DATA.request. The time interval between two consecutive AAL-DATA.indication primitives is constant and a function of the specific AAL service provided to the AAL user.

Description of parameters:
AAL_SDU: This parameter contains 1 bit of AAL user data to be transferred by the AAL between two communication AAL user peer entities.

Structure: This parameter is used to indicate the beginning or continuation of a block of AAL_SDUs when providing for the transfer of a structured bit stream between communicating AAL user peer entities (structured data transfer service). The length of the blocks is constant for each instance of the AAL service and is a multiple of 8 bits. This parameter takes one of the following two values: Start and Continuation. It is set to Start whenever the AAL_SDU being passed in the same primitive is the first bit of a block of a structured bit stream. Otherwise, it is set to Continuation. This parameter is used only when SDT service is supported.

Status: This parameter indicates whether the AAL_SDU being passed in the same indication primitive is judged to be nonerrored or errored. It takes one of the following two values: Valid or Invalid. The Invalid value may also indicate that the AAL_SDU being passed is a dummy value. The use of this parameter and the choice of the dummy value depend on the specific service provided.

TABLE 3.3 SAR Primitives

SAR-DATA.invoke (CSDATA, SCVAL, CSIVAL)	This primitive is issued by the sending CS entity to the sending SAR entity to request the transfer of a CSDATA to its peer entity.
SAR-DATA.signal (CSDATA, SNCK, SCVAL, CSIVAL)	This primitive is issued by the receiving SAR entity to the receiving CS entity to notify it of the arrival of a CSDATA from its peer CS entity.

Description of parameters:
CSDATA: This parameter represents the interface data unit exchanged between the SAR entity and the CS entity. It contains the 47-octet CS_PDU.

SCVAL: This 3-bit parameter contains the value of the sequence count associated with the CS_PDU contained in the CSDATA parameter.

CSIVAL: This 1-bit parameter contains the value of the CSI bit.

SNCK: This parameter is generated by the receiving SAR entity. It represents the results of the sequence number protection error check over the SAR_PDU header. It can assume the values of SN-Valid and SN-Invalid.

3.4   ATM Adaptation Layer Functions for VBR (or Bursty Data) Services

As seen in Fig. 3.5, AAL functions for VBR services such as SMDS and frame relay consist of a set of core functions and a set of optional functions. This AAL is now commonly referred to as AAL Type 3/4. As an example, SMDS over ATM uses AAL Type 3/4. The purpose of the ATM Adaptation Layer Type 4/3 Common Part (CPAAL3/4) protocol is to support the upper-layer data transfer needs while using the service of the ATM Layer. This protocol provides for the transport of variable-length frames (up to 65,535 octets in length) with error detection. The CPAAL3/4 provides service over preestablished connections. Termination of a CPAAL3/4 connection also coincides with termination of an ATM Layer service. The establishment and initialization of a CPAAL3/4 connection is performed by interaction with CPAAL3/4 Layer Management entities. There is a dual view of the AAL3/4 Layer.

1. View in terms of Service-Specific Parts and Common Part, as shown in the left-hand side of Fig. 3.8. Core functions are required by all bursty data applications; these functions are known as CP. Optional SSPs are selected as needed. For some applications the SSP is null, implying that the user of the AAL3/4 Layer utilizes the Common Part directly.

2. View in terms of a combination of SAR, the Common Part of the Convergence Sublayer, and SSP, as shown in the right-hand side of Fig. 3.8. SAR and the Common Part of the Convergence Sublayer taken together make up the CP; the Common Part of CS and SSP together form the CS. In other words, the Convergence Sublayer has been

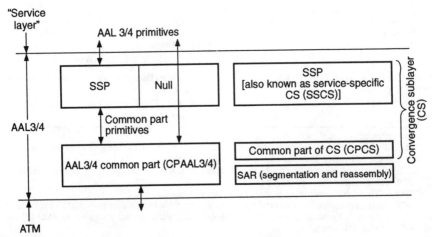

Figure 3.8 Model of AAL3/4. Left: CP/SSP view; right: CS/SAR view.

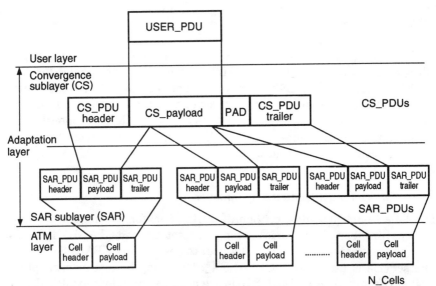

Figure 3.9 Adaptation Layer model for bursty data services.

subdivided into the Common Part CS (CPCS) and the Service-Specific CS (SSCS). In this view, functions are provided by the operation of two logical sublayers, the CS and the SAR. Figure 3.9 shows the operation of AAL3/4 in terms of the PDUs.

The SAR Sublayer is common to all VBR services using AAL3/4, whereas the Convergence Sublayer provides additional, service-specific functions (note that some VBR services may use AAL5). The functions of the Common Part are clearly common by definition. In addition to this, achieving the maximum commonality in the Convergence Sublayer protocol for bursty data services has also been an objective, as implied in Fig. 3.5. For these services, the user presents a variable-size PDU for transmission across the ATM network. The transmission is accomplished by using fixed-length cells to transport data in ATM, as discussed in Chap. 2. At the receiving end of the ATM connection, the user layer receives the PDU that has been reassembled by the SAR and CS protocols.

The discussion that follows looks at AAL3/4 first from a CP point of view (the left-hand model in Fig. 3.8), then from the SAR point of view (the right-hand side of Fig. 3.8). As noted, the functions of the CPAAL3/4 in this view have been grouped into two sublayers: CPAAL3/4 Segmentation and Reassembly (CPAAL3/4_SAR) and CPAAL3/4 Convergence Sublayer (CPAAL3/4_CS). The CPAAL3/4_SAR deals principally with the segmentation and reassembly of data units so that they can be mapped into fixed-length payloads of the ATM cells, while the CPAAL3/4_CS deals mainly with checking missassembled CPAAL3/4_CS_PDUs.

CPAAL3/4 Layer Management is responsible for the following capabilities: assignment of the CPAAL3/4 association necessary for the establishment of CPAAL3/4 connections between peer CPAAL3/4 entities, resetting the parameters and state variables associated with a CPAAL3/4 connection between peer CPAAL3/4 entities, and monitoring performance for the quality of the ATM connection service provided through notification of errors.

3.4.1 Services provided to the upper layer

The CPAAL3/4 provides, on behalf of its user, for the sequential and transparent transfer of variable-length, octet-aligned CPAAL3/4_SDUs from one corresponding CPAAL3/4 peer to one or more CPAAL3/4 peers. The service is unassured: CPAAL3/4_SDUs may be lost or corrupted. Lost or corrupted CPAAL3/4_SDUs are not recovered by the CPAAL3/4. As an option, corrupted CPAAL3/4_SDUs may be delivered to the remote peer with an indication of the error (this option is known as corrupted data delivery option).

Specifically, the functions performed by the CPAAL3/4 are[6]

- Data transfer between CPAAL3/4 peers
- Preservation of CPAAL3/4_SDUs (delineation and transparency of CPAAL3/4_SDUs)
- CPAAL3/4_SDU segmentation
- CPAAL3/4_SDU reassembly
- Error detection and handling (detects and handles bit errors, lost or gained information, and incorrectly assembled CPAAL3/4_SDUs)
- Multiplexing and demultiplexing (optional multiplexing of multiple CPAAL3/4 connections or interleaving of CPAAL3/4_CS_PDUs)
- Abort (termination of task in case of partially transmitted/received CPAAL3/4_SDUs)
- Pipelining (forwarding PDUs before the entire PDU is received)

This layer provides its user two services:

1. Message-mode service: In this service mode, the CPAAL3/4_SDU passed across the CPAAL3/4 interface is exactly equal to one CPAAL3/4 interface data unit (CPAAL3/4_IDU), as seen in Fig. 3.10.

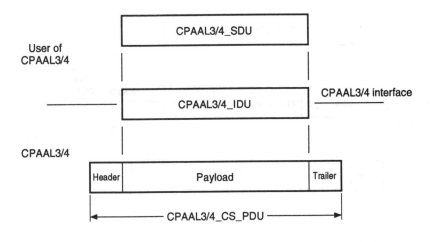

Figure 3.10   Message-mode service.

2. Streaming-mode service: In this service mode, the CPAAL3/4_SDU is passed across the CPAAL3/4 interface using one or more CPAAL3/4_IDUs. (IDUs are *interface data units*.) The transfer of these CPAAL3/4_IDUs across the CPAAL3/4 interface may occur separated in time. This service may pipeline the CPAAL3/4_SDU, that is, initiate the information transfer to the peer CPAAL3/4 entity before it has the complete CPAAL3/4_SDU available. This service includes an abort capability which discards a CPAAL3/4_SDU that is partially transferred across the CPAAL3/4 interface. All the CPAAL3/4_IDUs belonging to a single CPAAL3/4_SDU are transferred in one CPAAL3/4_PDU. See Fig. 3.11.

The primitives to support the service provided by the AAL are as follows (not all primitives are required by all services—e.g., ABORT is not used in message-mode service):

1. CPAAL3/4-UNITDATA.invoke (ID, M, ML, LP, CI)[*]
2. CPAAL3/4-UNITDATA.signal (ID, M, ML, RS, LP, CI)*
3. CPAAL3/4-U-ABORT.invoke
4. CPAAL3/4-U-ABORT.signal
5. CPAAL3/4-P-ABORT.signal

Note: If the SSP is null, then .invoke can be equated to .request and .signal can be equated to .indication. If the SSP is not null, then the function of the SSP is in fact used to map the .invoke to a .request and

---

*The items in parentheses are parameters—see Table 3.4.

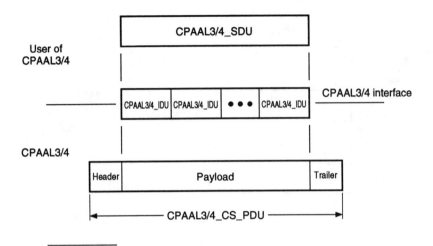

Figure 3.11 Streaming-mode service.

the .signal to an .indication. Table 3.4 provides additional information on these primitives.

Services from the ATM Layer. The CPAAL3/4 expects the ATM Layer (discussed in Chap. 2) to provide for the transparent and sequential transport of 48-octet CPAAL3/4 data units (that is, CPAAL3/4_SAR_PDUs) between communicating CPAAL3/4 peers over preestablished connections at a negotiated QOS. The information is transferred to the ATM Layer in the order in which it is to be sent, with no retransmission of lost or corrupted information.

Interaction with CPAAL3/4 Management entities. Management information is exchanged using five management primitives. See Ref. 4 for details.

3.4.2 SAR Sublayer functions

There is a single SAR function for all bursty data services. Hence, the SAR control fields that appear in each cell payload must be the same, regardless of the service and whether or not the fields are used by a particular application. A single SAR for these services leads to lower overall costs for equipment providers and network providers, and hence for end users (e.g., diagnostic generation, testing, and maintenance are simpler when only a single SAR function is used for all services).

The SAR control fields include the following:[6]

Segment_Type field to identify the cell payload as being beginning of message (BOM), continuation of message (COM), end of message (EOM), or only a single-segment message (SSM).

TABLE 3.4   CPAAL3/4 Primitives

CPAAL3/4-UNITDATA.invoke	Issued by a CPAAL3/4 entity to request the transfer of a CPAAL3/4_IDU over an existing CPAAL3/4 connection. This IDU is not subject to any flow control and is always transmitted. The transfer of the IDU is subject to the service mode being used (message versus streaming).
CPAAL3/4-UNITDATA.signal	Issued to a CPAAL3/4 entity to indicate the arrival of a CPAAL3/4_IDU over an existing CPAAL3/4 connection.
CPAAL3/4-U-ABORT.invoke	Issued by a CPAAL3/4 entity using streaming-mode service to request the termination of a CPAAL3/4_SDU that has been partially transferred. The issue of this primitive also causes the generation of an abort message by the CPAAL3/4 to its peer entity if the transmission of the message has already started. (This primitive is not used in message mode.)
CPAAL3/4-U-ABORT.signal	Issued by a CPAAL3/4 entity using streaming-mode service to indicate the termination of a partially delivered CPAAL3/4_SDU by instruction from its peer entity. (This primitive is not used in message mode.)
CPAAL3/4-P-ABORT.signal	Issued by a CPAAL3/4 entity using streaming-mode service to indicate to its user that a partially delivered CPAAL-3/4_SDU is to be discarded because of the occurrence of some error; it has local significance. (This primitive is not used in message mode.)

Description of parameters:

ID (Interface data): This parameter contains the interface data unit (CPAAL3/4_IDU) exchanged between CPAAL3/4 entities [it may be the entire CPAAL3/4_SDU (message mode) or segments (streaming mode)].

M (more): Used only in streaming mode to indicate whether the CPAAL3/4_IDU communicated in the ID parameter contains the ending segment of the CPAAL3/4_PDU (=0) or does not (=1).

ML (maximum length): Used only in streaming mode to indicate the maximum length of the CPAAL3/4_SDU; it has values from 0 to 65,535.

RS (reception status): Indicates that the CPAAL3/4_IDU delivered may be corrupted.

LP (loss priority): Indicates the loss priority assigned to the CPAAL3/4_SDU. Two levels of priority are supported, but how to map this parameter to and from the ATM_Submitted_Loss_Priority (discussed in Chap. 2) has not yet been worked out.

CI (congestion indication): Indicates the detection of congestion experienced by the received CPAAL3/4_SDU.

Sequence_Number field to improve the reassembly error detection process.

Message_ID (M_ID) field, which, for connectionless services, allows for the collection of the cell payloads that make up a CS PDU.

Cell Fill field that allows the identification of the fill within a cell payload. It can be used to locate the last octet in the end of message cell. The last octet in the EOM cell could also be identified from the length field associated with the PDU; additionally, data pipelining could be provided by a series of partially filled single-segment message cells. However, in the latter case, significant additional processing is required to reconstruct the original data unit compared with the case where partial fills are indicated by a cell-associated length field.

Error Control field which provides error detection capabilities across the adaptation header and the information payload. The error check is made across all 48 octets irrespective of whether the cell is fully or partially filled.

On transmission, the process is used by the sending CPAAL3/4 entity. The SAR Sublayer accepts variable-length CPAAL3/4_CS_PDUs from the Convergence Sublayer and maps each CPAAL3/4_CS_PDU into a sequence of CPAAL3/4_SAR_PDUs, by placing at most 44 octets of the CPAAL3/4_CS_PDU into a CPAAL3/4_SAR_PDU payload, along with additional control information, described below, used to verify the integrity of the CPAAL3/4_SAR_PDU payload on reception and to control the reassembly process. The sending CPAAL3/4 entity transfers the CPAAL3/4_SAR_PDUs to the ATM Layer for delivery across the network.

On reception, CPAAL3/4_SAR_PDUs are validated, and the user data in the CPAAL3/4_SAR_PDU (note that a CPAAL3/4_SAR_PDU can be partially filled) are passed to the Convergence Sublayer.

3.4.3 Convergence Sublayer functions

On transmission, the Convergence Sublayer accepts variable-length user protocol data units (USER_PDUs) from the service layer. The Convergence Sublayer prepends a 32-bit header to the USER_PDU, then appends from 0 to 3 pad octets to the USER_PDU to build it out to an integral multiple of 32 bits. Next, it appends a 32-bit trailer to the concatenated header, USER_PDU, and pad structure. This collection (the header, USER_PDU, pad, and trailer) is referred to as a CPAAL3/4_CS_PDU. The header and trailer fields are used to detect loss of data and to perform additional functions as required by the service user. After appending the trailer, the Convergence Sublayer passes the CPAAL3/4_CS_PDU to the SAR Sublayer for segmentation and then transmission.[6]

On reception, the Convergence Sublayer validates the collection of CPAAL3/4_SAR_PDU payloads received from the SAR Sublayer by using the information contained in the Convergence Sublayer header and trailer. It removes the pad octets, if any, and presents the validated CPAAL3/4_CS_PDU payload to the user (i.e., the service layer).

3.4.4 SAR Sublayer fields and format

The SAR Sublayer functions are implemented using a 2-octet adaptation header and a 2-octet adaptation trailer. The header and trailer, together with 44 octets of user information, make up the payload of the ATM cell. The sizes and positions of the fields are given in Fig. 3.12. The use of the error control field for error detection is mandatory. The 10-bit CRC has the capability of single-bit error correction over the 48 octets. If the underlying transmission system produces single-bit errors, error correction may be applied at the receiver.

Figure 3.12 shows the CPAAL3/4_SAR_PDU components of the Adaptation Layer, which include a SAR_PDU_Header and an SAR_PDU_Trailer. These two fields encapsulate the SAR_PDU_Payload, which contains a portion of the CPAAL3/4_CS_PDU.

The SAR_PDU_Header is subdivided into three fields: a Segment_Type field, a Sequence_Number field, and a Message Identification (MID) field. The SAR_PDU_Trailer is subdivided into two fields: a Payload_Length field and a Payload CRC field. Details of the purpose and encoding of each subfield follow.[6]

Segment_Type subfield. The 2-bit Segment_Type subfield is used to indicate whether a CPAAL3/4_SAR_PDU is a BOM, COM, EOM, or SSM. Table 3.5 shows the encodings for the Segment_Type subfield.

Sequence_Number subfield. Four-bits are allocated to the SAR_PDU Sequence_Number (SAR_SN) subfield, allowing the streams of

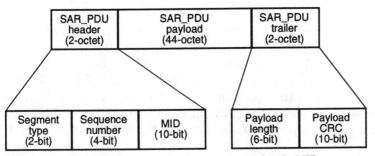

Figure 3.12 CPAAL3/4_SAR_PDU Sublayer format of AAL. MID = message identifier, or multiplexing identifier.

TABLE 3.5   Encoding of the Segment _Type Subfield

Segment_Type	Encoding
BOM	10
COM	00
EOM	01
SSM	11

CPAAL3/4_SAR_PDUs and CPAAL3/4_CS_PDUs to be numbered modulo 16. The SAR_SN is set to all 0s for the first CPAAL3/4_SAR_PDU associated with a given CPAAL3/4_CS_PDU (i.e., the BOM). For each succeeding CPAAL3/4_SAR_PDU of that CPAAL3/4_CS_PDU, the SAR_SN is incremented by 1 relative to the SAR_SN of the previous CPAAL3/4_SAR_PDU of the CPAAL3/4_CS_PDU. When reassembling a CPAAL3/4_CS_PDU, a state variable is maintained that indicates the value of the next expected SAR_SN for the CPAAL3/4_CS_PDU. If the value of the received SAR_SN differs from the expected value, the CPAAL3/4_SAR_PDU is dropped, the partially reassembled errored CPAAL3/4_CS_PDU is discarded, and any following CPAAL3/4_SAR_PDUs associated with this corrupted CPAAL3/4_CS_PDU are dropped.

The use of this function allows the detection of most consecutive losses of COM cells as soon as the following COM or EOM cell of the CPAAL3/4_CS_PDU is received. If the number of COMs of a given CPAAL3/4_CS_PDU that is lost is an integer multiple of 16, the SAR_SN cannot detect them. Therefore, the use of the length field at the CS Sublayer is still required to detect any modulo 16 consecutive losses of CPAAL3/4_SAR_PDUs that may occur during situations like network congestion or protection switching events.

In addition, the use of this function will allow for immediate detection of most cases of cell insertion.

The use of Sequence_Number to detect situations in which two CPAAL3/4_CS_PDUs are inadvertently merged into one and the resulting length matches the length field in the CPAAL3/4_CS_PDU trailer is weak. This is due to the fact that this error event requires that the lengths of the original CPAAL3/4_CS_PDUs be the same. This implies that the same number of CPAAL3/4_SAR_PDUs will probably be required to transport two CPAAL3/4_CS_PDUs. Therefore, the SAR_SNs of the received CPAAL3/4_SAR_PDUs will probably be consecutive, and so the SAR Sublayer will not detect this error event. As a result, the use of the Etag at the CS Sublayer is still required.

Message Identification (MID) subfield.   The 10-bit MID subfield is used to reassemble CPAAL3/4_SAR_PDUs into CPAAL3/4_CS_PDUs. All CPAAL3/4_SAR_PDUs of a given CPAAL3/4_CS_PDU will have the same MID. Note that this provides the basis for reassembly of discrete connectionless packets. Use of this subfield as the basis for a multiplexing or reassembly capability for connection-oriented services is for further study.

Payload_Length subfield.   The 6-bit Payload_Length subfield is coded with the number of octets from the CPAAL3/4_CS_PDU that are included in the current CPAAL3/4_SAR_PDU. This number has a value between 0 and 44 inclusive. This subfield is binary coded with the most significant bit left-justified. BOM and COM cells take the value 44; EOM cells take the values 4, 8, ..., 44; SSM cells take the values 8, 12, ..., 44.

SAR_PDU_Payload.   The CPAAL3/4_CS_PDU is left-justified in the SAR_PDU_Payload of the CPAAL3/4_SAR_PDU. Any part of the SAR_PDU_Payload that is not filled with CS information shall be coded as zeros.

Payload_CRC subfield.   The 10-bit Payload_CRC subfield is filled with the value of a CRC calculation that is performed over the entire contents of the CPAAL3/4_SAR_PDU payload, including the SAR_PDU_Header, the SAR_PDU_Payload, and the SAR_PDU_Trailer. The CRC-10 generating polynomial has the capability of single-bit error correction over the CPAAL3/4_SAR_PDU. The following generator polynomial is used to calculate the Payload_CRC:

$$G(x) = x^{10} + x^3 + 1$$

The CRC remainder is placed in the CRC subfield with the most significant bit left-justified in the CRC subfield.

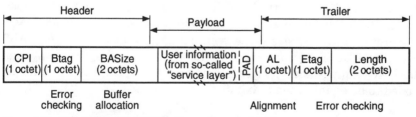

Figure 3.13   CPAAL3/4_CS_PDU Sublayer format of AAL.

3.4.5 Convergence Sublayer
fields and format

Figure 3.13 depicts the Convergence Sublayer format of the AAL3/4.

There are two Adaptation Layer control fields: the CS_PDU_Header and the CS_PDU_Trailer, both of which are 4 octets long. The CS_PDU_Header and CS_PDU_Trailer encapsulate the user's protocol data units (USER_PDU). In addition, there may be from 0 to 3 pad octets added to align the CPAAL3/4_CS_PDU with a 32-bit boundary.

The CS_PDU_Header is subdivided into three fields: an 8-bit Common Part Indicator field, an 8-bit Beginning Tag (Btag) field, and a 16-bit Buffer Allocation size (BAsize) field. Likewise, the CS_PDU_Trailer is also subdivided into three fields: an 8-bit filler field, an 8-bit End Tag (Etag) field, and a 16-bit Length field.[6]

Common Part Indicator subfield.   The 8-bit Common Part Indicator (CPI) subfield is used to identify the message type, i.e., to interpret subsequent fields for the CPAAL3/4-CS functions in the CPAAL3/4_CS_PDU header and trailer. It also indicates the counting unit for the values specified in the BAsize and Length fields.

CS_PDU Header—Btag subfield.   For a given CPAAL3/4_CS_PDU, the same value appears in the 8-bit Btag field of the CS_PDU_Header and in the Etag field in the CS_PDU_Trailer. This allows the identification of a BOM segment and an EOM segment, and hence all intervening COM segments, as belonging to the same CPAAL3/4_CS_PDU. This correlation is required to implement segment loss detection over a CPAAL3/4_CS_PDU. As each CPAAL3/4_CS_PDU is transmitted, the Etag value is changed so that the entire range of Etag field values (0 to 255) is cycled through before reuse to aid in this segment loss protection.

BAsize subfield.   The 16-bit Buffer Allocation size (BAsize) subfield is used to predict the buffer requirements for the CPAAL3/4_CS_PDU. Therefore, it must be greater than or equal to the true CPAAL3/4_CS_PDU length. This field is binary coded with the most significant bit left-justified in the subfield. If message-mode service is being provided, the BAsize value is encoded to be equal to the length of the USER_PDU field contained in the CPAAL3/4_CS_PDU Payload field. If streaming-mode service is being provided, the BAsize value is encoded to be equal to the maximum length of the CPAAL3/4_SDU.

USER_PDU field.   The variable-length USER_PDU field contains user information. It contains the CPAAL3/4_SDU. It is octet aligned, as it is limited in length to the value of the BAsize field multiplied by the value of the counting unit (as identified in the CPI field).

Pad Field.   The Pad field consists of 0, 1, 2, or 3 octets set to zero, so that the CPAAL3/4_CS_PDU is padded out to a 32-bit boundary.

AL.   This 8-bit subfield is used to achieve 32-bit alignment in the CPAAL3/4_CS_PDU trailer. This is strictly a filler octet and does not contain any additional information.

Etag subfield.   The 8-bit Etag subfield in the CPAAL3/4_CS_PDU trailer has the same value as the Btag subfield in the corresponding CPAAL3/4_CS_PDU header. As was mentioned earlier, the Btag and Etag subfields in the CS_PDU_Header and CS_PDU_Trailer are correlated in order to detect segment loss and misassembly. This field is binary coded with the most significant bit left-justified.

Length subfield.   The 16-bit Length subfield specifies the length, in octets, of the USER_PDU (that is, the length of the user information contained in the CPAAL3/4_CS_PDU Payload field). This field is binary coded with the most significant bit left-justified in the subfield. It is used in conjunction with the Btag and Etag fields for the purpose of detecting misassembled CPAAL3/4_CS_PDUs.

3.5   AAL Type 5

The goal of the AAL Type 5 is to support, in the most streamlined fashion, those capabilities that are required to meet upper-layer data transfer over an ATM platform. The AAL Type 5 Common Part (CPAAL5) protocol provides for the transport of variable-length frames (1 to 65,535 octets) with error detection (the frame is padded to align the resulting PDU with an integral number of ATM cells). A length field is used to extract the frame and detect additional errors not detected with the CRC-32 mechanism. ANSI had a Letter Ballot for AAL Type 5 Common Part at press time, and ITU-TS had a draft version of I.363 (Section 6); approval was expected.

The Convergence Sublayer has been subdivided into the Common Part CS (CPCS) and the Service-Specific CS (SSCS), as shown in Fig. 3.14. Different SSCS protocols, to support specific AAL user services or groups of services, may be defined. The SSCS may also be null, in the sense that it provides only for the mapping of the equivalent primitives of the AAL to CPCS and vice versa. SSCS protocols are specified in separate Recommendations, not in, say, ITU-T I.363. This discussion

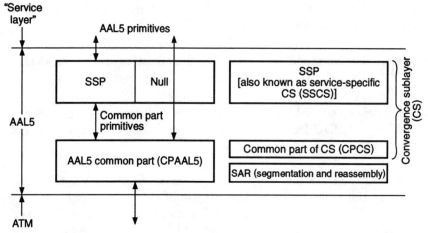

Figure 3.14 Structure of AAL Type 5.

therefore focuses on CPCS and SAR. Notice that CPAAL5 = SAR + CPCS. Also see Fig. 3.15.

3.5.1 Service provided by CPAAL5

The Common Part of AAL Type 5 provides the capability to transfer the CPAAL5_SDU from one CPAAL5 user to another CPAAL5 user through the ATM network. During this process, CPAAL5_SDUs may be corrupted or lost (in this case, an indication of the error is provided). Corrupted or

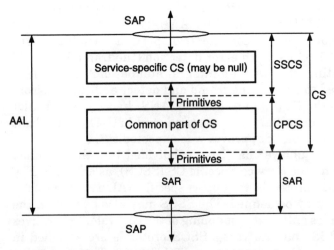

Figure 3.15 Another view of the structure of AAL Type 5.

lost CPAAL5_SDUs are not recovered by CPAAL5. CPAAL5 supports a message mode and a streaming mode. The message-mode service, streaming-mode service, and assured and nonassured operations as defined below for CPAAL5 are identical to those defined for AAL Type 3/4.

1. *Message-mode service.* The CPAAL5_SDU is passed across the CPAAL5 interface in exactly one Common Part AAL interface data unit (CPAAL5_IDU). This service provides the transport of fixed-size or variable-length CPAAL5_SDUs.

    a. In the case of small fixed-size CPAAL5_SDUs, an internal blocking/deblocking function in the SSCS may be applied; it provides the transport of one or more fixed-size CPAAL5_SDUs in one SSCS_PDU.
    b. In the case of variable-length CPAAL5_SDUs, an internal CPAAL5_SDU message segmentation/reassembling function in the SSCS may be applied. In this case, a single CPAAL5_SDU is transferred in one or more SSCS_PDUs.
    c. Where the above options are not used, a single CPAAL5_SDU is transferred in one SSCS_PDU. When the SSCS is null, the CPAAL5_SDU is mapped to one CPCS_SDU.

2. *Streaming-mode service.* The CPAAL5_SDU is passed across the CPAAL5 interface in one or more CPAAL5_IDUs. The transfer of these CPAAL5_IDUs across the CPAAL5 interface may occur separated in time. This service provides the transport of variable-length CPAAL5_SDUs. Streaming-mode service includes an abort service by which the discarding of an CPAAL5_SDU that has been partially transferred across the AAL interface can be requested.

    a. An internal CPAAL5_SDU message segmentation/reassembling function in the SSCS may be applied. In this case, all the CPAAL5_IDUs belonging to a single CPAAL5_SDU are transferred in one or more SSCS_PDUs.
    b. An internal pipelining function may be applied. It provides the means by which the sending CPAAL5 entity initiates the transfer to the receiving CPAAL5 entity before it has the complete CPAAL5_SDU available.
    c. Where option *a* is not used, all the CPAAL5_IDUs belonging to a single CPAAL5_SDU are transferred in one SSCS_PDU. When the SSCS is null, the CPAAL5_IDUs belonging to a single CPAAL5_SDU are mapped to one CPCS_SDU.

Both modes of service may offer the following peer-to-peer operational procedures:

- *Assured operations*. Every assured CPAAL5_SDU is delivered with exactly the data content that the user sent. The assured service is provided by retransmission of missing or corrupted SSCS_PDUs. Flow control is provided as a mandatory feature. The assured operation may be restricted to point-to-point AAL connections.

- *Nonassured operations*. Integral CPAAL5_SDUs may be lost or corrupted. Lost and corrupted CPAAL5_SDUs will not be corrected by retransmission. An optional feature may be provided to allow corrupted CPAAL5_SDUs to be delivered to the user (i.e., optional error discard). Flow control may be provided as an option.

Description of AAL connections.   The CPAAL5 provides the capability to transfer the CPAAL5_SDU from one AAL5-SAP to another AAL5-SAP through the ATM network. CPAAL5 users have the ability to select a given AAL5-SAP associated with the QOS required to transport that CPAAL5_SDU (for example, delay- and loss-sensitive QOS).

The CPAAL5 in nonassured operation also provides the capability to transfer the CPAAL5_SDUs from one AAL5-SAP to more than one AAL5-SAP through the ATM network.

CPAAL5 makes use of the service provided by the underlying ATM Layer. Multiple AAL connections may be associated with a single ATM-Layer connection, allowing multiplexing at the AAL; however, if multiplexing is used in the AAL, it occurs in the SSCS. The AAL user selects the QOS provided by the AAL through the choice of the AAL5-SAP used for data transfer.

Primitives for the AAL.   These primitives are service-specific and are contained in separate Recommendations on SSCS protocols.

The SSCS may be null, in the sense that it provides only for the mapping of the equivalent primitives of the AAL to CPCS and vice versa. In this case, the primitives for the AAL are equivalent to those for the CPCS but are identified as CPAAL5-UNITDATA.request, CPAAL5-UNITDATA.indication, CPAAL5-U-Abort.request, CPAAL5-U-Abort.indication, and CPAAL5-P-Abort.indication, consistent with the primitive naming convention at an SAP.

Primitives for the CPCS of the AAL.   As there is no SAP between the sublayers of the AAL5, the primitives are called .invoke and .signal instead of the conventional .request and .indication to highlight the absence of the SAP.

CPCS-UNITDATA.invoke and CPCS-UNITDATA.signal.   These primitives are used for data transfer. The following parameters are defined:

- Interface data (ID). This parameter specifies the interface data unit exchanged between the CPCS and the SSCS entity. The ID is an integral multiple of 1 octet. If the CPCS entity is operating in message-mode service, the ID represents a complete CPCS_SDU; when operating in streaming-mode service, the ID does not necessarily represent a complete CPCS_SDU.

- More (M). In message-mode service, this parameter is not used. In streaming-mode service, this parameter specifies whether the interface data communicated contains a beginning/continuation of a CPCS_SDU or the end of a complete CPCS_SDU.

- CPCS loss priority (CPCS-LP). This parameter indicates the loss priority for the associated CPCS_SDU. It can take only two values, one for high priority and the other for low priority. The use of this parameter in streaming mode is for further study. This parameter is mapped to and from the SAR-LP parameter.

- CPCS congestion indication (CPCS-CI). This parameter indicates that the associated CPCS_SDU has experienced congestion. The use of this parameter in streaming mode is for further study. This parameter is mapped to and from the SAR-CI parameter.

- CPCS user-to-user indication (CPCS-UU). This parameter is transparently transported by the CPCS between peer CPCS users.

- Reception status (RS). This parameter indicates that the associated CPCS_SDU delivered may be corrupted. This parameter is utilized only if the corrupted data delivery option is used.

Depending on the service mode (message- or streaming-mode service, discarding or delivery of errored information), not all parameters are required.

CPCS-U-Abort.invoke and CPCS-U-Abort.signal.   These primitives are used by the CPCS user to invoke the abort service. They are also used to signal to the CPCS user that a partially delivered CPCS_SDU is to be discarded by instruction from its peer entity. No parameters are defined. These primitives are not used in message mode.

CPCS-P-Abort.signal.   This primitive is used by the CPCS entity to signal to its user that a partially delivered CPCS_SDU is to be discarded because of the occurrence of some error in the CPCS or below. No parameters are defined. This primitive is not used in message mode.

Primitives for the SAR sublayer of the AAL.   These primitives model the exchange of information between the SAR sublayer and the CPCS.

As there is no SAP between the sublayers of the AAL5, the primitives are called .invoke and .signal instead of the conventional .request and .indication to highlight the absence of the SAP.

SAR-UNITDATA.invoke and SAR-UNITDATA.signal.   These primitives are used for data transfer. The following parameters are defined:

- Interface data (ID). This parameter specifies the interface data unit exchanged between the SAR and the CPCS entity. The ID is an integral multiple of 48 octets. It does not necessarily represent a complete SAR_SDU.

- More (M). This parameter specifies whether the interface data communicated contains the end of the SAR_SDU.

- SAR loss priority (SAR-LP). This parameter indicates the loss priority for the associated SAR interface data. It can take on two values, one for high priority and the other for low priority. This parameter is mapped to the ATM Layer's submitted loss priority parameter and from the ATM Layer's received loss priority parameter.

- SAR congestion indication (SAR-CI). This parameter indicates whether the associated SAR interface data has experienced congestion. This parameter is mapped to and from the ATM Layer's congestion indication parameter.

3.5.2 Functions, structure, and coding of AAL5

Functions of the SAR Sublayer.   The SAR Sublayer functions are performed on an SAR_PDU basis. The SAR Sublayer accepts variable-length SAR_SDUs which are integral multiples of 48 octets from the CPCS and generates SAR_PDUs containing 48 octets of SAR_SDU data. It supports the preservation of SAR_SDUs by providing for an "end of SAR_SDU" indication.

SAR_PDU structure and coding.   The SAR Sublayer function utilizes the ATM-Layer-user-to-ATM-Layer-user (AUU) parameter of the ATM Layer primitives to indicate that a SAR_PDU contains the end of a

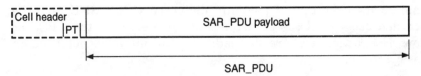

Figure 3.16 SAR_PDU format for AAL5. [*Note:* The payload type (PT) field belongs to the ATM header. It conveys the value of the AUU parameter end-to-end.]

SAR_SDU. A SAR_PDU where the value of the AUU parameter is 1 indicates the end of a SAR_SDU; a value of 0 indicates the beginning or continuation of a SAR_SDU. The structure of the SAR_PDU is shown in Fig. 3.16.

Convergence Sublayer. The CPCS has the following service characteristics.

- Nonassured data transfer of user data frames with any length measured in octets from 1 to 65,535 octets.
- The CPCS connection will be established by management or by the Control Plane.
- Error detection and indication (bit error and cell loss or gain).
- CPCS_SDU sequence integrity on each CPCS connection.

Functions of the CPCS. The CPCS functions are performed per CPCS_PDU. The CPCS provides several functions in support of the CPCS service user. The functions provided depend on whether the CPCS service user is operating in message or streaming mode.

1. *Message mode service.* The CPCS_SDU is passed across the CPCS interface in exactly one CPCS-IDU. This service provides the transport of a single CPCS_SDU in one CPCS_PDU.

2. *Streaming mode service.* The CPCS_SDU is passed across the CPCS interface in one or more CPCS-IDUs. The transfer of these CPCS-IDUs across the CPCS interface may occur separated in time. This service provides the transport of all the CPCS-IDUs belonging to a single CPCS_SDU into one CPCS_PDU. An internal pipelining function in the CPCS may be applied which provides the means by which the sending CPCS entity initiates the transfer to the receiving CPCS entity before it has the complete CPCS_SDU available. Streaming-mode service includes an abort service by which the discarding of a CPCS_SDU partially transferred across the interface can be requested.

Note: At the sending side, parts of the CPCS_PDU may have to be buffered if the restriction "interface data are a multiple of 48 octets" cannot be satisfied.

The functions implemented by the CPCS include:

1. *Preservation of CPCS_SDU.* This function provides for the delineation and transparency of CPCS_SDUs.

2. *Preservation of CPCS user-to-user information.* This function provides for the transparent transfer of CPCS user-to-user information.

3. *Error detection and handling.* This function provides for the detection and handling of CPCS_PDU corruption. Corrupted CPCS_SDUs are either discarded or optionally delivered to the SSCS. The procedures for delivery of corrupted CPCS_SDUs are for further study. When delivering errored information to the CPCS user, an error indication is associated with the delivery. Examples of detected errors would include received length and CPCS_PDU Length field mismatch including buffer overflow, an improperly formatted CPCS_PDU, and CPCS CRC errors.

4. *Abort.* This function provides for the means to abort a partially transmitted CPCS_SDU. This function is indicated in the Length field.

5. *Padding.* A padding function provides for 48-octet alignment of the CPCS_PDU trailer.

CPCS structure and coding. The CPCS functions require an 8-octet CPCS_PDU trailer. The CPCS_PDU trailer is always located in the last 8 octets of the last SAR_PDU of the CPCS_PDU. Therefore, a padding field provides for a 48-octet alignment of the CPCS_PDU. The

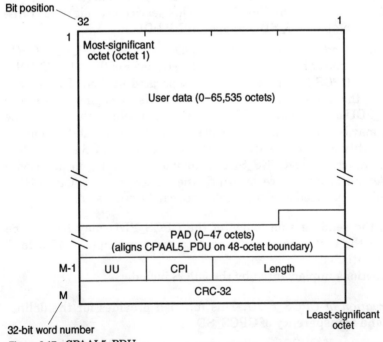

Figure 3.17 CPAAL5_PDU.

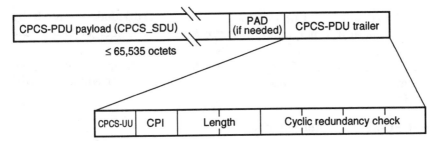

Figure 3.18 CPAAL5_PDU, another view.

CPCS_PDU trailer, the padding field, and the CPCS_PDU payload make up the CPCS_PDU.

The coding of the CPCS_PDU conforms to the coding conventions specified in 2.1 of Recommendation I.361. See Figs. 3.17 and 3.18.

1. *CPCS_PDU payload.* The CPCS_PDU payload is the CPCS_SDU.

2. *Padding (Pad) field.* Between the end of the CPCS_PDU payload and the CPCS_PDU trailer, there will be from 0 to 47 unused octets. These unused octets are called the padding (Pad) field; they are strictly used as filler octets and do not convey any information. Any coding is acceptable. This padding field complements the CPCS_PDU (including CPCS_PDU payload, padding field, and CPCS_PDU trailer) to an integral multiple of 48 octets.

3. *CPCS User-to-User Indication (CPCS-UU) field.* The CPCS-UU field is used to transparently transfer CPCS user-to-user information.

4. *Common Part Indicator (CPI) field.* One of the functions of the CPI field is to align the CPCS_PDU trailer to 64 bits. Other functions are for further study. Possible additional functions may include identification of Layer Management messages. When only the 64-bit alignment function is used, this field is coded as zero.

5. *Length field.* The Length field is used to encode the length of the CPCS_PDU payload field. The Length field value is also used by the receiver to detect the loss or gain of information. The length is binary coded as number of octets. A Length field coded as zero is used for the abort function.

6. *CRC field.* The CRC-32 is used to detect bit errors in the CPCS_PDU. The CRC field is filled with the value of a CRC calculation which is performed over the entire contents of the CPCS_PDU, including the CPCS_PDU payload, the Pad field, and the first 4 octets of the CPCS_PDU trailer. The CRC field shall contain the 1s complement of the sum (modulo 2) of

a. The remainder of $xk*(x^{31} + x^{30} + ... + x + 1)$ divided (modulo 2) by the generator polynomial, where k is the number of bits of the information over which the CRC is calculated.

b. The remainder of the division (modulo 2) by the generator polynomial of the product of x^{32} and the information over which the CRC is calculated.

The CRC-32 generator polynomial is:

$$G(x) = x^{32} + x^{26} + x^{23} + x^{22} + x^{16} + x^{12} + x^{11} + x^{10} + x^8 + x^7 + x^5 + x^4 + x^2 + x + 1$$

The result of the CRC calculation is placed with the least significant bit right-justified in the CRC field.

As a typical implementation at the transmitter, the initial content of the register of the device computing the remainder of the division is preset to all 1s and is then modified by division by the generator polynomial (as described above) of the information over which the CRC is to be calculated; the 1s complement of the resulting remainder is put into the CRC field.

As a typical implementation at the receiver, the initial content of the register of the device computing the remainder of the division is preset to all 1s. The final remainder, after multiplication by x^{32} and then division (modulo 2) by the generator polynomial of the serial incoming CPCS_PDU, will be (in the absence of errors)

$$C(x) = x^{31} + x^{30} + x^{26} + x^{25} + x^{24} + x^{18} + x^{15} + x^{14} + x^{12} + x^{11} + x^{10} + x^8 + x^6 + x^5 + x^4 + x^3 + x + 1$$

3.6   Frame Relay Service-Specific AAL

The Frame Relay Service-Specific ATM Adaptation Layer Convergence Sublayer (FR-SSCS) is positioned in the upper part of the ATM Adaptation Layer; it is located above the CPAAL5, as shown in Figs. 3.19 and 3.20. It is an example of an SSP. The purpose of the FR-SSCS protocol at an ATM CPE (that is, user's equipment) is to emulate the Frame Relaying Bearer Service (FRBS) in an ATM-based network (Fig. 3.19). On network nodes, the FR-SSCS is used for interworking between an ATM-based network and a Q.922-based Frame Relaying Network (Fig. 3.20).

The FR-SSCS protocol provides for the transport of variable-length frames with error detection.[*] The FR-SSCS provides its service over

---

[*]This discussion is based on Ref. 4.

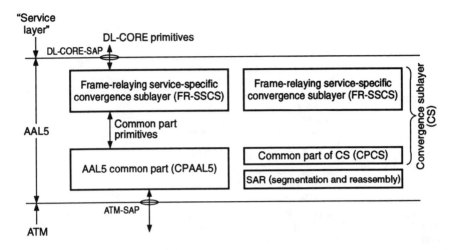

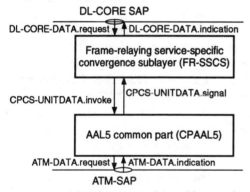

Figure 3.19 AAL5 for interworking of frame relay and ATM (in CPE).

preestablished connections with negotiated traffic parameters. An FR-SSCS connection represents the segment of an end-to-end frame relay (FR) connection over B-ISDN. At an ATM-based B-TE, the FR-SSCS connection is terminated at the point of termination of the FR-SSCS service and represents one end of the FR connection. Optionally, multiplexing may be performed at the FR-SSCS, allowing various FR-SSCS connections to be associated with a single CPAAL5 connection (and with the corresponding ATM connection). FR-SSCS connections within a CPAAL5 connection are uniquely identified by data link connection identifiers (DLCIs). The establishment (or provisioning) and initialization of an FR-SSCS connection is performed by interaction with FR-SSCS Layer Management (MFR-SSCS) entities. The traffic parameters of each FR-SSCS connection are determined at the time of its estab-

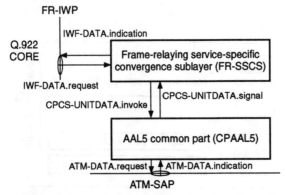

Figure 3.20 AAL5 for interworking of frame relay and ATM (in a network element supporting an interworking function). FR-IWP = frame relay interworking point.

lishment. The negotiated traffic parameters are bounded by the ATM Layer/CPAAL5 connection characteristics.

The FR-SSCS can indicate to its user that the receiver FR_SSCS_PDU has experienced congestion (forward congestion) or that an FR_SSCS_PDU traveling in the opposite (sending) direction has experienced congestion (backward congestion). The FR-SSCS allows for two discard eligibility priorities. The FR-SSCS user can request the discard eligibility (loss priority) associated with each FR_SSCS_SDU. The FR-SSCS uses the CPAAL5 message-mode service without the corrupted data delivery option and preserves the FR_SSCS_SDU sequence integrity.

The MFR-SSCS is responsible for the following actions: assignment of the FR_SSCS association necessary for the establishment or provisioning of FR-SSCS connections between peer FR-SSCS entities, resetting the parameters and state variables associated with a FR-SSCS connection when required, releasing the association created for a FR-SSCS connection between peer FR-SSCS entities, and performance monitoring of the quality of the FR-SSCS connection service provided through notification of errors (i.e., FR_SSCS_PDU discards resulting from errors in the FR_SSCS_PDU).

Service provided by the FR-SSCS. The FR-SSCS provides services to (1) the core service user (upper layer) at ATM-based B-TEs or (2) the Q.922-CORE Data Link Layer (Q.922-DLL) on network nodes at interworking functions (IWFs) points. Only item (1) is covered here.

The FR-SSCS provides the capability to transfer variable-length octet-aligned FR_SSCS_SDUs from one or more FR_SSCS users. The FR-SSCS Sublayer preserves the FR_SSCS_SDU sequence integrity within an FR-SSCS connection. During this process, FR_SSCS_SDUs may be lost or corrupted. Lost or corrupted FR_SSCS_SDUs are not recovered by the FR-SSCS. The FR-SSCS uses CPAAL5 message-mode service without the corrupted data delivery option.

FR-SSCS functions. The functions provided by the FR_SSCS include

Multiplexing/demultiplexing. This function provides for the optional multiplexing and demultiplexing of FR-SSCS connections into a single CPAAL5 connection. The number of FR-SSCS connections supported over a CPAAL5 connection is defined at connection establishment or provisioning. The default number of FR-SSCS connections when multiplexing is not supported is 1. Within a given FR-SSCS connection, sequence integrity is preserved.

Inspection of the FR_SSCS_PDU length. This function inspects the FR_SSCS_PDU to ensure that it consists of an integral number of octets and to ensure that it is neither too long nor too short.

Congestion control. These functions provide the means to notify the end user that congestion avoidance procedures should be initiated,

TABLE 3.6   DL-CORE Primitives

D L - C O R E - D A T A . r e q u e s t (DL_CORE_User_Data, Discard_Eligibility, DL_CORE_Service_User_Protocol_Control_Information)	This primitive is received from the FR-SSCS user to request the transfer of an FR_SSCS_SDU over the associated FR-SSCS connection.
D L - C O R E - D A T A . i n d i c a t i o n (DL_CORE_User_Data, Congestion_Encountered_Backward, Congestion_Encountered_Forward, DL_CORE_Service_User_Protocol_Information)	This primitive is used to the FR-SSCS user to indicate the arrival of an FR_SSCS_SDU from the associated connection.

Description of parameters:

DL_CORE_User_Data: This parameter specifies the FR_SSCS_SDU transported between the FR-SSCS user and the FR-SSCS. This parameter is octet-aligned and can range from 1 to a maximum of at least 4096 octets in length.

Discard_Eligibility: This parameter indicates the loss priority assigned to the FR_SSCS_SDU. Two levels of priority are identified: High and Low. A value of High indicates that the FR_SSCS_SDU may experience a better quality of service with respect to loss (i.e., minimal loss) than if the Discard_Eligibility parameter were set to Low.

DL_CORE_Service_Protocol_Information: This parameter specifies a 1-bit FR-SSCS/Q.922-DLL user control information to be transparently transferred between FR-SSCS/Q.922-DLL users.

Congestion_Encountered_Backward: This parameter indicates that an FR_SSCS_SDU has experienced congestion in the opposite (sending) direction, and therefore that an FR_SSCS_SDU sent on the corresponding connection may encounter congested resources. This parameter may take on two values: True or False. A value of True indicates that an FR_SSCS_SDU has experienced congestion in the opposite (sending) direction of the connection.

Congestion_Encountered_Forward: This parameter indicates that the received FR_SSCS_SDU has experienced congestion. This parameter may take two values: True or False. A value of True indicates that the FR_SSCS_SDU has experienced congestion.

where applicable (congestion control forward and congestion control backward). In addition, the functions provide the means for the end user and/or the network to indicate what frames should be discarded in a congestion situation.

Primitives. The information exchanged between the FR-SSCS and its user (for ATM-based B-TEs) is modeled by the primitives of Table 3.6 (which are the same DL-CORE primitives in Annex C of ITU-T Recommendation I.233.1).

Services expected from the CPAAL5. The FR-SSCS expects the CPAAL5 to provide the capability to transfer variable-length (from 3 to a maximum of at least 4100 octets) octet-aligned FR_SSCS_SDUs, with error detection and in sequence, between communicating FR-SSCS entities. Lost or corrupted FR_SSCS_PDUs are not expected to be recovered by the CPAAL5. Multicast services, derived from the ATM Layer, are expected.

The FR-SSCS entity expects the CPAAL5 to provide each FR_SSCS_PDU (CPAAL5_SDU) with the CP_Congestion_Indication (True or False) set to the value of the Congestion_Indication received by the ATM Layer with the last ATM_SDU conforming to the CPAAL5_SDU; and with the CP_Loss_Priority set to either Low, if any of the ATM_SDUs conforming to the CPAAL5_SDU was received with the Received_Loss_Priority parameter set to Low, or High otherwise.

The FR-SSCS entity passes each FR_SSCS_PDU (CPAAL5_SDU) with the CP_Loss_Priority set to the value of the Discard_Eligibility parameter received from the upper layer or the Q.922-DLL (High or Low), the CP_Congestion_Indication (True or False) always set to False, and the User_User_Indication parameter always set to zero.

3.7   Signaling ATM Adaptation Layer (SAAL)

This section describes the Signaling ATM Adaptation Layer (SAAL) for use at the UNI. SAAL is used in the Control Plane. (This topic could also have been treated in the next chapter, but it was decided to include it here with other AALs.)

The SAAL resides between the ATM Layer and Q.2931 in the user's equipment, specifically in the software implementing the Control Plane (i.e., the signaling capability). The purpose of the SAAL is to provide reliable transport of Q.2931 messages between peer Q.2931 entities (e.g., ATM switch and host) over the ATM Layer. The SAAL is composed of two sublayers, a Common Part and a Service-Specific

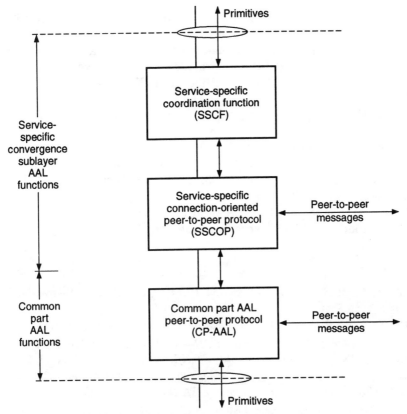

Figure 3.21   SAAL structure. (*Note:* This figure represents the allocation of functions and is not intended to illustrate sublayers as defined by OSI modeling principles.)

Part. The Service-Specific Part is further subdivided into a Service-Specific Coordination Function (SSCF) and a Service-Specific Connection-Oriented Protocol (SSCOP). Figure 3.21 illustrates the structure of the SAAL.[5]

The SAAL for supporting signaling uses the protocol structure illustrated in Fig. 3.21. The Common Part AAL protocol provides unassured information transfer and a mechanism for detecting corruption of SDUs. The AAL Type 5 Common Part protocol is used to support signaling. The AAL Type 5 Common Part protocol is specified in Draft Recommendation I.363.

The SAAL for supporting signaling at the UNI uses the AAL Type 5 Common Part protocol, discussed above, as specified in Ref. 7 with minor amendments.[8]

The Service-Specific Connection-Oriented Protocol (SSCOP) resides in the Service-Specific Convergence Sublayer (SSCS) of the SAAL. SSCOP is used to transfer variable-length service data units (SDUs) between users of SSCOP. SSCOP provides for the recovery of lost or corrupted SDUs. SSCOP is specified in ITU-T Recommendation Q.2110.[9]

The SAAL for supporting signaling utilizes SSCOP as specified in Q.2110.[9]

An SSCF maps the service of SSCOP to the needs of the SSCF user. Different SSCFs may be defined to support the needs of different AAL users. The SSCF used to support Q.93B at the UNI is specified in ITU-T Recommendation Q.2130.[10]

The external behavior of the SAAL at the UNI appears as if the UNI SSCF specified in Q.2130[10] were implemented.

References

1. CCITT I.362, *B-ISDN AAL Functional Description*, Geneva, Switzerland, 1992.

2. CCITT I.363, *B-ISDN AAL Specification*, Geneva, Switzerland, 1992.

3. ANSI T1.BCR-199x, *Broadband ISDN—ATM Adaptation Layer for Constant Bit Rate Services Functionality Specification*, New York, Nov. 13, 1992.

4. Bellcore, *Asynchronous Transfer Mode (ATM) and ATM Adaptation Layer (AAL) Protocols Generic Requirements*, TA-NWT-001113, Issue 2, July 1993.

5. B. Kittams, Bellcore, personal communication, May 1993.

6. T1S1.5/93-52, *Broadband Aspects of ISDN Baseline Document*, T1S1 Technical Subcommittee, August 1990, Chief Editor: Rajeev Sinha. Reissued February 1993, Chief Editor: Erwin Fandrich.

7. CCITT Document TD-XVIII/10 (AAL5), "AAL Type 5, Draft Recommendation Text for Section 6 of I.363," Geneva, Switzerland, Jan. 29, 1993.

8. ATM Forum, *ATM User-Network Interface Specification*, Version 3.0, August 1993.

9. ITU Document DT/11/3-28 [Q.SAAL1 (now Q.2110)], *Service-Specific Connection-Oriented Protocol (SSCOP) Specification*, Geneva, Switzerland, May 17, 1993.

10. ITU Document DT/11/3-XX [Q.SAAL2 (now Q.2130)], *Service-Specific Connection-Oriented Protocol (SSCOP) Specification*, Geneva, Switzerland, May 17, 1993.

User-to-Network Signaling

ATM principles and technologies can be utilized to support a variety of communication services, including cell relay service, frame relay service, SMDS, and circuit emulation. Cell relay service is being targeted at supporting evolving applications now being introduced commercially that require high transmission capacity. Such applications include distributed multimedia, videoconferencing, and distance learning and enterprisewide networks.

Cell relay service supports both on-demand switched virtual connections and nonswitched permanent virtual connections. PVCs are typically utilized by institutions between fixed corporate locations, for example, between data centers or regional hubs. In contrast with PVC service, SVC service affords maximum flexibility in establishing dynamic connections in support of the customer applications identified above and in Chap. 1, particularly when there are numerous dispersed locations or when the locations to which connectivity is required are not fixed. SVCs are established and disestablished using a *signaling protocol*. The protocol must be sufficiently flexible to support the connection types required for the new user applications. Such SVC capability is especially important for the new corporate work paradigm that utilizes informal dispersed groups, cooperative work, and just-in-time applications, all of which may require connectivity on a more ad hoc basis than traditional data communication applications. Some of the video, imaging, and multimedia applications now being introduced also require that cell relay service support not only point-to-point connections, but also point-to-multipoint and asymmetric (in terms of bandwidth) connections. In the future, there will also be a need for multipoint-to-multipoint connectivity.

This chapter describes some of the procedures required for dynamically establishing, maintaining, and clearing ATM network connections at the user-network interface. These procedures are defined in terms of call-control messages and the information elements carried in the call-control messages that are used to characterize the end-to-end ATM connection to be established through the network. The user conveys its SVC connectivity needs to a signaling partner in the network (typically at the switch); in turn, the local broadband switch sets up the appropriate connection(s) to the specified destination(s). The user signals the network using a protocol stack that resides in the Control Plane, as shown in Fig. 1.3; hence, the user's equipment must implement two stacks, one for the data transfer and one for signaling. This chapter focuses on the signaling stack.

4.1 Overview

Signaling is the act of transferring service-related information between the user and the network and among network entities. Unless the user is able to signal his or her needs to the network, he or she will not be able to receive the required services in a dynamic manner. The *signaling network* is the collection of physical facilities that carry the signaling information. Signaling takes place both between the user and the network, over the user-network interface, and between network elements, over the network node interface (NNI). In the access side (user to network), the signaling usually takes place over the same physical facility used for the actual information transport; in the NNI side, the signaling network can be a truly separate network. Signaling entities supporting protocol stacks up to the OSIRM Application Layer are required in the user's equipment to access the high-speed digital network services identified above. One of the most important call-control messages generated by the user's signaling stack is the SETUP message; it conveys to the network the user's connectivity needs. Initial emphasis for the signaling protocol is on bidirectional symmetric and asymmetric point-to-point and point-to-multipoint connections.

The signaling protocols covered below support the following ATM services, already discussed in previous chapters:

1. Class X service, which is a connection-oriented ATM transport service where the AAL, traffic type (VBR or CBR), and timing requirements are user-defined (i.e., transparent to the network). The user chooses

only the desired bandwidth and QOS with appropriate information elements in the SETUP message to establish a Class X connection.

2. Class A service, which is a connection-oriented, constant-bit-rate ATM transport service. Class A service has end-to-end timing requirements and may require stringent cell loss, cell delay, and cell delay variation performance. The user chooses the desired bandwidth and the appropriate QOS in the SETUP message to establish a Class A connection.

3. Class C service, which is a connection-oriented, variable-bit-rate ATM transport service. Class C service has no end-to-end timing requirements. The user chooses the desired bandwidth and QOS with appropriate information elements in the SETUP message to establish a Class C connection.

Signaling applies to two portions of an ATM network; the access side and the interswitch side (also known as the "trunk side").

Standards-making bodies such as the ITU-T, ANSI Committee T1S1, and the ATM Forum have finalized Phase 1 access signaling standards.* Q.2931 (commonly referred to as Q.93B), covering point-to-point virtual connections, became available at the end of 1993 (with actual publication in 1994).[†] A T1S1 specification based on the ITU-TS document is also expected in 1994. The *ATM Forum UNI Specification*, Issue 3, August 1993, covers both point-to-point and point-to-multipoint connections. Bellcore has published Issue 1 of TA-NWT-001111, *Broadband ISDN Access Signaling Generic Requirements* (August 1993),[‡] covering generic requirements for a nationally consistent service. There also is ongoing work on the trunk side; extensions to the ISDN User Part (ISUP) to enable it to control ATM connections are nearly completed. This chapter concentrates on the access side; Sec. 4.2.4 briefly discusses the interswitch side.

4.1.1 Signaling protocol stack

The signaling protocol stack that has to be implemented in the user's equipment and in the network peer consists of the following protocol layers, listed in decreasing order according to the OSIRM (see Fig. 4.1; aspects of this stack were already shown in Fig. 3.21):

---

*Phase 2 work using object-oriented methods for "multiconnection" calls was starting at press time.

[†]Work on Q.2931 in its present form dates back to 1988; however, it has as its basics the Q.931 standard, first published in 1980.

[‡]The initial version of this document, FA-NWT-001111, was issued by Bellcore in December 1991.

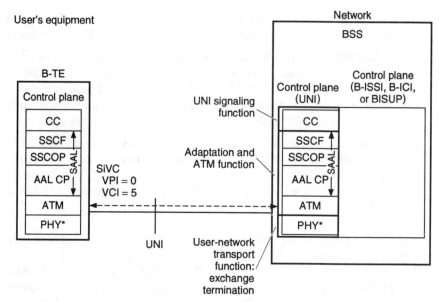

Figure 4.1 Signaling stack. B-TE = broadband terminal equipment; CC = call control; SSCF = Service-Specific Coordination Function; SSCOP = Service-Specific Connection-Oriented Protocol; AAL = ATM Adaptation Layer; CP = common part; SAAL = Signaling AAL; SiVC = signaling virtual channel; LT = line terminator; B-ISSI = broadband interswitch system interface; B-ICI = broadband intercarrier interface.

Layers 7–3	Call control; Q.93B
Layer 2a	Service-Specific Coordination Function [also known as Signaling ATM Adaptation Layer Level 2 (Q.2130)]
Layer 2b	Service-Specific Connection-Oriented Protocol [also known as Signaling ATM Adaptation Layer Level 1 (Q.2110)]
Layer 2c	ATM Adaptation Layer Type 5 Common Part
Layer 2d	ATM
Layer 1	DS3 framing or SONET framing

The protocol partners are the user signaling entity in the broadband terminal and the call processing entity in the network or, more specifically, in a broadband switching system. This discussion focuses on UNIs that support a *single* B-TE (such a B-TE, however, could terminate multiple non-ATM user terminals at the location in question, e.g., a LAN router); slight extensions exist for UNIs that support multiple B-TEs (these extensions being called "metasignaling").

4.1.2 Call control functions

For on-demand SVC service, cell relay service requires a mechanism to enable the user to inform the network of specific aspects of the user's desired connectivity needs. Hence, the signaling mechanism must support the transfer of "information elements" describing features of the service instanciation. Call control for point-to-point calls entails the following procedures: establishing a call at the originating interface, terminating a call (that is, establishing the call at the destination interface), clearing a call, and handling error conditions. Call control for point-to-multipoint calls entails the following procedures: adding a party at the originating interface, adding a party at the destination interface, clearing a call, and handling error conditions. The signaling is generally done during the call-establishment phase (except for multipoint calls where parties can be added or dropped as needed); the call-establishment phase is then followed by an information transfer phase, and finally by a call-release phase. The ITU-T Q.2931 protocol provides this capability for point-to-point connections, while the ATM Forum extends the protocol to point-to-multipoint connections. Table 4.1 lists some of the key information elements specifiable at call-establishment time. At call setup time, the user supplies information elements as well as constituent fields to describe the service required, including symmetry and traffic intensity (for example, peak cell rate, sustained cell rate, and burst length).

TABLE 4.1 On-Demand Information Elements Specifiable at Call Establishment

AAL parameters

ATM user cell rate*

Broadband bearer capability

Broadband low-layer compatibility

Broadband high-layer compatibility

Called party/parties number

Called party/parties subaddress

Calling party number

Calling party subaddress

Quality of service parameter

Transit network selection

*ATM cell rate indication may include both a peak rate and a sustained rate (defined as a fraction of the peak rate).

Note: For multipoint services, several of these parameters may be specified on a per origin-destination basis.

Current specifications (ITU-T Q.2931, ATM Forum UNI specification, Bellcore TA-NWT-001111) provide capabilities for supporting the dynamic establishing, maintaining, and clearing of ATM connections at the user-network interface. The following capabilities have been defined for the United States:

- Support of a point-to-point interface configuration
- Support of the cell relay bearer service
- Addressing and routing based on E.164 addresses
- Establishment of point-to-point virtual channel connections
- Establishment of unidirectional (outgoing from the source) point-to-multipoint virtual channel connections
- Symmetric and asymmetric bandwidth connections
- Symmetric and asymmetric quality of service connections
- Transport of network-transparent parameters: called party subaddress, calling party subaddress, broadband high-layer information, broadband low-layer information (including low-layer negotiation), and ATM Adaptation Layer parameter information (including, in the future, ATM Adaptation Layer parameter negotiation)

Table 4.2 identifies some of the key procedures to support these capabilities that are embodied in the signaling protocol.

The signaling apparatus discussed in this chapter applies to both public networks and appropriately configured private networks; our treatment takes the perspective of carrier-based networks, although the underpinning of the current view of ATM is that a single technology (including protocols) can synergistically support both private and public networks.

4.2   Transport of Signaling Messages

Signaling messages that the user and other network elements generate must be reliably transported between peers. On the UNI, at least two additional functions must be implemented (beyond what is available on a PVC UNI): (1) a call control function and (2) a Signaling ATM Adaptation Layer function, handling reliable communication above the ATM Layer. This section summarizes the underlying transport mechanism. The next section looks at the messages themselves in more detail.

4.2.1   Signaling ATM Adaptation Layer

(This topic was already treated at the end of Chap. 3.) The SAAL protocol and procedures define how to transfer the signaling informa-

TABLE 4.2 Key Procedures to Establish/Clear SVCs

Call/bearer control procedures for point-to-point calls

  Call/bearer establishment at the originating interface

    Call/bearer request

    Connection identifier (VPI/VCI) allocation/selection

    QOS and traffic parameters selection procedures

    Invalid call/bearer control information

    Call/bearer proceeding

    Notification of interworking at the originating interface

    Call/bearer confirmation indication

    Call/bearer connected

    Call/bearer rejection

    Transit network selection

  Call/bearer establishment at the destination interface

    Incoming call/bearer request

    Connection identifier (VPI/VCI) allocation/selection—destination

    QOS and traffic parameter selection procedures

    Call/bearer confirmation

    Called user clearing during incoming call establishment

    Call failure

    Call/bearer acceptance

    Active indication

  Call/bearer clearing

    Exception conditions

    Clearing initiated by the user

    Clearing initiated by the network

    Clear collision

    Restart procedure

    Handling of protocol error conditions

  User notification procedure

Call/bearer control procedures for point-to-multipoint calls

  Adding a party at the originating interface

  Added party establishment at the destination interface—point-to-point

  Call/bearer clearing

  Handling of error conditions

Note: This table is partially based on Refs. 1, 2, and 3.

tion for call and connection control within the cells of the ATM Layer on virtual channels used for signaling. The SAAL resides in the Control Plane. SAAL comprises a Common Part, which represents the functionality common to all users requiring a connection-oriented, variable-bit-rate information transfer, and a Service-Specific Part, which identifies the protocol and procedures associated with the signaling needs at the UNI. The SAAL provides reliable delivery of Q.2931 signaling messages. The Common Part protocol provides unassured information transfer and a mechanism for detecting corruption of information carried in the SAAL frames; the Service-Specific Part provides recovery. The Service-Specific Part is further subdivided into a Service-Specific Coordination Function and a Service-Specific Connection-Oriented Protocol. The SSCOP is used to transfer variable-length SDUs between its users. It provides for the recovery of lost or corrupted SDUs. The SSCF maps the service of SSCOP to the needs of the SSCF user. Three protocols in support of these functions that were nearing final status at press time are ITU-T Q.2130 (that is, SSCF), Q.2110 (that is, SSCOP), and I.363 (that is, AAL5 Common Part).

4.2.2   ATM Layer

The ATM Layer supports both signaling and user data, as covered in Chap. 2. A default bidirectional VCC known as signaling virtual channel (SiVC) is used for all access signaling, both user-initiated and network-initiated (i.e., call offering). The default bandwidth of the SiVC is 167 cells/s (corresponding to 64 kbits/s), upgradable to 3841 cells/s in steps of 167 cells/s.

The SiVC is used for all access signaling. Both access and network-side signaling protocol capabilities need to be implemented in the network to support SVC service.

The signaling information is transmitted using assured-mode AAL procedures. The protocol partners are the user signaling entity in the B-TE and the call processing entity in the network. The SiVC is identified by the preassigned value of VPI = 0, VCI = 5.

The Selective Broadcast Signaling Channel is a unidirectional VCC from network to user that is used to offer calls to specific B-TEs connected to the interface. This allows for multiple call-offering channels on a point-to-multipoint access interface, in such a way that signaling information to specific entities on the interface is segregated for performance, security, administrative, or other service-discrimination reasons. The VPI/VCI(s) for the Selective Broadcast Signaling Channel(s) are assigned dynamically as part of the metasignaling process.

The Broadcast Signaling Channel is a unidirectional VCC (from network to user) used to transmit call-offering messages to all the signaling entities sharing the UNI. The Broadcast Signaling Channel is used for BTE(s) that do not support selective broadcast call offering.

4.2.3 Physical Layer

The signaling information pertaining to connections supported across a UNI can flow over the facility associated with that UNI or over some other facility; at this time, only facility-associated signaling is supported. The facility may be DS3- or SONET-based.

4.2.4 Network-Side Signaling

Control Plane information may be transmitted *between switches* in a number of ways:

1. Using SiVCs allocated over the broadband interswitching system interface (B-ISSI) or the broadband intercarrier interface (B-ICI) to carry network signaling traffic (i.e., "per-trunk signaling")
2. Using the Common Channel Signaling System #7 Interface

Both alternatives are being addressed by the standards bodies. Alternative 2 is based on the existing CCS/SS#7 physical interfaces. It can also be used for interworking with narrowband network elements and in support of narrowband services (e.g., N-ISDN); these network elements are typically already connected to the existing signaling network. This alternative could also be used as a short-term mechanism to transport signaling messages relating to B-ISSI/B-ICI interfaces. The physical architecture implied by Alternative 1 utilizes "direct signaling trunks." See Fig. 4.2.

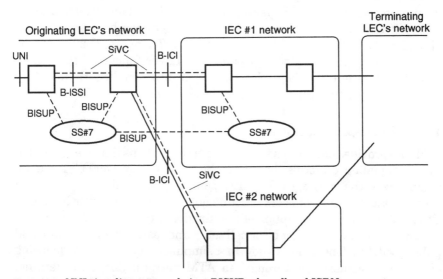

Figure 4.2 NNI signaling—general view. BISUP = broadband ISDN user part.

SiVCs over the B-ISSI and B-ICI would be permanent/semipermanent ATM connections, and would use the same lower-layer protocols. The SiVC channel assignment rules are implementation-specific. At the AAL, the SAAL is extended to provide the equivalent of SS#7 Level 2 service, particularly with respect to recovery under link failure. The existing SS#7 Level 3 service/protocol [i.e., Network Layer, specifically known as Message Transfer Part (MTP)], as well as the higher layers (e.g., the Signaling Connection Control Part), can be used with minor modifications.

Three protocol architecture proposals were being studied at press time:

1. Use of Broadband ISDN User Part (BISUP) over MTP-3, over MTP-2, over a physical facility

2. Use of BISUP over MTP-3, over SAAL, over ATM, over a physical facility

3. Use of Q.2931 over SAAL, over ATM, over a physical facility

(For more information on BISUP and MTP, see Ref. 4.) Standards and other specifications were underway in 1994.

4.3   UNI Signaling Messages

This section defines the call control messages for the Layer 3 call control procedures alluded to above. Messages are composed of information elements.

Note: Although Q.931, Q.933, and Q.2931 are loosely called network-layer protocols (also called Layer 3), they are not in fact identical to the OSI Network Layer. The call establishment messages can be more properly viewed as OSI Application Layer procedures. Therefore, Q.2931 can be interpreted as providing some Application Layer functionality, a small subset of Presentation and Session Layer functionality, rudimentary Transport Layer functionality, and Network Layer functionality.

4.3.1   Point-to-point messages

Table 4.3 provides definitions for the type of connections that are supported by the signaling protocols (based on the ATM Forum work).[1] Table 4.4 summarizes the messages for ATM point-to-point call and connection control that the protocol peers must be able to generate and/or interpret. Table 4.5 provides a description of the functionality of these messages.

Figures 4.3 and 4.4 depict basic call setup and teardown over private and public switches. These flows show in a simplified manner the sequencing of call control messages through an ATM network (for more detailed information on procedures, the reader is referred to Refs. 1, 2, and 4).

TABLE 4.3   ATM Connections

Multipoint-to-Point Connection
A multipoint-to-point connection where the bandwidth from the root node to the leaf node is zero, and the return bandwidth from the leaf node to the root node is nonzero.

Multipoint-to-Multipoint Connection
A multipoint-to-multipoint connection is a collection of associated ATM VC or VP links and their associated endpoint nodes, with the following properties:

1. All N nodes in the connection, called endpoints, serve as root nodes in a point-to-multipoint connection to all of the $(N - 1)$ remaining endpoints.

2. Each of the endpoints on the connection can send information directly to any other endpoint, but the receiving endpoint cannot distinguish which of the endpoints is sending information without additional (e.g., higher-layer) information.

Point-to-Multipoint Connection
A point-to-multipoint connection is a collection of associated ATM VC or VP links with associated endpoint nodes, with the following properties:

1. One ATM link, called the root link, serves as the root in a simple tree topology. When the root node sends information, all of the remaining nodes on the connection, called leaf nodes, receive copies of the information.

2. Each of the leaf nodes on the connection can send information directly to the root node. The root node cannot distinguish which leaf is sending information without additional (higher-layer) information.

3. The leaf nodes cannot communicate with one another directly with this connection type.

Point-to-Point Connection
A connection with only two endpoints.

4.3.2   Point-to-Multipoint Messages

Table 4.6 summarizes the additional messages for ATM point-to-multipoint call and connection control. Table 4.7 provides a description of the functionality of these messages.

4.4   SETUP Message Capabilities

As indicated earlier, the SETUP message is one of the more important messages, in that it embodies the functionality afforded to the user of the ATM network. This section provides a description of this message and some of the key information elements to describe this functionality. (For more information on the details of this message, the totality of its information elements, and other messages, the reader is referred directly to the standards;[1,2] the purpose of this section is to educate the reader as to the type of protocol format he or she should expect to find upon obtaining the standards themselves.)

TABLE 4.4   Messages for ATM Point-to-Point Call and Connection Control

Call establishment messages:

  CALL PROCEEDING

  CONNECT

  CONNECT ACKNOWLEDGE

  SETUP

Call clearing messages:

  RELEASE

  RELEASE COMPLETE

Miscellaneous messages:

  RESTART

  RESTART ACKNOWLEDGE

  STATUS

  STATUS ENQUIRY

Note: Q.2931 also uses an ALERTING message.

Note: This section is based in its entirety on the information found in Refs. 1 and 2 (and in many cases first published in Ref. 5).

The SETUP message is sent by the calling user to the network and by the network to the called user to initiate call establishment. Table 4.8 shows its constituent information elements.

Note: The ITU-T Q.2931 SETUP message carries additional information elements, particularly in support of ISDN interworking in order to facilitate videoconferencing using the H.261 standards.

Some of the key information elements that the user can include in this message in order to request services from an ATM network are discussed next. This material is for perusal purposes and to provide a sense of the functionality supported; the reader should refer to Refs. 1 and 2 for more information.

4.4.1   AAL Adaptation Layer parameters

This information element specifies the adaptation parameters that the user intends to use in his or her User Plane.[3,6]

The purpose of the ATM Adaptation Layer parameters information element is to indicate the requested ATM Adaptation Layer parameter values (end-to-end significance) for the ATM connection (as shown, for example, in Fig. 3.2). It contains the parameters selectable by the user for all AAL

---

*Do not confuse this User Plane AAL with the Control Plane SAAL discussed above.

TABLE 4.5 Message Significance

CALL PROCEEDING	This message is sent by the called user to the network or by the network to the calling user to indicate that the requested call establishment has been initiated and no more call establishment information will be accepted.
CONNECT	This message is sent by the called user to the network and by the network to the calling user to indicate call acceptance by the called user.
CONNECT ACKNOWL-EDGE	This message is sent by the network to the called user to indicate that the user has been awarded the call. It may also be sent by the calling user to the network to allow symmetrical call control procedures.
RELEASE	This message is sent by the user or the network to indicate that the equipment sending the message has disconnected the virtual connection (if any) and intends to release the virtual channel and the call reference. Thus the receiving equipment should release the virtual connection and prepare to release the call reference after sending a RELEASE COMPLETE.
RELEASE COMPLETE	This message is sent by the user or the network to indicate that the equipment sending the message has released the virtual channel (if any) and call reference, the virtual channel is available for reuse, and the receiving equipment shall release the call reference.
RESTART	This message is sent by the user or the network to request the recipient to restart (i.e., release all resources associated with) the indicated virtual channel or virtual channels controlled by the signaling virtual channel.
RESTART ACKNOWL-EDGE	This message is sent to acknowledge the receipt of a RESTART message and to indicate that the requested restart is complete.
SETUP	This message is sent by the calling user to the network and by the network to the called user to initiate call establishment.
STATUS	This message is sent by the user or the network in response to a STATUS ENQUIRY message or at any time to report certain error conditions.
STATUS ENQUIRY	This message is sent by the user or the network at any time to solicit a STATUS message from the peer Layer 3 entity. Sending a STATUS message in response to a STATUS ENQUIRY message is mandatory.

sublayers. The contents of this information element are transparent for the network, except for the case of interworking. See Table 4.9.

The ATM Adaptation Layer parameters information element may also be included in the CONNECT message to indicate that the called party in a point-to-point call (or the first leaf of a multipoint call) wishes to

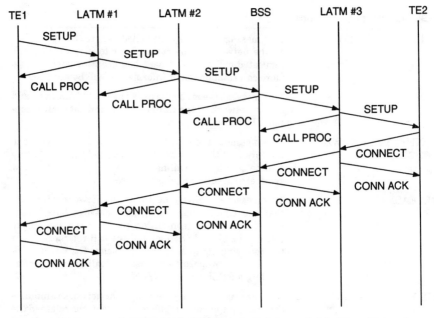

Figure 4.3 Call setup. LATM= local ATM switch (private switch). (*Note:* Network may contain no LATM switches and/or more than one BSS.)

indicate the forward and backward maximum CPCS-SDU size (for AAL3/4 and AAL5), reduce the value of the MID range (for AAL3/4), or indicate user-defined AAL information. (Refer to Chap. 3 for more information on AAL, if desired.)

Note: The AAL parameters information element shown in Table 4.9 is based on the version found in ITU-T Q.2931; at writing time the ATM

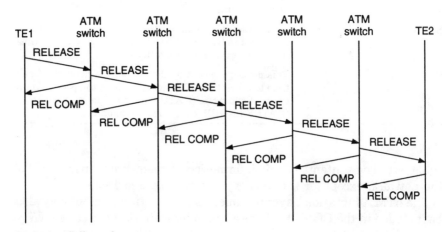

Figure 4.4 Call teardown.

TABLE 4.6   Messages for ATM Point-to-Multipoint Call and Connection Control

ADD PARTY

ADD PARTY ACKNOWLEDGE

ADD PARTY REJECT

DROP PARTY

DROP PARTY ACKNOWLEDGE

Forum had not yet harmonized its version of the AAL parameters information element (as shown in Ref. 1) with the one found in Q.2931. (The need for such harmonization is dictated by interworking considerations.) What the user community wants to avoid at all costs is a repeat of the lack of interoperability found in packet-switched networks and in integrated digital services networks.

TABLE 4.7   Message Significance

ADD PARTY	This message is sent to add a party to an existing connection.
ADD PARTY ACKNOWL-EDGE	This message is sent to acknowledge that the ADD PARTY request was successful.
ADD PARTY REJECT	This message is sent to acknowledge that the ADD PARTY request was not successful.
DROP PARTY	This message is sent to drop (clear) a party from an existing point-to-multipoint connection.
DROP PARTY ACKNOWL-EDGE	This message is sent in response to a DROP PARTY message to indicate that the party was dropped from the connection.

(text continues on page 120)

TABLE 4.8 Information Elements of SETUP Message (from ATM Forum Specification)

Information element	Direction of transmission	Type	Length (octets)
Protocol discriminator	Both	M	1
Call reference	Both	M	4
Message type	Both	M	2
Message length	Both	M	2
AAL parameters	Both	O^a	4–20
ATM user cell rate	Both	M	12–30
Broadband bearer capability	Both	M	6–7
Broadband high-layer information	Both	O^b	4–13
Broadband repeat indicator	Both	O^c	4–5
Broadband low-layer information	Both	O^d	4–17
Called party number	Both	M	e
Called party subaddress	Both	O^f	4–25
Calling party number	Both	O^g	4–26
Calling party subaddress	Both	O^h	4–25
Connection identifier	N → U	M	9
QOS parameter	Both	M	6
Broadband sending complete	Both	O^i	4–5
Transit network selection	U → N	O^j	4–8
Endpoint reference	Both	O^k	4–7

M = mandatory; O = optional.

[a]Included in the user-to-network direction when the calling user wants to pass ATM Adaptation Layer parameters information to the called user. Included in the network-to-user direction if the calling user included an ATM Adaptation Layer parameters information element in the SETUP message.

[b]Included in the user-to-network direction when the calling user wants to pass broadband high-layer information to the called user. Included in the network-to-user direction if the calling user included a broadband high-layer information element in the SETUP message.

[c]Included when two or more broadband low-layer information information elements are included for broadband low-layer information negotiation.

[d]Included in the user-to-network direction when the calling user wants to pass broadband low-layer information to the called user. Included in the network-to-user direction if the calling user included a broadband low-layer information information element in the SETUP message. Two or three information elements may be included in descending order of priority (i.e., highest priority first) if the broadband low-layer information negotiation procedures are used.

[e]Minimum length depends on the numbering plan. Maximum length is 25 octets.

[f]Included in the user-to-network direction when the calling user wants to indicate the called party subaddress. Included in the network-to-user direction if the calling user included a called party subaddress information element in the SETUP message.

[g]May be included by the calling user, or by the network to identify the calling user.

[h]Included in the user-to-network direction when the calling user wants to indicate the calling party subaddress. Included in the network-to-user direction if the calling user included a calling party subaddress information element in the SETUP message.

[i]It is optional for the user to include the broadband sending complete information element when enbloc sending procedures (i.e., complete address information is included) are used; its interpretation by the network is optional. It is optional for the network to include the broadband sending complete information element when enbloc receiving (i.e., complete address information is included) is used.

[j]Included by the calling user to select a particular transit network.

[k]Not used for point-to-point connection establishment. Must be included in SETUP messages involved in point-to-multipoint connection establishment.

TABLE 4.9 AAL Adaptation Layer Parameters[2, 3, 6]

Part A: ATM Adaptation Layer Parameters Information Element
(Octet Groups 1–5 for All AAL Types)

			Bits					
8	7	6	5	4	3	2	1	Octets
ATM Adaptation Layer parameters								
0	1	0	1	1	0	0	0	1
Information element identifier								
1 ext	Coding standard	IE instruction field						2
Length of AAL parameters contents								3
Length of AAL parameters contents (continued)								4
AAL type								5
Further content depending upon AAL type (see below)								6 etc.

Part B: ATM Adaptation Layer Parameters Information Element
(Octet Groups 6–12 for AAL Type 1)

			Bits					
8	7	6	5	4	3	2	1	Octets
Subtype identifier								6
1	0	0	0	0	1	0	1	
Subtype								6.1
CBR rate identifier								7
1	0	0	0	0	1	1	0	
CBR rate								7.1
Multiplier identifier								8*[a]
1	0	0	0	0	1	1	1	
Multiplier								8.1*[a]
Multiplier (continued)								8.2*[a]
Source clock frequency recovery method identifier								9*
1	0	0	0	1	0	0	0	
Source clock frequency recovery method								9.1*
Error correction method identifier								10*
1	0	0	0	1	0	0	1	

TABLE 4.9   AAL Adaptation Layer Parameters[2, 3, 6] (*Continued*)

Error correction method								10.1*
Structured data transfer identifier								11*
1	0	0	0	1	0	1	0	
Structured data transfer blocksize								11.1*
Structured data transfer blocksize (continued)								11.2*
Partially filled cells identifier								12*
1	0	0	0	1	0	1	1	
Partially filled cells method								12.1*

Part C: ATM Adaptation Layer Parameters Information Element
(Octet Groups 6–9 for AAL Type 3/4)

			Bits					
8	7	6	5	4	3	2	1	Octets
Forward maximum CPCS-SDU size identifier								6*[b]
1	0	0	0	1	1	0	0	
Forward maximum CPCS-SDU size								6.1*
Forward maximum CPCS-SDU size (continued)								6.2*
Backward maximum CPCS-SDU size identifier								7*[b]
1	0	0	0	0	0	0	1	
Backward maximum CPCS-SDU size								7.1*
Backward maximum CPCS-SDU size (continued)								7.2*
MID size range identifier								8*
1	0	0	0	0	0	1	0	
MID range (lowest MID value)								8.1*
MID range (lowest MID value) (continued)								8.2*
MID range (highest MID value)								8.3*
MID range (highest MID value) (continued)								8.4*
SSCS type identifier								9*
1	0	0	0	0	1	0	0	
SSCS type								9.1*

TABLE 4.9   AAL Adaptation Layer Parameters[2, 3, 6] *(Continued)*

Part D: ATM Adaptation Layer Parameters Information Element
(Octet Groups 6–8 for AAL Type 5)

			Bits					
8	7	6	5	4	3	2	1	Octets
Forward maximum CPCS-SDU size identifier								6*[c]
1	0	0	0	1	1	0	0	
Forward maximum CPCS-SDU size								6.1*
Forward maximum CPCS-SDU size (continued)								6.2*
Backward maximum CPCS-SDU size identifier								7*[c]
1	0	0	0	0	0	0	1	
Backward maximum CPCS-SDU size								7.1*
Backward maximum CPCS-SDU size (continued)								7.2*
SSCS type identifier								8*
1	0	0	0	0	1	0	0	
SSCS type								8.1*

Part E: ATM Adaptation Layer Parameters Information Element
(Octet Group 6 for User-Defined AAL)

			Bits					
8	7	6	5	4	3	2	1	Octets
User-defined AAL information								6*
User-defined AAL information								6.1*
User-defined AAL information								6.2*
User-defined AAL information								6.3*

*Optional octets.

[a]These octets are present only if octet 7.1 indicates "$n \times 64$ kbits/s" or "$n \times 8$ kbits/s."

[b]If the forward maximum CPCS-SDU size is included, the backward maximum CPCS-SDU size must be included. If the backward maximum CPCS-SDU size is included, the forward maximum CPCS-SDU size must be included.

[c]If the forward maximum CPCS-SDU size is included, the backward maximum CPCS-SDU size must be included. If the backward maximum CPCS-SDU size is included, the forward maximum CPCS-SDU size must be included.

The actual encoding of the fields follows.

Coding standard (octet 2)

Bits 7 6	Meaning
0 0	ITU-TS (CCITT) standardized

IE instruction field (octet 2)

Bits 5 4 3 2 1	Meaning
0 0 0 0 0	IE instruction field is not significant

AAL type (octet 5)

Bits 8 7 6 5 4 3 2 1	Meaning
0 0 0 0 0 0 0 1	AAL Type 1
0 0 0 0 0 0 1 0	AAL Type 2*
0 0 0 0 0 0 1 1	AAL Type 3/4
0 0 0 0 0 1 0 1	AAL Type 5
0 0 0 1 0 0 0 0	User-defined AAL

*For AAL Type 2, no further parameters are specified beyond the ones given in Table 4.9, Part A.

All other values are reserved.

Subtype (octet 6.1 for AAL Type 1)

Bits 8 7 6 5 4 3 2 1	Meaning
0 0 0 0 0 0 0 1	Voice-band signal transport based on 64 kbits/s, G.711/G.722 (*Note:* for further study, see Rec. I.363)
0 0 0 0 0 0 1 0	Circuit transport (see Rec. I.363, Sec. 2.5.1.1)
0 0 0 0 0 1 0 0	High-quality audio signal transport (*Note:* for further study, see Rec. I.363)
0 0 0 0 0 1 0 1	Video signal transport (*Note:* for further study, see Rec. I.363)

All other values are reserved.

CBR rate (octet 7.1 for AAL Type 1)

Bits 8 7 6 5 4 3 2 1	Meaning
0 0 0 0 0 0 0 1	64 kbits/s
0 0 0 0 0 1 0 0	1,544 kbits/s (DS1)
0 0 0 0 0 1 0 1	6,312 kbits/s (DS2)
0 0 0 0 0 1 1 0	32,064 kbits/s
0 0 0 0 0 1 1 1	44,736 kbits/s (DS3)
0 0 0 0 1 0 0 0	97,728 kbits/s
0 0 0 1 0 0 0 0	2,048 kbits/s (E1)
0 0 0 1 0 0 0 1	8,448 kbits/s (E2)
0 0 0 1 0 0 1 0	34,368 kbits/s (E3)
0 0 0 1 0 0 1 1	139,264 kbits/s
0 1 0 0 0 0 0 0	$n \times 64$ kbits/s
0 1 0 0 0 0 0 1	$n \times 8$ kbits/s

All other values are reserved.

Multiplier (octets 8.1 and 8.2 for AAL Type 1 and $n \times 64$ kbits/s or $n \times 8$ kbits/s indication in octet 7.1). This is an integer representation of multiplier values between 2 and $2^{16} - 1$ for $n \times 64$ kbits/s and an integer representation of multiplier values between 1 and 7 for $n \times 8$ kbits/s.

Source clock frequency recovery method (octet 9.1 for AAL Type 1)

Bits 8 7 6 5 4 3 2 1	Meaning
0 0 0 0 0 0 0 0	Null (synchronous circuit transport)
0 0 0 0 0 0 0 1	Synchronous residual time stamp (SRTS) method (asynchronous circuit transport) (cf. Rec I.363, Sec. 2.5.2.2.1)
0 0 0 0 0 0 1 0	Adaptive clock method (cf. Rec. I.363, Sec. 2.5.2.2.1)

All other values are reserved.

Error correction method (octet 10.1 for AAL Type 1)

Bits 8 7 6 5 4 3 2 1	Meaning
0 0 0 0 0 0 0 0	Null (no error correction is provided)
0 0 0 0 0 0 0 1	A forward error correction method for loss-sensitive signal transport (cf. I.363, Sec. 2.5.2.4.1)
0 0 0 0 0 0 1 0	A forward error correction method for delay-sensitive signal transport (*Note:* for further study, cf. I.363)

All other values are reserved.

Structured data transfer blocksize (octets 11.1 and 11.2 for AAL Type 1). This is a 16-bit integer representation of values between 1 and 65,535, i.e., $2^{16} - 1$. This parameter represents the block size of SDT CBR service.

Partially filled cells method (octet 12.1 for AAL Type 1)

Bits 8 7 6 5 4 3 2 1	Meaning
0 0 0 0 0 0 0 0 through 0 0 1 0 1 1 1 0	Integer representation of the number of leading octets of SAR-PDU payload in use (values between 1 and 47) (*Note:* for further study; cf. Rec. I.363)

All other values are reserved.

Forward maximum CPCS-SDU size (octets 6.1 and 6.2 for AAL Type 3/4 and Type 5). This is a 16-bit integer representation of the values between 1 and 65,535, i.e., $2^{16} - 1$. This parameter indicates the maximum CPCS-SDU size sent in the direction from the calling user to the called user.

Backward maximum CPCS-SDU size (octets 7.1 and 7.2 for AAL Type 3/4 and Type 5). This is a 16-bit integer representation of the values between 1 and 65,535, i.e., $2^{16} - 1$. This parameter indicates the maximum CPCS-SDU size sent in the direction from the called user to the calling user.

MID range (octets 8.1, 8.2, 8.3, and 8.4 for AAL Type 3/4). These are integer representations of the lowest value (octets 8.1 and 8.2) and the highest value (octets 8.3 and 8.4) of the MID range; only values between 0 and 1023 are valid.

SSCS type (octet 9.1 for AAL Type 3/4; octet 9.1 for AAL Type 5)

Bits 8 7 6 5 4 3 2 1	Meaning
0 0 0 0 0 0 0 0	Null
0 0 0 0 0 0 0 1	Data SSCS based on SSCOP (assured operation)
0 0 0 0 0 0 1 0	Data SSCS based on SSCOP (nonassured operation)
0 0 0 0 0 1 0 0	Frame relay SSCS

All other values are reserved.

User-defined AAL information (octets 6 to 6.3 for user-defined AAL). The use and coding of octets 6 to 6.3 is according to user-defined requirements.

Note: In case of the absence of parameters, the following default values will apply:

Subtype	No default (mandatory for AAL Type 1)
CBR rate	No default (mandatory for AAL Type 1)
Multiplier	No default (mandatory for CBR rate $n \times 64$ kbits/s and $n \times 8$ kbits/s)
Clock recovery	Default = null
Error correction	Default = null
SDT blocksize	Default = null (= no SDT)
Partially filled cells	Default = 47 octets
Forward maximum CPCS-SDU size	Default = 65,535
Backward maximum CPCS-SDU size	Default = 65,535
MID range	Default = 0–0 (no multiplexing via MID field)
SSCS type	Default = null

4.4.2 ATM user cell rate

The purpose of the ATM user cell rate information element is to communicate the set of traffic parameters for a requested connection. See Table 4.10. The network uses this information

- As input to the Connection Admission Control, to decide if there are sufficient resources available to support the requested connection
- To set the relevant Usage Parameter Controls for the connection in order to support traffic policing and traffic contracting (see Chap. 6).

TABLE 4.10 ATM User Cell Rate Information Element[a,b]

8	7	6	5	4	3	2	1	Octets
Bits								
ATM user cell rate								
0	1	0	1	1	0	0	1	1
Information element identifier								
1 ext	Coding standard	IE instruction field						2
Length of ATM user cell rate contents								3
Length of ATM user cell rate contents (continued)								4
1	0	0	0	0	0	1	0	5*
Forward peak cell rate identifier (CLP = 0)								
Forward peak cell rate								5.1*
Forward peak cell rate (continued)								5.2*
Forward peak cell rate (continued)								5.3*
1	0	0	0	0	0	1	1	6*
Backward peak cell rate identifier (CLP = 0)								
Backward peak cell rate								6.1*
Backward peak cell rate (continued)								6.2*
Backward peak cell rate (continued)								6.3*
1	0	0	0	0	1	0	0	7
Forward peak cell rate identifier (CLP = 0 + 1)								
Forward peak cell rate								7.1[c]
Forward peak cell rate (continued)								7.2[c]
Forward peak cell rate (continued)								7.3[c]
1	0	0	0	0	1	0	1	8
Backward peak cell rate identifier (CLP = 0 + 1)								
Backward peak cell rate								8.1[c,d]
Backward peak cell rate (continued)								8.2[c,d]
Backward peak cell rate (continued)								8.3[c,d]
1	0	0	0	1	0	0	0	9*[e]
Forward sustainable cell rate identifier (CLP = 0)								
Forward sustainable cell rate								9.1*[e]
Forward sustainable cell rate (continued)								9.2*[e]

TABLE 4.10 ATM User Cell Rate Information Element[a,b] **(Continued)**

Forward sustainable cell rate (continued)								9.3*[e]
1	0	0	0	1	0	0	1	10*[e]
Backward sustainable cell rate identifier (CLP = 0)								
Backward sustainable cell rate								10.1*[e]
Backward sustainable cell rate (continued)								10.2*[e]
Backward sustainable cell rate (continued)								10.3*[e]
1	0	0	1	0	0	0	0	11*[e]
Forward sustainable cell rate identifier (CLP = 0 + 1)								
Forward sustainable cell rate								11.1*[e]
Forward sustainable cell rate (continued)								11.2*[e]
Forward sustainable cell rate (continued)								11.3*[e]
1	0	0	1	0	0	0	1	12*[e]
Backward sustainable cell rate identifier (CLP = 0 + 1)								
Backward sustainable cell rate								12.1*[e]
Backward sustainable cell rate (continued)								12.2*[e]
Backward sustainable cell rate (continued)								12.3*[e]
1	0	1	0	0	0	0	0	13*[e]
Forward maximum burst size identifier (CLP = 0)								
Forward maximum burst size								13.1*[e]
Forward maximum burst size (continued)								13.2*[e]
Forward maximum burst size (continued)								13.3*[e]
1	0	1	0	0	0	0	1	14*[e]
Backward maximum burst size identifier (CLP = 0)								
Backward maximum burst size								14.1*[e]
Backward maximum burst size (continued)								14.2*[e]
Backward maximum burst size (continued)								14.3*[e]
1	0	1	1	0	0	0	0	15*[e]
Forward maximum burst size identifier (CLP = 0 + 1)								
Forward maximum burst size								15.1*[e]
Forward maximum burst size (continued)								15.2*[e]
Forward maximum burst size (continued)								15.3*[e]
1	0	1	1	0	0	0	1	16*[e]
Backward maximum burst size identifier (CLP = 0 + 1)								

TABLE 4.10 ATM User Cell Rate Information Element[a,b] **(Continued)**

Backward maximum burst size								16.1*[e]
Backward maximum burst size (continued)								16.2*[e]
Backward maximum burst size (continued)								16.3*[e]
1	0	1	1	1	1	1	0	17*[f]
Best effort indicator								
1	0	1	1	1	1	1	1	18*[g]
Traffic management options identifier								
0	0	0	0	0	0	Tagging backward	Tagging forward	18.1*[g]
Reserved								

[a]All the parameters are position-independent. The term "forward" indicates the direction from the calling user to the called user. The term "backward" indicates the direction from the called user to the calling user.
[b]The traffic parameters encoded in this information element do not include OAM cells.
[c]If only the peak cell rate for CLP = 0 + 1 is specified, the network resource allocation assumes that the entire peak cell rate can be used for CLP = 0.
[d]For point-to-multipoint calls, the backward peak cell rate (CLP = 0 + 1) value is coded as 0. No other backward traffic descriptors are included.
[e]If forward sustainable cell rate (CLP = 0), forward sustainable cell rate (CLP = 0 + 1), backward sustainable cell rate (CLP = 0), or backward sustainable cell rate (CLP = 0 + 1) is included, the corresponding maximum burst size is included. Similarly, if forward maximum burst size (CLP = 0), forward maximum burst size (CLP = 0 + 1), backward maximum burst size (CLP = 0), or backward maximum burst size (CLP = 0 + 1) is included, the corresponding sustainable cell rate is included.
[f]QOS class 0 is used with the best effort indication. The interpretation of the forward peak cell rate (CLP = 0 + 1) parameter and the backward peak cell rate (CLP = 0 + 1) parameter is modified by the best effort indication.
[g]When these octets are not present, it is assumed that tagging is not requested.

Coding standard (octet 2)

Bits	
7 6	**Meaning**
0 0	ITU-TS (CCITT) standardized*
1 1	Standard defined for the network (either public or private) present on the network side of the interface.[†]

*This codepoint is used when the combinations of traffic parameter subfields in Tables 4.11 and 4.12 are used.
[†]This codepoint can be used to specify additional experimental parameters. These parameters may be used to provide a more detailed traffic characterization (e.g., average cell rate, average burst size, etc.).

IE instruction field (octet 3)

Bits	
5 4 3 2 1	**Meaning**
0 0 0 0 0	IE instruction field is not significant

Forward/backward peak cell rate (octets $i.1$ to $i.3$, where i may have values 5, 6, 7, or 8). The forward and backward peak cell rate parameters indicate the peak cell rate, expressed in cells per second.

Forward/backward sustainable cell rate (octets $i.1$ to $i.3$, where i may have values 9, 10, 11, or 12). The forward and backward sustainable cell rate parameters indicate the sustainable cell rate, expressed in cells per second.

Forward/backward maximum burst size (octets $i.1$ to $i.3$, where i may have values 13, 14, 15, or 16). The forward and backward maximum burst size parameters indicate the maximum burst size, expressed in cells.

Best effort indication (octet 17). This octet is included when the best effort QOS class is requested.

Tagging backward (octet 18.1). The tagging backward parameter is coded as 1 when tagging is requested in the backward direction and as 0 when tagging is not requested.

Tagging forward (octet 18.1). The tagging forward parameter is coded as 1 when tagging is requested in the forward direction and as 0 when tagging is not requested.

The valid combinations of the traffic descriptor subfields in the ATM user cell rate information element are shown in Tables 4.11 and 4.12. Table 4.11 shows the valid combinations of traffic parameter subfields for a given direction (i.e., the forward direction may use one combination of traffic descriptors, while the backward direction uses a different combination). Total information element length will depend upon the combinations of traffic parameter subfields chosen for each direction. Table 4.12 shows the valid combination of traffic parameter subfields for the best effort QOS class (best effort service* always applies to both directions of the connection).

4.4.3 Broadband bearer capability

The purpose of the broadband bearer capability information element is to indicate a requested broadband connection-oriented bearer service to be provided by the network. The three bearer services supported are Broadband Connection-Oriented Bearer Type A (BCOB-A), Broadband

---

*"Best effort" is one of the QOS options being considered for CRS as contrasted to a "guaranteed" service. It is similar to the way the Internet IP protocol/service works. See Chap. 6.

TABLE 4.11 Allowable Combinations of Traffic Parameters in a Given Direction[1]

Allowable combinations of traffic parameter subfields in the ATM user cell rate information element for a given direction
Peak cell rate, CLP = 0 Peak cell rate, CLP = 0 + 1
Peak cell rate, CLP = 0 Peak cell rate, CLP = 0 + 1 Tagging = tagging requested
Peak cell rate, CLP = 0 + 1 Sustainable cell rate, CLP = 0 Maximum burst size, CLP = 0
Peak cell rate, CLP = 0 + 1 Sustainable cell rate, CLP = 0 Maximum burst size, CLP = 0 Tagging = tagging requested
Peak cell rate, CLP = 0 + 1
Peak cell rate, CLP = 0 + 1 Sustainable cell rate, CLP = 0 + 1 Maximum burst size, CLP = 0 + 1

Connection-Oriented Bearer Type C (BCOB-C), and Broadband Connection-Oriented Bearer Type X (BCOB-X). These correspond directly to the service classes A, C, and X introduced at the beginning of this chapter (Class X supports cell relay service).

Table 4.13 shows the layout of this important information element.

Coding standard (octet 2)

Bits	
7 6	Meaning
0 0	ITU-TS (CCITT) standardized

IE instruction field (octet 2). This field is currently coded as 00000 to indicate that the IE instruction field is not significant.

TABLE 4.12 Combination of Traffic Parameters for Best Effort[1]

Combination of traffic parameter subfields in the ATM user cell rate information element for best effort	Total information element length in octets (including overhead)
Peak cell rate forward, CLP = 0 + 1 Peak cell rate backward, CLP = 0 + 1 Best effort indication	13

TABLE 4.13 Broadband Bearer Capability Information Element[1,2]

			Bits					
8	7	6	5	4	3	2	1	Octets
Broadband bearer capability								
0	1	0	1	1	1	1	0	1
Information element identifier								
1 ext	Coding standard		IE instruction field					2
Length of B-BC contents								3
Length of B-BC contents (continued)								4
0/1 ext	0 Spare	0	Bearer Class					5
1 ext	0 Spare	0	Traffic type			Timing requirements		5a*[a]
1 ext	Susceptibility to clipping		0	0 Spare	0	User Plane connection configuration		6

[a]This octet will be present only if Bearer Class X is indicated in octet 5.

Bearer class (octet 5)

Bits 5 4 3 2 1	Meaning
0 0 0 0 1	BCOB-A
0 0 0 1 1	BCOB-C
1 0 0 0 0	BCOB-X

Reserved (octet 5a). This field is reserved for indication of the connection mode for bearer class X.

Traffic type (octet 5a)

Bits 5 4 3	Meaning
0 0 0	No indication
0 0 1	Constant bit rate
0 1 0	Variable bit rate

Timing requirements (octet 5a)

Bits 2 1	Meaning
0 0	No indication
0 1	End-to-end timing required
1 0	End-to-end timing not required
1 1	Reserved

Susceptibility to clipping (octet 6).   This field is coded as 00 when the User Plane information is not susceptible to clipping, and as 01 when it is.

User Plane connection configuration (octet 6).   This field is coded as 00 for point-to-point connections and as 01 for point-to-multipoint connections.

4.4.4   Quality of service parameter

The purpose of the quality of service parameter information element is to request and indicate the quality of service class for a connection that the user wishes the network to set up. QOS classes are described in more detail in Chap. 6. See Table 4.14.

Coding standard (octet 2).   This field is coded as 11, indicating the standard defined for the network (either public or private) present on the network side of the interface.

TABLE 4.14   Quality of Service Parameter Information Element[1,2]

8	7	6	5	4	3	2	1	Octets
				Bits				
Quality of service parameter								
0	1	0	1	1	1	0	0	1
Information element identifier								
1 ext	Coding standard	IE instruction field						2
Length of quality of service parameter contents								3
Length of quality of service parameter contents (continued)								4
QOS class forward								5
QOS class backward								6

IE instruction field (octet 2). This field is currently coded as 00000 to indicate that the IE instruction field is not significant.

QOS class forward (octet 5)*

Bits 8 7 6 5 4 3 2 1	Meaning
0 0 0 0 0 0 0 0	QOS class 0—unspecified QOS class (best effort)
0 0 0 0 0 0 0 1	QOS class 1
0 0 0 0 0 0 1 0	QOS class 2
0 0 0 0 0 0 1 1	QOS class 3
0 0 0 0 0 1 0 0	QOS class 4

*The cell relay services currently defined and under consideration by carriers support only two QOS classes: QOS Class I (with cell loss ratio in the 10^{-10} range) and QOS class II (with cell loss ratio in the 10^{-7} range).

QOS class backward (octet 6)*

Bits 8 7 6 5 4 3 2 1	Meaning
0 0 0 0 0 0 0 0	QOS class 0—unspecified QOS class (best effort)
0 0 0 0 0 0 0 1	QOS class 1
0 0 0 0 0 0 1 0	QOS class 2
0 0 0 0 0 0 1 1	QOS class 3
0 0 0 0 0 1 0 0	QOS class 4

*The cell relay services currently defined and under consideration by carriers support only two QOS classes: QOS Class I (with cell loss ratio in the 10^{-10} range) and QOS class II (with cell loss ratio in the 10^{-7} range).

4.4.5   Other information elements

Broadband high-layer information. The function of the broadband high-layer information element is to provide a capability to be used for compatibility checking by an addressed entity (e.g., a remote user or an interworking unit). The broadband high-layer information element is carried transparently (as, for example, is the case for the AAL parameter) by an ATM network between the call originating party (e.g., the calling user) and the addressed party. For the public UNI, the availability of this information element must be negotiated with the network provider. At a public UNI, the network provider has the option of not supporting this element in the SETUP message. At a private UNI (e.g., private switches, hubs, etc., used, for example, in ATM-based LANs), support for this information element is considered to be mandatory.[1]

Broadband low-layer information.   The function of the broadband low-layer information element is to provide a capability to be used for compatibility checking by an addressed entity (e.g., a remote user or an interworking unit or a high-layer function network node addressed by the calling user). The broadband low-layer information element is carried transparently by an ATM network between the call originating entity (e.g., the calling user) and the addressed entity. Support of this information element by the network is mandatory.[1,2,5,7]

References

1. ATM Forum, *ATM User-Network Interface Specification*, Version 3.0, August 1993.

2. ITU-TS Recommendation Q.2931: *B-ISDN User-Network Interface Layer 3 Specification for Basic Call / Bearer Control*, Geneva, Switzerland, December 1993.

3. Bellcore (D. Minoli), "Q.93B AAL Information Element Format," CCITT/ITU-T Meeting, Melbourne, Australia, February 1993.

4. D. Minoli and G. H. Dobrowski, *Understanding Signaling: The Road to Cell Relay and Frame Relay Services,* Artech House, Norwood, Mass., 1994.

5. Bellcore Framework Advisory FA-NWT-001111, *Broadband ISDN Access Signaling Framework Generic Criteria for Class II Equipment*, December 1991.

6. D. Minoli, "Alignment of the AAL IE," Contribution to the ATM Forum, Stockholm, Sweden, November 1993.

7. Bellcore Technical Advisory TA-NWT-001111, *Broadband ISDN Access Signaling Generic Requirements*, August 1993.

5

Cell Relay Service: A Formal Description

There is now considerable interest in cell relay service. This chapter presents a formal definition of cell relay service, based on the concepts presented in Chap. 1 through 4. Sections 5.1 through 5.8 are based verbatim on a contribution made to the ANSI T1 Committee.[1] Section 5.9 provides some additional information. In the material that follows, the expression "for further study" means that the indicated feature is not yet supported in ANSI standards; such a feature may or may not actually be under consideration for further development or may already be resolved in standards issued by other bodies. Note that in the contribution, CRS is called cell relay bearer service (CRBS) to emphasize the fact that the service is a pure transport service; that is, no "supplementary" capabilities are included in the description. Some additional material is found in the remaining sections. Chapter 6 provides more details on CRS.

This contribution provided a formal description of CRS. Its purpose was to propose an ANSI standard for cell relay service. Such efforts begin with a Stage 1 Service Description. The proposed standard is expected to be useful for end users, software application developers, and hardware manufacturers.

5.1 Scope, Purpose, and Application

This standard explains the asynchronous transfer mode–based cell relay bearer service from the user's perspective. The scope of this standard includes point-to-point, point-to-multipoint, and multipoint-to-multipoint connection arrangements; symmetric and asymmetric connections; bidirectional and unidirectional transmission; and permanent and on-demand establishment of connections.

This standard is based on ITU-T (formerly CCITT) Recommendations F.811, I.211, and I.361.

5.1.1 Purpose

This standard supplies the service user with a description of what these services provide, along with possible options. This also provides the basis for the division of functionality and the subsequent development/particularization of standardized protocols to support this service.

5.1.2 Application

This standard applies to a B-ISDN as described in the ITU-T Recommendations of the I series.

5.2 Normative References

The following standards contain provisions which, through reference in this text, constitute provisions of this standard.

ITU-T Recommendation I.150, *B-ISDN ATM Functional Characteristics*, 1992.

ITU-T Recommendation I.211, *B-ISDN Service Aspects*, 1992.

ITU-T Recommendation I.311, *B-ISDN General Network Aspects*, 1992.

ITU-T Recommendation I.361, *B-ISDN ATM Layer Specification*, 1992.

ITU-T Recommendation I.371, *Traffic Control and Congestion Control in B-ISDN*, 1992.

ITU-T Recommendation I.413, *B-ISDN UNI Specification*, 1992.

ITU-T Recommendation F.811, *Broadband Connection-Oriented Bearer Service*, 1992.

ITU-T Recommendation E.164, *Numbering Plan in the ISDN Era*, 1990.

ANSI American National Standard for Telecommunications T1.5ATM, *B-ISDN ATM Layer Cell Transfer—Performance Parameters*, 199x.

5.3 Definitions

5.3.1 Access reference configuration

The access reference configuration used in this description is consistent with the definition provided in ITU-T Recommendation I.413.

5.3.2 Broadband terminal (BT)

As used in this description, the BT incorporates functions equivalent to those described in I.413 for the Broadband Network Termination 2 (B-NT2) functional group. (B-NT2 functions include but are not limited to concentration, switching, and resource management.)

5.3.3 Service performance parameters

In this description, such terms as cell error ratio, severely errored cell block ratio, cell loss ratio, cell misinsertion rate, cell transfer delay, mean cell transfer delay, and cell delay variation are defined consistent with ANSI T1.511-1994.

5.3.4 Network

In this description, "network" refers to all telecommunications equipment that has any part in processing a call. It may include the local exchange, transit exchanges, and B-NT2, but it does not include the BTs and is not limited to the public network or any particular set of equipment.

5.3.5 Reference load signaling processing delay for point-to-point call establishment

This is the difference between the time an incoming user service request message is delivered by the incoming Physical Layer to the incoming Data Link Layer at the serving switch or any other switch supporting CRBS, and the time an outgoing setup message is delivered by the outgoing Data Link Layer to the outgoing Physical Layer.

5.3.6 Reference load signaling processing delay for call teardown

This is the difference between the time an incoming user disconnect message is delivered by the incoming Physical Layer to the incoming Data Link Layer at the serving switch or any other switch supporting CRBS, and the time an outgoing disconnect is delivered by the outgoing Data Link Layer to the outgoing Physical Layer.

5.3.7 Service profile

In this description, the service profile is a collection of information maintained by a network to provide service to access a signaling entity; it is network-specific. The collection of information can contain details on a nonstandard protocol stack used by the user, terminal subscription data, directory number, supplementary service information, and other user or service data, as defined by a specific network.

5.3.8 Service provider

This is a company, organization, administration, business, etc., that sells, administers, maintains, charges for, etc., the service. The service provider may or may not be the provider of the network.

5.4 General Description

The ATM Layer CRBS provides a connection-oriented sequence-preserving cell-based communication service between two or more BTs, including BTs within the network, at a variety of access rates and information transfer rates.

Cells are 53 octets in length and conform with ITU-T Recommendation I.361. Access rate aspects are addressed in ITU-T Recommendation I.211. Supported U.S. access rates include $n \times 64$ kbits/s aggregate for $2 \leq n \leq 672$, n even; 64 kbits/s; DS1; DS2; DS3; STS-1; STS-3c; and STS-12c. The physical access channel can be a T1/DS1-, T3/DS3- or SONET-based (STS-3c or STS-12c) facility.

The actual CRBS service transfer rate can be expressed in cells per second. For a given access, the peak instantaneous aggregate cell rate multiplied by 424 must be less or equal to the access rate expressed in bits per second. Nominal oversubscription may be permitted. Supported U.S. peak cell rates for each connection are appropriate values in the range $150 <$ cell transfer rate per second $< 1{,}470{,}000$. The actual CRBS payload transfer rate is a function of the access rate, the transfer rate, and the protocol control information (PCI) utilized.

CRBS supports communication at a negotiated peak rate or at a negotiated sustained rate which is less than the peak rate but may approach or be equal to the peak rate during a (short) burst interval.

The transfer of cells that is supported in CRBS can take place in a bidirectional symmetric, bidirectional asymmetric, or unidirectional fashion, either for point-to-point, point-to-multipoint, or multipoint-to-multipoint connection arrangements. The service can be provided over permanent (provisioned) connections or over switched (on-demand) connections.

The service is defined at the user-network interface (UNI) for a single BT on such an interface. CRBS is defined to operate between ATM Layer entities in BTs (see Recommendation I.321), providing for transparent transfer of ATM cells. At the ATM Layer, cells are relayed from the ATM Layer entity in the source ("origin") BT, through ATM Layer entities in the network, to the ATM Layer entity in the "destination" BT. In the Control Plane, a call/bearer control protocol may be used to establish, maintain, and release calls and bearers in the User Plane for on-demand establishment of connections.

From the network's perspective, there is only one entity on the BT side of the UNI. This is referred to as *point-to-point access*. Point-to-point access does not preclude the user's equipment from acting as an aggregator of other tributary devices present at the location where the UNI terminates. The network's transport of subaddress information in support of tributary devices connected to the BT is for further study.

The cell header conforms to ITU-T Recommendation I.361 and includes the capability to specify a virtual channel identifier (VCI)/virtual path identifier (VPI), a payload type indicator, a cell loss priority, and a header check sequence. The VCIs/VPIs, which are locally significant, act as logical channel identifiers for the virtual channels (VCs) and virtual paths (VPs). The combined bit representation of the VPI/VCI field in the cell header represents the logical identifier of the bearer channel. The VPI portion of the combined VPI/VCI field can be viewed as a hierarchical channel identification mechanism; hence, a VP can be considered a set of VCs. Multiple VCs and/or VPs may be supported over a single UNI.

Within a VP, the different VCs can have different transfer rates; however, the aggregate rate must be less than or equal to the maximum bandwidth available over the physical interface. The VCs (in different VPs) defined over a given UNI can represent connections to remote destinations which are on different remote physical interfaces.

The maximum number of VPIs and/or VCIs that may be supported at the UNI is network-specific, and may be further constrained by subscription. Some VPIs and VCIs may be reserved for specific operation or signaling functions.

Destinations are identified by a suitable addressing scheme, e.g., ITU-T E.164. A VC and/or VP between two BTs is called a (virtual) connection. As in the case of the origin BT, from the network point of view, a destination is composed of a single BT. Access VPIs/VCIs can be assigned by the network or, optionally, can be negotiated. The appropriate mapping or set of mappings of VPIs/VCIs is undertaken by the network to achieve the desired connectivity with the destination associated with the given address. The scope of the set of supported addressing structures and encodings is for further study.

Traffic management (traffic control and/or congestion control) may be applied over each connection; this depends on both the quality of service

(QOS) selected/supported and the state of the network. Traffic management is particularly applicable to links (access and interswitch) where the VPs/VCs support variable-bit-rate traffic and/or where nominal oversubscription of bandwidth across multiple VCs/VPs in a link is allowed. Attributes that characterize traffic are defined in ITU-T Recommendations I.311 and I.371. Goals as to what cell loss may be sustained for compliant cells may be viewed as integral to the definition of CRBS. Additionally, operation, administration, and maintenance (OAM) and customer network management functions are supported.

CRBS can be provided on demand or as a subscription option. In either case, a set of "elements" describing the characteristics of the virtual connection is made available to the network entity supporting the service. Each element is composed of a set of identifiable fields that represent a parametric description of the element's desired action. For on-demand CRBS, these elements represent negotiable aspects of the service. See Table 5.1. For subscribed CRBS, a subset of these elements represents characteristics to be used in provisioning the service.

For on-demand cases, the service requires a mechanism to enable the user to signal to the network the need for the service and to transfer *information elements* describing features of the service instanciation; this is done during a call-establishment phase. This is followed by an information transfer phase, and finally by a call-release phase. The characteristics of the call can be declared only at call establishment and cannot be subsequently changed during the call. Signaling for renegotiation of call characteristics is for further study.

TABLE 5.1 On-demand CRBS Information Elements Specifiable at Call Establishment

AAL parameters

ATM user cell rate*

Broadband bearer capability

Broadband low-layer compatibility

Broadband high-layer compatibility

Called party/parties number

Called party/parties subaddress

Calling party number

Calling party subaddress

Quality of service parameter

Transit network selection

*ATM cell rate indication may include both a peak rate and a sustained rate (defined as a fraction of the peak rate).

Note: For multipoint services, several of these parameters may be specified on a per origin-destination basis.

A user specifies information elements as well as constituent fields to describe the service required, including symmetry and traffic intensity. Traffic intensity is characterized by attributes such as peak cell rate, sustained cell rate, and burst length. The network will police the user traffic to ascertain that it is within the stipulated range. The exact mechanism for describing the traffic stream, and the mechanism utilized by the network to police the traffic, is currently under study. The user can set a bit in each cell (the cell loss priority bit) to indicate that the network may, in case of congestion, discard the cell.

A service profile capability may also be supported by some networks. The service profile associated with a specific user is a network-resident database that contains service information (including some of the information listed in Table 5.1, but not limited to it) that can be used as part of the call establishment phase. The information can only be updated by the service provider. The possibility of user-updatable service profiles is for further study.

5.4.1 Basic service capabilities

The CRBS operates at the B-ISDN ATM layer. Cells are transported to the destination(s) with a level of assurance consistent with the selected QOS class, of which a number of classes may be available. The network provides a high assurance for

1. The sequentiality of the cell stream
2. Cell integrity, which includes correctness of the payload, assurance that the cell will be delivered, and assurance that a received cell is for the intended destination
3. Low delay in establishing and releasing on-demand calls
4. Low end-to-end delay for the delivery of the first user cell
5. Low variation in intercell delay

Aspects of the metrics are described in Chap. 6.

In addition to the transport functionality identified above, CRBS includes OAM/customer network management functions; interworking functions may also be supported. These functions are discussed in the appropriate sections.

In the following service descriptions, the term *outbound* refers to cells flowing from a user to the network; the term *inbound* refers to cells flowing from the network to the user. The term *cell transfer rate* refers to the peak rate or the sustained rate, as appropriate.

5.4.2   Bidirectional symmetric
point-to-point (BSPP) service

At a given interface, a network-registered user (known generically as the origin) can specify

1. The identity of the party with which the origin wishes to establish an ATM layer bearer service (known generically as the destination).

2. A requested cell transfer rate, QOS class, and other connection parameters, which are identical for both the origin-destination and destination-origin channels. The possibility of origin-network and/or origin-destination negotiation of requested cell transfer rate, QOS class, and other connection parameters, and related procedures, is for further study.

3. A preferred/exclusive/network-selected VPI/VCI for local identification of the connection. *Preferred* refers to the user's preference for the specified VPI/VCI, but also the user's willingness to accept another label supplied by the network. *Exclusive* refers to the user's firm requirement for the specified VPI/VCI—if the VPI/VCI is not available, service is not to be enacted. *Network-selected* refers to the case in which the user has no say on the label, since it is completely selected by the network.

The cells submitted by the origin are delivered to the specified destination, in accordance with points 1 to 5 in Sec. 5.4.1. The cells submitted by the destination are delivered to the origin, in accordance with points 1 to 5 in Sec. 5.4.1.

Multiple VCs between the origin and the destination can be requested via distinct service requests. In addition, at a UNI, the different VCs need not all be BSPP connections, but can be any mix discussed in Sec. 5.4.

If no parties need to be added to an existing BSPP session, then the service is realizable as a single ATM connection; if parties do need to be added then the service is realized as two unidirectional point-to-point connections (Fig. 5.1).

5.4.3   Bidirectional asymmetric
point-to-point (BAPP) service

At a given interface, the origin can specify

1. The identity of the destination party with which the origin wishes to establish an ATM Layer bearer service.

2. An origin-destination cell transfer rate, QOS class, and other connection parameters, as well as a destination-origin cell transfer rate,

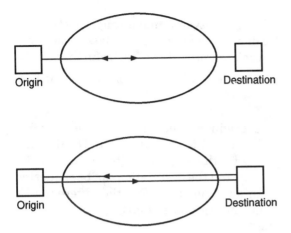

Figure 5.1 BSSP Service. Top: single-connection realization for nonadditive environments; bottom: dual-connection realization for additive environments.

QOS class, and other connection parameters; the parameters may be different for the two directions. The possibility of origin-network and/or origin-destination negotiation of requested cell transfer rate, QOS class, and other connection parameters, and related procedures, is for further study.

3. A preferred/exclusive/network-selected VPI/VCI for local identification of the connection.

The cells submitted by the origin are delivered to the specified destination, in accordance with points 1 to 5 in Sec. 5.4.1. The cells submitted by the destination are delivered to the origin, in accordance with points 1 to 5 in Sec. 5.4.1.

Multiple VCs between the origin and the destination can be requested via distinct service requests. In addition, at a UNI, the different VCs need not all be BAPP connections, but can be any mix discussed in Sec. 5.4.

5.4.4 Unidirectional point-to-point (UPP) service

At a given interface, the origin can specify

1. The identity of the destination party with which the origin wishes to establish an ATM Layer bearer service.

2. An origin-destination cell transfer rate, QOS class, and other connection parameters, with no connection resources for the destination-ori-

gin path. The possibility of origin-network and/or origin-destination negotiation of requested cell transfer rate, QOS class, and other connection parameters, and related procedures, is for further study.

3. A preferred/exclusive/network-selected VPI/VCI for local identification of the connection.

The cells submitted by the origin are delivered to the specified destination, in accordance with points 1 to 5 in Sec. 5.4.1. The destination is not allowed to supply cells for the origin over this connection.

Multiple VCs between the origin and the destination can be requested via distinct service requests. In addition, at a UNI, the different VCs need not all be UPP connections, but can be any mix discussed in Sec. 5.4.

5.4.5   Bidirectional symmetric point-to-multipoint (BSPM) service

At a given interface, the origin can specify

1. The identity of a set of destinations with which the origin wishes to establish an ATM Layer bearer service. The destinations are identified via separate service requests, a group-addressing scheme, or a reference to a service profile.

2. A requested cell transfer rate, QOS class, and other connection parameters, which are identical for all the origin-destination connections. The possibility of origin-network and/or origin-destination negotiation of requested cell transfer rate, QOS class, and other connection parameters, and related procedures, is for further study.

3. A preferred/exclusive/network-selected VPI/VCI for local identification of the outbound connection. A set of preferred/exclusive/network-selected VPIs/VCIs for local identification of each inbound connection is also specified. The issue of how to specify the required set of inbound VPIs/VCIs in the case where separate service requests are not utilized is for further study.

The issue of whether destinations can be added during the information transfer phase and the issues of who authorizes the adds and how a BSPM connection is identified are for further study. However, users can abandon the call autonomously at any time. The issue of whether the other participants of the call need to be informed of the defection and how to accomplish this, is for further study.

The cells submitted by the origin are delivered to the specified destinations, in accordance with points 1 to 5 in Sec. 5.4.1. The network provides (distributed) replication for optimized delivery of cells without requiring the origin to supply duplicate copies of the cells.

The cells submitted by any destination are delivered to the origin, in accordance with points 1 to 5 in Sec. 5.4.1; these cells are not automatically (directly) delivered to the other destinations. The cells arriving at the origin are delivered over the appropriate inbound VPI/VCI.

If multiple destinations' (leaves') information is multiplexed to a single VC associated with the origin (root), the origin cannot demultiplex the cells in the ATM Layer; if needed, this demultiplexing must be done at a higher layer (Fig. 5.2).

Multiple VCs between the origin and a destination can be requested via distinct service requests. In addition, at a UNI, the different VCs need not all be BSPM connections, but can be any mix discussed in Sec. 5.4.

5.4.6 Bidirectional asymmetric point-to-multipoint (BAPM) service

At a given interface, the origin can specify

1. The identity of a set of destinations with which the origin wishes to establish an ATM Layer bearer service. The destinations are identi-

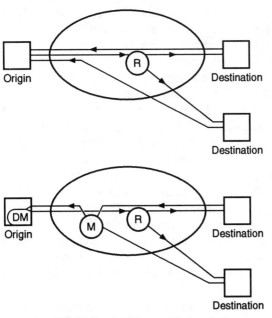

Figure 5.2 BSPM Service. Top: multiple-origin-connection realization; Bottom: single-origin-connection realization (demuxing beyond ATM is needed). R = replication function; M = multiplexing function; DM = demultiplexing function.

fied via separate service requests, a group-addressing scheme, or a reference to a service profile.

2. An origin-destinations cell transfer rate, QOS class, and other connection parameters, as well as a different cell transfer rate, QOS class, and other connection parameters for the destinations-origin connection. The case in which the origin-destination cell transfer rate, QOS class, and other connection parameters are different for each destination and for each destination-origin connection (namely, a completely asymmetric case) is for further study. The possibility of origin-network and/or origin-destinations negotiation of requested cell transfer rate, QOS class, and other connection parameters, and related procedures, is also for further study.

3. A preferred/exclusive/network-selected VPI/VCI for local identification of the outbound connection. A set of preferred/exclusive/network-selected VPIs/VCIs for local identification of each inbound connection. The issue of how to specify the required set of inbound VPIs/VCIs in the case where separate service requests are not utilized is for further study.

The issue of whether destinations can be added during the information transfer phase and the issues of who authorizes the adds and how a BSPM connection is identified are for further study. However, users can abandon the call autonomously at any time. The issue of whether the other participants of the call need to be informed of the defection, and how to accomplish this, is for further study.

The issue of how to specify the cell transfer rate, QOS class, and other connection parameters for each destination in the case where separate service requests are not utilized is for further study.

The cells submitted by the origin are delivered to the specified destinations, in accordance with points 1 to 5 in Sec. 5.4.1. The network provides (distributed) replication for optimized delivery of cells without requiring the origin to supply duplicate copies of the cells.

The cells submitted by any destination are delivered to the origin, in accordance with points 1 to 5 in Sec. 5.4.1; these cells are not automatically (directly) delivered to the other destinations. The cells arriving at the origin are delivered over the appropriate inbound VPI/VCI.

Each traffic source is responsible for ascertaining that there is logical speed consistency between itself and the party (parties) with which it wishes to communicate. The network may or may not provide buffering in support of speed conversion.

If multiple destinations' (leaves') information is multiplexed to a single VC associated with the origin (root), the origin cannot demultiplex the cells in the ATM Layer; if needed, this demultiplexing must be done at a higher layer.

Multiple VCs between the origin and a destination can be requested via distinct service requests. In addition, at a UNI, the different VCs need not all be BAPM connections, but can be any mix discussed in Sec. 5.4.

5.4.7   Unidirectional point-to-multipoint (UPM) service

At a given interface, the origin can specify

1. The identity of a set of destinations with which the origin wishes to establish an ATM Layer bearer service. The destinations are identified via separate service requests, a group-addressing scheme, or a reference to a service profile.

2. An origin-destination cell transfer rate, QOS class, and other connection parameters for each destination, with no connection resources for the destinations-origin connections. The possibility of origin-network and/or origin-destinations negotiation of requested transfer cell rate, QOS class, and other connection parameters, and related procedures, is for further study.

3. A preferred/exclusive/network-selected VPI/VCI for local identification of the outbound connection. A set of preferred/exclusive/network-selected VPIs/VCIs for local identification of each inbound connection is also specified. The issue of how to specify the required set of inbound VPIs/VCIs in the case where separate service requests are not utilized is for further study.

The issue of whether destinations can be added during the information transfer phase and the issues of who authorizes the adds and how a UPM connection is identified are for further study. However, users can abandon the call autonomously at any time. The issue of whether the other participants of the call need to be informed of the defection, and how to accomplish this, is for further study.

The cells submitted by the origin are delivered to the specified destinations, in accordance with points 1 to 5 in Sec. 5.4.1. The network provides (distributed) replication for optimized delivery of cells without requiring the origin to supply duplicate copies of the cells. The destinations are not allowed to supply cells for the origin over this connection.

Multiple VCs between the origin and a destination can be requested via distinct service requests. In addition, at a UNI, the different VCs need not all be UPM connections, but can be any mix discussed in Sec. 5.4.

5.4.8 Bidirectional symmetric multipoint-to-multipoint (BSMM) service

The description that follows assumes that there are N users that need to be connected in a "complete graph on N nodes" fashion. The case where each user i needs to be connected to a (different) subset S_i is for further study.

At a given interface, *each* origin can specify

1. The identity of a set of destinations with which the origin wishes to establish an ATM Layer bearer service. The destinations are identi- fied via separate service requests, a group-addressing scheme, or a reference to a service profile.

2. A requested cell transfer rate, QOS class, and other connection parameters, which are identical for all the origin-destination connec- tions supported by this origin. The possibility of origin-network and/or origin-destinations negotiation of requested cell transfer rate, QOS class, and other connection parameters, and related procedures, is for further study.

3. A preferred/exclusive/network-selected VPI/VCI for local identifica- tion of the outbound connection. A set of preferred/exclusive/network- selected VPIs/VCIs for local identification of each inbound connection is also specified. The issue of how to specify the required set of inbound VPIs/VCIs in the case where separate service requests are not utilized is for further study.

The issue of whether destinations can be added during the informa- tion transfer phase and the issues of who authorizes the adds and how a BSMM connection is identified are for further study. However, users can abandon the call autonomously at any time. The issue of whether the other participants of the call need to be informed of the defection, and how to accomplish this, is for further study.

The cells submitted by *each* origin are delivered to the specified destinations, in accordance with points 1 to 5 in Sec. 5.4.1. The network provides (distributed) replication for optimized delivery of cells without requiring the origin to supply duplicate copies of the cells.

The cells submitted by any destination are delivered to the origin, in accordance with points 1 to 5 in Sec. 5.4.1; these cells are *also* delivered to the other destinations. The network provides (distributed) replication for optimized delivery of cells without requiring the origin to supply duplicate copies of the cells. The inbound cells arriving at any origin are delivered over the appropriate inbound VPI/VCI.

If multiple destinations' (leaves') information is multiplexed to a single VC associated with the origin (root), the origin cannot demultiplex the cells in the ATM Layer; if needed, this demultiplexing must be done at a higher layer (Fig. 5.3).

Multiple VCs between the origin and a destination can be requested via distinct service requests. In addition, at a UNI, the different VCs need not all be BSMM connections, but can be any mix discussed in Sec. 5.4.

5.4.9 Bidirectional asymmetric multipoint-to-multipoint (BAMM) service

For further study.

5.4.10 Unidirectional multipoint-to-multipoint (UMM) service

The description that follows assumes that there are N users that need to be connected in a "complete graph on N nodes" fashion. The case where each user i needs to be connected to a (different) subset S_i, is for further study.

At a given interface, *each* origin can specify

1. The identity of a set of destinations with which the origin wishes to establish an ATM Layer bearer service. The destinations are identi-

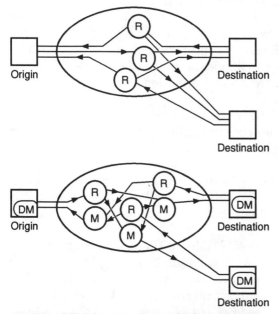

Figure 5.3 BSMM service. Top: multiple-connection realization; bottom: single-connection realization (demuxing beyond ATM is needed). R = replication function; M = multiplexing function; DM = demultiplexing function.

fied via separate service requests, a group-addressing scheme, or a reference to a service profile.

2. A requested cell transfer rate, QOS class, and other connection parameters, which are identical for all the origin-destination connections supported by this origin. The possibility of origin-network and/or origin-destinations negotiation of requested cell transfer rate, QOS class, and other connection parameters, and related procedures, is for further study.

3. A preferred/exclusive/network-selected VPI/VCI for local identification of the outbound connection. A set of preferred/exclusive/network-selected VPIs/VCIs for local identification of each inbound connection from the multiple destinations is also specified. The issue of how to specify the required set of inbound VPIs/VCIs in the case where separate service requests are not utilized is for further study.

The issue of whether destinations can be added during the information transfer phase and the issues of who authorizes the adds and how a UMM connection is identified are for further study. However, users can abandon the call autonomously at any time. The issue of whether the other participants of the call need to be informed of the defection, and how to accomplish this, is for further study.

The cells submitted by *each* origin are delivered to the specified destinations, in accordance with points 1 to 5 in Sec. 5.4.1. The network provides (distributed) replication for optimized delivery of cells without requiring the origin to supply duplicate copies of the cells. The cells arriving at any destination from any destination are delivered over the appropriate inbound VPI/VCI.

If multiple destinations' (leaves') information is multiplexed to a single VC associated with the origin (root), the origin cannot demultiplex the cells in the ATM Layer; if needed, this demultiplexing must be done at a higher layer.

Multiple VCs between the origin and a destination can be requested via distinct service requests. In addition, at a UNI, the different VCs need not all be UMM connections, but can be any mix discussed in Sec. 5.4.

Note: The distinction between BSMM and UMM is as follows: Given a specific origin O and a specific destination D, in BSMM, O can send cells to D, and D can return cells over the same connection; in UMM, O can send cells to D, but D cannot return cells to O over the same connection (however, D can send cells to O over another connection). UMM connections can also be considered as the (independent) overlay of multiple UPM connections.

5.4.11 Service management capabilities

Service management capabilities exist at two levels: Layer Management capabilities and Management Plane capabilities. Layer (specifically, ATM Layer) Management capabilities deal with issues such as loopback, performance monitoring, alarm surveillance, etc. Management Plane capabilities deal with service aspects, such as changing subscription parameters, obtaining billing information, reconfiguring VPs/VCs, etc.

Layer Management capabilities should be implementable either in-band, using specialized cells, or using an out-of-band process known as broadband local management interface (B-LMI).* The issue of the need for a B-LMI is for further study. Management Plane capabilities are supported via a separate customer network management (CNM) protocol such as OSINM or SNMP.

5.5 Procedures

5.5.1 Provision/withdrawal

By arrangement with service provider.

5.5.2 Normal procedures

Provisioned CRBS.

Activation/deactivation/registration.   By arrangement with service provider.

Invocation and operation.   By arrangement with service provider.

Connection release.   By arrangement with service provider.

On-demand CRBS.

Activation/deactivation/registration.   By arrangement with service provider.

Invocation and operation.   User-network signaling is done on a VCI allocated to the signaling function. The call/bearer control protocol is contained in ITU-T Recommendation Q.2931. The AAL in support of UNI signaling for CRBS is AAL Type 5.

Procedures required.   Table 5.2 depicts some of the key procedures required to support on-demand CRBS. The actual procedures conform to the procedures included in ITU-T Recommendation Q.93B.

---

*This interface is also referred to as the interim LMI (ILMI).

TABLE 5.2 Key Procedures Required to Support On-Demand CRBS

Call/bearer Control Procedures For Point-to-Point Calls

  Call/bearer establishment at the originating interface

    Call/bearer request

    Connection identifier (VPI/VCI) allocation/selection

    QOS and traffic parameters selection procedures

    Invalid call/bearer control information

    Call/bearer proceeding

    Notification of interworking at the originating interface

    Call/bearer confirmation indication

    Call/bearer connected

    Call/bearer rejection

    Transit network selection

  Call/bearer establishment at the destination interface

    Incoming call/bearer request

    Connection identifier (VPI/VCI) allocation/selection—destination

    QOS and traffic parameter selection procedures

    Call/bearer confirmation

    Called user clearing during incoming call establishment

    Call failure

    Call/bearer accept

    Active indication

  Call/Bearer clearing

    Exception conditions

    Clearing initiated by the user

    Clearing initiated by the network

    Clear collision

    Restart procedure

    Handling of protocol error conditions

  User notification procedure

Call/Bearer Control Procedures for Point-to-Multipoint Calls

  Adding a party at the originating interface

  Add party establishment at the destination interface—point-to-point

  Call/bearer clearing

  Handling of error conditions

Connection establishment for UPP, BSPP, BAPP.   The connection is originated by the user requesting the bearer service from the network; the request includes a number identifying the called user. (The connection establishment procedures are consistent with the procedures embodied in ITU-T Recommendation Q.2931.) Other information for the bearer service and for use by the network or by the called user may be provided. This information includes information transfer characteristics, etc.

After initiating a connection request, the requesting user will receive an acknowledgment that the network is able to process the request. The requested party will receive an indication of the arrival of an incoming call for the bearer service.

When an indication is received by the network that the requested party is being informed of this connection request, the network will notify the requesting party.

When the requested party accepts the connection and the connection is established in the network, an indication of the connection establishment is sent by the network to the requesting party.

Possible procedures during the communication phase for UPP, BSPP, BAPP.   None.

Connection release procedures for UPP, BSPP, BAPP.   Either or both users may terminate the connection by either or both users by sending a request to the network. If one user terminates a connection, an appropriate indication is sent to the other user.

Connection establishment/release for UPM, BSPM, BAPM.   As needed.

Connection establishment/release for UMM, BSMM, BAMM.   For further study.

5.5.3 Exceptional procedures

As needed.

5.6 Quality of Service

CRBS can be provided based on a number of QOS classes. A QOS class is defined in terms of specific parameters associated with some or all of the following end-to-end performance measures (defined in ANSI T1.511-1994):

- Cell error ratio
- Severely errored cell block ratio
- Cell loss ratio
- Cell misinsertion rate
- Cell transfer delay

- Mean cell transfer delay
- Cell delay variation
- Signaling processing delay for point-to-point call establishment
- Signaling processing delay for call teardown

Two QOS classes are initially supported. (The issue of whether more than two QOS classes are needed to support various applications is for further study.) The "higher-quality" CRBS QOS class has consistently tighter limits on these end-to-end performance measures than the "lower-quality" QOS class. The user of CRBS shall be able to negotiate the QOS class using the appropriate signaling procedures given in Sec. 5.5 or by arrangement with the service provider.

5.7   Network Capabilities for Charging

It shall be possible for the service provider to charge accurately for this service.

5.8   Interworking Requirements

ATM Level interworking refers to mapping ATM cells to the apparatus of another bearer service. Complexity arises when the two bearer services support different levels of services. For example, one bearer service may include flow control and another may not.

Interworking between CRBS and the following are under consideration:

1. Unrestricted dedicated digital service (e.g., T1, T3 link)
2. N-ISDN (H11, H12)
3. N-ISDN-based voice service
4. Frame-mode bearer service
5. Connectionless service

The issue of how interworking is accomplished is beyond the scope of the definition of CRBS.

5.9   Some Additional Information

5.9.1   Functionality outside the scope of CRS

Although the CRS provides a high assurance for the delivery of cells, the user must be prepared to deal with the following (rare) contingencies:

1. A cell is delivered out of sequence.
2. There is an error in the payload.
3. A cell is lost or duplicated.
4. A cell is delivered erroneously.
5. The delay in establishing and releasing an on-demand call exceeds an expected threshold.
6. The end-to-end delay for the delivery of the first user cell exceeds an expected threshold.
7. The variation in intercell delay exceeds an expected threshhold.

Higher-layer functionality is required to deal with these contingencies. This functionality, including adaptation functions, error correction, etc., is *beyond the scope of CRS*, and must be handled separately. See Table 5.3. For example, adaptation functions may be required; how adaptation is accomplished, however, is not part of CRS.

5.9.2 Customer service management capabilities

ATM-Layer operations capabilities.   End-to-end operations administration and maintenance capabilities need to be supported. For VPs, operation

TABLE 5.3 Upper-Layer Functionality: Functions beyond CRS*

Handle cell delivered out of sequence

Handle error in the payload

Handle lost or duplicated cell

Handle misrouted cell (foreign cell received)

Handle a problem related to signaling

Handle timing/jitter problems

Handle security (e.g., encryption, authentication)

Handle BTE portability

Handle address conversion

Handle transcoding

Handle ATM-Level interworking

Adaptation of cell stream to other higher-layer streams/ protocols, e.g., AAL5, TCP/IP, IBM APPN, etc.

Demultiplex ATM stream when cells arrive from multiple remote destinations over a single virtual connection

*Partial list.

functions are supported via specially marked ATM cells, which are transmitted over VCs with specific VCI values (these are known as F4 flows). For VCs, operation functions are supported via cells marked with an appropriate codepoint in the Payload Type Indicator field (these are known as F5 flows). The functions supported were shown in Table 2.6. This topic is treated in more detail in Chap. 10.

Broadband local management interface. Bidirectional exchange of management information between a UNI Management entity in the user's equipment and an equivalent peer in the network is for further study. Table 5.4 depicts some of the key functions to be supported.

Customer network management capabilities. The following list identifies possible customer network management features supported by CRBS:

1. Receive unsolicited event notifications.
2. Retrieve UNI configuration information.
3. Retrieve VP/VC configuration information.
4. Retrieve "network configuration," e.g., who is in the multipoint call.
5. Retrieve performance information.
6. Retrieve usage information.
7. Request event notification.
8. Request network intervention.
9. Initiate tests.
10. Trouble report administration.
11. Support security policies.

Figure 5.4 depicts the customer network management system in the CRS context.

5.9.3 CRS applications requiring AALs

Table 5.5 provides a partial list of applications that may utilize CRS; user-provided adaptation functions are required (as observed, CRS signaling will carry user-supplied AAL information end-to-end if this is provided by the origin).

TABLE 5.4   B-LMI Functions Associated with CRS

Physical Layer	Interface index
	Interface address
	Transmission type
	Media type
	Operational status
ATM Layer	Maximum number of VPCs
	Maximum number of VCCs
	VPI/VCI address width
	Number of configured VPCs
	Number of configured VCCs
	Port type
ATM Layer statistics	ATM cells received
	ATM cells dropped on receive side
	ATM cells transmitted
VP connection	VPI value
	Shaping traffic descriptor
	Policing traffic descriptor
	Operational status
	QOS category
VC connection	VPI/VCI value
	Shaping traffic descriptor
	Policing traffic descriptor
	Operational status
	QOS category

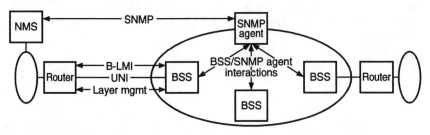

Figure 5.4   Positioning of SNMP and B-LMI.

TABLE 5.5 Upper-Layer Functionality: Technical Characteristics of Applications that May Utilize CRS, with a View to Required User Adaptation*

Constant-bit-rate video

Constant-bit-rate image

Constant-bit-rate data

Constant-bit-rate voice

Constant-bit-rate audio

Constant-bit-rate multimedia (combination of video, image, data, voice, audio)

Variable-bit-rate video (with timing)

Variable-bit-rate image (with timing)

Variable-bit-rate data (with timing)

Variable-bit-rate voice (with timing)

Variable-bit-rate audio (with timing)

Variable-bit-rate multimedia (combination of video, image, data, voice, audio) (with timing)

Variable-bit-rate video (without timing—e.g., messaging)

Variable-bit-rate image (without timing)

Variable-bit-rate data (without timing)

Variable-bit-rate voice (without timing)

Variable-bit-rate audio (without timing)

Variable-bit-rate multimedia (combination of video, image, data, voice, audio) (without timing)

Variable-bit-rate emulation of packet-mode bearer services

Variable-bit-rate emulation of frame-mode bearer services

Unspecified/unrestricted bit-rate characteristics

*Partial list.

Reference

1. D. Minoli, *Proposed Cell Relay Bearer Service Stage 1 Description,* T1S1.1/93-136-R1 (Revision 1), ANSI Committee T1 (T1S1.1), Somerset, N.J., June 7–11, 1993.

6

Cell Relay Service:
Traffic and Performance

Chapter 5 provided a macro-level functional view of cell relay service, in terms of how cells submitted by the user are "moved" through an ATM network. This chapter takes a more microscopic view of the service, looking at the actual treatment of individual cells by an ATM network, particularly one supporting multiple fastpacket services. The protocols discussed in the previous chapters form the logical supporting infrastructure upon which cell relay service rests.

Specifically, this chapter covers a number of traffic and performance factors associated with cell relay service. Traffic shaping, ATM performance parameters, QOS classes, and aspects of traffic contracts are covered. This material is based on a number of standards, such as ITU-T Q.2931, ITU-T I.356, and the ATM Forum UNI Specification (1993), and is included here in order to promulgate understanding of ATM and facilitate its introduction in the corporate environment. A markovian model for studying some aspects of customer behavior vis-a-vis QOS is also provided in the last section of the chapter. Figure 6.1 depicts a physical view of a basic CRS network; all of the performance parameters discussed in this chapter can be located by the reader on such a prototypical network.

6.1 CRS Cell Transfer Rates

As already discussed, CRS connections support two types of traffic: constant bit rate and variable bit rate. The traffic parameters required to inform the network of the type of connection desired (as implied in

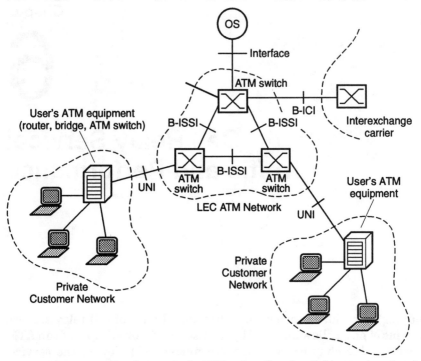

Figure 6.1 Typical cell relay network. BSS = broadband switching system (carrier's switch).

Sec. 4.4.2) are the peak cell rate (PCR) for CBR connections, and the PCR, the sustainable cell rate (SCR), and the maximum burst size (MBS) for VBR connections. At call setup the user provides these values to the network using the SETUP message.[*]

In the industry proposals that have been published, the values for PCR and SCR supported by CRS are expressed as specific numbers of cells per second. Although in theory a large range of values can be selected for inclusion in the SETUP message (150 ≤ PCR value ≤ 1,470,000, as seen in Chap. 5), only a small subset of values is actually allowed by the networks being planned at this time. The number of PCR values offered is kept small in order to simplify implementation. (It is possible that additional values will be offered in the future.)

Users requesting CRS connections to support CBR traffic must specify a PCR from the available values (say, for example, 177; 354; 1062; 2124; 4248; 8496; 16,992; 122,698; etc.) via the signaling process. The PCR traffic parameter specifies an upper bound on the cell rate that can be

---

[*]For PVC service, the traffic parameters are established at service ordering time (this is also known as "service provisioning time," in carriers' terminology).

submitted on a CRS connection. Network enforcement of this bound allows the service provider to allocate sufficient resources to ensure that performance objectives (QOS) can be achieved for *all* users of the network.

Users requesting CRS connections to support VBR traffic must specify two values: PCR and SCR. The PCR values are selected from the available values for equivalent bandwidths (say 177, 354, 1062, 2124, 4248, etc.); additional PCR values that allow VBR to provide transport for a variety of data flows, such as those generated by commonly used LANs, and to support SMDS over multiservice UNIs are also available. Users requesting CRS connections to support VBR traffic must specify a SCR in addition to the PCR (the SCR applies only to VCCs and not VPCs). The SCR defines the "average throughput" of a connection (i.e., the rate averaged over a time interval). Allowed values of the SCR could be a set of given values (e.g., 10 percent of the PCR, 50 percent of the PCR, 100 percent of the PCR). Associated with the SCR is a burst tolerance (BT) traffic parameter which limits the time a user may send traffic bursts beyond the "average rate" before cells become candidates for being tagged for potential discard by the service provider. Hence, the BT is defined as the amount of time a user may send data at the PCR before the cells are tagged. The BT can be expressed in terms of a maximum burst size in cells by the following equation:

$$BT = (MBS - 1) \left(\frac{1}{SCR} - \frac{1}{PCR} \right)$$

(A typical value for BT is 210.) See Fig. 6.2. Note that, as seen in Sec. 4.4.2, the user could in theory communicate the MBS at call establishment time; in practice, the carrier will stipulate how much BT is actually allowed.

6.2 Traffic Shaping

6.2.1 Ingress traffic shaping

Ingress policing functions at an ATM switch monitor incoming traffic at a network (i.e., at point A in Fig. 6.3) to protect the network against sources that exceed the bandwidth they have requested at call setup time (as discussed in Chap. 4). To do this, the service provider performs a function known as usage parameter control (UPC). UPC is defined as the set of actions taken by the service provider to monitor and control traffic in the network ingress direction of a UNI. The user of CRS is affected by the UPC function as it operates on the traffic carried by a VCC or VPC using the PCR, SCR, and MBS traffic parameters described earlier and in Sec. 4.4.2. The generic cell rate algorithm (GCRA) has

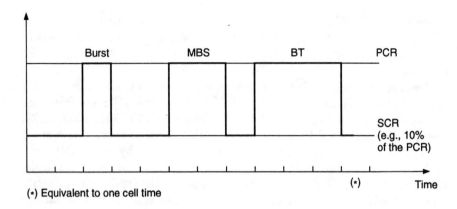

(*) Equivalent to one cell time

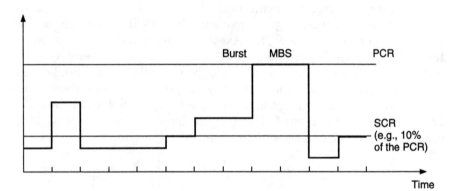

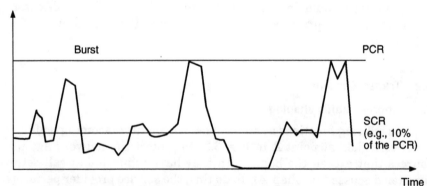

Figure 6.2 PCR versus SCR. Top: simplified view; middle: more typical view; bottom: actual traffic.

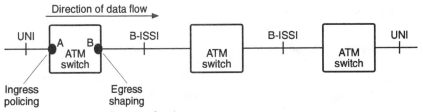

Figure 6.3   Ingress and egress shaping.

been identified by ITU-TS and the ATM Forum as an approach for unambiguously specifying cell conformance (the implementation of the UPC function does *not require* use of the GCRA itself, but the UPC must have similar algorithmic characteristics).

In applications such as LAN interconnection, the user's packets typically have the same level of importance and therefore are submitted to the ATM network as CLP = 0 cells (after being processed at the AAL). Since traffic from multiple workstations is multiplexed on a given VP, there may not be a traffic shaper on the user side of the UNI (this may particularly be the case at the private UNI). In such applications, it is desirable for the network to accept and/or tolerate some amount of nonconformance of the CLP = 0 stream; to do so, it tags the nonconforming cells by setting CLP = 1 for them. This way, users do not have to be pessimistic in their traffic description, and therefore excessive overallocation for bursty data applications may be avoided.

In enforcing the PCR, the UPC function is designed to tolerate a certain amount of cell delay variation CDV_{TOL} (say 250 μs) before identifying cells as exceeding the PCR. The GCRA operating with an *increment parameter* of 1/PCR and a limit parameter of CDV_{TOL} can identify cells which do not conform to the PCR. Cells transmitted across the UNI that are identified as nonconformant by the GCRA may be discarded by the CRS network, if necessary. For VBR applications of CRS, the user specifies a value of SCR for the connection which applies to cells with CLP = 0.[*] In this case, the GCRA operating with an increment parameter of 1/SCR and a limit parameter of BT identifies cells that do not conform to the SCR. Cells not conforming to the SCR will have the value of the CLP bit set to 1 by the ingress network switch. This is called cell tagging. Network equipment will start to discard cells having CLP = 1 when necessary (e.g., in congested situations).

---

[*]Current thinking is not to use CLP across the UNI; i.e., to force the user to set the field to zero.

6.2.2 Egress traffic shaping

There is also the need to do egress policing, especially where the ATM switch supports multiple fastpacket services, notably SMDS (this issue is treated in more detail in Chap. 7). The QOS contracted with users at call setup time must be guaranteed by the ATM platform. In an ATM multiservice platform, the QOS provided to users of each service must be at least as good as the QOS offered to users of physically separate platforms.

In the network, multiple user connections through a multiservice ATM switch can be multiplexed into a single connection for transport through the ATM network. Once a sending ATM switch allows excess traffic from one connection (or group of connections) to use additional resources, the user that is not able to utilize "its" resources will experience a lower QOS. An egress shaping mechanism ensures that a sending ATM switch (i.e., at point B in Fig. 6.3) does not exceed the peak bandwidth allocated to one connection (or group of connections).

In a multiservice network, traffic engineering for a service, done discretely, could affect the QOS experienced by users of *other* services being transported across a multiservice broadband interswitching system interface (B-ISSI). In this case, there must be a mechanism to guarantee (with a high probability) that a load condition on one service does not exceed a peak bandwidth allocation for that service on the given B-ISSI. In particular, this points to the need for a traffic enforcement mechanism for SMDS at B-ISSIs (and at B-ICIs) *that are carrying multiple services*. This mechanism is designed to operate at the packet level to maximize the effectiveness of the discarding algorithm—i.e., *if necessary,* entire PDUs are discarded rather than discarding a few cells from each of several PDUs. An alternative is to segregate SMDS traffic by allocating full B-ISSI and B-ICI interfaces to SMDS transport; this solution, however, is deemed to be less desirable.

As an example of a multiservice ATM platform and the policing issues, consider the case depicted in Fig. 6.4. In this illustrative example, the B-ISSI supports three VPCs. VPC A carries SMDS traffic between the two ATM switches, VPC B carries FRS traffic between the two ATM switches, and VPC C carries CRS traffic supporting constant-bit-rate applications between the two ATM switches. Based on traffic engineering decisions, VPC A supports the interswitch traffic load of 15 SMDS customers accessing the network at DS3 rates; to achieve multiplexing gains, VPC A is assigned a peak bandwidth equivalent to 45 Mbits/s. Similarly, VPC B multiplexes 25 FRS connections with an aggregate peak bandwidth equivalent to five DS3s; to achieve multiplexing gains, the equivalent of 45 Mbits/s is assigned to VPC B. VPC C supports 28 CRS constant-bit-rate connections equivalent to 45 Mbits/s.

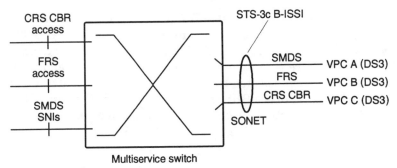

Figure 6.4 A multiservice ATM switch.

Under steady-state conditions, this engineering of the trunking pool is adequate, since all the user connections being multiplexed (i.e., in VPC A and VPC B) are bursty in nature and do not fully use their potential bandwidth. However, during a brief time interval (perhaps, lasting a few seconds), two or more of the SMDS customers may send traffic at the DS3* rate, which is a legal amount of traffic. Since VPC A has been allocated only the equivalent bandwidth of a DS3 trunk, the excess traffic must use the other B-ISSI resources (buffer space and cell slots on the SONET frame), which may be needed by VPC B and VPC C. Because constant-bit-rate applications, such as video, do not tolerate degradation, the customers using this service will be affected by the burst of SMDS traffic. This example shows that the ATM switch should perform an egress shaping function on the traffic to be carried across VPC A, to protect the constant-bit-rate applications from experiencing degradation of service.

When ATM switches that provide intermediate ATM cell switching functions (e.g., the middle switch in Fig. 6.3) use peak-rate allocation, only the source of the connection (e.g., the ATM switch to which the user is directly connected) has to undertake egress shaping. Intermediate ATM switches need not do egress shaping because the cell flow already abides by the desired traffic profile. Peak-rate allocated connections include all VPCs provisioned across a B-ISSI as well as individual VCCs over a B-ISSI not associated with a VPC. The output cell rate of a connection is described using two parameters: peak rate in cells per second and cell delay variation (CDV) tolerance. The CDV tolerance is a parameter used to limit the size of a burst of cells belonging to a single connection. CDV tolerance is necessary to limit cell bursts that, because of the long idle periods that result from burstiness, would otherwise

---

*This figure is used for simplicity; the maximum SMDS traffic from a user accessing the network over a DS3 interface is 34 Mbits/s.

comply with the long-term peak rate. The peak rate of the connection depends on the type of traffic carried across the connection. An ATM switch controls the output cell rate of a VC that requires peak bandwidth allocation, to make sure that it conforms with the peak rate and CDV tolerance that have been selected by the carrier. An ATM switch must provision connections across a B-ISSI in such a way that the sum of the peak bandwidths of all virtual connections that require peak bandwidth allocation does not exceed the line rate of the B-ISSI.

6.3   Quality of Service Principles

6.3.1   Introduction

The discussion that follows is based directly on I.356, I.371, Q.2931, and the ATM Forum UNI specification. It aims at describing quantifiable quality of service metrics to support the deployment of public CRS networks and related tariffing efforts. Several well-defined "events" are used in defining the ATM cell transfer performance parameters, as listed in Table 6.1.

6.3.2   ATM performance parameters

This section summarizes ATM cell transfer performance parameters, particularly those defined in ITU-T I.356. The cell events and cell transfer outcomes defined in Table 6.1 are used in defining these performance parameters. These parameters and their classification into the ITU-T I.330 framework are shown in Table 6.2.

Cell error ratio.   This parameter is defined as follows:

$$\frac{\text{Errored cells}}{\text{Successfully transferred cells} + \text{errored cells}}$$

An errored cell event occurs when a successfully delivered cell contains one or more bit errors in its payload. As no ATM Layer error checking is performed on cell payloads, it is expected that errored cell events will occur with the same frequency as Physical Layer bit errors as a result of background error events. Errored cell events are not directly visible to the ATM Layer, but are observed at the AAL.

Successfully transferred cells and errored cells contained in cell blocks counted as severely errored cell blocks are excluded from the population used in calculating the cell error ratio. This is done in an attempt to avoid biasing the cell error ratio measure toward burst error events; instead it is targeted toward background events.

TABLE 6.1   Events and Outcomes Used in Performance Definition

Cell exit event	Event that occurs when the first bit of an ATM cell has completed transmission out of an end-user device to a private ATM network element across the "private UNI" measurement point, or out of a private ATM network element to a public ATM network element across the "public UNI" measurement point, or out of an end-user device to a public ATM network across the "public UNI" measurement point.
Cell entry event	Event that occurs when the last bit of an ATM cell has completed transmission into an end-user device from a private ATM network element across the "private UNI" measurement point, or into a private ATM network element from a public ATM network element across the "public UNI" measurement point, or into an end-user device from a public ATM network element across the "public UNI" measurement point.
Successful cell transfer outcome	The cell corresponding to the transmitted cell is received within a specified time T_{max}. The binary content of the received cell conforms exactly to the corresponding cell payload, and the cell is received with a valid header field after header error control procedures are completed.
Errored cell outcome	The cell corresponding to the transmitted cell is received within a specified time T_{max}. However, the binary content of the received cell payload differs from that of the corresponding transmitted cell or the cell is received with an invalid header field after header error control procedures are completed.
Lost cell outcome	No cell corresponding to the transmitted cell is received within a specified time T_{max}. (Examples include "never showed up" and "late.")
Misinserted cell outcome	A cell for which there is no corresponding transmitted cell is received.
Severely errored cell block outcome	M or more lost cell outcomes, misinserted cell outcomes, or errored cell outcomes are observed in a received cell block of N cells transmitted consecutively on a given connection.

Note: This table is based on Refs.1 and 2.

TABLE 6.2 ATM Performance Parameters

	Accuracy	Speed	Dependability
Cell error ratio	x		
Severely errored cell block ratio	x		
Cell loss ratio			x
Cell misinsertion rate	x		
Cell transfer delay		x	
Mean cell transfer delay		x	
Cell delay variation		x	
Service availability			x
Mean time to service restoral			x
Mean time between service outages			x

Severely errored cell block ratio.   This parameter is defined as follows:

$$\frac{\text{Severely errored cell blocks}}{\text{Total transmitted cell blocks}}$$

A cell block is a sequence of N cells transmitted consecutively on a given connection. A severely errored cell block outcome occurs when more than M error cell, lost cell, or misinserted cell outcomes are observed in a received cell block. For practical measurement purposes, a cell block normally corresponds to the number of user information cells transmitted between successive OAM cells (see Chap. 10).

Cell loss ratio.   This parameter is defined as follows:

$$\frac{\text{Lost cells}}{\text{Total transmitted cells}}$$

Again, lost and transmitted cells contained in severely errored cell blocks are excluded from the cell population in computing cell loss ratio, in an effort to avoid bias due to large error bursts. In practice, network cell loss ratio objectives will be different for different types of connections and for different settings of the CLP bit of the cell header.

Cell misinsertion rate.   This parameter is defined as follows:

$$\frac{\text{Misinserted cells}}{\text{Time interval}}$$

Again, severely errored cell blocks are excluded from the calculation of the cell misinsertion rate. This performance parameter has been defined as a rate (rather than as a ratio) because the mechanism producing misinserted cells is independent of the number of transmitted cells received on the corresponding connection. A cell misinsertion event can occur when a line burst error causes multiple errors in a cell header in such a way as to (1) cause the HEC mechanism to pass the corrupted header and (2) have the resultant corrupt VPI/VCI value be valid for some other active virtual connection. This event will be seen as a cell loss event on the VC in which it was transmitted, and as a misinserted cell event on the VC on which it is received.

Cell transfer delay.   The cell transfer delay is defined as the elapsed time between a cell exit event at measurement point 1 (MP_1) (e.g., at the source UNI) and the corresponding cell entry event at measurement point 2 (MP_2) (e.g., the destination UNI) for a particular connection. The cell transfer delay between two measurement points is the sum of the total inter-ATM node transmission delay and the total ATM node processing delay between MP_1 and MP_2.

The components of cell transfer delay in a VCC or VPC include

- Emission delay (e.g., at DS3 rates, emission delay is approximately 9 μs)
- Propagation delays (approximately 1 ms per 100 fiber miles)
- Processing delays at intermediate ATM nodes (e.g., switching/multiplexing delays)
- Queuing delays at intermediate ATM nodes

In practice, the cell transfer delay across a network may be dominated by the propagation delay component.

Mean cell transfer delay.   This parameter is defined as the arithmetic average of a specified number of cell transfer delays for one or more connections.

Cell delay variation.   Cell delay variation (CDV) is concerned with the variability of delay across an ATM network. It is a measure of how much the cell transfer delay experienced by any cell differs from a reference value of cell transfer delay associated with a specific virtual connection. Equivalently, CDV can be thought of as a measure of the variability of intercell arrival times. Objectives for CDV are typically expressed in terms of quantiles of the cumulative distribution function of CDV.

Cell delay variation is a key parameter for planning the performance of delay-sensitive applications, such as CBR applications. If the CDV exceeds a preset limit associated with the buffer capacity of a receiver, an underflow condition will result at the receiver, causing the next cell to be declared "lost" and initiating cell loss recovery procedures. To an end application, this will be identical to a cell loss event. Thus, it is important that designers of such receivers have a thorough understanding of the limiting CDV performance of a cell relay service.

There are two performance parameters used to characterize cell delay variation: the 1-point cell delay variation (1-point CDV) and the 2-point cell delay variation (2-point CDV).[1] The 1-point CDV describes variability in the pattern of cell arrival events observed at a single measurement point with reference to the negotiated peak rate $1/T$, as defined in ITU-T I.371. The 1-point CDV for cell k (y_k) at a measurement point is defined as the difference between the cell's reference arrival time (c_k) and its actual arrival time (a_k) at the measurement point: $y_k = c_k - a_k$. The reference arrival time (c_k) is defined as follows:

$$c_0 = a_0 = 0$$

$$c_{k+1} = \begin{cases} c_k + T & \text{if } c_k \geq a_k \\ a_k + T & \text{otherwise} \end{cases}$$

Positive values of the 1-point CDV correspond to cell clumping; negative values correspond to gaps in the cell stream. The reference arrival time defined above eliminates the effect of gaps and provides a measurement of cell clumping.

The 2-point CDV describes variability in the pattern of cell arrival events observed at the output of a connection portion (MP_2) with reference to the pattern of the corresponding events observed at the input to the connection portion (MP_1). The 2-point CDV for cell k (v_k) between two measurement points (MP_1 and MP_2) is the difference between the absolute cell transfer delay of cell k (x_k) between the two MPs and a defined reference cell transfer delay ($d_{1,2}$) between MP_1 and MP_2; that is, $v_k = x_k - d_{1,2}$. The absolute cell transfer delay (x_k) of cell k between MP_1 and MP_2 is the same as the cell transfer delay. The reference cell transfer delay ($d_{1,2}$) between MP_1 and MP_2 is the absolute cell transfer delay experienced by a reference cell between the two MPs.

Service availability (SA).   Service availability is defined as the percentage of scheduled service time in which the service is usable by end users. Overall service availability is dependent on four main factors:

- The proportion of time in which the accuracy objectives are met
- The frequency of switching equipment outages
- The frequency of transport system outages
- Restoral times for outages

Mean time to service restoral (MTTSR).   The MTTSR is the average amount of time, averaged over multiple outage events, from loss of service to complete restoral of service. MTTSR is highly influenced by operations procedures. As such, specific MTTSR objectives are set by individual operating entities.

Mean time between service outages (MTBSO).   MTBSO is the average time, averaged over multiple outage events, between the onset of periods of service unavailability. The MTBSO is related to the service availability (SA) and the MTTSR by the following relationship:

$$\text{MTBSO} = \frac{\text{MTTSR}}{1 - \text{SA}/100}$$

As the MTTSR is operating entity-dependent, so is the MTBSO.

6.3.3 Quality of service provided by the ATM Layer

A user of an ATM connection (a VCC or a VPC) can choose one of a number of QOS classes supported by the network, on a per-call basis. As noted in Chap. 4, up to five classes are permitted in the ATM Forum specification; however, at the current time only two classes are under active consideration: Class I (corresponding to Class 1 below) and Class II (corresponding to Class 3 below). The performance provided by the network should meet (or exceed) the performance parameter objectives of the QOS class requested by the ATM user.

It should be noted that a single VPC may carry VC links of various QOS classes. The QOS of the VPC must meet the most demanding QOS of the VC links carried, as defined in I.150. The QOS class associated with a given ATM connection is indicated to the network at the time of connection establishment and will not change for the duration of that ATM connection.

6.4 QOS Classes

A QOS class can be defined with explicitly specified performance parameters (specified QOS class) or with no specified performance parameters (referred to as an unspecified QOS class; also known as a "best effort" class[*]). A specified QOS class has a set of performance parameters

---

[*]The "best effort" service (also called "Class Y" or "available bit rate") provides, in general, the same type of service supported by a protocol such as IP (Internet Protocol): for a smaller network fee, the user inputs a cell into the network and then "prays" that it gets to the other end. Hopefully, it will get there enough times so that the CLR is one with

specified and the objective values for each performance parameter identified. Examples of performance parameters that could be specified in a QOS class are cell transfer delay, cell delay variation, and cell loss ratio.

As presently foreseen, performance parameters other than the cell loss ratio would apply to the aggregate cell flow of an ATM connection. However, within a specified QOS class, up to two cell loss ratio parameters may be specified. If a specified QOS class does contain two cell loss ratio parameters, then one parameter is for all CLP = 0 cells and the other is for all CLP = 1 cells of the ATM connection. A QOS class could contain, for example, the following performance parameters: mean cell transfer delay, a cell delay variation, a cell loss ratio on CLP = 0 cells, and a cell loss ratio on CLP = 1 cells. An unspecified QOS class can also be supported.

For the purpose of early ATM implementation, the PVC management capability can be used by the network to report the QOS classes across the UNI. For a switched connection, the signaling protocol's information elements can be used to communicate the QOS class across the UNI.

6.4.1 Specified QOS classes

A specified QOS class provides a quality of service to an ATM virtual connection (VCC or VPC) defined in terms of a subset of the ATM performance parameters above. Initially, a CRS network provider will probably define objective values for a subset of the ATM performance parameters of Sec. 6.3 for at least one of the following service classes (first introduced in Chap. 1):

Service Class A: Circuit emulation, constant-bit-rate video

Service Class B: Variable-bit-rate audio and video

Service Class C: Connection-oriented data transfer

Service Class D: Connectionless data transfer

---

which the user can live. Class Y is an ATM bearer service where the transfer characteristics provided by the network may change subsequent to connection establishment. A user that adapts its traffic to the changing transfer characteristics (in a closed-loop manner) will experience a low CLR. The user specifies a maximum required bandwidth to the network at call establishment time; however, the bandwidth available from the network may, theoretically, become small or even zero during the course of the call. Class Y is not intended to support constant bit rate applications (such as real-time video); rather, it is aimed at "elastic" applications such as traditional LAN interconnection, file transfer, and interactive terminal traffic. In contrast, Class X service guarantees the bandwidth negotiated at call setup time and the CLR intrinsic in the selected QOS class.

(In the future, more QOS classes may be defined, even for a given service class described above.) The following specified QOS classes are currently defined:[1]

Specified QOS Class 1. Support a QOS that will meet Service Class A performance requirements. This class aims at yielding performance comparable to current digital private line performance.

Specified QOS Class 2. Support a QOS that will meet Service Class B performance requirements. This class is targeted at packetized video and audio in teleconferencing and multimedia applications.

Specified QOS Class 3. Support a QOS that will meet Service Class C performance requirements. This class is intended for interoperation of connection-oriented protocols, such as frame relay.

Specified QOS Class 4. Support a QOS that will meet Service Class D performance requirements. This class is intended for interoperation of connectionless protocols, such as IP or SMDS.

The two actual QOS classes under consideration by (some) carriers are as follows (as specified in Bellcore TA-NWT-001110, TA-NWT-001408, TA-NWT-001409, and TA-NWT-001501; see Fig. 1.9)

Class 1: $CLR \leq 1.7 \times 10^{-10}$; CTD (99th percentile) = 150 µs; CDV (10^{-10} quantile) = 250 µs

Class 2: $CLR \leq 10^{-7}$; CTD (99th percentile) = 150 µs; CDV (10^{-10} quantile) = 250 µs.

Note: When an ATM platform supports other fastpacket services, such as SMDS and frame relay service, the performance goals of those services must also be met. (These may be expressed in terms of PDU transfer delay, undelivered PDUs, undelivered frames, etc.)

6.4.2 Unspecified QOS class

The unspecified QOS class is characterized by having no objectives specified for the performance parameters (these internal performance parameter objectives need not be constant during the duration of a call). However, the network provider may determine a set of internal objectives for the performance parameters.

An example application of the unspecified QOS class is the support of "best effort" service. For this type of service, the user selects the best effort capability, the unspecified QOS class, and only the traffic parameter for the peak cell rate on CLP = 0 + 1 (read as "CLP equal 0 or 1"). This class can be used to support users that are capable of regulating the traffic flow into the network and adapting to time-variable available resources.[1]

6.5 Factors Affecting ATM QOS Performance Parameters

This section provides a discussion of items being considered by carriers in setting QOS performance parameter objectives. The objective is to have maximum commonality between public and private networks. This section is based partially on the ATM Forum UNI Specification,[1] Bellcore's TA-TSV-001409,[3] Bellcore TA-NWT-001110,[4] and other documents and standards.

6.5.1 Sources of QOS degradation

Propagation delay.   This is the delay introduced by the physical media (fiber, radio, etc.) which transport the bits making up ATM cells between UNIs and between ATM switches. This affects public and private networks, and is linearly proportional to the distance between source and sink. Private networks may extend from the desktop to international distances, while public networks generally extend from metropolitan to international distances.

Transmission media errors.   These are the random and/or bursty bit errors that are introduced by factors affecting the physical media (e.g., lightning affecting a radio channel). The background error rate is highly influenced by the physical media type (e.g., single-mode fiber, multimode fiber, unshielded twisted pair, etc.) and by the transmission method.

Switch architecture.   The architecture of the switch can have significant effects on performance. Factors include the switch matrix design, the buffering strategy, and the switch characteristics under load. The choice of switch matrix design may influence the loss under heavy load conditions. The approach to how the buffer capacity of a port supporting the UNI on an ATM switch is managed may differ across switch architectures: the buffer capacity may be dedicated to a single port, it may be shared between multiple ports, or some combination thereof. Chapter 11 describes differences among switch architectures.

Buffer capacity.   This is the actual capacity of the buffer (typically expressed as a number of cells) at a port supporting the UNI, within an ATM matrix, or in other elements of an ATM switch. Clearly, larger buffers are less prone to cell loss, but at the possible expense of larger delays.

Traffic load.   This is the load offered by the set of ATM VPC/VCCs on the same route as the VPC/VCC under consideration. One would expect the performance on routes approaching or exceeding rated capacity to be inferior to that experienced on underutilized links.

Number of nodes in tandem.   This is the number of ATM switching nodes that a particular VPC or VCC traverses. Each additional node adds a switch with limited buffers and links that can be susceptible to media errors and traffic overloads.

Resource allocation.   This is the capacity allocated to a VPC/VCC or to a set of VPC/VCCs, such as the set of VPC/VCCs on a given route that are assigned a given QOS class.

Failures.   These are events that affect availability, such as port failures, module failures, switch failures, or link failures. Even with standby components, transfers between failing equipment or circuits may introduce cell loss.

6.5.2 Impact of QOS degradation on performance parameters

Table 6.3 summarizes how various sources of degradation can affect the performance parameters.

Cell error ratio and severely errored cell block ratio.   The cell error ratio is expected to be primarily influenced by the error characteristics of the physical media. The severely errored cell block ratio is also influenced by the error characteristics of the physical media and by buffer overflows. Error characteristics may also be a function of the physical

TABLE 6.3 Degradation of QOS Parameters

Attribute	Cell error ratio (CER)	Cell loss ratio (CLR)	Cell misinsertion rate (CMR)	Mean cell transfer delay (MCTD)	Cell delay variation (CDV)
Buffer capacity		Yes		Yes	Yes
Failures		Yes			
Media errors	Yes	Yes	Yes		
Number of tandem nodes	Yes	Yes	Yes	Yes	Yes
Propagation delay				Yes	
Resource allocation		Yes		Yes	Yes
Switch architecture		Yes		Yes	Yes
Traffic load		Yes	Yes	Yes	Yes

distance and the characteristics of the media. Transmission protection switching and rearrangements may also introduce errors.

Cell loss ratio.   Cell loss events are caused by errors in the cell header (in turn caused by physical media errors), buffer overflows, and UPC actions. Cells may also be lost because of failures, protection switching, and path reconfiguration.

Some networks may not provide large buffers or multiple levels of priority, since transmission capacity and resources may be relatively inexpensive. Therefore, cell loss ratios may be higher than in a more sophisticated network. For example, a lost higher-level PDU can be detected in a much shorter time in a LAN than in a WAN. Therefore, higher-layer protocol retransmissions can be initiated sooner, and thus a given loss ratio will have less impact on higher-layer application throughput in local-area networks than in wide-area networks. Buffering strategies in wider-area or lower-speed networks may be more complex than in local, high-speed networks. Transmission capacity resources are relatively more expensive. Multiple levels of delay priority, and possibly relatively large buffers, may be implemented. The number of nodes in tandem also affects the cell loss ratio because of the possibility of overflow in any buffer between the source and the destination.[1]

Cell misinsertion rate.   Cell misinsertion events are caused by undetected/miscorrected errors in the cell header. Thus, this performance parameter is expected to be primarily influenced by physical media errors, primarily large error bursts such as those experienced during a facility switchover initiated by a physical media protection switch. The likelihood that an undetected/miscorrected cell header error maps into a valid VPI/VCI is dependent upon the number of VPI/VCI values that are assigned and being actively used. The number of active ATM sources is often less for a private network than for a public network, decreasing the likelihood of an undetected/miscorrected cell header error in a cell that is incorrectly misinserted into some other VPI/VCI cell stream.

Cell transfer delay.   Cell transfer delay is affected by propagation delay and queuing, routing, and switching delays; these factors are likely to differ for local and wide area networks. In a local private network, the mean cell transfer delay may be dominated by emission, queuing, and routing times. In WANs, the mean cell transfer delay is dominated by propagation delay over longer distances, at least for the highest-priority class; over shorter distances, or for lower-priority classes, delay may conceivably be high during periods of significant network load.

The propagation delay for local networks is on the order of 0.1 to 10 μs. Queuing delays are likely to be very small in high-performance ATM LANs (see Chap. 9), as long as statistical multiplexing procedures do not induce burst-scale congestion. Depending on the transmission media and on distance, the emission time may dominate the propagation time; for example, for media operating at the DS3 rate, the emission time of a cell is approximately 9 μs. Additional services, such as ATM cell routing, may introduce additive delay that ranges from insignificant to something on the order of microseconds. Routing of higher-layer protocols usually requires many microseconds. For WANs, the mean cell transfer delay can be on the order of tens of microseconds for metropolitan areas and tens of milliseconds for national and international areas as a result of propagation delay.

Cell delay variation. Specification of CDV is essential for obtaining desired constant-bit-rate performance, so important for circuit emulation services and/or video. Its value is necessary for the dimensioning of the elastic buffer required at the terminating end of the connection to absorb the accumulated CDV. Values of 750 μs delay for absorbing the accumulated CDV from the ingress public UNI to the egress public UNI for both DS1 and DS3 circuit emulation services have been suggested. As an implementation practice, the receiver CDV tolerance is designed to handle the case where a connection traverses three networks, each having three switches in tandem.

6.6 Traffic Contracts

A traffic contract specifies the negotiated traffic parameters (e.g., PCT, SCR, BT) for each direction of transmission of a connection at a UNI; it defines the method of determining conformance to the contract; and it specifies the carrier's actions in case of nonconformance.[1,2] The traffic contract consists of

1. The values of PCR, SCR, and BT to be supported for the connection

2. The connection's QOS class

3. A conformance definition (e.g., based on the GCRA)

4. The definition of a compliant connection

In the traffic contract, the cell delay variation tolerance specified at the UNI is defined in relation to the PCR by the GCRA; the burst tolerance specified at the UNI is defined in relation to the SCR, also by the GCRA.

The GCRA used in the contract is an algorithm that can be viewed as a continuous-state leaky bucket algorithm or as a virtual scheduling algorithm. The GCRA is defined by the flowchart in Fig. 6.5. The GCRA is parametrized on two variables: the increment parameter I and the limit parameter L. The algorithm is shown as GCRA (I, L). The virtual scheduling updates a theoretical arrival time (TAT), which is the "nominal" arrival time of the cell assuming equally spaced cells when the source is active. If the actual arrival time is not "too" early relative to the TAT (specifically, if the actual arrival time is after TAT $- L$), then the cell is conforming; otherwise it is nonconforming. The continuous-state leaky bucket algorithm can be viewed as a finite-capacity buffer (bucket) whose real-valued content drains out at a continuous rate of 1 unit of content per unit time and whose content is increased by the increment I for each conforming cell. Equivalently, it can be viewed as the workload in a finite-capacity queue or as a real-valued counter. If at a cell arrival the contents of the buffer are less than or equal to a limit value L, then the cell is conforming; otherwise it is nonconforming. The maximum capacity of the buffer (counter) is $L + I$.

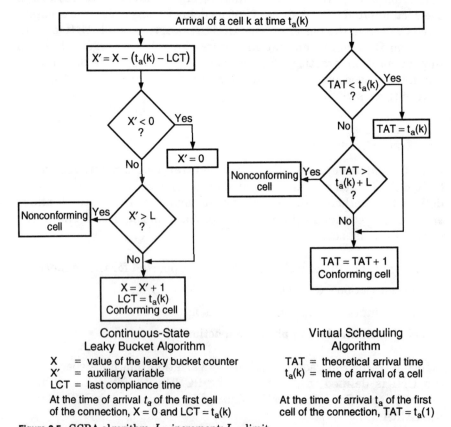

Figure 6.5 GCRA algorithm. I = increment; L = limit.

The GCRA of Fig. 6.5 is used to define the relationship between the PCR and the CDV tolerance, and between the CSR and the burst tolerance. In addition, for the cell flow of an ATM connection, the GCRA is used to specify conformance (at a UNI) to declared values of the above two tolerances as well as declared values of the traffic parameters peak cell rate and sustainable cell rate and burst tolerance.

As noted, for each cell arrival, the GCRA determines whether the cell is conforming with the traffic contract of the connection; hence, the GCRA is used to provide the formal definition of traffic conformance to the traffic contract. However, note that although traffic conformance is defined in terms of the GCRA, the carrier is not obligated to use this algorithm for the usage parameter control function.

6.7 Modeling Quality of Service Classes

This section discusses some of the issues that must be taken into consideration when developing a QOS/pricing scheme for cell relay service. The bottom line of the discussion is that the network must be managed so as to keep the QOS within stipulated limits. This is not a novel concept: Telephone networks have always been managed at the teletraffic level.

Some carriers have contemplated two classes of cell relay services:

Class 1: No QOS guarantees, but lower price (C_1)

Class 2: Guaranteed QOS, but higher price (C_2)

The concern is that users may volitionally switch between classes, creating an unstable environment. In particular, the concern is that so long as there are only a few users, all users will subscribe to Class 1. As more and more users join Class 1, the QOS degenerates, until some users decide to migrate to Class 2; however, in doing so, they (basically by themselves paying more) improve the QOS of the users that remained in Class 1, which further annoys these users that have decided to switch.

The answer to this potential instability is simple: The carrier must monitor the network so that the QOS for Class 1 always remains within $QOS_{1,L} \leq QOS \leq QOS_{1,R}$ and $d(QOS_{1,L}, QOS_{1,L}) \leq d_1$, with d_1 small. Also, the carrier must ensure that the QOS for Class 2 always remains within $QOS_{2,L} \leq QOS \leq QOS_{2,R}$ and $d(QOS_{2,L}, QOS_{2,R}) \leq d_2$, with d_2 small. Namely, by its traffic engineering actions, the carrier must ensure that there are no large swings in the QOS values. This is achieved by properly and judiciously adding trunk resources as needed (not before they are needed, not after they are needed). Additionally, the carrier could levy charges for switching from class to class, thereby discouraging the phenomenon of *balking and reneging*. Also, the carrier could impose requirements on the minimum stay in a given class (i.e., the user is not allowed to switch more than, say, once a month). If this requirement cannot be *imposed* outright, at least it could be *made available* with an inducement, so that the user could choose it of his or her own accord. For example, today carriers offer month-to-month tariffs, but also offer tariffs for 1-, 3-, 5-, and 7-year user commitments. In these cases, a user who agrees to remain subscribed to the service is afforded a discount.

Below we provide a model to show the importance of properly managing QOS. The model aims at showing the principles involved, rather than being totally encompassing; more detailed models along these lines can be developed.

6.7.1 Markovian model

Figure 6.6 depicts the Markov chain model studied (a more sophisticated model showing the arrival of customers for C_1 and C_2 can be developed, but this is not done at this time). *As always, one is interested in calculating/maximizing profit.*

This model assumes that the carrier had allocated N_1 trunk resources to Class C_1 and N_2 trunk resources to Class C_2, with $N - N_1 - N_2$ trunk resources held in reserve, to be allocated as needed. At time s_0, in state S_0 there were U_1 active users subscribing to C_1 and U_2 active users subscribing to C_2. Assume that users in C_1 were paying t_1 to present a cell to the switch, and users in C_2 were paying t_2 ($t_2 \geq t_1$). Assume that there is an operations cost O_1 to keep a resource allocated to C_1, O_2 to keep a resource allocated to C_2, and O_3 to simply keep a resource in reserve ($O_3 \neq 0$).

Then,

$$\text{Revenue}_{S0} = U_1 t_1 + U_2 t_2$$
$$\text{Cost}_{S1} = N_1 O_1 + N_2 O_2 + (N - N_1 - N_2)O_3$$
$$\text{Profit}_{S1} = \text{Revenue}_{S0} - \text{Cost}_{S0}$$

Now assume that with probability a_1, a new Class 1 user joins the network, moving the system to state S_1. Then

$$\text{Revenue}_{S1} = (U_1 + 1)t_1 + U_2 t_2$$
$$\text{Cost}_{S1} = N_1 O_1 + N_2 O_2 + (N - N_1 - N_2)O_3$$
$$\text{Profit}_{S1} = \text{Revenue}_{S1} - \text{Cost}_{S1}$$

However, this additional traffic may cause a degradation in QOS. Hence, the carrier, having monitored the traffic statistics, should (be inclined to) adjust the trunking bandwidth by taking a trunk from the reserved pool and adding it to support Class 1 users. Assume that the

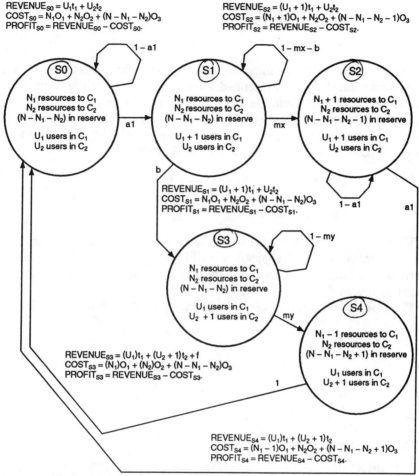

REVENUE$_{S0}$ = U$_1$t$_1$ + U$_2$t$_2$
COST$_{S0}$ = N$_1$O$_1$ + N$_2$O$_2$ + (N – N$_1$ – N$_2$)O$_3$
PROFIT$_{S0}$ = REVENUE$_{S0}$ – COST$_{S0}$.

REVENUE$_{S2}$ = (U$_1$ + 1)t$_1$ + U$_2$t$_2$
COST$_{S2}$ = (N$_1$ + 1)O$_1$ + N$_2$O$_2$ + (N – N$_1$ – N$_2$ – 1)O$_3$
PROFIT$_{S2}$ = REVENUE$_{S2}$ – COST$_{S2}$.

REVENUE$_{S1}$ = (U$_1$ + 1)t$_1'$ + U$_2$t$_2$
COST$_{S1}$ = N$_1$O$_1$ + N$_2$O$_2$ + (N – N$_1$ – N$_2$)O$_3$
PROFIT$_{S1}$ = REVENUE$_{S1}$ – COST$_{S1}$.

REVENUE$_{S3}$ = (U$_1$)t$_1$ + (U$_2$ + 1)t$_2$ + f
COST$_{S3}$ = (N$_1$)O$_1$ + (N$_2$)O$_2$ + (N – N$_1$ – N$_2$)O$_3$
PROFIT$_{S3}$ = REVENUE$_{S3}$ – COST$_{S3}$.

REVENUE$_{S4}$ = (U$_1$)t$_1$ + (U$_2$ + 1)t$_2$
COST$_{S4}$ = (N$_1$ – 1)O$_1$ + N$_2$O$_2$ + (N – N$_1$ – N$_2$ + 1)O$_3$
PROFIT$_{S4}$ = REVENUE$_{S4}$ – COST$_{S4}$.

Figure 6.6 Markov chain model of two classes of service.

carrier had inclination (probability) mx to do this (m = management), and so move to a state S$_2$. In S$_2$,

$$\text{Revenue}_{S2} = (U_1 + 1)t_1 + U_2 t_2$$
$$\text{Cost}_{S1} = (N_1 + 1)O_1 + N_2 O_2 + (N - N_1 - N_2 - 1)O_3$$
$$\text{Profit}_{S2} = \text{Revenue}_{S2} - \text{Cost}_{S2}$$

Or, the carrier could do nothing (letting the system remain in the same state). Or, the user might consider switching to the more expensive class C$_2$, after paying a transfer fee f. With probability b, the system moves to state S$_3$, with

$$\text{Revenue}_{S3} = (U_1)t_1 + (U_2 + 1)t_2 + f$$
$$\text{Cost}_{S3} = (N_1)O_1 + (N_2)O_2 + (N - N_1 - N_2)O_3$$
$$\text{Profit}_{S3} = \text{Revenue}_{S3} - \text{Cost}_{S3}$$

However, this migration may cause an improvement in the QOS of Class C_1 beyond what the carrier intended. Hence, the carrier, having monitored the traffic statistics, *should* (be inclined to) adjust the trunking bandwidth by removing a trunk from the Class C_1 pool and returning it to the reserved state. Assume that the carrier had inclination (probability) my to do this (m = management) and so move to a state S_4. In S_4,

$$\text{Revenue}_{S4} = (U_1)t_1 + (U_2 + 1)t_2$$
$$\text{Cost}_{S4} = (N_1 - 1)\, O_1 + N_2 O_2 + (N - N_1 - N_2 + 1)O_3$$
$$\text{Profit}_{S4} = \text{Revenue}_{S4} - \text{Cost}_{S4}$$

Then the modeled system moves back to state S0. Refer to Fig. 6.5. for a pictorial view. The problem is highly multidimensional: many parameters affect the decision, including the cost of the resources, the transfer fee, and the user tariffs.

The transition matrix $\tilde{M}$ of the underlying Markov chain is as follows:

	S0	S1	S2	S3	S4
S0	$1 - a_1$	a_1	0	0	0
S1	0	$1 - mx - b$	mx	b	0
S2	a_1	0	$1 - a_1$	0	0
S3	0	0	0	$1 - my$	my
S4	1	0	0	0	0

6.7.2 Closed-form solution

One is interested in the steady-state probability of finding the system in states S_0, S_1, etc. Call these probabilities $\tilde{p} = (p_0, p_1, p_2, p_3, p_4)$. Then one can compute the expected profit as

$$EP = p_0{}^* \text{Profit}_{S0} + p_1{}^* \text{Profit}_{S1} + p_2{}^* \text{Profit}_{S2} + p_3{}^* \text{Profit}_{S3} + p_4{}^* \text{Profit}_{S4}$$

One would then choose a strategy which maximizes the expected profit. For example, the carrier could "play" with its willingness to add or remove resources, the transition fee, and the tariffs for the two classes. We have

$$\tilde{p} = \tilde{M}\,\tilde{p},$$

or

$$(1 - a_1)\, p_0 + a_1 p_2 + p_4 = p_0$$
$$a1\, p_0 + (1 - mx - b)\, p_1 = p_1$$

$$mxp_1 + (1 - a_1) p_2 = p_2$$
$$bp_1 + (1 - my) p_3 = p_3$$
$$myp_3 = p_4$$

Also,

$$p_0 + p_1 + p_2 + p_3 + p_4 = 1$$

After some considerable algebra, one obtains

$$p_0 = \frac{my^*(b + my)}{b^*my + my^2 + a_1{}^*my + mx^*my + b^*a_1 + b^*a_1{}^*my}$$

$$p_1 = p_0 \left(\frac{a_1}{b + my} \right)$$

$$p_2 = p_0 \left(\frac{mx}{b + my} \right)$$

$$p_3 = p_0 \left(\frac{b^*a_1}{my^*(b + my)} \right)$$

$$p_4 = p_0 \left(\frac{b^*a_1}{b + my} \right)$$

The expected profit is calculated as indicated above.

6.7.3 Numerical examples

The problem has 15 dimensions (variables); hence it will be difficult to draw generalized conclusions. Any interested party can obtain the software from the authors and conduct any sensitivity study of interest.

The tables preceding show some examples. Table 6.4 depicts input strategy/transition variables, as well as tariff and network engineering/cost variables. The vector $\tilde{p}$ is calculated, followed by the revenue, the cost, and the profit in each state. The expected profit is shown last.

Keeping all the variables equal to the case of Table 6.4, but varying my, one obtains the results shown in Table 6.5.

This table implies that in order to maximize the profit (given the 14 other assumptions), the carrier should not remove a facility from Class 1 and place it in the pool of unused/reserved resources (if the operational cost to keep the facility in service were higher and the cost to keep it in reserve were low, this result would probably not be true). Keeping all the variables equal to the case of Table 6.4, but varying mx, one obtains the results shown in Table 6.6.

TABLE 6.4   Markovian Model in Closed Form

a_1	0.4	
mx	0.1	$(mx + b \leq 1)$
b	0.2	
my	0.2	

Calculation:

p_0	0.290
p_1	0.290
p_2	0.072
p_3	0.290
p_4	0.058
Total	1.000

u_1	20
u_2	10
t_1	3
t_2	5
N_1	20
N_2	10
$N - N_1 - N_2$	20
O_1	2
O_2	3
O_3	1
f	1

	S_0	S_1	S_2	S_3	S_4
Revenue	110	113	113	116	115
Costs	90	90	91	90	89
Profit	20	23	22	26	26

S_0: status quo
S_1: new user
S_2: resource added
S_3: user moves
S_4: resource removed

Expected profit: 23.10

TABLE 6.5   Removing a Facility from Class 1

my	Expected profit
0.01	25.6746303
0.05	24.7242798
0.1	23.9761905
0.2	23.1014493

my = probability of downsizing Class C_1's trunk bundle.

The optimum profit (given the 14 other assumptions) is achieved when $b = 1$ and $mx = 0$, namely, when the carrier does not add a resource to C_1, although a new Class 1 user (lower QOS customer) arrived, and the carrier allows the user to move up to Class C_2 ($b =1$); the carrier also should not remove a facility from C_1 (naturally this all depends on the tariff for C_2, t_2, and the fee—for different values a different action may be better). (The global optimum is obtained by adjusting my from 0.2 as in Table 6.5 to 0.01—profit goes from 23.90 to 25.99.)

The next few tables shows what happens when the tariffs t_1 and t_2 are increased by an order of magnitude. The examples corresponding to Tables 6.4, 6.5, and 6.6 are shown in Tables 6.7, 6.8, and 6.9.

The last table basically shows that the expected revenue is almost independent of mx; the maximum profit is made when the user is allowed to switch class ($b = 1$).

References

1. *ATM User-to-Network Interface Specification*, Version 3.0, ATM Forum, August 1993.
2. ITU-T Recommendation I.356, *B-ISDN ATM Layer Cell Transfer Performance*, Geneva, Switzerland, July 1993.
3. TA-TSV-001409, *Generic Requirements for Exchange Access PVC Cell Relay Service*, Bellcore, Livingston, N.J., 1993.
4. TA-NWT-001110, *Broadband ISDN Switching System Generic Requirements, Issue 2*, Bellcore, Livingston, N.J., 1993.

TABLE 6.6   Carrier's Maximum Profit

a_1	0.4	
mx	See below	$(mx + b \leq 1)$
b	0.2	
my	0.2	

mx	Expected profit
0.00	23.18 ← Optimum
0.05	23.14
0.10	23.10
0.80	22.73

a_1	0.4	
mx	See below	$(mx + b \leq 1)$
b	0.5	
my	0.2	

mx	Expected profit
0.00	23.65 ← Optimum
0.10	23.58
0.20	23.52

a_1	0.4	
mx	See below	$(mx + b \leq 1)$
b	1.0	
my	0.2	

mx	Expected profit
0.00	23.90 ← Optimum of all three optima above

TABLE 6.7   Markovian Model in Closed Form

$a1$	0.4	
mx	0.1	$(mx + b \leq 1)$
b	0.2	
my	0.2	
Calculation:		
p_0	0.290	
p_1	0.290	
p_2	0.072	
p_3	0.290	
p_4	0.058	
Total	1.000	
u_1	20	
u_2	10	
t_1	30	
t_2	50	
n_1	20	
n_2	10	
$n - n_1 - n_2$	20	
o_1	2	
o_2	3	
o_3	1	
f	1	

	S_0	S_1	S_2	S_3	S_4
Revenue	1100	1130	1130	1151	1150
Costs	90	90	91	90	89
Profit	1010	1040	1039	1061	1061

Expected profit: 1038.53623

TABLE 6.8   Removing a Facility from Class 1

my	Expected profit
0.01	1060
0.05	1051
0.1	1045

TABLE 6.9 **Carrier's Maximum Profit**

a_1	0.4	
mx	See below	$(mx + b \leq 1)$
b	0.2	
my	0.2	

mx	Expected profit
0.00	1038.50
0.10	1038.53
0.20	1038.56
0.80	1038.69 ← Optimum

a_1	0.4	
mx	See below	$(mx + b \leq 1)$
b	0.5	
my	0.2	

mx	Expected profit
0.00	1041.82 ← Optimum
0.50	1041.52

a_1	0.4	
mx	See below	$(mx + b \leq 1)$
b	1.0	
my	0.2	

mx	Expected profit
0.00	1043.60 ← Optimum of all three optima above

Chapter

7

Support of
Fastpacket Services
and CPE

This chapter examines five areas that are related to the support of fastpacket services and CPE over an ATM platform; issues related to both the network and the user equipment are examined. The topics covered are

1. Multiservice ATM switches

2. Remote multiplexer nodes (also called service multiplexers)

3. Support of frame relay service on an ATM platform

4. Support of TCP/IP over ATM

5. ATM data exchange interface (ATM DXI)

7.1 Multiservice Broadband
Switching Systems

Carriers have the objective of deploying a single broadband platform that is able to support a variety of services, including CRS, frame relay, and SMDS. This objective is driven by the desire to minimize capital expenditures and operations costs. The deployment of an integrated platform eliminates duplicate transmission and switching facilities, staff, operations systems, maintenance procedures, and so on. Reference 1 makes the case for integration very clear.

Figure 7.1 depicts an early arrangement with an ATM switch terminating multi-protocol user equipment and distinct service-spe-

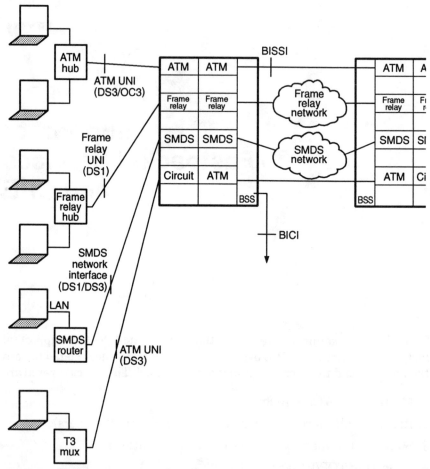

Figure 7.1 Early arrangement with ATM switch terminating multiprotocol user equipment and distinct service-specific networks. BICI = broadband intercarrier interface; BISSI = broadband interswitching system interface.

cific networks. Figure 7.2 shows an early arrangement with the ATM switch terminating multiprotocol user equipment and distinct service-specific networks; some networks (e.g., frame relay) have been replaced by ATM.

Corporate communication planners may employ multiprotocol routers to protect their invested base, while utilizing an ATM WAN. This is illustrated in Figure 7.3, where the ATM switch supports a multiservice UNI. Figure 7.4 shows a strategy receiving considerable attention from service providers: here the carrier provides a multiprotocol service multiplexer, enabling the user to protect its invested base, while the carrier utilizes ATM. Figure 7.5 illustrates one "high-end" scenario in

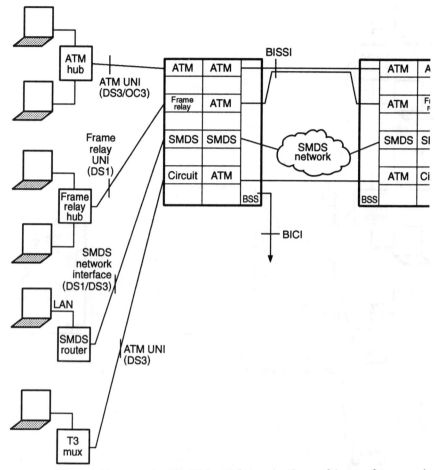

Figure 7.2 Early arrangement with ATM switch terminating multiprotocol user equipment and distinct service-specific networks; some networks (e.g., frame relay) have been replaced by ATM.

which the corporate manager has replaced the entire enterprise network with one based on ATM and is relying on the public network for the WAN connectivity.

Figure 7.6 depicts the type of full-feature multiservice ATM switch for which carriers have issued requests for proposals.

7.2 Remote Multiplexer Nodes

7.2.1 Functionality

A hierarchy of functional elements in support of ATM deployment has been defined as follows:

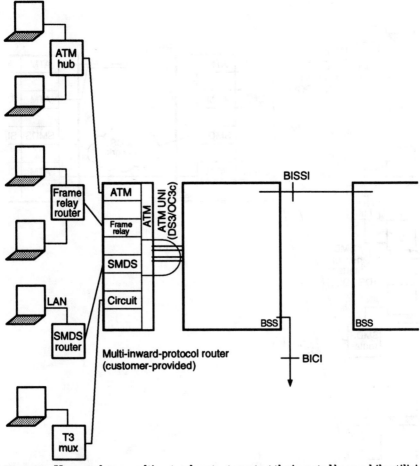

Figure 7.3 User employs a multiprotocol router to protect the invested base, while utilizing ATM WAN.

1. Customer premises node
2. Distribution/drop
3. Remote multiplexer node (RMN)
4. Subfeeder
5. Access node
6. Feeder
7. Local exchange node
8. Interexchange
9. Transit exchange node

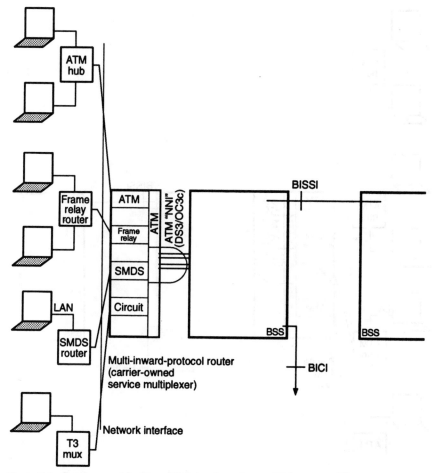

Figure 7.4 Carrier provides a multiprotocol service multiplexer, enabling user to protect the invested base while the carrier utilizes ATM.

The RMN, under discussion, is defined in Bellcore's FA-NWT-001109, *Broadband ISDN Transport Network Elements Framework Generic Criteria*, as follows (see Fig. 7.7):

The RMN is a SONET mux/demux pair which provides a variety of standard Customer Premises Network (CPN) interfaces. It is useful in the concentration of various CPN signals onto a single fiber optic pipe, thus reducing the amount of fiber required in the sub-feeder or feeder. The RMN could be located on customer premises, in the distribution network, or in a CO. The customer side of the RMN would support DS1/DS3 interfaces BISDN UNI ... and SIP. On the network side, the RMN supports various SONET interfaces. An initial, minimum set of functions ... would be the SONET multiplexing/de-

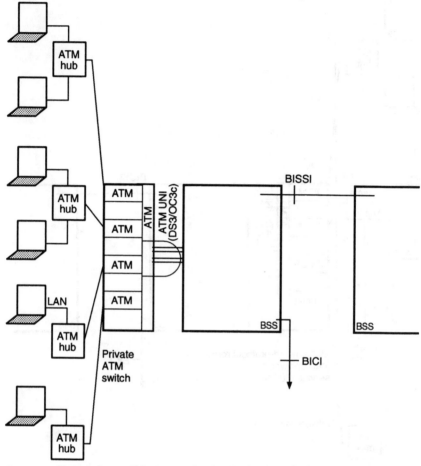

Figure 7.5 User replaces all devices with ATM devices and uses an ATM WAN.

multiplexing functions ... A more advanced form ... would include ATM-related functions.

In some (but not necessarily all) ATM deployment circumstances, it might make sense to go beyond SONET multiplexing and support basic remote ATM multiplexing (but without call control), as provided by an RMN; also, it may be possible to make the case for deployment of feeder-based interworking[*] (e.g., provide frame relay interworking units). Carriers that need an architectural building block that supports remote ATM switching with call processing could use, alternatively, a

---

[*]This type of interworking can also be done at the BSS, as shown in Fig. 7.1 and 7.2.

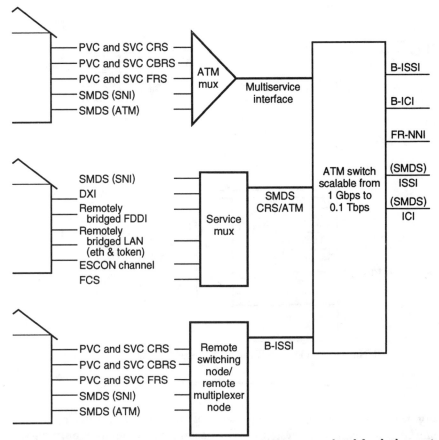

Figure 7.6 Full-feature multiservice ATM switches being contemplated for deployment. SNI = subscriber network interface; CBRS = CBR service (circuit emulation); FCS = fiber channel standard.

low-end ATM switch in lieu of an RMN, and connect it to the CO-based ATM switch over a B-ISSI interface (this is in fact the architecture of Fig. 7.6).

More recently, the discussion has focused on the use of large "core" switches located at the CO or some LATA-level hub, in conjunction with smaller "edge" switches located closer to the user. Smaller switches support new distance-limited services such as LAN emulation.

7.2.2 Economic justification

As the density of customers using ATM increases, RMN functions (i.e., ATM-based remote digital terminals supporting ATM multiplexing and interworking of ATM with other services, such as FRS) become more economically justified. The technical functionality of RMNs is relatively well understood. The business justification for RMN technology *support-*

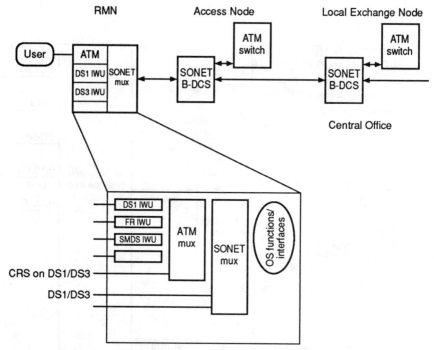

Figure 7.7 RMN as defined in FA-NWT-001109.

ing remote switching with call control and complex interfaces to a plethora of operations systems[*] will become more obvious only as the penetration of ATM increases. A full-fledged RMN would need

- SONET multiplexing functions
- ATM multiplexing functions
- Interworking capabilities
- Remote switching
- Open interfaces to the ATM switch
- Call control capabilities, including trunk-side signaling
- Direct access to OSs, beyond basic OS-NE surveillance/provisioning functions

---

[*]The RMN being discussed here is one that does more than just a basic SONET/ATM multiplexing or user interface support (e.g., FRS), which is in fact planned for deployment in some networks.

All of this can make such a device expensive. The following ordered list offers a possible deployment plan, in increasing order of sophistication, functionality, and complexity:

1. Deploy a SONET multiplexer.
2. Deploy an ATM multiplexer without call control.
3. Deploy a small ATM switch in the feeder plant to act as RMN.
4. Deploy an ATM multiplexer with call control using a vendor-proprietary interface to the ATM switch.
5. Deploy an ATM multiplexer with call control using an open interface to the ATM switch and with full OS connectivity.

Approaches 1 to 4 may be adequate for near-term fastpacket applications.

Some of the ATM services under consideration include LAN emulation (the cost/benefit tradeoff of using an evolving technology to emulate a 25-year-old legacy technology, and hence the market penetration of such emulation service, remains to be demonstrated—this is an example of technology push rather than market pull). These services are distance-limited in the sense that any carrier devices utilized to support the user LAN and FDDI emulation would have to reside only a few hundred meters from the user. Therefore these services would necessitate a RMN (also called a service node, in this context).

Another issue affecting the need for RMNs is whether ATM will be used mostly by commercial data users (fastpacket applications) or also to deliver residential video, for video-on-demand applications.

The economic tradeoff of using RMSs depends on

- The economies of scale (these become important when the population of users grows)
- The cost of transport versus the cost of switching
- Facility availability
- Maintenance and operations costs

Density-based analysis of remote switching modules deployment timetable. This discussion assumes that at first ATM will be found effective, and hence utilized, only by data users. U.S. LAN deployment was estimated at 600,000 systems in 1993, of which 20 percent were strictly local (or 30 on average for each of the 20,000 U.S. serving COs, as measured by deployed switches). As an optimistic estimate, one can assume that ultimately (say by 1998) 50 percent of these LANs will use ATM for WAN communication (the number may be lower). This implies

(600,000)*(0.80)*(0.5)/20,000 = 12 LANs per CO that will utilize WAN ATM access lines by 1998, on average.

If one assumes that the number of LANs will double by then, that would mean 24 LANs per CO requiring WAN ATM. Some COs will have more customers, while others will have less; for example, one could assume that the top 1,000 COs had twice as many as the average CO. This would imply 24 or 48 LANs for these COs, corresponding with the earlier assumptions.

Note that the estimate of 12 LANs per CO requiring WAN ATM access lines by 1998 equates to 240,000 ATM access lines in the United States by 1998. (Again, these estimates do not take into account the use of ATM to deliver consumer video; it is possible that RMNs will be required to support residential video services.)

These technical and business considerations are dependent on at least three factors:

1. The cost-effectiveness of multiplexing in the access plant considering the technical advantage of doing so; namely, a comparison of the cost of connecting users to the CO over a purely SONET infrastructure with the cost/savings involved in ATM multiplexing.

2. The time horizon under consideration. For example, some network optimization capabilities may not be needed now, but such capabilities may be needed at a future date, assuming that the market has validated customer interest in the services so that there is a stable, growing, and paying customer base.

3. The type of services that the user community chooses to adopt for its enterprise networking needs. For example, if ATM-based on-demand residential video services would benefit from and/or necessitate RMN capabilities, then the question of the need for RMNs should be correlated with how widely deployed such service is expected to become in the time horizon under scrutiny.

Some aspects of the decision-making approach are as follows:

1. An explicit need should be demonstrable.

2. An explicit advantage should be demonstrable.

3. The simplest possible solution should be sought; complexity for the sake of generality does not afford the carriers an explicit competitive advantage.

When a CO *switch* costs $10 million, it makes sense to find a way to meet this need with another architectural element that costs much less than the switch. However, when the ATM switch costs, say, $50,000, the carrier may find it completely cost-effective to meet this need for distributed switching by using a low-end switch, rather than developing an entirely new architectural element.

As Fig. 7.8 depicts graphically, there are no economic/engineering incentives/advantages to introducing access multiplexing when there are only a few users. This may be the case initially, as cell relay services begin to be introduced, particularly if the user equipment is expensive and/or the service is available only at DS3. Also, if cell relay service is targeted to (high-end) data users, it is likely that the user population will initially be small.

Figure 7.9 shows graphically that access multiplexing may not be effective when the population of users is not clustered, but is scattered geographically all around the CO. This may be the case initially, as cell relay services begin to be introduced, particularly if these are targeted only to data users.

Figure 7.10 shows graphically that access multiplexing may not be effective when the population of ATM users is very close to the CO. This also may be the case initially, as cell relay services begin to be introduced, as these may be targeted to major metropolitan markets, such as New York City, Atlanta, etc. (Parts of the country which have lower population density may be in a different situation.)

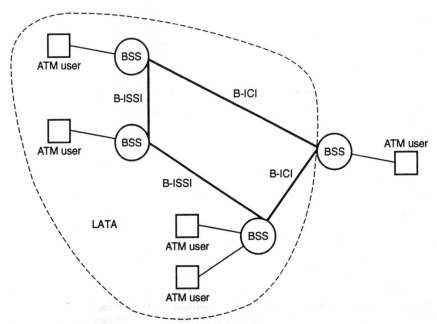

Figure 7.8 Access multiplexing may not be effective when the population of users is sparse (except for distance-limited service support).

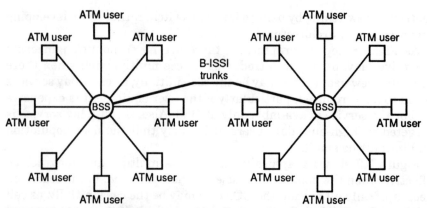

Figure 7.9 Access multiplexing may not be effective when the population of users is not in any specific part of town (except for distance-limited service support). BSS = broadband switching system (ATM switch).

Figure 7.11 shows graphically that access multiplexing may be done using specialized multiplexing when the cost of a switch is very high. However, if the cost of the switch is low, then a low-end switch can be employed, and there is no need to develop a whole new architectural element.

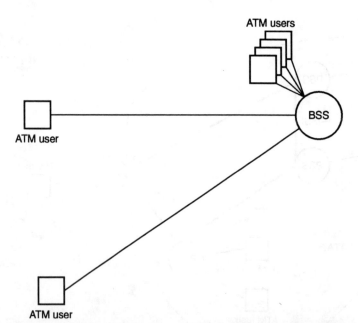

Figure 7.10 Access multiplexing may not be effective when the population of users is very close to the switching office (except for distance-limited service support). BSS = broadband switching system (ATM switch).

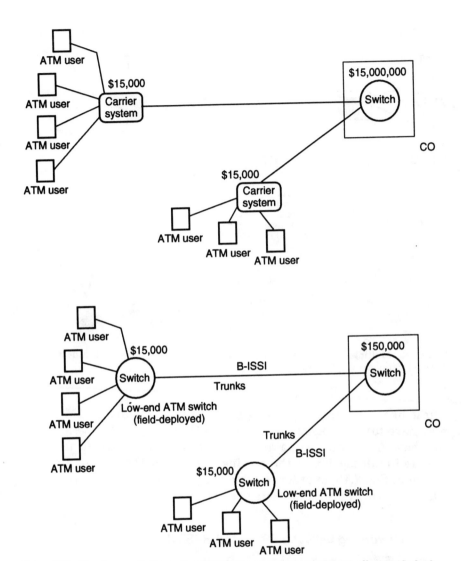

Figure 7.11 Development of new functional elements is not economically justified when the cost of the switch is very low. Top: Traditional situation; bottom: ATM situation.

Figure 7.12 shows that when the majority of the traffic is destined for locations that are not connected to the same RMN, there is no real advantage to ATM access multiplexing. Studies have shown that of high-speed data communication, 25 percent is for intrabuilding communication, 20 percent for intra-LATA communication, and 55 percent for inter-LATA communication. Hence, beyond the physical economics of the loop plant, there may not be overwhelming advantages to remote multiplexing.

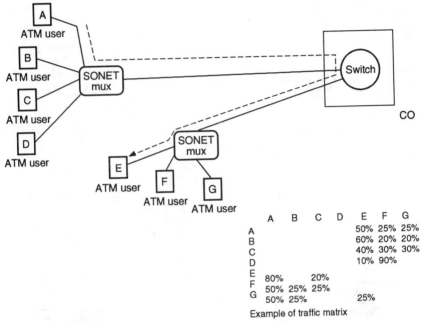

	A	B	C	D	E	F	G
A					50%	25%	25%
B					60%	20%	20%
C					40%	30%	30%
D					10%	90%	
E	80%		20%				
F	50%	25%	25%				
G	50%	25%			25%		

Example of traffic matrix

Figure 7.12 Multiplexing is not effective when a major portion of the traffic is destined for remote locations (except for distance-limited service support).

It is likely that initially, users that require access to an ATM switch may have to use tandem techniques, as there may be only a few COs that have ATM switches. In this case it may be advantageous to do the required multiplexing at the serving CO, rather than in the field, as shown in Fig. 7.13, in order to achieve economies of scale, particularly when there are only a few users per CO.

7.3   Interworking between FRBS and B-ISDN

In this section interworking between frame relaying bearer service (FRBS) and the connection-oriented variable-bit-rate services provided by Class C service of B-ISDN is described. This discussion is based on ITU-T I.555.[2] It is provided to illustrate some of the issues that come into play at the ATM switch (that is, the BSS) in supporting multiple fastpacket services.

One wants to be able to achieve interworking between frame relaying and B-ISDN services with the following provisos:

- Mapping of the frame relaying loss priority and congestion control indications

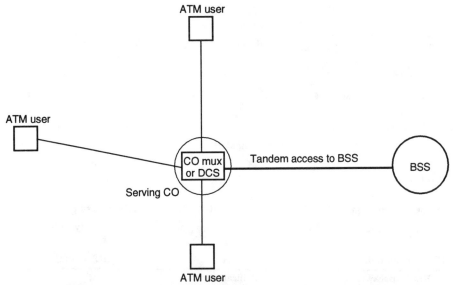

Figure 7.13 Field-based multiplexing is not effective when ATM switch is accessed via tandem means (except for distance-limited service support).

- Negotiation procedures for frame relaying frame size
- Message-mode unassured operation without flow control
- Immediate transfer of user data once the connection has been established, using AAL parameter negotiation procedures

Figure 7.14 represents the interworking arrangements considered. Interworking between FRBS and B-ISDN Class C services is performed either by call control mapping or by provisioning. Since in both the ISDN and the B-ISDN, call control is handled in a separate call control plane, it is assumed that similar call control functions are used. The interworking between the respective signaling systems is for further study (i.e., it has not yet been worked out and/or there is no agreement yet). Table 7.1

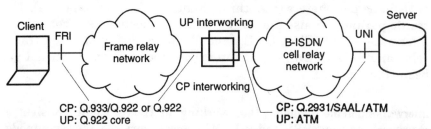

Figure 7.14 Interworking between frame relay and ATM. CP = control plane; UP = user plane.

TABLE 7.1 Quick Comparison of Frame Relay Service and Cell Relay Service

	Frame relay	Cell relay
Connection types	Virtual connections	Virtual paths, virtual connections
Local address	DLCI	VPI/VCI
Connection establishment	Provisioning (PVC) or call control (SVC)	Provisioning (PVC) or call control (SVC)
PDU length	Variable	Fixed (48 + 5 octets)
Delineation method	Flag-delineated	HEC cell-delineation method
Traffic descriptor	Multiparameter (CIR, B_C, B_E, T)	Multiparameter (PCR, SCR, B_T)
Priority indication	Discard eligibility (D/E)	Cell loss priority (CLP)
Error protection	CRC-16 over entire frame	Header only (plus AAL functions)
Congestion indication	FECN, BECN	EFCI (PT coding)

BECN: Backward explicit congestion notification
CIR: Committed information rate
DLCI: Data link connection identifier
EFCI: Explicit forward congestion indication
FECN: Forward explicit congestion notification

provides a comparison between frame relay service and cell relay service, to facilitate this discussion.

7.3.1 Interworking requirements

The identified interworking arrangement is between FRBS and B-ISDN Class C, message mode, nonassured operation.

Interworking in the C Plane. Call control mapping is provided in such a way that U-Plane connections are established and released in both interworking networks, with interconnection in the interworking function (IWF). C-Plane procedures must provide for the negotiation of U-Plane parameters (e.g., throughput, maximum frame size). The traffic parameters used for frame relay connections are committed information rate (CIR), B_c, B_e, and T. The mapping between frame relay and B-ISDN traffic descriptors (covered in Chap. 6) has not yet been standardized.

Interworking in the U Plane. Interworking in the U Plane consists of interworking the FRBS and B-ISDN Class C services, message mode, unassured operation, with two sets of service conditions:

- The B-ISDN supports the FRBS (defined in ITU-T I.233.1).
- The B-ISDN supports another service (e.g., CRS) with which FRBS can interwork.

In particular, B-ISDN Class C, message mode, unassured operation provides basic functions (see Table 7.2) similar to those provided by the frame relaying core service.

7.3.2 Network interworking (scenario 1)

Figure 3.3 (top part) represents the case where B-ISDN is interposed between frame relaying networks to provide a high interconnection capability. In this case, the frame relaying networks are users of B-ISDN.

TABLE 7.2 Provision of Core Frame Relay Functions in the Equivalent B-ISDN Service

FRBS	B-ISDN Class C, message mode, Unassured		
I.233.1 core functions	ATM functions	SAR and CPCS functions (AAL5)	FR-SSCS functions
Frame delimiting, alignment, and transparency		Preservation of CPCS_SDU	
Frame muxing/de-muxing using the DLCI field	Muxing/demuxing using VPI/VCI		Muxing/demuxing using the DLCI field
Inspection of the frame to ensure that it consists of an integral number of octets			Inspection of the frame to ensure that it consists of an integral number of octets
Inspection of the frame to ensure that it is neither too long nor too short			Inspection of the frame to ensure that it is neither too long nor too short
Detection (but not recovery) of trans-mission errors		Detection (but not recovery) of trans-mission errors	
Congestion control forward	Congestion control forward		Congestion control forward
Congestion control backward			Congestion control backward
Command/response			Command/response
Congestion control discard eligibility	Cell loss priority		Congestion control discard eligibility

The FR-SSCS, as shown in Fig. 3.3, supports the frame relaying core functions of Recommendation I.233.1. Table 7.2 illustrates the division of functions among FR-SSCS, CPCS, the SAR Sublayer, and the ATM Layer. AAL Type 5 (SAR and CPCS) is used for frame relaying and B-ISDN interworking. The FR-SSCS is defined in Recommendation I.365.1. The FR-SSCS_PDU has exactly the same structure as the Q.922 core frame without the flags, zero-bit insertion, and FCS, as specified in Recommendation I.363.

There are two schemes for multiplexing FRBS connections over B-ISDN:

- A number of frame relaying logical connections are multiplexed into a single ATM virtual channel connection. Multiplexing is accomplished at the FR-SSCS sublayer using data link connection identifiers (DLCIs).

- Each frame relaying logical connection is mapped to a single ATM virtual channel connection, and multiplexing is accomplished at the ATM Layer using VPI/VCIs.

In both multiplexing schemes, the FRBS connections are identified by the Q.922 core DLCI. The FR-SSCS links are identified by VPI/VCIs and FR-SSCS DLCIs for the first multiplexing scheme. The FR-SSCS links are identified by VPI/VCIs for the second multiplexing scheme (the DLCI value at the FR-SSCS does not convey additional information). All the above-mentioned link identifiers have only local significance, and their values have to be negotiated at call setup or by subscription for both sides of the IWF. The first scheme of multiplexing (DLCI-based multiplexing) may be used only for FRBS VCs that terminate on the same ATM-based end system (i.e., end users of IWFs). FRBS VCs from a single source that terminate on different ATM-based end systems must be mapped to different ATM connections. In this case, the second scheme of multiplexing or a combination of the two schemes can be used.

The recommended congestion management strategy for the multiplexing methods is as follows: At the ingress point of the B-ISDN, in the first scheme, the VCC may be composed of a large number of frame relaying connections multiplexed to form a VCC; in the second scheme, a VPC may be composed of a large number of VCCs carrying frame relay traffic. If the number of FR connections or the number of VCCs is in fact large, then according to the law of large numbers, the resultant combined over the ATM VCC or the VPC behaves almost as a constant bit rate. As a consequence, statistical smoothing of the aggregate traffic at the ingress point of the B-ISDN will enable resource management on peak bandwidth allocation of the VCC or VPC, respectively, to achieve acceptable efficiency. The FR network congestion management would then operate as usual.

The forward explicit congestion notification (FECN) and backward explicit congestion notification (BECN) parameter values are not mapped to the AAL5 CPCS and ATM Layers. However, congestion indications generated by the B-ISDN will be taken into account when generating FECN/BECN towards the frame relay networks. This approach provides an averaged QOS over all ATM connections for frame relay carriage, and uses the preventative control of network resource management concept described in Recommendations I.370 and I.371.

The interworking between FR and B-ISDN is performed as follows:

- The information fields of the PDUs are transferred unchanged between the FR Service-Specific Convergence Sublayer and the Q.922 core.

- The protocol control information (PCI) derived from the headers of the two interworked protocols (Q.922 and FR-SSCS) is exchanged via parameters in primitives. These parameters are processed to create the header of the PDU in each of the interworked protocols. In the FR-SSCS, some of these parameters are also mapped to the parameters exchanged with the AAL5 CPCS. The format of the header of the interworked protocol is defined in Recommendation Q.922. The use of the B-ISDN network by the frame relaying network is not visible to the end users. The end-user protocols remain intact.

7.3.3 Network interworking (scenario 2)

Figure 3.3 (bottom part) represents the case where a B-ISDN terminal using FRBS (according to Recommendation Q.922 core) is connected via the B-ISDN to an IWF for accessing a FR terminal on a FR network. The IWF is the same as that described in the previous scenario. The mapping of parameter values of the primitives among Q.922, FR-SSCS, and AAL5 CPCS is described later.

Services interworking applies when a frame relaying service user interworks with a B-ISDN service user, and the B-ISDN service user performs no frame relaying specific functions and the frame relaying service user performs no B-ISDN service functions. All interworking functionalities are performed by the IWF. Since the B-ISDN terminal does not support the I.233.1-type core service, higher-layer interworking functions may be needed.

Interworking of loss priority and congestion management. Interworking of loss priority and congestion management is achieved through mappings to/from FR and B-ISDN.

Discard eligibility and loss priority at the interworking function
Loss priority mapping in the FR-to-B-ISDN direction. The DE parameter value in the Q.922 core frame is mapped into the DE parameter

value in the FR-SSCS-PDU header and into the CPCS-LP parameter value of the CPCS-UNITDATA.invoke primitive.

Loss priority mapping in the B-ISDN-to-FR direction.   If the parameter value of CPCS-LP is 0 and DE = 0 in the FR-SSCS-PDU header, then DE is set to 0 in the Q.922 core frame.

If DE = 1 in the FR-SSCS-PDU, then DE is set to 1 in the Q.922 core frame, irrespective of the CPCS-LP parameter value of the CPCS-UNIT-DATA.signal primitive.

The mapping of CPCS-LP = 1 and DE = 0 in the FR-SSCS_PDU to DE 1 in the Q.922 core frame has not yet been standardized.

Congestion indication mapping.

Congestion indication mapping in the FR-to-B-ISDN direction.   T h e FECN in the Q.922 core frame is mapped into the FR-SSCS_PDU header FECN. The CPCS-CI parameter value of the CPCS-UNITDATA.invoke primitive is set to 0 by the FR-SSCS (thus separate indications exist for congestion occurring in the ATM network and the FR network).

Congestion indication mapping in the B-ISDN-to-FR direction.   If the CPCS-CI parameter value of the CPCS-UNITDATA.signal primitive is 0 and the FR-SSCS_PDU header FECN = 0, then FECN is set in the Q.922 core frame. If the FR-SSCS_PDU header FECN = 1, then FECN is set to 1 in the Q.922 core frame, irrespective of the CPCS-CI parameter value of the CPCS-UNITDATA.signal primitive.

If the CPCS-CI parameter value of the CPCS-UNITDATA.signal primitive is 1 and the FR-SSCS_PDU header FECN = 0, then FECN is set to 1 in the Q.922 core frame.

7.4   IP over ATM

A specification for transmitting IP datagrams over ATM networks exists in RFC1577.[3] This specification is summarized here to expose the reader to the general principles involved in this type of networking. The discussion that follows is extracted from Ref. 3.[*]   For background information on IP and ARP the reader may consult Ref. 4 or other references.

7.4.1   Introduction

The goal of RFC1577 is to allow compatible and interoperable implementations for transmitting IP datagrams and ATM Address Resolution Protocol (ATMARP) requests and replies over ATM Adaptation Layer 5 (AAL5). RFC1577 defines only the operation of IP and address resolu-

---

[*]This material is included with the permission of the author of RFC1577, Mark Laubach.

tion over ATM, and is not meant to describe the operation of ATM networks. Any reference to virtual connections, permanent virtual connections, or switched virtual connections applies only to virtual channel connections used to support IP and address resolution over ATM, and thus are assumed to be using AAL5. RFC1577 places no restrictions or requirements on virtual connections used for other purposes.

Initial deployment of ATM provides a LAN-segment replacement for

1. Local area networks (e.g., Ethernets, token rings, and FDDI)
2. Local-area backbones between existing (non-ATM) LANs
3. Dedicated circuits or frame relay PVCs between IP routers

In item 1, local IP routers with one or more ATM interfaces will be able to connect islands of ATM networks. In item 3, public or private ATM wide area networks will be used to connect IP routers, which in turn may or may not connect to local ATM networks. ATM WANs and LANs may be interconnected.

Private ATM networks (local or wide area) will use the private ATM address structure specified in The ATM Forum UNI specification. This structure is modeled after the format of an OSI Network Service Access Point Address. A private ATM address uniquely identifies an ATM endpoint. Public networks will use either the address structure specified in ITU-TS recommendation E.164 or the private network ATM address structure. An E.164 address uniquely identifies an interface to a public network.

The characteristics and features of ATM networks are different than those found in LANs:

- ATM provides a virtual connection (VC) switched environment. VC setup may be done on either a permanent virtual connection (PVC) or dynamic switched virtual connection (SVC) basis. SVC call management signaling is performed via implementations of the Q.2931 protocol.

- Data to be passed by a VC is segmented into 53 octet quantities called cells (5 octets of ATM header and 48 octets of data).

- The function of mapping user protocol data units (PDUs) into the information field of the ATM cell and vice versa is performed in the ATM Adaptation Layer (AAL). When a VC is created a specific AAL type is associated with the VC. There are four different AAL types, which are referred to individually as "AAL1," "AAL2," "AAL3/4," and "AAL5." The AAL type is known by the VC endpoints via the call setup mechanism and is not carried in the ATM cell header. For PVCs the AAL type is administratively configured at the endpoints when the connection (circuit) is set up. For SVCs, the AAL type is communicated along the VC path via Q.2931 as part of call setup establishment and the endpoints use the signaled information for configuration. ATM switches generally do not care about the AAL type of VCs. The AAL5 format specifies a packet format with a maximum size of (64K – 1) octets of user data. Cells for an AAL5 PDU are transmitted first to last, the last cell indicating the end of the PDU. ATM standards guarantee that on a given VC, cell ordering is preserved end-to-end.

- ATM Forum signaling defines point-to-point and point-to-multipoint connection setup. Multipoint-to-multipoint VCs are not yet specified by ITU-TS or ATM Forum.

- An ATM Forum ATM endpoint address is either encoded as an NSAP address (NSAPA) or is an E.164 public UNI address. In some cases, both an ATM endpoint address and an E.164 public UNI address are needed by an ATMARP client to reach another host or router. Since the use of ATM endpoint addresses and E.164 public UNI addresses by ATMARP are analogous to the use of Ethernet addresses, the notion of "hardware address" is extended to encompass ATM addresses in the context of ATMARP, even though ATM addresses need not have hardware significance. ATM Forum NSAPAs use the same basic format as U.S. GOSIP NSAPAs.

RFC1577 describes the initial deployment of ATM within "classical" IP networks as a direct replacement for local area networks (Ethernets) and for IP links which interconnect routers, either within or between administrative domains. The "classical" model here refers to the treatment of the ATM host adapter as a networking interface to the IP protocol stack operating in a LAN-based paradigm.

Characteristics of the classical model are as follows:

- The same maximum transmission unit (MTU) size is used for all VCs in a logical IP subnetwork (LIS).

- Default LLC/SNAP encapsulation of IP packets.

- End-to-end IP routing architecture stays the same.

- IP addresses are resolved to ATM addresses by use of an ATMARP service within the LIS; ATMARPs stay within the LIS. From a client's perspective, the ATMARP architecture stays faithful to the basic ARP model.

- One IP subnet is used for many hosts and routers. Each VC directly connects two IP members within the same LIS.

Future specifications are expected to describe the operation of IP over ATM when ATM networks become globally deployed and interconnected.

The deployment of ATM into the Internet community is just beginning and will take many years to complete. During the early part of this period, it is expected that deployment will follow traditional IP subnet boundaries for the following reasons:

- Administrators and managers of IP subnetworks will tend to initially follow the same models as they currently have deployed. The mindset of the community will change slowly over time as ATM increases its coverage and builds its credibility.

- Policy administration practices rely on the security, access, routing, and filtering capability of IP Internet gateways, i.e., firewalls. ATM will not be allowed to "back door" around these mechanisms until ATM provides better management capabilities than the existing services and practices.

- Standards for global IP over ATM will take some time to complete and deploy.

RFC1577 details the treatment of the classical model of IP and ATMARP over ATM. RFC1577 does not preclude the subsequent treatment of ATM networks within the IP framework as ATM becomes globally deployed and interconnected; this will be the subject of future documents. RFC1577 does not address issues related to transparent data link layer interoperability.

7.4.2   IP subnetwork configuration

In the LIS scenario, each separate administrative entity configures its hosts and routers within a closed logical IP subnetwork. Each LIS operates and communicates independently of other LISs on the same ATM network. Hosts connected to ATM communicate directly to other hosts within the same LIS. Communication to hosts outside of the local LIS is provided via an IP router. This router is an ATM endpoint attached to the ATM network that is configured as a member of one or more LISs. This configuration may result in a number of disjoint LISs operating over the same ATM network. Hosts of differing IP subnets must communicate via an intermediate IP router even though it may be possible to open a direct VC between the two IP members over the ATM network.

The requirements for IP members (i.e., hosts and routers) operating in an ATM LIS configuration are

- All members have the same IP network/subnet number and address mask.

- All members within a LIS are directly connected to the ATM network.

- All members outside of the LIS are accessed via a router.
- All members of a LIS must have a mechanism for resolving IP addresses to ATM addresses via ATMARP and vice versa via InATMARP when using SVCs.
- All members of a LIS must have a mechanism for resolving VCs to IP addresses via InATMARP when using PVCs.
- All members within a LIS must be able to communicate via ATM with all other members in the same LIS; i.e., the virtual connection topology underlying the intercommunication among the members is fully meshed.

The following list identifies a set of ATM specific parameters that must be implemented in each IP station connected to the ATM network:

- *ATM hardware address (atm$ha).* The ATM address of the individual IP station.
- *ATMARP request address (atm$arp-req).* atm$arp-req is the ATM address of an individual ATMARP server located within the LIS. In an SVC environment, ATMARP requests are sent to this address for the resolution of target protocol addresses to target ATM addresses. That server must have authoritative responsibility for resolving ATMARP requests of all IP members within the LIS. If the LIS is operating with PVCs only, then this parameter may be set to null and the IP station is not required to send ATMARP requests to the ATMARP server.

It is recommended in RFC1577 that routers providing LIS functionality over the ATM network also support the ability to interconnect multiple LISs. Routers that wish to provide interconnection of differing LISs must be able to support multiple sets of these parameters (one set for each connected LIS) and be able to associate each set of parameters to a specific IP network/subnet number. In addition, it is recommended in RFC1577 that a router be able to provide this multiple LIS support with a single physical ATM interface that may have one or more individual ATM endpoint addresses.

7.4.3 Packet format

Implementations must support IEEE 802.2 LLC/SNAP encapsulation. LLC/SNAP encapsulation is the default packet format for IP datagrams.

It is recognized in RFC1577 that other encapsulation methods may be used. However, in the absence of other knowledge or agreement, LLC/SNAP encapsulation is the default. Also, the future deployment of end-to-end signaling within ATM that will allow negotiation of encapsulation method on a per-VC basis. Signaling negotiations are beyond the scope of RFC1577.

7.4.4   MTU size

The default MTU size for IP members operating over the ATM network shall be 9180 octets. The LLC/SNAP header is 8 octets; therefore, the default ATM AAL5 protocol data unit size is 9188 octets. In classical IP subnets, values other than the default can be used if and only if all members in the LIS have been configured to use the nondefault value.

It is recognized in RFC1577 that the future deployment of end-to-end signaling within ATM that will allow negotiation of MTU size on a per-VC basis.

7.4.5   Address resolution

Address resolution within an ATM logical IP subnet shall make use of the ATM Address Resolution Protocol (ATMARP) and the Inverse ATM Address Resolution Protocol (InATMARP) as defined in RFC1577. ATMARP is the same protocol as the ARP protocol with extensions needed to support ARP in a unicast server ATM environment. InATMARP is the same protocol as the original InARP protocol but applied to ATM networks. All IP stations must support these protocols as updated and extended in RFC1577. Use of these protocols differs depending on whether PVCs or SVCs are used.

7.4.6   Permanent virtual connections

An IP station must have a mechanism (e.g. manual configuration) for determining what PVCs it has, and in particular which PVCs are being used with LLC/SNAP encapsulation. The details of the mechanism are beyond the scope of RFC1577.

All IP members supporting PVCs are required to use the Inverse ATM Address Resolution Protocol (InATMARP) on those VCs using LLC/SNAP encapsulation. In a strict PVC environment, the receiver shall infer the relevant VC from the VC on which the InATMARP request (InARP_REQUEST) or response (InARP_REPLY) was received. When the ATM source and/or target address is unknown, the corresponding ATM address length in the InATMARP packet must be set to zero, indicating a null length; otherwise, the appropriate address field should be filled in and the corresponding length set appropriately.

It is the responsibility of each IP station supporting PVCs to revalidate [ATM]ARP table entries as part of the aging process.

7.4.7 Switched virtual connections

SVCs require support for ATMARP in the nonbroadcast, nonmulticast environment that ATM networks currently provide. To meet this need a single ATMARP server must be located within the LIS. This server must have authoritative responsibility for resolving the ATMARP requests of all IP members within the LIS.

The server itself does not actively establish connections. It depends on the clients in the LIS to initiate the ATMARP registration procedure. An individual client connects to the ATMARP server using a point-to-point VC. The server, upon the completion of an ATM call/connection of a new VC specifying LLC/SNAP encapsulation, will transmit an InAT-MARP request to determine the IP address of the client. The InATMARP reply from the client contains the information necessary for the AT-MARP server to build its ATMARP table cache. This information is used to generate replies to the ATMARP requests it receives.

The ATMARP server mechanism requires that each client be administratively configured with the ATM address of the ATMARP server atm$arp-req as defined earlier in RFC1577. There is to be one and only one ATMARP server operational per logical IP subnet. It is recommended in RFC1577 that the ATMARP server also be an IP station. This station must be administratively configured to operate and recognize itself as the ATMARP server for a LIS. The ATMARP server must be configured with an IP address for each logical IP subnet it is serving to support InATMARP requests.

It is recognized in RFC1577 that a single ATMARP server is not as robust as multiple servers which synchronize their databases correctly. This document is defining the client-server interaction by using a simple, single server approach as a reference model, and does not prohibit more robust approaches which use the same client-server interface.

7.4.8 ATMARP and InATMARP
packet format

Internet addresses are assigned independently of ATM addresses. Each host implementation must know its own IP and ATM address(es) and must respond to address resolution requests appropriately. IP members must also use ATMARP and InATMARP to resolve IP addresses to ATM addresses when needed.

The ATMARP and InATMARP protocols use the same hardware type (ar$hrd), protocol type (ar$pro), and operation code (ar$op) data formats as the ARP and InARP protocols. The location of these fields within the ATMARP packet are in the same byte position as those in ARP and InARP packets. A unique hardware type value has been assigned for

ATMARP. In addition, ATMARP makes use of an additional operation code for ARP_NAK. The remainder of the ATMARP/InATMARP packet format is different from the ARP/InARP packet format.

The ATMARP and InATMARP protocols have several fields that have the following format and values:

ar$hrd	16 bits	Hardware type
ar$pro	16 bits	Protocol type
ar$shtl	8 bits	Type and length of source ATM number (q)
ar$sstl	8 bits	Type and length of source ATM subaddress (r)
ar$op	16 bits	Operation code (request, reply, or NAK)
ar$spln	8 bits	Length of source protocol address (s)
ar$thtl	8 bits	Type and length of target ATM number (x)
ar$tstl	8 bits	Type and length of target ATM subaddress (y)
ar$tpln	8 bits	Length of target protocol address (z)
ar$sha	q octets	Source ATM number
ar$ssa	r octets	Source ATM subaddress
ar$spa	s octets	Source protocol address
ar$tha	x octets	Target ATM number
ar$tsa	y octets	Target ATM subaddress
ar$tpa	z octets	Target protocol address

where

ar$hrd   Assigned to ATM Forum address family; it is 19 decimal (0x0013).

ar$pro   See assigned numbers for protocol type number for the protocol using ATMARP (IP is 0x0800).

ar$op   The operation type value (decimal):

ARP_REQUEST = 1
ARP_REPLY = 2
InARP_REQUEST = 8
InARP_REPLY = 9
ARP_NAK = 10

ar$spln   Length in octets of the source protocol address. For IP, ar$spln is 4.

ar$tpln   Length in octets of the target protocol address. For IP, ar$tpln is 4.

ar$sha   Source ATM number (E.164 or ATM Forum NSAPA).

ar$ssa   Source ATM subaddress (ATM Forum NSAPA).

ar$spa   Source protocol address.

ar$tha   Target ATM number (E.164 or ATM Forum NSAPA).

ar$tsa   Target ATM subaddress (ATM Forum NSAPA).

ar$tpa   Target protocol address.

ATM addresses in Q.2931 (as defined by The ATM Forum UNI 3.0 signaling specification) include a "Calling Party Number Information Element" and a "Calling Party Subaddress Information Element." These information elements (IEs) should map to ATMARP/InATMARP source ATM number and source ATM subaddress, respectively. Furthermore, ATM Forum defines a "Called Party Number Information Element" and a "Called Party Subaddress Information Element." These IEs map to ATMARP/InATMARP target ATM number and target ATM subaddress, respectively.

The ATM Forum defines three structures for the combined use of number and subaddress:

	ATM number	ATM subaddress
Structure 1	ATM Forum NSAP	Null
Structure 2	E.164	Null
Structure 3	E.164	ATM Forum NSAP

IP members must register their ATM endpoint address with their ATMARP server using the ATM address structure appropriate for their ATM network connection: i.e., LISs implemented over ATM LANs following ATM Forum UNI 3.0 should register using Structure 1; LISs implemented over an E.164 "public" ATM network should register using Structure 2. A LIS implemented over a combination of ATM LANs and public ATM networks may need to register using Structure 3. Implementations based on RFC1577 must support all three ATM address structures.

ATMARP and InATMARP requests and replies for ATM address structures 1 and 2 must indicate a null ATM subaddress; i.e., ar$sstl.type = 1 and ar$sstl.length = 0 and ar$tstl.type = 1 and ar$tstl.length = 0. When ar$sstl.length and ar$tstl.length = 0, the ar$tsa and ar$ssa fields are not present.

The ATMARP packet format presented in RFC1577 is general in nature in that the ATM number and ATM subaddress fields should map directly to the corresponding Q.2931 fields used for ATM call/connection setup signaling messages. The IP over ATM Working Group of the IETF expects ATM Forum NSAPA numbers (Structure 1) to predominate over E.164 numbers (Structure 2) as ATM endpoint identifiers within ATM LANs. The ATM Forum's VC routing specification is not complete at this time and therefore its impact on the operational use of ATM Address Structure 3 is undefined. The ATM Forum will be defining this relationship in the future. It is for this reason that IP members need to support all three ATM address structures.

7.4.9 ATMARP/InATMARP
packet encapsulation

ATMARP and InATMARP packets are to be encoded in AAL5 PDUs using LLC/SNAP encapsulation. The format of the AAL5 CPCS-SDU payload field for ATMARP/InATMARP PDUs is shown in Table 7.3.

The LLC value of 0xAA-AA-03 (3 octets) indicates the presence of a SNAP header. The OUI value of 0x00-00-00 (3 octets) indicates that the following two bytes is an Ethertype. The Ethertype value of 0x08-06 (2 octets) indicates ARP. The total size of the LLC/SNAP header is fixed at 8 octets. This aligns the start of the ATMARP packet on a 64-bit boundary relative to the start of the AAL5 CPCS-SDU.

The LLC/SNAP encapsulation for ATMARP/InATMARP presented in RFC1577 is consistent with the treatment of multiprotocol encapsulation of IP over ATM AAL5 and in the format of ATMARP over IEEE 802 networks.

Traditionally, address resolution requests are broadcast to all directly connected IP members within a LIS. It is conceivable that in the future larger-scale ATM networks may handle ATMARP requests to destinations outside the originating LIS, perhaps even globally; issues raised by ATMARPing outside the LIS or by a global ATMARP mechanism are beyond the scope of RFC1577.

7.4.10 IP broadcast address

ATM does not support broadcast addressing, therefore there are no mappings available from IP broadcast addresses to ATM broadcast services. This lack of mapping does not restrict members from transmit-

TABLE 7.3 Payload Format for ATMARP/InATMARP PDUs

LLC 0xAA-AA-03
OUI 0x00-00-00
Ethertype 0x09-06
ATMARP/InATMARP packet

ting or receiving IP datagrams specifying any of the four standard IP broadcast address forms. Members, upon receiving an IP broadcast or IP subnet broadcast for their LIS, must process the packet as if addressed to that station.

7.4.11 IP multicast address

ATM does not support multicast address services, therefore there are no mappings available from IP multicast addresses to ATM multicast services. Current IP multicast implementations (i.e., MBONE and IP tunneling) will continue to operate over ATM-based logical IP subnets if operated in the WAN configuration.

7.5 Asynchronous Transfer Mode Data Exchange Interface

This section discusses the asynchronous transfer mode data exchange interface (ATM DXI), which has been developed and promulgated by The ATM Forum.[5] The ATM DXI allows data terminal equipment (DTE) (such as a router) and data communications equipment (DCE) [such as an ATM Channel Service Unit (CSU*)] to cooperate to provide a UNI for ATM networks; this is expected to expedite introduction to ATM services

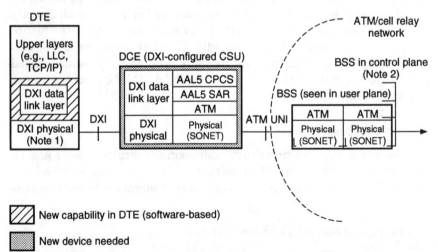

Figure 7.15 The function and role of a DXI-configured CSU. [*Note 1:* Typically preexisting physical interfaces such as V.35 and High-Speed Serial Interface (HSSI) (EIA/TIA 612/613). *Note 2:* See Fig. 4.1 for more detail. *Note 3:* Mode 1a and 1b type (see text.)]

---

*Some also use the more precise term data service unit (DSU). We use the more commonly used terminology.

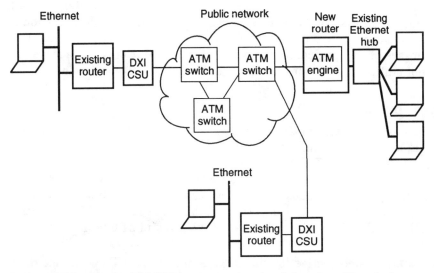

Figure 7.16 The use of a DXI CSU in a corporate network (as a transition step).

in user environments, since users do not have to completely replace existing equipment. Figure 7.15 depicts the positioning of a DXI-configured CSU in an enterprise network. Also see Fig. 7.16. The user does not have to employ this device if the user does not want to. For example, an ATM-configured router may embody all the required ATM functionality in the router. However, there are situations in which the user wants to retain an existing (but programmable) router. With this approach, the user loads appropriate software (probably supplied by the DXI CSU vendor) into the router and adds in the DXI-configured CSU, enabling the user to gain access to an ATM network. DXI-configured CSUs were used in SMDS (these CSUs implemented the SMDS protocols, though, not the ATM protocols). In SMDS a number of router vendors took this approach; others built complete routers (implementing the entire SMDS stack). Over time, the importance of DXI will decrease.

The ATM DXI defines the data link protocol and physical layers which handle data transfer between the DTE and the DCE. This enables the DTE to continue to use the protocol it has been using; the DCE provides the required functions (AAL, ATM, and PHY) to connect to an ATM network. The DXI also defines the local management interface (LMI) and management information base (MIB) for the ATM DXI. All modes of the DXI are capable of transparently supporting Service-Specific Convergence Sublayers and other higher layers. The DXI, however, addresses only the Common Part Convergence Sublayer per ITU-T Recommendation I.363. The DTE/DCE uses the V.35, EIA/TIA 449/530, and/or EIA/TIA 612/613 [high-speed serial interface (HSSI)] physical interface. This overview tutorial discussion is based completely on Ref. 5; implementers and readers who require the complete details should refer to the original ATM Forum documentation, as the description that follows is of pedagogical (not implementation) value only[*]; this material is not sufficient by itself for one to generate DXI software code.

7.5.1 DXI functions

The implementation of the ATM UNI is split between the DTE and the DCE, as illustrated in Fig. 7.17. Three operating modes (1a, 1b, and 2) have been defined. These are examined in turn.

The DXI frame address (DFA) is contained in the DXI frame header. The DFA is used to pass the ATM virtual path identifier and virtual channel identifier addressing information between the DTE and the DCE. The DFA is 10 bits in Mode 1a (and 1b) and 24 bits in Mode 2.

Mode 1a. The objective for the DTE is to transport DTE service data units via the ATM network to an appropriate peer entity. The DTE_SDU corresponds to the information field for the AAL protocol being used. With reference to Fig. 7.18, the DTE will encapsulate its DTE_SDU into a DXI frame. The DCE performs the ATM Adaptation Layer 5 Common Part Convergence Sublayer (AAL5 CPCS), functionality, AAL5 Segmentation and Reassembly (AAL5 SAR) functionality, and ATM Layer functionality, as well as the ATM UNI Physical Layer functions. Mode 1a supports (1) up to 1023 virtual connections; (2) AAL5 only; (3) up to 9232 octets (DTE_SDU); and (4) 16-bit FCS (between the DTE and DCE).

Mode 1b. This mode includes the features of Mode 1a, with the addition of support for AAL3/4 on individually configurable virtual connections. Figure 7.19 illustrates processing of AAL3/4. The DTE first performs the AAL3/4 CPCS encapsulation, then further encapsulates that AAL3/4

---

[*]This material is included with permission from The ATM Forum.

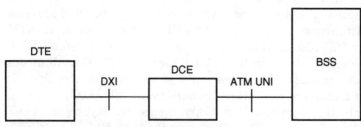

Figure 7.17 ATM DXI. (*Copyright © 1993 The ATM Forum.*)

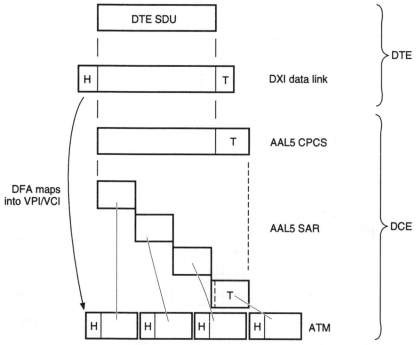

Figure 7.18 Mode 1a and Mode 1b processing for AAL5. (*Copyright © 1993 The ATM Forum.*)

CPCS_PDU into a DXI frame. The DCE then performs the AAL3/4 Segmentation and Reassembly (AAL3/4 SAR), the ATM Layer functionality, and the ATM UNI functionality. Mode 1b processing of AAL5 is as shown in Fig. 7.18. The Physical Layer functions are not shown. This mode supports up to 1023 virtual connections; it supports AAL3/4 for at least one virtual connection and AAL5 for other virtual connections. This DXI accepts up to 9232 octets (DTE_SDU) when using AAL5 and up to 9224 octets (DTE_SDU) when using AAL3/4. Sixteen-bit FCS (between the DTE and DCE) is used.

(*Note*: The DCE/DTE need only support AAL3/4 for a single VPI/VCI to be compliant. For example, it is acceptable for the DTE/DCE to support AAL3/4 only in support of a particular service across a single well-known VPI/VCI—e.g., VPI = 0, VCI = 15).

Mode 2.   The DTE performs the AAL3/4 CPCS encapsulation and further encapsulates that AAL3/4 CPCS_PDU into a DXI frame. The DCE performs one of the following:

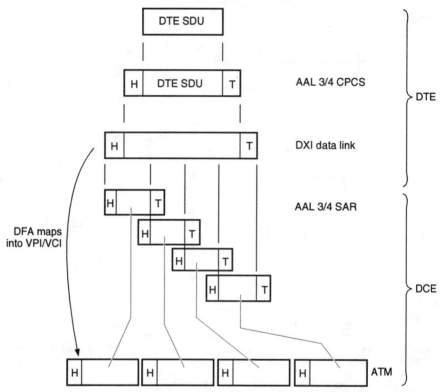

Figure 7.19 Mode 1b DXI for AAL3/4. (*Copyright © 1993 The ATM Forum.*)

1. For VPI/VCI values indicating an AAL5 virtual connection, the DCE strips off the AAL3/4 CPCS header/trailer and encapsulates the remainder of the PDU into an AAL5 CPCS_PDU as shown in Fig. 7.20. The DCE then performs the AAL5 SAR and ATM Layer functionality and the ATM UNI functionality. The Physical Layer functions are not shown.

2. For VPI/VCI values indicating an AAL3/4 virtual connection, the DCE performs AAL3/4 SAR and ATM Layer functionality as shown in Fig. 7.21, as well as ATM UNI functionality.

This mode supports up to 16,777,215 ($2^{24} - 1$) virtual connections; it supports AAL5 and AAL3/4, one per virtual connection. The DTE_SDU can be as large as 65,535 ($2^{16} - 1$) octets; it uses a 32-bit FCS between the DTE and the DCE.

7.5.2   DXI Data Link Layer protocol

The Data Link Layer defines the method by which the DXI frames and their associated addressing (DFA) are formatted for transport over the

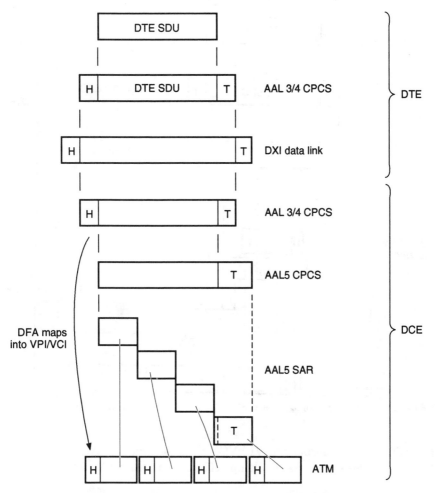

Figure 7.20   Mode 2 processing for AAL5. (*Copyright © 1993 The ATM Forum.*)

Physical Layer between the DTE and the DCE. The protocol is dependent on the mode selected, as described below.

Mode 1a.   For data transmission to the ATM network, the DTE generates the DXI header which contains the DFA, encapsulates the DTE_SDU into a DXI (data link) frame, and transports the resulting frame to the DCE. The DCE then strips off the DXI frame encapsulation to gain access to the DTE_SDU and associated DFA. The DCE encloses the DTE_SDU in an AAL5 CPCS_PDU and segments the result into AAL5 SAR_PDUs. The DTE maps (as noted in Fig. 7.23[*])

_____

*Refer to The ATM Forum specification for a detailed explanation of the fields of this data link frame.

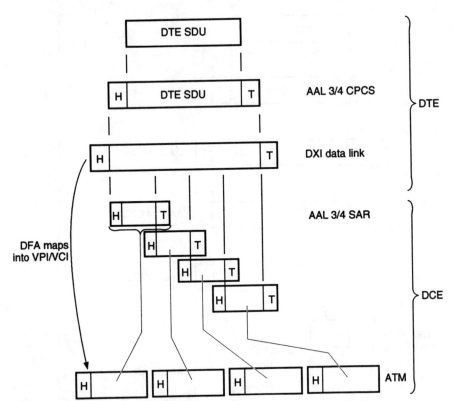

Figure 7.21   Mode 2 processing for AAL3/4. (*Copyright © 1993 The ATM Forum.*)

the DFA to the appropriate VPI/VCI, thus forming the ATM cells. The DCE then transmits the resulting ATM cells to the ATM network.

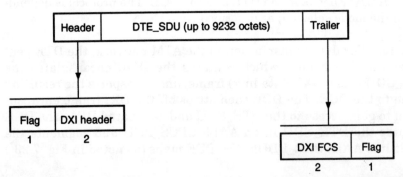

Figure 7.22   Modes 1a and 1b data link frame for AAL5. (*Copyright © 1993 The ATM Forum.*)

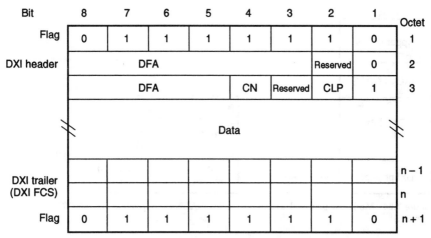

Figure 7.23   Modes 1a and 1b data link frame (detail). (*Copyright © 1993 The ATM Forum.*)

For data transmission from the ATM network to the DTE, the reverse process is followed. Figure 7.15 showed the protocol stacks, and Fig. 7.18 showed the process.

DXI frame encapsulation.   The DTE_SDU, for AAL5, is encapsulated with the DXI frame header and trailer, as shown in Fig. 7.22. (It is the intent of this encapsulation to emulate standard frame relay encapsulation. Using it as the basis advances the primary goal of the ATM DXI effort: to provide an expedient ATM access method while requiring minimal changes to the installed base of equipment.)

The flag, DXI header field, and DXI trailer field are shown in more detail in Fig. 7.23.

Mode 1b.   This mode consists of Mode 1a with the addition of support for the AAL3/4 on at least one individually configured virtual connection. With reference to Fig. 7.19, the DTE will form the AAL3/4 CPCS protocol data units, generate the associated address, encapsulate these in the DXI frame, and transport the resulting frame to the DCE. The DCE then strips off the DXI frame encapsulation to gain access to the AAL3/4 CPCS_PDU and associated DFA. The DCE segments the AAL3/4 CPCS_PDU into AAL3/4 SAR_PDUs and translates the DFA to the appropriate VPI/VCI, thus forming the ATM cells. The DCE then performs the appropriate ATM UNI processing and transmits the resulting ATM cells to the ATM network.

For data transmission from the ATM network to the DTE, the reverse process is followed. Figure 7.24 shows the protocol stacks for AAL3/4

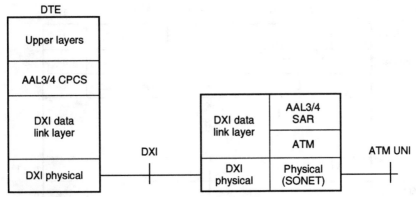

Figure 7.24 Mode 1b protocol architecture for AAL3/4. (*Copyright © 1993 The ATM Forum.*)

use. Figure 7.19 showed the process. For AAL5, the protocol stack is as in Fig. 7.15.

For Mode 1b using AAL3/4, the AAL3/4 CPSC_PDU is encapsulated with the DXI frame header and trailer as shown in Fig. 7.25.

Mode 2. For VPI/VCI values indicating an AAL5 virtual connection, the DTE forms the AAL3/4 CPCS_PDU, generates the associated address, encapsulates these in a DXI frame, and transports the resulting frame to the DCE. The DCE then strips off the DXI frame encapsulation to gain access to the AAL3/4 CPCS_PDU and associated DFA. The DCE

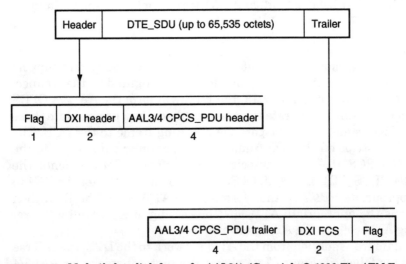

Figure 7.25 Mode 1b data link frame for AAL3/4. (*Copyright © 1993 The ATM Forum.*)

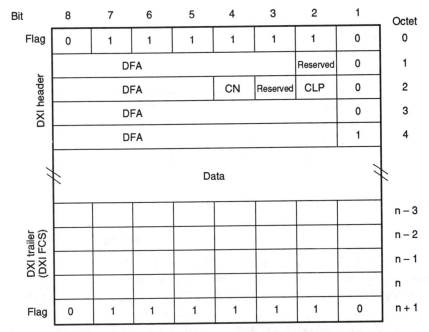

Figure 7.26 Mode 2 data link frame (detail). (*Copyright © 1993 The ATM Forum.*)

will then strip off the header/trailer of the AAL3/4 CPCS_PDU, but retain the DFA, and encapsulate the DTE_SDU within an AAL5 CPCS_PDU. Then the AAL5 SAR functions are performed. The DCE translates the DFA to the appropriate VPI/VC. The DCE then performs the ATM Physical Layer processing. The fields are shown in Fig. 7.26.

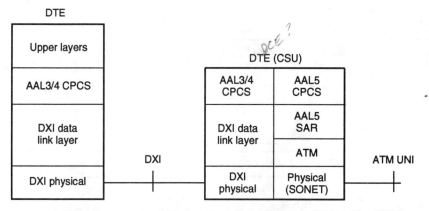

Figure 7.27 Mode 2 protocol architecture for AAL5. (*Copyright © 1993 The ATM Forum.*)

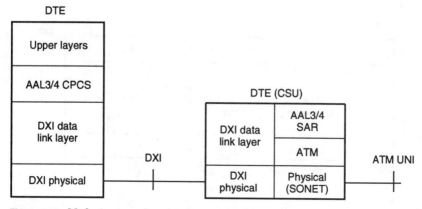

Figure 7.28 Mode 2 protocol architecture for AAL3/4. (*Copyright © 1993 The ATM Forum.*)

For data transmission from the ATM network to the DTE, the reverse process is followed. Figure 7.27 shows the protocol stack.

For VPI/VCI values indicating an AAL3/4 virtual connection, the DTE forms the AAL3/4 CPCS_PDU, generates the associated address, encapsulates these in a DXI frame, and transports the resulting frame to the DCE. The DCE then strips off the DXI frame encapsulation to gain access to the AAL3/4 CPCS_PDU and associated DFA, then performs the AAL3/4 SAR functions. The DCE then translates the DFA to the appropriate VPI/VCI. The DCE then performs the ATM Physical Layer processing.

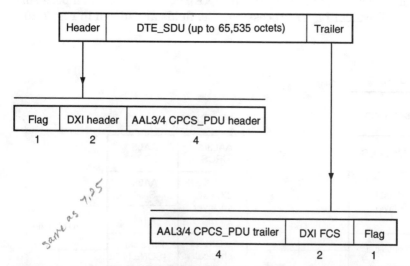

Figure 7.29 Mode 2 data link frame. (*Copyright © 1993 The ATM Forum.*)

For data transmission from the ATM network to the DTE, the reverse process is followed. Figure 7.28 shows the protocol stacks. Figure 7.21 shows the process.

DXI frame encapsulation.   The PDU is encapsulated with the DXI frame header and trailer as shown in Fig. 7.29.

The flag, DXI header, and DXI trailer fields are shown in more detail in Fig. 7.26.*

This discussion provided only an overview of DXI; implementers and readers who require the complete details should refer to Ref. 5 for a more extensive treatment of this topic.*

7.5.3 Local management interface

The ATM DXI local management interface operates in conjunction with the DXI, and it defines the protocol for exchanging management information across the DXI. The ATM DXI LMI supports exchange of DXI-specific, AAL-specific, and ATM UNI-specific management information. The DXI is the interface between a DTE (e.g., a router or hub) and the ATM DCE (e.g., a data service unit), and the ATM UNI is the user-network interface originated and terminated at the ATM DCE.

This definition of the LMI assumes a one-to-one relationship between the DXI and UNI. Other configurations require other management techniques.

The ATM DXI LMI is designed to support a management station running Simple Network Management Protocol and/or a switch running ILMI (Interim Local Management Interface). Therefore, it is assumed that an SNMP proxy agent residing in the DTE is responsible for determining when to query the ATM DCE in response to an SNMP request received from the management station. It is also assumed that an ILMI proxy agent residing in the DTE is responsible for determining when to query the ATM DCE in response to an ILMI request received from the switch. The DXI LMI protocol is a simple, adaptable, and generic means of providing the end customer with network management information that meets the needs of the application while minimizing effort and delay in realizing these requirements. This approach to the LMI does not imply compliance with the SNMP network management requirements.

References

1. TA-NWT-001110, *Broadband-ISDN Switching System Generic Requirements*, Bellcore Technical Advisory, Issue 2, Livingston, N.J., August 1993.

---

*Refer to The ATM Forum specification for a detailed explanation of the fields of this data link frame.

2. ITU-T Draft Recommendation I.555, *Frame Relaying Bearer Service Inter-working*, Geneva, Switzerland, February 1993.

3. M. Laubach, *Classical IP and ARP over ATM*, RFC1577, IETF, January 1994.

4. D. Minoli, *1st, 2nd, and Next Generation LANs*, McGraw-Hill, New York, 1994.

5. Document ATM_FORUM/93-590R1, *ATM Data Exchange Interface (DXI) Specification*, Release 0.12, June 15, 1993.

8

ATM Interworking: Support of Basic Multimedia

This chapter discusses some basic aspects of ATM support of multimedia. The presentation focuses on supporting voice requirements as well as $n \times 64$-kbits/s clear-channel service (which in turn can be used to support videoconferencing, for example, using the H.200 series of CCITT/ITU Recommendations). Much remains to be done to support general multimedia applications over ATM networks, including an assessment of the needed QOS, AAL issues (for example, to support MPEG and MPEG II video), end-end synchronization when using networks from multiple carriers (for example, spanning two or more LATAs), two-way symmetric point-to-multipoint and multipoint-to-multipoint connectivity, and cost-effectiveness factors. Yet (some) carriers are already deploying large ATM-based networks to support K-12 two-way video-based distance learning covering entire states, and business videoconfererencing networks, making this issue of multimedia support an important one. Multimedia proper, with an emphasis on communications issues and video schemes that need to be supported, has been treated in more detail in Ref. 1.

This chapter is divided into two major subsections examining two specific multimedia-related issues: (1) support of voice services (Sec. 8.1) and (2) support of $n \times 64$-kbits/s clear-channel services (Sec. 8.2). The reader may wish to skim this chapter on first reading. Detailed information is included for those readers that might have to implement such systems.

8.1   Support of Voice over ATM

This section examines how a broadband switching system can support voice communication. An overview of the various architectures for the interworking of ATM-based voice with existing voice networks, as well as the rationale for selecting a specific architecture, are presented. Functionality required in the user's equipment is discussed. Voice requirements strictly within an ATM network (i.e., ATM end-to-end without interworking) are also examined.

8.1.1   Architectures

Some multimedia applications utilizing ATM services may have a telephonic voice component that needs to be satisfied at one end outside the B-ISDN environment. Such ATM-based applications require a mechanism to interwork with existing voice services, narrowband ISDN (N-ISDN) in particular. The phrase "voice over ATM" refers here to the interworking between (1) a user accessing the network over an ATM UNI and supplying an information stream over a specified virtual connection, consisting (solely) of digitized 3.1-kHz or 7-kHz speech,[*] and (2) an ISDN-based voice network. The initial goal of this interworking is to achieve "backward compatibility" for limited voice-over-ATM capabilities; supplementary (e.g., Q.932-based) voice services over ATM are not considered.

The dynamics of user applications, CPE capabilities, CPE costs, and ATM transport costs will ultimately determine when it is economical to provide these capabilities to customers and when customers might elect to employ them. As a practical matter, voice over ATM must be cost-effective to the end user compared to separate POTS (plain old telephone service) lines terminating on the user's CPE (these costs are in the neighborhood of $25 per month plus $6 per hour).

Figure 8.1 depicts interworking at the conceptual level. An assumption made here (embodied in Fig. 8.1) is that the BSS does not directly terminate N-ISDN customers' basic rate or primary rate interfaces. This assumption implies that the BSS is not assumed to have the functionality equivalent to a Class 5 CO switch. The model is that voice is received over an ATM UNI. Another assumption is that any interworking with a POTS switch is done via a N-ISDN switch (see Fig. 8.2; this assumption is not mandatory, but it simplifies BSS and CPE requirements).

This discussion only addresses a single active voice connection over a VC in the UNI (in order not to have to worry about $n \times 64$ structured

---

[*]Other VCs on the same UNI may contain other traffic.

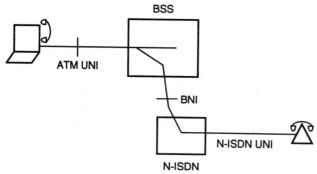

Figure 8.1   Interworking of BSS with a narrowband switch, conceptual view. BNI = broadband-to-narrowband interface.

signals, which require a more complex AAL mechanism, namely, P protocol data units and non-P protocol data units in AAL1, discussed in Chap. 3). If multiple voice connections are required, multiple VCs can be used (instead of a single VC carrying an $n \times 64$ signal).

Architecturally, the question is: What are the characteristics of the broadband-to-narrowband interface (BNI)? Such characteristics have to be specified for the User Plane of the BNI as well as for the Control Plane. Different (interworking) functionality is required in the BSS and/or N-ISDN switch, depending on the choices made. The BNI can consist of any of the following:

1. B-ISDN UNI

2. B-ISDN NNI

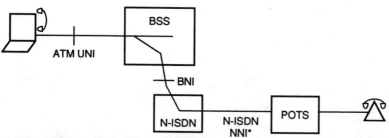

*Existing interface/specification

Figure 8.2   Interworking of a broadband switching system with a POTS switch is accomplished via a N-ISDN switch. BNI = broadband-to-narrowband interface.

3. N-ISDN UNI-like

4. N-ISDN NNI

5. Other, including proprietary

In the first instance (see Fig. 8.3), the interworking function is assumed to take place in the N-ISDN switch; Q.2931 is used between the BSS and the N-ISDN switch. Note the relaying functions both in the User Plane and in the Control Plane. The user signals the BSS; it in turn signals the N-ISDN switch using ATM protocols. Also note that the N-ISDN switch runs a stack toward the ultimate user (assuming that this is ISDN-based).

In the second instance (see Fig. 8.4), the interworking function is assumed to take place in the N-ISDN switch; the B-ISSI protocol is implemented between the BSS and the N-ISDN switch. The figure depicts Q.2931 as the protocol used, however, it can also be B-ISUP over SAAL. (Another option—not shown—is to signal outside the B-ISSI, and use instead the SS 7 network with B-ISUP over MTP 3, as discussed in Chap. 4.) The user signals the BSS; it in turn signals the N-ISDN switch using ATM protocols. Also note that the N-ISDN switch runs a stack toward the ultimate user (assuming that this is ISDN-based).

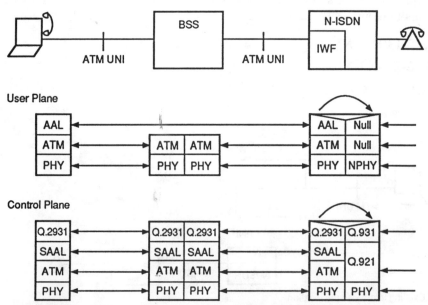

Figure 8.3 BNI implemented as a B-ISDN UNI. IWF = interworking function; NPHY = N-ISDN PHY.

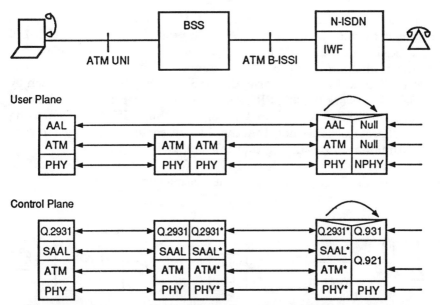

Figure 8.4 BNI implemented as a B-ISDN B-ISSI. IWF = interworking function; NPHY = N-ISDN PHY. [*B-ISSI protocol suite: Q.2931, or B-ISUP over SAAL.]

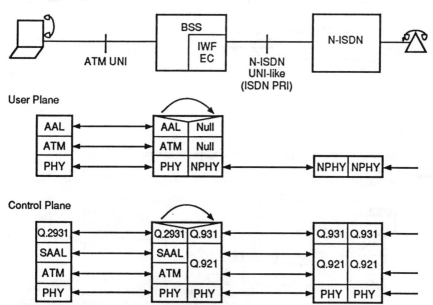

Figure 8.5 BNI implemented as a N-ISDN UNI-like. IWF = interworking function; NPHY = N-ISDN PHY; EC = echo control.

234   Chapter Eight

In the third instance (see Fig. 8.5), the interworking function is assumed to take place in the BSS. The interface is called N-ISDN UNI-like because the BSS is not expected to terminate local loops, but it can use N-ISDN UNI protocols (primary rate interface, in particular) over the trunk. In this scenario, the BSS is acting as a PBX as seen by the ISDN network (Q.931, PRI, subservient numbering, etc.). The user signals the BSS; the BSS in turn signals the N-ISDN switch using N-ISDN protocols. Also note that the N-ISDN switch runs a stack toward the ultimate user (assuming that this is ISDN-based).

This case has a variant, shown in Fig. 8.6. In this variant, the interface is seen as an ISDN primary rate interface/basic rate interface "nailed

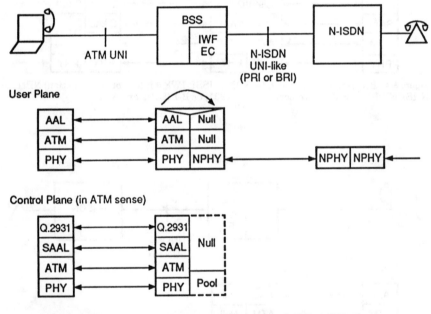

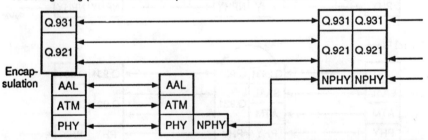

Figure 8.6 BNI implemented as a N-ISDN UNI-like with in-band ISDN signaling over the ATM access virtual channel. IWF = interworking function; NPHY = N-ISDN PHY; EC = echo control.

up" from the BSS to the ISDN switch. The user signals the BSS using Q.2931; upon such request, the BSS allocates a pre-nailed-up channel from the pool (an equivalent "derived D channel") to the user, so that the user can signal the N-ISDN switch using encapsulated N-ISDN protocols. Also note that the N-ISDN switch runs a stack toward the ultimate user (assuming that this is ISDN-based).

There is yet another variant of this scenario (not shown) in which the derived signaling channel is nailed up all the way from the user to the N-ISDN switch. (This scenario is similar to that shown in Fig. 8.6, except that the ATM Control Plane stack does not exist.) In the previous case, the user signals the BSS on demand to make available a pooled facility (i.e., a nailed-up channel from the BSS to the N-ISDN switch); in this case the PVC nailed-up signaling channel is always there.

In the fourth instance, the interworking function is assumed to take place in the BSS, using N-ISDN NNI protocols (see Fig. 8.7). This is similar to the second scenario, except that the interworking burden is placed on the BSS. The user signals the BSS using Q.2931; upon such request, the BSS signals the N-ISDN switch over SS 7 links to establish the voice call. Also note that the N-ISDN switch runs a stack toward the ultimate user (assuming that this is ISDN-based).

Lastly, vendor-proprietary methods could be used, as depicted in Fig. 8.8. The user signals the BSS using Q.2931; upon such request, the BSS

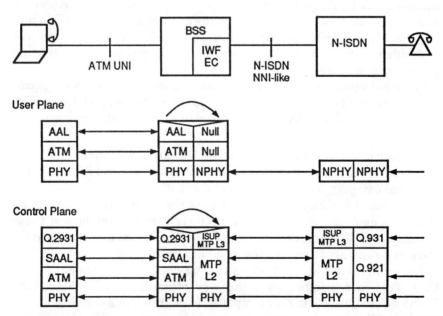

Figure 8.7   BNI implemented as a N-ISDN NNI-like. IWF = interworking function; NPHY = N-ISDN PHY; EC = echo control.

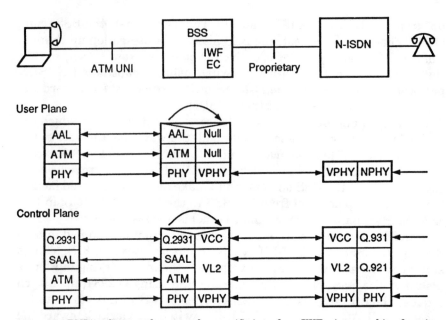

Figure 8.8 BNI implemented as a vendor-specific interface. IWF = interworking function; NPHY = N-ISDN PHY; VCC = vender-specific call control; VL2 = vendor-specific Layer 2; VPHY = vendor-specific PHY; EC = echo control.

signals the N-ISDN switch using a proprietary protocol stack. Also note that the N-ISDN switch runs a stack toward the ultimate user (assuming that this is ISDN-based). Notice that this approach requires the embedded N-ISDN switch to support this (new) protocol, necessitating some sort of upgrade.

There is a variant of this scenario (not shown) in which the vendor-specific protocol runs end-to-end, namely, directly between the user and the N-ISDN switch (in this case the BSS is not involved in voice-related signaling).

Discussion of Scenarios. Each of these scenarios has advantages and disadvantages. These advantages and disadvantages can fit either in a technical category, a business category, or both.

The scenario of Figs. 8.3 and 8.4 puts the interworking burden on currently deployed switches. It is unlikely that the vendors of these switches can be persuaded to make the necessary investment in hardware and software to ensure this compatibility.

The scenario of Fig. 8.5 places the interworking requirement on the BSS. This is consistent with the way other types of interworking functions currently being contemplated (e.g., frame relay) will be implemented. This scenario is the recommended approach. In the User Plane, access is accomplished by pseudo-circuit emulation[*] of individual speech-oriented bearer channels using AAL capabilities in the CPE and at the BSS. The user needs to employ Q.2931 signaling in the ATM Control Plane. Interworking of the signaling channel (Q.2931 to Q.931) occurs at the BSS. The narrowband bearer capability (N-BC) information element (IE) must be included in the broadband SETUP message; this IE will be used by the BSS to launch a N-ISDN SETUP message (this functionality is currently supported in Q.2931, but not in the ATM Forum's SETUP message shown in Chap. 4). The BNI is an ISDN circuit-switched primary rate bearer channel. One of the disadvantages of this scenario is that the BSS must play a role in the call setup process by intercepting, converting, and interpreting the narrowband signaling messages, as implied by the Control Plane stack shown in Fig. 8.5.

The scenario of Fig. 8.6 is similar to the scenario of Fig. 8.5, except that a pseudo-circuit-emulated connection is supported transparently through the BSS between the user equipment and the N-ISDN switch. This user-to-N-ISDN transparent channel is set up between the user and the BSS over a signaling path that *terminates in the BSS* (thus, B-ISDN-to-N-ISDN signaling interworking is not supported in the BSS). Note that the user station still needs to support Q.2931. It is assumed that a pool of (pre-)nailed-up DS0 channels exists between the BSS and the N-ISDN switch. A trunk is selected by the BSS to establish the transparent path from the user to the N-ISDN switch. After the path is set up, the user initiates an in-band N-ISDN signaling exchange with the N-ISDN switch. The disadvantage of this approach is that the user equipment now needs to support *both signaling stacks* (one for B-ISDN and one for N-ISDN). Another possibility emerges from this discussion (not shown in Fig. 8.6, but already alluded to): Have a few DS0 VCs predefined (i.e., PVC-like) from the user, through the BSS, to the N-ISDN to be used to establish voice calls; this requires the user to have a Q.931 stack but not a Q.2931 stack active in the voice station (presumably the user would have a Q.2931 stack somewhere, given that the user is a B-ISDN user by assumption).

The scenario of Fig. 8.7 is a more sophisticated version of the scenario of Fig. 8.6, as the N-ISDN switch treats the BSS as a peer switch, via a

---

[*]As noted in Sec. 4.4.1, the AAL subtype for an AAL1 connection (first defined in Table 1.2) supports the following encodings: "null," "voice–based on 64 kbits/s," "circuit emulation (synchronous)," "circuit emulation (asynchronous)," "high-quality audio," and "video." We refer here to the "voice–based on 64 kbits/s" and the "high-quality audio" capabilities, used in conjunction with a CBR traffic type and a BCOB-A bearer class, as pseudo-circuit emulation; this nomenclature distinguishes these cases from the other four AAL subtypes in the CBR/BCOB-A arrangement (and, clearly, from BCOB-C or BCOB-X bearer classes and/or from VBR traffic types).

NNI, rather than as a simple PBX-like concentrator. However, the protocol machinery is more complex.

The scenario of Fig. 8.8 has the disadvantage of being vendor-specific, thereby limiting global interoperability.

Recommended architecture.   Based on this discussion, the scenario of Fig. 8.5 is the approach to take to support voice over ATM. See Table 8.1.

AAL issues.   Figure 8.5 shows that AAL capabilities are needed in both the CPE and the BSS. At press time, standards groups had not settled on a choice of AAL type for voice service. AAL Type 1 provides cell sequencing for lost/misinserted cell detection and (optionally) timing recovery (using the synchronous residual time stamp, or SRTS, technique) for applications that have stringent jitter requirements. (This was covered in Chap. 3.)

AAL Type 1 provides more-than-sufficient error protection and timing recovery functions to support voice. With the very low cell loss/misinsertion ratios expected in ATM networks, error detection is not considered necessary for single-channel voice support. Also, at 64 kbits/s, synchronous clock recovery may not be necessary for voice. Instead, receiver-specific methods of recovering timing from buffer fill observation may suffice. Thus, from a technical point of view, AAL Type 1 functions may not be strictly necessary for voice. However, even if these capabilities are not strictly needed for voice, it may make sense to use AAL1 coding so that all DS0 signals have the same payload/cell rates. Specifically, 64-kbits/s unrestricted digital information (data) will presumably take advantage of AAL1 error detection. Thus, in order not to have different cell rates for 64-kbits/s voice and 64-kbits/s data, it may make sense to

TABLE 8.1 Proposed BNI for Voice over ATM at the Physical Architecture Level

Interworking capability:

- Located at the BSS
- Broadband-to-narrowband interface defined to be an ISDN PRI
- BSS looks like a PBX to N-ISDN

User Plane access:

- Pseudo-circuit emulation using AAL1 capabilities in the CPE and at the BSS (AAL-supported BCOB-A CBR path between CPE and BSS)
- ISDN circuit-switched primary rate channel between BSS and the N-ISDN switch

Signaling: User employs Q.93B signaling in ATM Control Plane

- Bearer capability IE included in the broadband SETUP message
- Bearer capability IE used by the BSS to launch a N-ISDN SETUP message

use AAL1 coding for voice for commonality. The costs of using SRTS compared with those of receiver-specific timing recovery methods for voice are not yet well understood.

As noted, the AAL1 functionality supports a Structured capability in order to establish the boundaries of a group of octets, for example in the $n \times 64$ kbits/s case. This is a more complicated framing protocol that utilizes alternating non-P and P protocol data units. The P protocol data units provide a pointer which indicates the beginning of the structure of octets (these issues were discussed in Chap. 3). Given the assumption of carrying a single voice channel over a VC, the Structured mechanism is not required.

In conclusion, AAL1 without Structure support can be used. Explicit source clock frequency recovery mechanisms do not have to be used for single-channel 64-kbits/s voice signals. Instead, a receive buffer may be used to smooth out cell delay variations; the buffer may impose some fixed maximum delay (of the order of 2 to 4 ms) for this smoothing function without introducing adverse delay problems, particularly when the partial-fill method described below is utilized. (*Note*: When cells are filled with 16 octets of speech, cells arrive at a rate of one cell every 2 ms or two cells every 4 ms; this allows the buffer mechanism at the receiving station a certain amount of slack in reading out cells at a constant rate.)

ATM cell fill issues.   Figure 8.5 shows that ATM capabilities are needed in both the CPE and the BSS. This section examines issues associated with the transport of speech information; the material could have been included in the next section, on CPE, but the choice was made to cover it here.

Two candidate solutions are feasible:[2]

- *Partial cell fill.* The broadband voice interworking unit (IWU) at the CPE or at the interface to a narrowband network would partially fill cells with less than the 47 (or 48) cell payload octets available. A value of 16-octet cell payload filling introduces a 4-ms round-trip delay as a result of cell construction. This delay would be considered acceptable.

- *Full cell fill.* The broadband voice interworking unit at the CPE (and at the interface to a narrowband network) would fill cells with 47 octets (voice samples). This would introduce a round-trip delay of approximately 12 ms, and will require echo cancellation at the IWU between the broadband and narrowband networks.

  Echo cancelers compute an echo estimate for each direction of a voice channel. This estimate is then subtracted (i.e., removed) from the send-path signal; this cancels the echo and leaves only the near-end speech to be transmitted to the distant end. Typically the canceler constructs a mathematical echo estimate on the near-end path after 200 ms worth of speech.

There are advantages and disadvantages to both approaches. The discussion that follows focuses on these considerations, followed by the suggested approach.

Partial fill with only 16 cells could be justified as follows: ATM is characterized by a degree of overhead, not only at the AAL level, but also at the ATM, at the transmission convergence (mapping), and at the physical medium–dependent (SONET) levels. STS-3c has 27 octets of overhead 8000 times a second, or about 2 Mbits/s. Additional overhead may be encountered in the cell mapping procedure. Another 14 Mbits/s (approximately) of overhead is generated at the ATM Layer. Another potential 3 Mbits/s (approximately) of overhead is generated by the AAL1 protocol, for an approximate total of 19 Mbits/s on a STS-3c UNI. While a sense of efficiency and elegance would ostensibly suggest filling the voice cells, at the practical level, this efficiency may be of limited practical consequence compared to the 19 Mbits/s of already existing overhead. Carrying a single voice channel over the UNI would produce additional overhead of 128 kbits/s [instead of 8000/47 = 170 fully filled cells per second, we now need to send 8000/16 = 500 partially filled cells, for a penalty of (500*47 − 170*47)*8 = 128 kbits/s]. Compared to 20 Mbits/s, 128 kbits/s is a trivial incremental percentage of overhead, namely (20.12 − 20)/20 or 0.6 percent more. Carrying 10 voice channels over the UNI would produce additional overhead of 1.3 Mbits/s. Comparing 1.3 Mbits/s to 20 Mbits/s gives an incremental percentage of (21.3 − 20)/20 or 6.5 percent more. Carrying 20 voice channels over the UNI would produce additional overhead of 2.6 Mbits/s. Comparing 2.6 Mbits/s to 20 Mbits/s gives an incremental percentage of (22.6 − 20)/20, or 13 percent more. Additionally, the overhead affects the access line, which, in practice, already allocates the bandwidth, whether it is utilized or not.

Given these observations, one simple approach to voice interworking would be to carry cells with 16-octet fill. This approach eliminates much of the cellularization delay at the source. The BSS can pipeline the voice octets to the N-ISDN switch, eliminating the need for BSS-based echo cancellation functions resulting from the delays incurred by the cellularization process (more on this below). *This approach eliminates the need to deploy echo cancelers in conjunction with the voice interworking function at the BSS.* This approach would make sense when the volume of internetworked voice over ATM is small, as indications are (multimedia use of ATM will eventually generate more voice, but this will probably be carried end-to-end over ATM).

Using 47-octet cell fill (full fill) entails the additional complexity and cost of echo cancellation. The considerations for choosing between partial fill and full cell fill (with echo cancelers) are discussed below.

Time to market.   Partial fill is easier to implement than full cell fill (from a network equipment perspective). Thus, it is reasonable to assume that systems implementing partial fill could be commercially available before systems employing echo cancelers to achieve full cell fill.

Initial equipment costs.   The impact of either option on CPE that supports single-channel voice (e.g., a multimedia workstation on an ATM LAN or an MCU associated with an ATM UNI) should be minimal. It is not unreasonable for CPE to be able to support either full or partial fill. It is expected that multimedia terminals on ATM LANs will probably use audio of higher than telephony quality (for intra-LAN networking), either multiplexed together with other media (as in H.261) or in fully filled cells.

The impact on network equipment is clear: Full cell fill requires the implementation of an echo cancellation function at the point of interworking between the broadband and narrowband networks, whereas partial fill does not. 1980s-vintage stand-alone echo cancelers operate on an entire T1 transmission system and cost approximately $1500 to $2000 (that is, approximately $60 to $80 per circuit). However, most of this cost has little to do with the actual echo cancellation (DSP) function; these stand-alone devices must (1) have their own power supplies, cases, etc.; (2) terminate and regenerate a DS1 signal; and (3) support external (maintenance) interfaces. At least one switch manufacturer has integrated echo canceler functions directly into (toll switch) trunk interface circuits, at a far lower per-line cost. An estimate of the (integrated) cost increment associated with echo cancellation is $10 to $40 per circuit (inversely related to the number of circuits sharing a single DSP echo canceler). In the architecture advocated in this paper, these narrowband circuits are used as part of a BSS-to-ISDN CO interface, and are thus shared (like trunk circuits) by all potential voice-over-ATM users. Assuming a typical 5:1 line-to-trunk ratio, this implies that the incremental equipment costs of full cell fill amount to $2 to $8 per equivalent voice line.

The echo control function must be integrated into the ATM-to-narrowband interworking equipment (that is, one should not have to rely on utilizing stand-alone echo cancelers in conjunction with the ATM-to-narrowband interworking equipment). It is not strictly required that echo cancellation functions be performed at this interworking point; however, looking into the ATM-to-narrowband interface from a suitable (i.e., impairment-free) ATM reference point, the equivalent echo return loss on any connection should exceed 30 dB. In practice, this may necessitate the use of echo cancelers integrated into the interworking function. If echo cancelers are included at the interworking point, they should have the following properties:

- They should conform to CCITT Recommendation G.165.
- The cancellation function is to be performed in one direction of transmission only. That is, the echo to be canceled is the far-end echo, if present.
- The echo cancelers should be capable of handling echoes with a tail delay of at least 32 ms.
- The BSS must be able to either (1) disable the echo canceler associated with any narrowband circuit or (2) route around the canceler-equipped circuits based on the bearer capability specified in the bearer capability IE (this is important not for voice transport but for ATM-to-narrowband data interworking).

Usage costs.   From both a carrier and an end-user perspective, full fill and partial fill are roughly equivalent in terms of usage. Partial fill "wastes" approximately 128 kbits/s per voice channel, but this is a relatively trivial amount if the true application for initial voice over ATM is backward compatibility with N-ISDN for low volumes of traffic. If the volume of traffic were high, it would be in the end user's best interest to have full cell fill, since the 128 kbits/s waste is incurred (in this architecture) solely on the user's access line.

To summarize this discussion, partial fill has the advantages of potentially earlier commercial availability and slightly lower per-line network equipment costs, whereas full cell fill has the advantage of using less bandwidth over the UNI. CPE should be capable of implementing either, or even both.

8.1.2 User equipment needed

AAL and ATM fill.   These issues are identical to those described for the BSS.

Voice digitization.   To properly support voice in an ATM environment, the user's terminal equipment must meet several functional requirements. First, to ensure compatibility with existing networks, the terminal equipment must support standard 64-kbits/s mu-law PCM encoding (ITU Recommendation G.711). CPE may optionally support 7-kHz audio (ITU Recommendation G.722). *Note*: Other voice coding schemes (e.g., G.721/ADPCM; J.41/15-kHz PCM; J.42/7-kHz PCM) are also possible.

Echo control in CPE. In a traditional telephone network, echo arises in the form of reflected energy back to the user when there is a mismatch of impedance of an analog loop termination (e.g., at the two to four wire hybrid). If the path is sufficiently short that the propagation delay is small, then the echo will reach the user quickly enough not to cause a problem (the propagation delay is 1/186 ms/mi). Delay can also be introduced by signal processing equipment (e.g., A/D conversion, buffering, switching, etc.). If the path includes several pieces of equipment which raise the delay to several milliseconds, then echo can begin to become a problem. Finally, there may be far-end injection of signal: for example, when the sender's voice is delivered over a full-duplex speakerphone, some of the output signal is picked up by the speakerphone's microphone and returned to the sender tens of milliseconds later.

Since the architecture discussed in this chapter is completely digital, the issues of impedance mismatch are not critical contributing factors. However, the buffering of the voice before it is sent onto the UNI could become a problem if

1. The digitized buffered signal is applied to the earpiece of the handset at the same time it is transmitted on the UNI. (This should not occur, since it does not make sense to convert the voice to a digital signal, then buffer it to cellularize it, then reconvert it in order to apply it to the earpiece; the earpiece signal should come directly from the handset without further processing. Even if the signal is applied at transmission time, it should not constitute a problem if the buffering time is only 4 ms or thereabouts.)

2. The signal is reinserted at the remote end and carried all the way back to the sender. Two mitigating factors come into play: (a) Even if the signal was reinjected, it should not constitute a problem if the buffering time is only 4 ms or thereabouts, so that the round-trip delay is small, and (b) Specifications for echo control are utilized in the design of the CPE.

To ensure that the far-end user experiences acceptable performance, the terminal equipment should be designed to meet the specification for echo control set forth in EIA/TIA-579,[3] which requires the weighted acoustic echo path loss (a measure of the attenuation of echoed signals) of the digital telephone set to be at least 45 dB. Transmit/receive loudness rating should also be consistent with EIA/TIA-579.[3]

8.1.3 Summary of requirements to support Interworking

CPE. The user's terminal equipment must be able to construct protocol data units for the following User Plane protocol stack:

AAL   AAL1 without Structure. Explicit source clock frequency recovery mechanisms are not used; instead, a receive buffer (imposing some fixed maximum delay) is used to smooth out cell delay variations.

ATM   Full fill of 47 speech octets per cell; 1 voice channel per VC.

PHY   Same PHY employed in the user's UNI.

The user's voice equipment (or the adjunct station of which the voice unit is part must be able to construct protocol data units for the following Control Plane protocol stack:

Q.2931   Call control capabilities with support for N-ISDN bearer capability.

SAAL   SSCF, SSCOP, AAL5 Common Part.

ATM   Normal operation.

PHY   Same PHY employed in the user's UNI.

The CPE must be designed to follow the following specification:

Echo control   Meet the specification set forth in EIA/TIA-579.

Network and network interface requirements. In summary, the network must support a SVC ATM UNI with a voice CPE meeting the requirements described above. Interworking is to be supported at the BSS. AAL1 must be supported. Full cell fill is utilized. Buffers are provided to support smoothing in order to meet cell delay variation tolerance requirements. Lost cells are replaced with dummy cells at the interworking unit.

Note: Full cell fill with AAL Type 1 format will require echo cancelers. These can be located at the interworking site, as described above.

The equivalent echo return loss on any connection should exceed 30 dB. If echo cancelers are included at the interworking point, they should have the following properties: (1) they should conform to ITU Recommendation G.165; (2) the cancellation function is to be performed in one direction of transmission only; (3) the echo cancelers should be capable of handling echoes with a tail delay of at least 32 ms; and (4) the BSS must be able to disable the echo canceler associated with any narrowband circuit, or route around the canceler-equipped circuits based on the bearer capability specified in the bearer capability IE.

More specifically, one has the following requirements:

UNI User Plane capabilities at BSS. In the origination-to-destination path, the IWU must be able to disassemble protocol data units built on the following User Plane protocol stack, for usage by the interworking relaying function:

AAL	AAL 1 without Structure. Explicit source clock frequency recovery mechanisms are not used; instead, a receive buffer (imposing some fixed maximum delay) is used to smooth out cell delay variations.
ATM	Full fill of 47 speech octets per cell; 1 voice channel per VC.
PHY	Same PHY employed in the user's UNI.

In the destination-to-origination path, the IWU must be able to assemble protocol data units built on the User Plane protocol stack just shown (for usage by the interworking relaying function).

UNI Control Plane capabilities at BSS. In the origination-to-destination path, the IWU must be able to disassemble protocol data units built on the following Control Plane protocol stack, for usage by the interworking relaying function:

Q.2931	Call control capabilities with support for N-ISDN bearer capability.
SAAL	SSCF, SSCOP, AAL5 Common Part.
ATM	Normal operation.
PHY	Same PHY employed in the user's UNI.

In the destination-to-origination path, the IWU must be able to assemble protocol data units built on the Control Plane protocol stack just shown (for usage by the interworking relaying function).

BNI User Plane capabilities at BSS. In the origination-to-destination path, the IWU must be able to disassemble protocol data units built on the following User Plane protocol stack toward the N-ISDN switch, for usage by the interworking relaying function:

PHY	ISDN circuit-switched primary rate bearer channel—ISDN User Plane.

In the destination-to-origination path, the IWU must be able to assemble protocol data units built on the User Plane protocol stack just shown (for usage by the interworking relaying function).

BNI Control Plane capabilities at BSS. In the origination-to-destination path, the IWU must be able to disassemble protocol data units built on the following Control Plane protocol stack, for usage by the interworking relaying function:

Q.931   UNI requests are mapped to N-ISDN call control protocols using the bearer capability obtained over the ATM UNI.

Q.921   Normal operation.

PHY   ISDN circuit-switched primary rate bearer channel—ISDN Control Plane.

In the destination-to-origination path, the IWU must be able to assemble protocol data units built on the Control Plane protocol stack just shown (for usage by the interworking relaying function).

8.1.4 Voice entirely within an ATM network

There are cases in which one wants to support voice entirely within an ATM network (i.e., ATM end-to-end without interworking). The current implicit assumption is that multimedia over ATM will be supported by CPE multiplexing of the video, voice, image, and data components. See Fig. 1.16 for an example. This predicament arises from the fact that no synchronization of distinct VCs is currently supported by network elements. Even VCs within a given VP are not necessarily guaranteed to be temporally synchronized. It appears likely that for many real-time multimedia applications, AAL1 will be used. Store-and-forward multimedia applications (e.g., messaging) could use AAL5 or some other adaptation protocol.

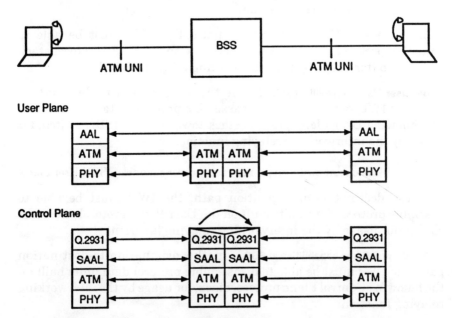

Figure 8.9 Voice support within an ATM network.

A voice call that is not part of a multimedia session can be supported over an ATM UNI to another ATM UNI, generally using the same techniques discussed earlier. Figure 8.9 depicts the architectural view. The key aspects of voice support are as follows:

- The originator uses Q.2931 signaling in the Control Plane to establish the end-to-end bidirectional symmetric SVC connection (see the next section for some information on the encoding of fields in the SETUP message).

- Voice samples are produced according to G.711, echo control according to EIA/TIA-579.

- Both originator and receiver utilize AAL1 over ATM in the User Plane, with receive-end buffering for timing.

- There is full fill of 47 speech octets per cell, with one voice channel per VC.

- The network does not provide any echo cancellation (full-duplex speakerphones must provide adequate echo management to avoid reinjection of signal).

In the interworking case discussed earlier, the BSS recognized the request over the UNI as a voice request by the presence of the narrow-band bearer capability IE. This IE is utilized by the N-ISDN switch to complete the call. This IE is not strictly necessary for a voice connection that is entirely provided over ATM. However, if the narrowband bearer capability IE is not utilized, another mechanism may be required to identify the VC as a voice-carrying VC: although the BSS does not necessarily need to know the nature of the VC content, the receiving equipment, which supports multiple VCs over the interface, needs to know that AAL1 logic must be provided on top of the local ATM Layer for this particular VC (other AALs may be active for other VCs over the UNI). One mechanism is to make the AAL parameters IE mandatory for voice-carrying channels; the subtype field can be coded for voiceband based on 64 kbits/s (see Sec. 4.4.1). However, many of the other fields in this IE are not needed (they are needed for more general $n \times 64$ channels using clock recovery). This implies some inefficiency. Another way to identify VCs as voice-carrying channels would be to reserve a small number of VCs per interface for voice applications.

As implied above, the AAL parameters IE for the voice-over-ATM case (i.e., as in Fig. 8.5) may be sent for the purpose of setting up the VC between the user equipment and the interworking point. In the case considered in this section, the AAL parameters IE is sent end-to-end (see Chap. 4).

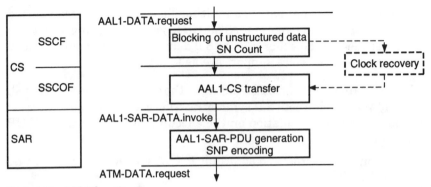

Figure 8.10 AAL1 functions.

8.1.5 Signaling considerations

Voice ATM Adaptation Layer functions. Efforts have been underway to define adaptation functions for a number of "services," such as, signaling, SMDS, etc. Chapter 3 indicated that adaptation functions can be divided into CS and SAR. CS has been further subdivided into two sublayers: SSCOF (Service-Specific Connection-oriented Function) and SSCF (Service-Specific Coodination Function). See Fig. 8.10.

Some key AAL1 functions are

- *The blocking/count process.* This assembles 376-bit (47-octet) AAL1_SDUs into an AAL1_CS_PDU and generates a sequence count value (SN) associated with each AAL1_CS_PDU.

- The *clock recovery process.*

- *The AAL1-CS transfer process.* This assembles the AAL1_CS_PDU components to pass them to the AAL1-SAR within an AAL1-SAR-DATA.signal primitive. The CSI (if used) is assigned at this point.

- *The AAL1_SAR_PDU generation process.* This accepts AAL1-SAR-DATA.invoke primitives from the AAL1-CS transfer process and (1) constructs AAL1_SAR_PDUs from the component parts and (2) generates the ATM-DATA.request primitives.

- *The SNP encoding process.* This generates the SNP field to protect the SN field against bit errors.

To support voice, one effectively needs to specify a voice-based AAL (VAAL). Such a VAAL may have the following features:

The *Sending* VAAL's SSCF supports the blocking /count process but not the clock recovery process.

The *Sending* VAAL's SSCOF supports the transfer process.

The *Sending* VAAL's SAR supports the PDU generation process and the SNP encoding process.

The *Receiving* VAAL's SAR supports a PDU receiving process and a SNP error check process.

The *Receiving* VAAL's SSCOF supports a SN checking process and a "concealment" process of repeating the last PDU if a cell is lost.

The *Receiving* VAAL's SSCF supports a locally timed buffering process used to achieve clocking and a deblocking process.

SETUP message IE encodings.   Certain key IEs in the SETUP message need to be coded specifically for voice.

Broadband bearer capability IE.   Coded as follows:
  Bearer class = BCOB-A
  Traffic type = CBR
  Timing requirements = End-to-end timing not required

Bearer capability IE.   If used, this IE will be coded consistent with the Q.931 rules.

ATM user cell rate.   Forward and backward peak cell rate are coded as 173 cells per second.

QOS class.   Code for the highest class.

AAL parameters.   Code as follows:
  AAL type = AAL 1
  Subtype = Voice band based on 64 kbits/s, or high-quality audio
  CBR rate = 64 kbits/s
  Clock recovery = Null
  Structured data transfer = Null
  Error correction = Null

All other pertinent fields (call reference, called party number, calling party number, etc.). Consistent with Q.2931 specifications.

8.1.6   Supporting voice over a non-N-ISDN far-end platform

Figure 8.2 depicted interworking of the BSS with a POTS switch via a N-ISDN "intermediary." In some cases this N-ISDN capability may not exist; a BSS-to-POTS interface may be needed. Figure 8.11 depicts the proposed arrangement. (It assumes that the switch is digital.)

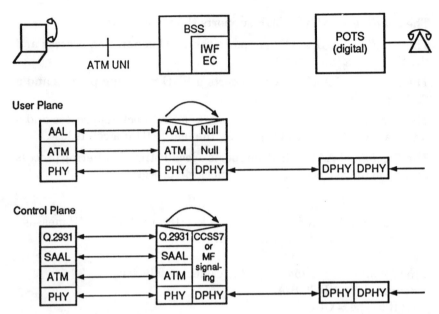

Figure 8.11 Support of ATM-to-POTS voice. IWF = interworking function; EC = echo control; DPHY = DS0-based Physical Layer.

The User Plane interworking function is similar to that described in Fig. 8.5 except that DS0s rather than B channels are utilized (the user-to-BSS interface is identical to that of Fig. 8.5). The Control Plane BSS interworking functions over the BSS-to-POTS interface must support a traditional signaling apparatus: the signaling can be in-band (associated) MF or can be via CCSS7. The Control Plane user-to-BSS interface is similar to that described earlier; the AAL parameters IE is utilized to set up the VC between the user and the interworking point in the BSS. Echo control is needed in the BSS.

8.2   Interworking with Narrowband ISDN

One wants to be able to interwork a broadband switching system to N-ISDN in order to support $n \times 64$-kbits/s services—for example, for ITU H.200-based videoconferencing. Architectural issues, signaling considerations that need to be taken into account, and the ITU-T's view on providing 64-kbits/s circuit-mode ISDN services are examined in this section. The purpose of the section is to identify technical solutions for this internetworking functions needed by the N-ISDN interworking unit (N-IWU) located at the BSS.

8.2.1 Architectures

Some multimedia applications utilizing ATM services may have a component that needs to be satisfied over N-ISDN; examples include H.261 videoconferencing, voice, and other sub-DS1 usages. Such ATM-based applications require a mechanism to interwork seamlessly with existing N-ISDN services. The phrase "N-ISDN over ATM" refers here to the interworking between (1) a user accessing the network over an ATM UNI and supplying an information stream over a specified VC, consisting of a circuit-emulated* data stream and (2) an N-ISDN network.

Note: Other VCs on the same UNI may contain other traffic.

Figure 8.12 depicts interworking at the conceptual level. The assumption embodied in Fig. 8.12 is that the BSS does not directly terminate N-ISDN customers' basic rate or primary rate UNIs. The model is that circuit-emulated $n \times$ 64-kbits/s ($2 \le n \le 24$) information is received over an ATM UNI.

As in the voice case, the BNI can consist of any of the following:

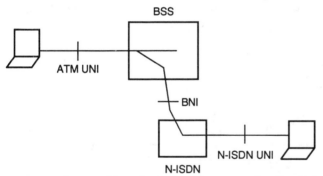

Figure 8.12 Interworking of a BSS with a narrowband switch, conceptual view. BNI = broadband-to-narrowband interface.

---

*The AAL subtype for an AAL1 connection supports a "null" encoding plus the following encodings: "voice–based on 64 kbits/s," "circuit emulation (synchronous)," "circuit emulation (asynchronous)," "high-quality audio," and "video." Hence, when the subtype is not "voice–based on 64 kbits/s," "high-quality audio," or "video," only three options remain: "null," "circuit emulation (synchronous)," and "circuit emulation (asynchronous)." *Circuit emulation* is used here to describe an AAL1 connection with a CBR traffic type and a BCOB-A bearer class. Alternatively, one would have to employ the phraseology "CBR-based BCOB-A VC with null AAL1 subtype."

Some have used circuit emulation to refer to a capability where all the Physical Layer from one system such as DS1, including the user-transparent information (e.g., transmission overhead; alarms; operations, administration, and maintenance information) is encapsulated along with the user information. Since the 64-kbits/s clear-channel interworking does not include transmission-channel overhead, this formulation of the definition would not apply. However, in this discussion, the more tightly defined meaning of circuit emulation implied by the previous discussion is employed.

1. B-ISDN UNI

2. B-ISDN NNI

3. N-ISDN UNI-like

4. N-ISDN NNI

5. Other, including proprietary

In the first instance (scenario 1), the interworking function is assumed to take place in the N-ISDN switch; ATM UNI protocols are used between the BSS and the N-ISDN switch. This entails a relaying function in both the User Plane and the Control Plane. The user signals the BSS; the BSS in turn signals the N-ISDN switch using ATM protocols. Also note that the N-ISDN switch runs a stack toward the ultimate user.

In the second instance (scenario 2), the interworking function is assumed to take place in the N-ISDN switch; the B-ISSI protocol is implemented between the BSS and the N-ISDN switch. Q.2931 can be used in the signaling plane, however, B-ISUP over SAAL may also be used (another option is to signal outside the B-ISSI, and use instead the SS 7 network with B-ISUP over MTP 3; also refer to Chap. 4). The user signals the BSS; the BSS in turn signals the N-ISDN switch using ATM

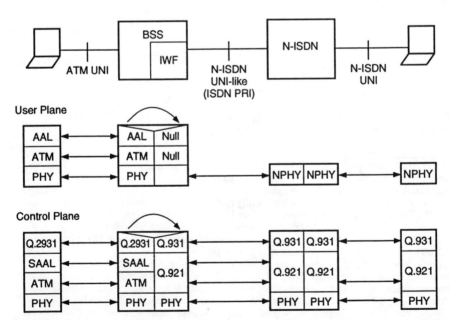

Figure 8.13   BNI implemented as a N-ISDN UNI-like. IWF = interworking function; NPHY = N-ISDN PHY.

protocols. Also note that the N-ISDN switch runs a stack toward the ultimate user.

In the third instance (scenario 3, depicted in Fig. 8.13), the interworking function is assumed to take place in the BSS. The interface is called N-ISDN UNI-like because the BSS is not expected to terminate local loops, but it can use N-ISDN UNI protocols (primary rate interface, in particular) over the trunk. In this scenario, the BSS is acting as a PBX as seen by the N-ISDN network (Q.931, PRI, subservient numbering, etc.). The user signals the BSS; the BSS in turn signals the N-ISDN switch using N-ISDN protocols. Also note that the N-ISDN switch runs a stack toward the ultimate user. Once the path is established, the N-IWU translates the circuit-emulated stream into a bit stream that is applied directly to a "real" $n \times 64$-kbits/s channel (from a pool of channels available between the BSS and the N-ISDN switch).

This case has a variant (scenario 3a): The interface is seen as an ISDN primary rate interface/basic rate interface "nailed up" via circuit emulation from end user to ISDN switch. The user signals the BSS using ATM protocols; upon such request, the BSS allocates a pre-nailed-up channel from the pool (an equivalent "derived D channel") to the user, so that the user can signal the N-ISDN switch using encapsulated N-ISDN protocols. There is yet another variant of this scenario (scenario 3b) in which the derived signaling channel is nailed up all the way from the user to the N-ISDN switch. (This scenario is similar to the previous one, except that the ATM Control Plane stack does not exist.) In the previous case, the user signals the BSS on demand to make available a pooled facility (i.e., a nailed-up channel from the BSS to the N-ISDN switch); in this case the PVC nailed-up signaling channel is always there.

In the fourth instance (scenario 4), the interworking function is assumed to take place in the BSS, using N-ISDN NNI protocols. This is similar to scenario 2, except that the interworking burden is placed on the BSS. The user signals the BSS using ATM protocols; upon such request, the BSS signals the N-ISDN switch over SS 7 links to establish the call. Also note that the N-ISDN switch runs a stack toward the ultimate user.

Lastly, vendor-proprietary methods could be used (scenario 5). The user signals the BSS using ATM protocols; upon such request, the BSS signals the N-ISDN switch using a proprietary protocol stack. Also note that the N-ISDN switch runs a stack toward the ultimate user. Notice that this approach requires the embedded N-ISDN switch to support this (new) protocol, necessitating some sort of upgrade. There is another a variant of this scenario in which the vendor-specific protocol runs end-to-end, namely directly between the user and the

N-ISDN switch. (In this case the BSS is not involved in N-ISDN-related signaling.)

Discussion of scenarios.   Each of these scenarios has advantages and disadvantages.

The first two scenarios (scenarios 1 and 2) put the interworking burden on currently deployed switches. It is unlikely that the vendors of these switches can be persuaded to make the necessary investment in hardware and software to ensure this compatibility.

The scenario of Fig. 8.13 (scenario 3) places the interworking requirement on the BSS. This is consistent with the way other types of interworking functions currently being contemplated (e.g., frame relay) will be implemented, hence it is the best approach. In the User Plane, access is accomplished by circuit emulation of clear bearer channels using AAL capabilities in the CPE and at the BSS. The user needs to employ Q.2931 signaling in the ATM Control Plane. Interworking of the signal channel (Q.2931 to Q.931) occurs at the BSS. The narrowband bearer capability (N-BC) information element (IE) must be included in the broadband SETUP message; this IE will be used by the BSS to launch a N-ISDN SETUP message (this functionality is currently supported in Q.2931, but not in the ATM Forum's specification). The BNI is a N-ISDN circuit-switched primary rate interface structure. One of the disadvantages of this scenario is that the BSS must play a role in the call setup process by intercepting, converting, and interpreting the narrowband signaling messages, as implied by the Control Plane stack shown in Fig. 8.13.

Scenario 3a is similar to scenario 3, except that a circuit-emulated connection is supported transparently through the BSS between the user equipment and the N-ISDN switch. This user-to-N-ISDN transparent channel is set up between the user and the BSS over a signaling path that *terminates in the BSS* (thus, B-ISDN-to-N-ISDN signaling interworking is not supported in the BSS). Note that the user station still needs to support Q.2931. It is assumed that a pool of (pre-)nailed-up DS0 channels exists between the BSS and the N-ISDN switch. A trunk is selected by the BSS to establish the transparent path from the user to the N-ISDN switch. After the path is set up, the user initiates an in-band N-ISDN signaling exchange with the N-ISDN switch. The disadvantage of this approach is that the user equipment now needs to support *both signaling stacks* (one for B-ISDN and one for N-ISDN). Another possibility emerges from this discussion: Have a few DS0 VCs predefined (i.e., PVC-like) from the user, through the BSS, to the N-ISDN to be used to establish calls; this requires the user to have a Q.931 stack but not a Q.2931 stack active in CPE (presumably the user would have a Q.2931 stack somewhere, given that the user is a B-ISDN user by assumption).

TABLE 8.3 Proposed Physical Architecture

Interworking capability:

- Located at the BSS

- Broadband-to-narrowband interface defined to be an ISDN PRI

- BSS looks like a PBX to N-ISDN

User Plane access:

- Circuit emulation using AAL capabilities in the CPE and at the BSS (AAL-circuit-emulated path between CPE and BSS using Structured format, asynchronous emulation, and explicit source clock frequency recovery achieved with SRTS techniques)

- ISDN circuit-switched primary rate interface structure between BSS and the N-ISDN switch

Signaling: User employs Q.2931 signaling in ATM Control Plane

- Narrowband bearer capability IE included in the B-SETUP message

- Narrowband bearer capability IE used by the BSS to launch a N-ISDN SETUP message

Scenario 4 is a more sophisticated situation, as the N-ISDN switch treats the BSS as a switch, via a NNI, rather than as a simple PBX-like concentrator; however, the protocol machinery is more complex.

Scenario 5 has the disadvantage of being vendor-specific, thereby limiting global interoperability.

Best architecture.   Based on this discussion, the scenario of Fig. 8.13 appears to be the approach to take to support N-ISDN interworking. See Table 8.3.

AAL issues.   Figure 8.13 shows that AAL capabilities are needed in both the CPE and the BSS. This section examines issues associated with the AAL.

AAL type.   At press time, standards groups had not yet settled on a choice of AAL type for N-ISDN clear channel service. AAL Type 1 provides cell sequencing for lost/misinserted cell detection and (optionally) timing recovery (using the synchronous residual time stamp or other techniques) for applications that have stringent jitter requirements.

AAL Type 1 provides error protection and timing recovery functions to support low speed circuit-emulated bearer services. The AAL1 functionality supports a Structured capability in order to establish the boundaries of a group of octets, for example in the $n \times 64$-kbits/s case. This is a more complicated framing protocol than the unstructured form; it utilizes alternating non-P and P protocol data units. The P protocol data units provide a pointer which indicates the beginning of the structure of octets.

ATM cell fill Issues.   Figure 8.13 shows that ATM capabilities are needed in both the CPE and the BSS. Two candidate solutions are feasible at the ATM Layer:

- *Partial cell fill.* The broadband interworking unit at the CPE or at the interface to a narrowband network would partially fill cells with less than the 47 (or 48) cell payload octets available. A value of 16-octet cell payload filling introduces a 4-ms round-trip delay as a result of cell construction.
- *Full cell fill.* The broadband interworking unit at the CPE (and at the interface to a narrowband network) would fill cells with 47 octets. This would introduce a round-trip delay of approximately 12 ms. Based on efficiency considerations, full cell fill may be used.

8.2.2   Summary of requirements

CPE.   The user's terminal equipment must be able to construct protocol data units built on the following User Plane protocol stack:

AAL   AAL1 with Structure. Explicit source clock frequency recovery is achieved with SRTS techniques.

ATM   Full fill of 47 octets per cell.

PHY   Same PHY employed in the user's UNI.

The user's equipment must be able to construct protocol data units built on the following Control Plane protocol stack:

Q.2931   Call control capabilities with support for N-ISDN bearer capability.

SAAL   SSCF, SSCOP, AAL5 Common Part.

ATM   Normal operation.

PHY   Same PHY employed in the user's UNI.

Network and network Interface requirements.   The network must support a SVC ATM UNI with a N-ISDN CPE meeting the requirements described above. Interworking is to be supported at the BSS. AAL1 must be supported. Explicit source clock frequency recovery is achieved with SRTS techniques. Lost cells are replaced with dummy cells at the interworking unit.

The BSS recognizes the request over the UNI as a $n \times$ 64-kbits/s request by the presence of the narrowband bearer capability IE. This IE is utilized by the N-ISDN switch to complete the call. The N-IWU needs to know that AAL1 logic needs to be provided on top of the local ATM Layer for a particular VC (other AALs may be active for other VCs over the UNI). One mechanism is to make the AAL parameters IE mandatory for N-ISDN-carrying channels; the subtype field can be coded for circuit emulation—synchronous. Other AAL IE fields need to be appropriately coded (e.g., CBR rate). "Synchronous" implies the availability of a network clock which can be used to derive clocks at both ends. It is unlikely that a B-ISDN island network based on SONET would be slaved to a N-ISDN clock; hence, AAL-based clock recovery must be supported. To support clock recovery, the subtype field can be coded for circuit emulation—asynchronous. Other AAL IE fields need to be appropriately coded (e.g., CBR rate and clock recovery type).

More specifically, one has the following requirements:

UNI User Plane capabilities at BSS. In the origination-to-destination path, the N-IWU must be able to disassemble protocol data units built on the following User Plane protocol stack, for usage by the interworking relaying function:

AAL   AAL1 with Structure. Explicit source clock frequency recovery is achieved with SRTS techniques.

ATM   Full fill of 47 octets per cell.

PHY   Same PHY employed in the user's UNI.

In the destination-to-origination path, the N-IWU must be able to assemble protocol data units built on the User Plane protocol stack just shown (for usage by the interworking relaying function).

UNI Control Plane capabilities at BSS. In the origination-to-destination path, the N-IWU must be able to disassemble protocol data units built on the following Control Plane protocol stack, for usage by the interworking relaying function:

Q.2931   Call control capabilities with support for N-ISDN bearer capability.

SAAL   SSCF, SSCOP, AAL5 Common Part.

ATM   Normal operation.

PHY   Same PHY employed in the user's UNI.

In the destination-to-origination path, the N-IWU must be able to assemble protocol data units built on the Control Plane protocol stack just shown (for usage by the interworking relaying function).

BNI User Plane capabilities at BSS. In the origination-to-destination path, the N-IWU must be able to disassemble protocol data units built on the following User Plane protocol stack toward the N-ISDN switch, for usage by the interworking relaying function:

PHY   ISDN circuit-switched primary rate interface structure—ISDN User Plane.

In the destination-to-origination path, the N-IWU must be able to assemble protocol data units built on the User Plane protocol stack just shown (for usage by the interworking relaying function).

BNI Control Plane capabilities at BSS. In the origination-to-destination path, the N-IWU must be able to disassemble protocol data units built on the following Control Plane protocol stack, for usage by the interworking relaying function:

Q.931   UNI requests are mapped to N-ISDN call control protocols using the N-ISDN bearer capability obtained over the ATM UNI.

Q.921   Normal operation.

PHY   ISDN circuit-switched primary rate interface structure—ISDN Control Plane.

In the destination-to-origination path, the N-IWU must be able to assemble protocol data units built on the Control Plane protocol stack just shown (for usage by the interworking relaying function).

8.2.3 Signaling considerations

N-ISDN ATM Adaptation Layer functions. In Sec. 8.1.5, the AAL1 functions were listed. One can specify a N-ISDN-based AAL (NAAL) by assigning the following functions:

The *Sending* NAAL's SSCF supports the blocking /count process but not the clock recovery process.

The *Sending* NAAL's SSCOF supports the transfer process.

The *Sending* NAAL's SAR supports the PDU generation process and the SNP encoding process.

The *Receiving* NAAL's SAR supports a PDU receiving process and a SNP error check process.

The *Receiving* NAAL's SSCOF supports a SN checking process and a "concealment" process of repeating the last PDU if a cell is lost.

The *Receiving* NAAL's SSCF supports a locally timed buffering process used to achieve clocking and a deblocking process.

SETUP message IE encodings.   This section describes how certain key IEs in the SETUP message are coded.

Broadband bearer capability IE. Coded as follows:
  Bearer class = BCOB-A
  Traffic type = CBR
  Timing requirements = End-to-end timing required

Bearer capability IE. If used, this IE will be coded consistent with the Q.931 rules.

ATM user cell rate. Forward and backward peak cell rate are coded as $n \times 173$ cells per second for $n \times 64$-kbits/s bearer service.

QOS class. Code for the highest class.

AAL parameters. Code as follows:
  AAL type = AAL1
  Subtype = Circuit emulation (synchronous)
  Clock recovery = SRTS and structured data transfer combined
  Error correction = Null
  CBR rate = $n \times 64$-kbits/s

All other pertinent fields (call reference, called party number, calling party number, etc.). Consistent with Q.2931 specifications.

8.2.4   ITU-TS View for Provision of 64-kbits/s Circuit-Mode ISDN Services

The material that follows is summarized from Section 6 and Annex E of the December 1993 working draft of ITU-T Q.2931.[4] This information is included to give the reader a sense of the ITU's views on interworking.

(1) Provision of 64-kbits/s-based circuit-mode ISDN services in B-ISDN and signaling interworking between N-ISDN and B-ISDN.   Section 6 of Q.2931 describes the particular features required to provide 64-kbits/s-based circuit-mode ISDN services in B-ISDN and signaling interworking between B-ISDN and N-ISDN. For the 64-kbits/s-based circuit-mode services, the term *N-ISDN services* is also used. This term includes the circuit-mode services described in the I.200 series of Recommendations and supported by the Q.931 protocol. For these services, interworking between B-ISDN and N-ISDN is possible.

In order to ease signaling interworking between B-ISDN and N-ISDN, separate services-related information elements are defined for N-ISDN services and B-ISDN services. For the provision of N-ISDN services, the Q.931 information elements *bearer capability, high-layer compatibility,* and *low-layer compatibility* are used in B-ISDN. In the B-ISDN these

TABLE 8.4 Information Elements in B-ISDN to Provide N-ISDN Services

	IEs used to describe network-relevant bearer attributes	IEs used to describe lower-layer attributes (transparent for B-ISDN)	IEs used to describe high-layer attributes (transparent for B-ISDN)
N-ISDN-related information elements	N-BC	N-LLC	N-HLC
B-ISDN-related information elements	Broadband bearer capability (B-BC) supplemented by: ATM user cell rate QOS parameter End-to-end transit delay	AAL parameters	—

information elements are designated as narrowband bearer capability (N-BC), narrowband low-layer compatibility (N-LLC), and narrowband high-layer compatibility (N-HLC). For their application in B-ISDN, the Q.931 information elements are modified according to the Q.2931 coding rules. For the provision of B-ISDN services, new information elements are used. Table 8.4 shows the information elements required for the provision of N-ISDN services in B-ISDN.

One major advantage of taking the Q.931 information elements nearly unchanged in B-ISDN is a significant simplification of interworking between B-ISDN and N-ISDN. Another important benefit is that by dividing the service-related attributes into N-ISDN- and B-ISDN-related parts, a decoupling of the B-ISDN specific information elements from the evolution of the Q.931-based information elements is achieved.

The reason for taking the Q.931 information elements for the provision of N-ISDN services in even a pure B-ISDN environment is that a B-ISDN user cannot know in advance whether the destination of a call will be a B-ISDN (Q.2931) or a N-ISDN (Q.931) terminal. Therefore, no distinction is made between the provision of N-ISDN services in a pure B-ISDN environment and the provision of these services in the case of interworking with N-ISDN.

Information elements for N-ISDN services in B-ISDN. When N-ISDN services are provided in a B-ISDN environment, in principle the information elements of Q.93B (e.g., called party number) are used in the same way as for B-ISDN specific services. However, for the service-related attributes listed in Table 8.4, Q.931 information elements are reused for the N-ISDN services as described below. The following subsections only describe the use of the service-related information elements in the SETUP message. However, in case of service negotiation, they may also be included in the first response message returned to the call-initiating entity.

Bearer-service-related information. The B-BC information element is always included in the SETUP message. This information element is mandatory for all services, and it is interpreted by the B-ISDN. For N-ISDN services, the N-BC information element is also mandatory in the SETUP message. Unlike the B-BC information element, however, the N-BC information element is transported transparently through the B-ISDN.

The N-BC information element is included in the SETUP message even if no interworking takes place, since the user is not able to know in advance whether the receiver of the SETUP message will be a B-ISDN (Q.2931) or a N-ISDN (Q.931) terminal.

For N-ISDN services, a value for the ATM cell rate is selected such that the bit rate of the N-ISDN service (64 kbits/s or $n \times 64$ kbits/s) can be transported as the payload (i.e., excluding the ATM and AAL overhead) of the ATM cells.

Low-layer information. If required for the description of the N-ISDN services, the N-LLC information element is included in the SETUP message.

The N-LLC information element is transported transparently through the B-ISDN. For the provision of N-ISDN services, the inclusion of the AAL parameter information element in the SETUP message is required, specifying AAL Type 1.

Higher-layer information. If required for the description of the N-ISDN service, the N-HLC information element is included in the SETUP message. The N-HLC information element is also transported transparently through the B-ISDN.

Interworking N-ISDN to B-ISDN. Section 6.3 of Q.2931 describes the functions performed by a terminal adapter (TA) or network adapter (NA) when initiating a connection from a N-ISDN to a B-ISDN user.

The objective is that Q.931 information elements simply be relayed through the B-ISDN by the TA or the NA.

Bearer-service-related information. The Q.931 BC information element is mapped to the Q.2931 N-BC information element by the TA or the NA by simply inserting the third octet containing the IE instruction field. The Flag bit in this octet is set to 0; i.e., the normal error-handling procedures as defined in Q.2931 subclause 5.7 apply. In addition, the B-BC information element is created by the TA or NA, indicating Bearer Class A and the value "yes" for the susceptibility to clipping field. The ATM user cell rate and the QOS parameter information elements are also generated by the TA or NA, after evaluating the information of the Q.931 BC information element.

Low-layer compatibility information. The Q.931 LLC information element (if present) is mapped to the N-LLC information element by the TA or NA without change of content. Again, the new octet 3 is inserted as described above. The AAL parameter is generated by the TA or NA, indicating AAL Type 1.

High-layer compatibility information. The Q.931 HLC information element (if present) is mapped to the N-HLC information element by the TA or NA without change of content. Again, the new octet 3 is inserted as described above.

The N-HLC information element is transported transparently through the B-ISDN in most cases.

Interworking B-ISDN to N-ISDN. If a B-TE initiates a call to a N-TE, only N-ISDN services will be processed and forwarded by the NA. If a B-ISDN specific service is requested by the B-TE towards the N-ISDN, then the call will be rejected by the NA with the cause "Service option not available, unspecified."

Bearer-service-related information. The B-BC, the ATM user cell rate, and the QOS parameter information element are discarded by the NA as there are no corresponding Q.931 IEs.

The N-BC information element is mapped to the Q.931 BC information element by the NA by removing its third octet, without causing other changes to the content.

If no N-BC information element is present, then a B-ISDN service shall be assumed and the call is rejected with the cause "Service option not available, unspecified."

Low-layer compatibility information. The N-LLC information element (if included) is mapped to the Q.931 LLC information element by the NA by simply removing its third octet, without any content change.

The AAL parameter information element is discarded by the NA.

If a B-LLI information element is detected by the NA, then the call is rejected with the cause "Service option not available, unspecified."

High-layer compatibility information. The N-HLC information element (if included) is mapped to the Q.931 HLC information element by the NA by simply removing its third octet, without any content change.

If a B-HLC information element is detected by the NA, then the call is rejected with the cause "Service option not available, unspecified."

Overlap sending and receiving. B-ISDN terminal equipment uses en-block sending. This implies, from the B-TE perspective, the mandatory inclusion of the Sending complete information element in the SETUP message. Since overlap receiving is an allowed procedure in N-ISDN, this procedure is also supported in B-ISDN for incoming calls from the N-ISDN. The Q.93B protocol also supports overlap sending in order to allow terminal equipment designed for the N-ISDN to be connected to the B-ISDN via a terminal adapter or via a customer's network. The procedures of Q.93B for overlap sending and receiving are described below.

If overlap sending is used, the SETUP message contains either

1. No called number information

2. Incomplete called number information

3. Called number information which the network cannot determine to be complete

On receipt of such a SETUP message, the network starts a timer (timer T302), sends a SETUP ACKNOWLEDGE message to the user, and enters the Overlap Sending state. When the SETUP ACKNOW-LEDGE message is received, the user enters the Overlap Sending state and optionally starts another timer (timer T304). After receiving the SETUP ACKNOWLEDGE message, the user sends the remainder of the call information (if any) in one or more INFORMATION messages. The called party number information is provided by the user in the called party number information element.

If the user employs timer T304, the user restarts T304 when each INFORMATION message is sent.

The call information in the message that completes the information sending may contain a "sending complete" indication (i.e., the Sending complete information element). The network restarts timer T302 on receipt of every INFORMATION message which does not contain a sending complete indication.

When a user which implements overlap receiving determines that a received message contains either

1. No called number information

2. Incomplete called number information

3. Called number information which the user cannot determine to be complete and when the user

the user starts timer T302, sends a SETUP ACKNOWLEDGE message to the network, and enters the Overlap Receiving state. When the SETUP ACKNOWLEDGE message is received, the network stops timer T303, starts timer T304, enters the Overlap Receiving state, and sends the remainder of the call information (if any) in one or more INFORMATION messages, starting timer T304 when each INFORMATION message is sent. The called party number information is provided in the called party number information element. The call address information may contain a sending complete indication (i.e., the sending complete information element).

If the network can determine that sufficient call setup information will be received by the called user by sending the next INFORMATION message, Q2931 recommends that this INFORMATION message contain the Sending complete information element.

The user starts timer T302 on receipt of every INFORMATION message which does not contain a Sending complete indication.

Following the receipt of a Sending complete indication, or the determination that sufficient call information has been received, the user stops timer T302 (if implemented) and sends a CALL PROCEEDING message to the network. Alternatively, depending on internal events, the user may send an ALERTING or CONNECT message to the network.

The CALL PROCEEDING message in this case causes the originating exchange to send a CALL PROCEEDING message to the originating user, if not already sent.

At the expiration of timer T302 the user either:

1. Sends a CALL PROCEEDING, ALERTING, or CONNECT message if sufficient information has been received.

2. Initiates clearing with cause No. 28, "invalid number format (incomplete number)," if it determines that the call information is definitely incomplete.

At the expiration of timer T304, the network initiates call clearing with cause No. 28, "invalid number format (incomplete number)," sent to the calling user and cause No. 102, "recovery on timer expiry," sent to the called user. If, following the receipt of a SETUP message or during overlap receiving, the user determines that the received call information is invalid (e.g., invalid called party number), it initiates call clearing with a cause such as one of the following:

#1   "Unassigned (unallocated) number";

#3   "No route to destination";

#22   "Number changed";

#28   "Invalid number format (incomplete number)."

Upon receipt of the completed call information, the user may perform further compatibility checking functions.

Notification of interworking. Interworking of B-ISDN with N-ISDN requires the support of the progress indicator values specified in Recommendation Q.931 by the B-ISDN.

The following principles apply:

1. In the case of interworking with N-ISDN, all progress indicator values applying for N-ISDN interworking are relayed to B-ISDN and then transported transparently through the B-ISDN.

2. In the case of a call leaving or entering B-ISDN at the NA, the NA does not generate a Q.931 and Q.93B progress indicator information element. The Q.931 progress indicator information element is mapped to the Q.93B progress indicator information element by adding or removing octet 3, depending on the direction of the call.

(2) Mapping functions to support 64-kbits/s-based circuit-mode ISDN services in B-ISDN and interworking between N-ISDN and B-ISDN (Q.931/Q.93B)

Use of the N-LCC and the B-LLI information elements in B-ISDN. The N-LCC and B-LLI information elements used in Q.2931 as described by the following items:

1. The N-LLC information element is used to determine end-to-end attributes on N-ISDN circuit-mode services supported in a B-ISDN. This information element is not used for B-ISDN specific services. In particular, this information element is used
   - By a B-ISDN terminal emulating a N-ISDN service
   - Between a TA (connecting a N-ISDN-TE to B-ISDN) and a B-ISDN network

2. For B-ISDN specific services, the B-LLI information element is used consistent with Q.93B.

3. Either the N-LLC or the B-LLI information element is used in a call, but not both.

4. If B-ISDN specific terminals which do not support emulation of N-ISDN services are connected to a B-ISDN, only the B-LLI information element is used, not the N-LLC information element.

The use of the N-LLC and B-LLI information elements is illustrated in Fig. 8.14.

Mapping functions between B-ISDN-related information elements and N-ISDN related information elements. This section specifies the processing and the detailed mapping of the service-related information elements performed by a network adapter (NA) installed between a B-ISDN and a N-ISDN. The communications scenario is described in Recommendation I.580, Annex A, scenario B. It should be noted that the functions and the mapping described in this section also apply to a

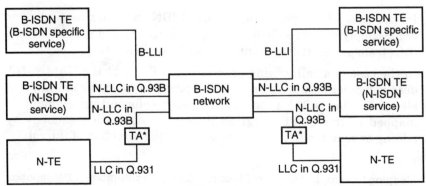

Figure 8.14 Illustration of the N-LLC and B-LLI IEs in Q.2931.[4] (*The LLC information is transferred transparently across the TA except for changes required by the different coding rules.)

terminal adapter (TA) at the UNI connecting a N-ISDN terminal to a B-ISDNnetwork.

Interworking functions between N-ISDN and B-ISDN are only provided for circuit-mode 64-kbits/s-based N-ISDN services. Interworking functions to support packet-mode and frame-mode bearer services are for further study.

For the interworking functions between N-ISDN and B-ISDN, the following principles apply:

1. If B-ISDN specific service is requested at the Q.93B side of the NA, the call is rejected.

2. If the NA receives a request for a N-ISDN service at its Q.931 side, it selects an ATM user cell rate for the B-ISDN side which is able to carry the 64-kbits/s (or $n \times$ 64-kbits/s) bit rate of the N-ISDN service.

3. If the NA receives a request for a N-ISDN service at its Q.931 side, it selects Bearer Class A (CBR, CO, end-to-end timing required) and AAL Type 1 as default values for the B-ISDN side. The value for the field "susceptibility to clipping" in the B-BC is set to "yes."

4. In the direction from Q.93B to Q.931, the NA places the information elements to be transferred to the N-ISDN side into ascending order as required by Q.931.

Detailed mapping functions for the direction Q.93B to Q.931. The detailed mapping functions performed by the NA for the direction from Q.93B to Q.931 are illustrated by the examples given below.

TABLE 8.5 Mapping Performed by the NA for the 3.1-kHz Audio Bearer Service (Direction Q.93B to Q.931)[4]

Q.93B: emulation of the N-ISDN bearer service 3.1-kHz audio	Q.931: 3.1-kHz audio bearer service

N-BC:
  3.1-kHz audio
  Circuit mode
  64 kbits/s
  G.711 mu-law
	BC:
	  3.1-kHz audio
	  Circuit mode
	  64 kbits/s
	  G.711 mu-law

N-HLC:
  Optional
	HLC:
	  Present, if provided

N-LLC:
  Optional
	LLC:
	  Present, if provided

B-BC:
  Bearer Class A
  Susceptibility to clipping
	(Discarded)

ATM user cell rate: Equal to 64 kbits/s	(Discarded)
Quality of service: Unspecified QOS class	(Discarded)
AAL parameters: AAL Type 1	(Discarded)

The NA relays the N-BC, N-LLC, and N-HLC information elements transparently to the N-ISDN. No further processing is required, except for changes needed to accommodate the different coding rules. The B-BC, ATM user cell rate, QOS parameter, and AAL parameter information elements are only B-ISDN-related and are therefore not needed by the NA to generate the N-ISDN-related information elements. These information elements are discarded. Table 8.5 illustrates the case of a B-ISDN user requesting the N-ISDN bearer service "3.1-kHz audio." Table 8.6 illustrates the case of a B-ISDN user requesting N-ISDN telephony teleservice.

Detailed mapping functions for the direction Q.931 to Q.93B. The detailed mapping functions performed by the NA for the direction from Q.931 to Q.93B are illustrated by the examples given below.

The NA relays the BC, LLC, and HLC information elements transparently to the B-ISDN. No further processing is required, except for changes needed to accommodate the different coding rules. The B-BC, ATM user cell rate, QOS parameter, and AAL parameter information elements are generated by the NA using default values

TABLE 8.6   Mapping Performed by the NA for the N-ISDN Telephony Teleservice (Direction Q.93B to Q.931)[4]

Q.93B: emulation of the N-ISDN telephony teleservice	Q.931: telephony teleservice
N-BC: Speech Circuit mode 64 kbits/s G.711 mu-law	BC: Speech Circuit mode 64 kbits/s G.711 mu-law
N-HLC: First high-layer characteristics identified to be used in the call. High-layer protocol profile: telephony	HLC: First high-layer characteristics identified to be used in the call. High-layer protocol profile: telephony
N-LLC: Optional	LLC: Present, if provided
B-BC: Bearer Class A Susceptibility to clipping	(Discarded)
ATM user cell rate: Equal to 64 kbits/s	(Discarded)
Quality of service: Unspecified QOS class	(Discarded)
AAL parameters: AAL Type 1	(Discarded)

and the information provided by the Q.931 information elements. The "susceptibility to clipping" field of the B-BC information element in Q.93B is always set to "yes." Table 8.7 illustrates the case of a N-ISDN user requesting the 3.1-kHz audio bearer service. Table 8.8 illustrates the case of a N-ISDN user requesting the telephony teleservice.

References

1. D. Minoli and B. Keinath, *Distributed Multimedia: Through Broadband Communication Services*, Artech House, Norwood, Mass., 1994.

2. W. O. Covington, Jr., and M. E. Vitella, "Voice Transport on an ATM Broadband Network," *GLOBECOM '89*, pp. 1921–1925.

3. EIA/TIA-579, *Acoustic-to-Digital and Digital-to-Acoustic Transmission Requirements for ISDN Terminals*, Electronics Industry Association, March 1991.

4. ITU-T Draft Recommendation Q.93B, "B-ISDN User-Network Interface Layer 3 Specification for Basic Call/Bearer Control," February 1993.

TABLE 8.7 Mapping Performed by the NA for Audio Bearer Service (Direction Q.931 to Q.93B)[4]

Q.931: 3.1-kHz audio bearer service	Q.93B: emulation of the audio bearer service
BC: 3.1-kHz audio Circuit mode 64 kbits/s G.711 mu-law	N-BC: 3.1-kHz audio Circuit mode 64 kbits/s G.711 mu-law
HLC: Optional	N-HLC: Present, if provided
LLC: Optional	N-LLC: Present, if provided
—	B-BC: Bearer Class A Susceptibility to clipping
—	ATM user cell rate: Equal to 64 kbits/s
—	Quality of service: Unspecified QOS class
—	AAL parameters: AAL Type 1

TABLE 8.8 Mapping Performed by the NA for the Telephony Teleservice (Direction Q.931 to Q.93B)[4]

Q.931: telephony teleservice	Q.93B: emulation of telephony teleservice
BC: Speech Circuit mode 64 kbits/s G.711 mu-law	N-BC: Speech Circuit mode 64 kbits/s G.711 mu-law
HLC: First high-layer characteristics identified to be used in the call. High-layer protocol profile: telephony	N-HLC: First high-layer characteristics identified to be used in the call. High-layer protocol profile: telephony
LLC: Optional	N-LLC: Present, if provided
—	B-BC: Bearer Class A Susceptibility to clipping
—	ATM user cell rate: Equal to 64 kbits/s
—	Quality of Service: Unspecified QOS class
—	AAL parameters: AAL Type 1

9

Third-Generation LANs

9.1 Introduction

Efforts[*] are now underway to develop customer premises networks (namely, LANs) that support very high speeds and at the same time are compatible with evolving public network communication architectures such as B-ISDN and cell relay.[1,2] This eliminates (or minimizes) the cost of ancillary equipment such as bridges, routers, and gateways to provide an N-layer relaying function (in OSIRM terminology) between the private network and the public network. This section provides a summary view of these proposals. This work has been done under the auspices of the ATM Forum. Many leading vendors are now pushing ATM instead of FDDI to provide high bandwidth to the desktop.[3] As many as a dozen vendors should have products by the end of 1994, and more by 1995.

First-generation LANs emerged in the late 1970s and early 1980s. They supported 10 Mbits/s on metallic media and were employed mostly to provide local data transmission for business applications such as E-mail and word processing. These LANs are now being called "legacy" LANs by many industry observers. Second-generation LANs, in the form of FDDI-based systems, emerged in the late 1980s and early 1990s. They supported 100-Mbits/s on fiber media (with some possible extensions to metallic media) and have been employed mostly to support campus-based LAN backbone interconnection and data applications. Although FDDI II[†] can support iso-

---

[*]This chapter is based on D. Minoli's *1st, 2nd, and Next Generation LANs*, McGraw-Hill, New York, 1994.

[†]Readers interested in a more extensive treatment of FDDI and FDDI II may consult the cited reference.

chronous traffic (voice and compressed digital video), its total throughput has remained in the 100-Mbits/s range; additionally, there has been little movement in terms of products or deployment.

ATM is the technology of choice for evolving B-ISDN public networks, which are beginning to appear and will see increased deployment in the near future (see Chap. 11), but ATM will also penetrate next-generation LANs at the core, as a premises technology. These LANs are now under development to support a variety of new applications such as desk-to-desk videoconferencing, multimedia conferencing, multimedia messaging, distance learning, imaging tasks (including computer-aided design and manufacturing), animation, data fusion, cooperative work (for example, joint document editing), and supercomputer access.[4–8]

Desk-to-desk videoconferencing might be done at 384 kbits/s or even 1.544 Mbits/s. A network supporting 20 to 30 such users (a typical workgroup and LAN configuration) would need a *sustained* throughput of 10 to 45 Mbits/s; additionally, these isochronous applications are delay-sensitive and so may not be able to make optimal use of a contention (Ethernet) or token-based data transfer discipline. Some high-quality graphics applications may require as much as 45 Mbits/s per user. Should 20 to 30 such users need simultaneous access to a server (for example, a group of radiologists reviewing X-rays), the sustained throughput would have to be 1.2 Gbits/s. These rates are in line with the B-ISDN/cell relay rates of 155 Mbits/s (also known as STS-3c, Synchronous Transport Signal Level 3 Concatenated) and 622 Mbits/s (STS-12c).

There are four goals for third-generation LANs:[1]

1. Provide the real-time transport capabilities necessary for multimedia applications (particularly for video signals).

2. Provide scalable throughput that can be grown both on a per-device basis and on an aggregate basis. Per-device scalability allows a few devices to receive more bandwidth if their applications warrant it. Aggregate scalability allows migration in terms of attached devices.

3. Facilitate interworking between LANs and WANs. Currently, routers and bridges (whether using T1 technology, frame relay, or SMDS) need to undertake relatively major protocol conversion in order to provide access to WAN services. These differences in LAN and WAN technology have slowed the extension of truly distributed LAN-based computing to environments beyond a campus.

4. Use, to the extent possible, evolving ATM/B-ISDN standards. This has the advantage of (a) expediting development and deployment of

the technology, since a set of about two dozen ATM/B-ISDN standards is already available, and (b) keeping the cost down, since chips developed for SONET and the ATM protocol can be utilized.

Three User Plane protocol layers are needed to undertake communication in a LAN environment (as was the case for CRS WANs covered in the previous chapters):

1. The ATM Layer
2. The Physical Layer
3. The ATM Adaptation Layer

The function of the AAL is to insulate the upper layers of the LAN application protocols (e.g., TCP/IP) from the details of the ATM mechanism. A very simple adaptation layer has been designed to support efficient cellularization and integrate smoothly into existing upper-layer protocols.[9] This AAL is AAL Type 5 [known initially as Simple and Efficient Adaptation Layer (SEAL)], already discussed in Chap. 3.

In addition, a mechanism is needed in the "signaling plane" in order to manage connections among users. In a departure from connectionless IEEE-based MAC communication, initial directions in ATM-based LANs are to use connection-oriented communication (this would make the LAN consistent with current B-ISDN services). As covered in Chap. 4, connection-oriented communication requires a call setup phase; signaling is needed to accomplish this. Connections can be made on a PVC basis (particularly for early 1993–94 products, called Phase I) and on an SVC basis (1995 and beyond products, called Phase II).

The goal is to bring ATM to the desktop using twisted-pair cable; however, initial work focused on fiber-based media. The 1993 ATM UNI specification[10] included a definition of five physical UNIs,* as follows:

- SONET-based fiber-optic UNI (public and private) operating at STS-3c (155.52 Mbits/s). This UNI uses single-mode fiber.
- DS3 (44.736 Mbits/s) C-Bit Parity UNI (public and private).
- 4B/5B FDDI-based (100 Mbits/s; 125 Mbaud) fiber-optic private UNI. This UNI uses multimode fiber.
- 8B/10B FCS-based (155 Mbits/s; 194.4 Mbaud) fiber-optic private UNI. This UNI uses multimode fiber.
- European E3 (34.368 Mbits/s) and E4 (139.264 Mbits/s) UNI (public)

*As of early 1994 there was a proposal to support a private UNI as 51.84 Mbits/s on UTP Type 3 as well as 155.52 Mbits/s on UTP Type 5.

9.2   Local ATM Technology

Local ATM refers to the application of ATM technology to premises-based communication.

9.2.1   Local ATM environment

The environment to which LATM is directed is composed of four entities:

1. User devices (including servers and hosts)

2. User-owned ATM switches (possibly in hubs)

3. Internetworking devices such as routers

4. The public ATM/B-ISDN/cell relay network

Figure 9.1 (from Ref.1) depicts this environment from a topological perspective. Devices connect to ATM switches over a point-to-point link. This interface is referred to as I_1. If desired, devices can have physical connectivity to multiple premises ATM switches; however, each interface has a unique address. The physical connection between premises switches is described by interface I_2. The interface between the local ATM switch and the public B-ISDN network is called I_3 (a device connecting directly the B-ISDN network, without the services of a local ATM switch, also employs interface I_3). This implies that a device could implement interfaces I_1 and I_3, while a premises ATM switch must implement all three interfaces. Table 9.1 provides some early requirements for these interfaces.

The initial LATM switches will probably support at most 100 or so users; that number could grow in the future. Some vendors could also include a multiprotocol router function (i.e., process network layer PDUs like IP PDUs). WAN communication is supported either through the public B-ISDN, particularly for discrete remote terminals without a remote premises ATM switch, or over a non-B-ISDN communication service, through an intermediate router mechanism.

In a LATM network, devices can obtain provisioned (and later signaled) device-to-device(s) ATM connection(s). Hence, device pairs which need to communicate either establish PVCs (by way of assigned VPIs/VCIs) or set up a SVC link as needed. Devices are identified by an addressing scheme now under definition. Protocols and services at three layers need to be defined, as follows:

- Physical Layer–to–ATM Layer services
- Physical Layer–to–Physical Layer protocols

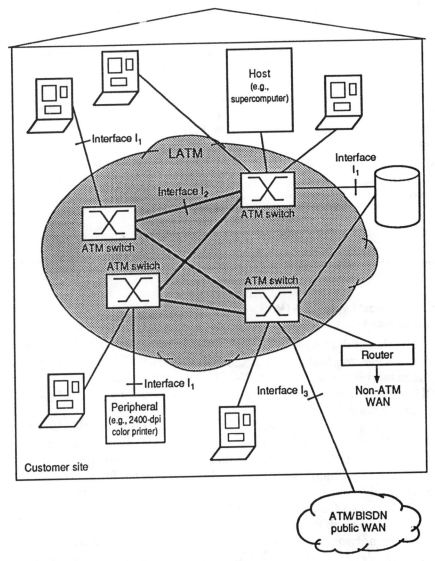

Figure 9.1 ATM-based LANs.

- ATM Layer–to–AAL services
- ATM Layer–to–ATM Layer protocols
- AAL–to–higher-layer services
- AAL–to–AAL protocols

TABLE 9.1   LATM Interface Profiles

	Interface I_1	Interface I_2	Interface I_3
Physical medium	Multimode and single-mode fiber, twisted pair	Multimode and single-mode fiber, twisted pair	Single-mode fiber
Physical Layer Protocol	DS3, SONET, FCS	DS3, SONET, FCS	DS3, SONET
ATM VPI/VCI Space	Small	Medium	Large
AAL	AAL5	AAL5	AAL5
Signaling plane functions	Initially, device-to-device PVCs	Switch-to-switch signaling capabilities	Initially: PVCs
	Future, device-to-device SVCs		Future: signaling used by public network

9.2.2   Physical Layer–to–ATM Layer services

The function of the Physical Layer is to move incoming PHY SDUs (i.e., cells) between two peer systems supporting the same Physical Layer. As is the case with any layer, the PHY-SDU is prepended with layer-specific PCI in order to transmit it to the peer entity. As noted earlier, four media format are used.[10]

One of the formats receiving a lot of initial attention is the 155.52-Mbits/s SONET-based format. Suppliers were hoping to (re)utilize existing chipsets developed for SONET equipment. The PCI includes transmission overhead like HEC, performance monitoring, and alarm bits. As seen in Table 9.1, both multimode (50/125 μm and 62/125 μm) and single-mode fiber is supported in the premises wiring; however, only single-mode is supported over the public network UNI. Only cells which have headers without bit errors are delivered to the higher layer with an *indication primitive* over the PHY-SAP. The use of twisted-pair wiring for local communication is under active research, with proposals for standards at 25, 50, 100, and 155 Mbits/s.

The Physical Layer comprises a TC and a PMD Sublayer, as discussed in Chap. 2. PMD functions include encoding of the bits into an appropriate electrical or optical signal. Bit transmission, symbol alignment, and timing extraction functions are supported in this sublayer. Timing for the SONET TC is (initially) 155.52 Mbits/s +/– 20 parts per million (ppm) at I_3 and 155.52 Mbits/s +/– 50 ppm at I_1 and I_2. The PMD also specifies the type of fibers, the transmitter/receiver wavelength, the receiver sensitivity, and the power budget (attenuation and dispersion) parameters. The optical connector type and its performance characteristics are also specified.

The TC Sublayer provides convergence functions to the SONET structure (adapts the cells for transmission over the transmission structure). The TC Sublayer generates and recovers transmission frames. Transmission frames are generated by adding the PCI to the cells (PHY-SDUs) received across the SAP. These cells are then accommodated within the payload structure of SONET or FCS. Data transmission functions of TC facilitate the movement of bits over the physical channel. Data reception functions perform the inverse process of data transmission. Cell delineation functions identify the cell boundaries within a bit stream. HEC generation functions calculate the HEC over the PHY-SDU's header. HEC processing functions allow the receiving peer entity to determine cell header errors and possibly correct single-bit errors; the HEC field can also be used for cell framing recovery. The TC Sublayer also provides line scrambling/descrambling to enhance clock recovery, minimize false cell framing, and enable the user to submit long transparent sequences of 0s (generator polynomial: $x^{43} + 1$).

Two TC approaches are proposed for support by LATM: (1) SONET/DS3(PLCP) and (2) the block-coded scheme used in the FCS (see Fig. 2.11). Under the SONET TC, ATM cells are mapped into the SONET synchronous payload envelope (SPE) (but, clearly, not in the overhead octets). Since cells "slide" within the SONET frame (the latter being 2340 octets, not an integral multiple of the 53-octet cell), a mechanism is required to establish the beginning of a cell. This is done by indicating in the overhead's H4 field the offset to the closest cell which follows (this counter is less than or equal to 52).

The "user plane/signaling plane" operation of the TC sublayer of the PHY Layer is as follows. On a UNITDATA.request from the ATM Layer, it generates the HEC and then the necessary physical transmission frame. The PMD is responsible for actual transmission. At the receiving end, the TC Sublayer extracts the SDU from the received PDU, and, if the HEC mechanism shows a valid header, a UNITDATA.indication to its ATM Layer is provided.

The PHY Layer also has a SAP to the Management Plane. Indications for such events as loss of signal, loss of frame, loss of cell delineation, uncorrectable HEC, far-end failure, and alarm condition are provided.

9.2.3 Physical Layer–to–Physical Layer protocols

We identify this protocol with the SONET structure in effect between peer TC sublayers. SONET at STS-3c provides cell transport at 149.760 Mbits/s and an actual payload throughput of 135.632 Mbits/s.

In the STS-3c frame (270 octets × 9 octets = 2430 octets per 125 μs), only the following transmission overhead octets are used (these reside in the first 9 octets × 9 octets): A1, A2, B1, C1 (in the Section Overhead), B2, H1, H2, H3, K2, and Z2 (in the line overhead). In the path overhead, only octets J1, B3, C2, G1, and H4 are used.

In LATM applications, the section overhead supports the following functions: frame alignment (A1, A2), frame identifier (C1), and section error monitoring (B1). Line overhead supports the following functions: line error monitoring (B2), pointer and concatenation (H1 and H2), and line performance monitoring and alarm indication (K2, Z2). The Path Overhead supports trace (J1), path error monitoring (B3, G1), and cell offset (H4). Figure 9.2 depicts the SONET frame for STS-1. Figure 9.3 shows the carriage of ATM frames within the underlying SONET frame. See Ref. 11 for an extensive treatment of SONET.

9.2.4 ATM Layer–to–AAL services

The ATM Layers provide for the transfer of cells (ATM SDUs) in support of the AAL. Both a point-to-point and a point-to-multipoint transmission service are supported. Initially, the ATM connection needs to be an already established PVC (with specified cell loss ratio, throughput, cell delay, and other transmission performance parameters); in Phase II equipment, the ATM connections will be signaled as required. Local ATM switches do not need to monitor or enforce throughput (measured as the number of cells per time unit), although public B-ISDN switches will. Proper sequencing of cells is provided, except possibly for gaps generated by lost cells (no retransmssion mechanism is supported) or corrupted cells (which are not relayed by an intermediate node which detects the corruption by means of the HEC).

Over the ATM-SAP, two primitives are supported: ATM-DATA.request and ATM-DATA.indication. The ATM-DATA.request primitive initiates the transfer of an ATM-SDU to the peer entity in the target device. In addition to the data, a cell priority parameter is passed down to the ATM Layer. The ATM-DATA.indication primitive alerts the AAL to the arrival of an ATM-SDU. In addition to the data, a congestion indication is set if the cell passes through a portion of the network experiencing congestion.

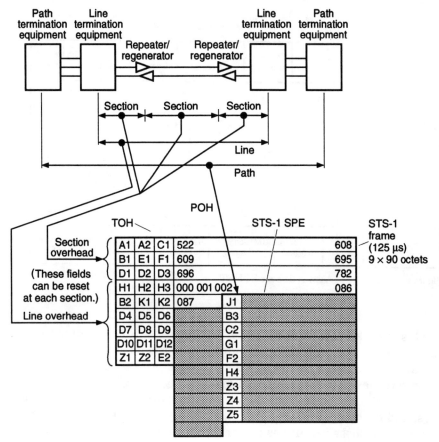

Figure 9.2 SONET frame.

9.2.5 ATM Layer–to–ATM Layer protocols

One can view the protocol as the mechanism embodied in the cell frame structure, plus additional procedures to deal with exceptional cases (e.g., header missing a field, encoding of a specific field not allowed, etc.)

9.2.6 AAL Layer–to–higher-layer services

The function of the AAL is to provide Data Link Layer capabilities to the higher layers, utilizing the services of the ATM Layer. It accepts upper-layer (e.g., TCP/IP) PDUs (varying from 0 to 65,535 octets) and transmits them to a peer AAL with error detection. The protocol aims at being efficient and simple. The protocol being used is known as Data Transfer AAL or AAL Type 5. One of the key functions of this layer is segmentation/reassembly of data into cells, as discussed extensively in Chap. 3.

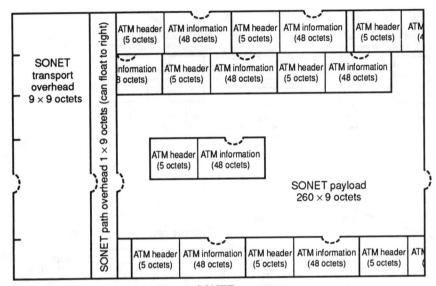

Figure 9.3 Carriage of ATM cells over SONET.

This layer accepts an AAL-UNITDATA.request from the upper layer and issues an AAL-UNITDATA.indication to the upper layer. A variety of parameters needs to be passed with these primitives as part of the service request. There is a SAP to Layer Management functions to create and remove AAL connections; to report errors; to set connection parameters, and for other functions. Again, a variety of parameters need to be passed with these primitives as part of the service request.

The AAL expects the ATM Layer to provide the multiplexing and transport of segments of 48 octets between AAL entities. This is done through an ATM-DATA.request and ATM-DATA.indication. The ATM-DATA.request primitive includes one data segment, a loss priority indication, and an SDU-type. The ATM-DATA.indication includes a data segment, the SDU type (0 = continuation, 1 = last), and any indication of congestion.

Six key AAL functions in the LATM context are

1. AAL-PDU generation by transmitter AAL. This function adds the appropriate padding to make the entire AAL-PDU (including the length field, control field, and CRC-32) divisible by 48. It also concatenates these fields to the PDU.

2. CRC generation by transmitter AAL.

3. Segmentation by transmitter AAL. This function generates successive blocks of 48 octets (beginning with the most significant octet). All

segments except the last one are submitted to the ATM Layer (with the AAL-DATA.request) with the ATM SDU-type set to zero.

4. Reassembly by receiver AAL. This function enables reconstruction of the AAL-PDU from the segments received via ATM.indication primitives. Successive blocks are appended until one (supposedly the last one) with an SDU-type bit set to 1 (for end of message). If there are no problems [lost cells, dropped cells, delayed cells, foreign (misrouted) cells], the PDU can be reconstructed; otherwise error procedures must be initiated. The determination of whether a problem was encountered or not is achieved using the CRC mechanism.

5. CRC validation. This receiver function computes a CRC-32 over the entire "working" AAL-PDU (by the concatenation of incoming ATM payloads). If the test passes, it follows that the "working" PDU has been correctly assembled.

6. AAL-SDU recovery. This receiver function identifies the AAL-SDU boundaries within the AAL-PDU using the length field (to identify which octets, if any, make up the pad).

9.2.7 AAL-to-AAL protocol

Procedures associated with the functions described in the previous sections (protocol state machine, error conditions, etc.) have been defined. The protocol supports "unassured" data transfer, but does detect transmission errors. No addressing is supported, since the VPI/VCI capability of the ATM Layer does this.

As AAL Type 5 was being defined in B-ISDN standards bodies, the protocol was partitioned into an upper sublayer [Service Specific Part (SSP)], which can be null (in most instances), and a lower sublayer called the Common Part (see Chap. 3).

9.2.8 Signaling

As discussed in Chap. 4, dynamic ATM connections require a signaling capability. The ATM Forum specification provides the basis for the type of signaling required by LATM networks.[10] In fact, the signaling has been designed to be consistent with the signaling that will be used over the evolving public broadband network (based on ITU-T Q.2931).

Third-generation "gigabit" LANs developed to support high-population multimedia are reverting to relying on connection-oriented techniques based on B-ISDN, as described in the earlier sections. In this environment, pairs of users can establish PVCs or SVCs over which high-data-rate communication with high frame-to-frame autocorrelation can take place efficiently. PVC-based methods, however, become restrictive from a management perspective as the number of users increases. Hence, SVC-based methods are being developed.

In SVC-based LATM communication, two (multimedia) terminals requiring communication go through a call setup phase, after which communication can take place (note again that this is not the case in a first- or second-generation LAN). The design objective is to keep this setup phase as short as possible, say 50 or 100 ms; a long setup phase (say 5 to 10 s) would impede communication. Signaling is required to communicate the user requests (call control and bearer/bandwidth control information) to a bandwidth manager, typically the (L)ATM switch. In addition, these techniques are necessary when communicating over a B-ISDN WAN. Additional functions include multiparty conference coordination, flow control, etc.

9.2.9 Multiprotocol carriage over ATM

In a general "multiplexed" ATM VC, say a WAN link carrying LAN traffic (TCP/IP for first- or second-generation LANs) as well as other traffic, there is a need to identify which protocol is being carried. The Internet Engineering Task Force has been working on multiprotocol interconnection. There are three approaches to accommodate connectionless traffic, identified in their Internet Draft, *Multiprotocol Interconnect over ATM AAL 5*:[12,13]

1. In the LLC/SNAP encapsulation method, multiple protocols (e.g. NetWare IPX, XNS, IP, AppleTalk, and IEEE 802.5 Bridged PDUs) may be carried over a single virtual channel connection. Protocol identification of the AAL5-SDU content is by use of an IEEE 802.2 LLC header, usually followed by an IEEE 802.1a SNAP header (see Chap. 3). This approach allows interworking with IEEE 802 LANs.

2. In the NLPID/SNAP method, multiple protocols may be carried over a single virtual channel connection. The ISO/IEC TR 9577 Network Layer Protocol ID (NLPID), sometimes in conjunction with a SNAP header, is used for protocol identification. This approach allows ATM–frame relay internetworking.

3. In the null encapsulation, only one protocol is carried on a virtual channel connection. Protocol identification is done by means of Q.2931 signaling. This approach conserves overhead (for example, it permits an IP packet containing a TCP ACK packet to consume exactly one ATM cell).

References

1. *Network Compatible ATM for Local Network Applications*, Phase 1, Version 1.0, April 1992, Anonymous FTP (Internet) at ftp.apple.com pub/latm/nclatm.ps or thumper.bellcore.com pub/latm/nclatm.ps.

2. J. B. Lyles and D. C. Swinehart, "The Emerging Gigabit Environment and the Role of Local ATM," *IEEE Communications Magazine*, April 1992, pages 52 ff.

3. S. Kolodziej, "ATM Gains Supplier Interest," *Lightwave*, August 1992, pages 1 ff.

4. *IEEE Communication Magazine*, Special Issue on Multimedia Communications, May 1992.

5. C. E. Catlett, "In Search of Gigabit Applications," *IEEE Communications Magazine*, April 1992, pages 42 ff.

6. N. K. Cheung, "The Infrastructure for Gigabit Computer Networks," *IEEE Communications Magazine*, April 1992, pages 60 ff.

7. H. T. Kung, "Gigabit Local Area Networks: A Systems Perspective," *IEEE Communications Magazine*, April 1992, pages 79 ff.

8. P. Newman, "ATM Technology for Corporate Networks," *IEEE Communications Magazine*, April 1992, pages 90 ff.

9. Z. Wang and J. Crowcroft, "SEAL Detects Cell Misordering," *IEEE Network*, July 1992, pages 8 ff.

10. The ATM Forum, *ATM User-Network Interface Specification*, Version 3.0, Interop/ATM Forum, Mountain View, Calif., August 1993,

11. D. Minoli, *Enterprise Networking, Fractional T1 to SONET, Frame Relay to B-ISDN*, Artech House, Norwood, Mass., 1993.

12. Internet Engineering Task Force, *Multiprotocol Interconnect over ATM AAL 5*, Anonymous FTP, nic.ddn.mil, nnsc.nsf.net, ftp.nisc.sri.com, July 1992.

13. D. Grossman, T1S1.2-92-315, T1S1 Contribution.

10

Network Management

10.1 Introduction

As ATM standards have been agreed upon and ATM equipment has become available, ATM network management has emerged as a critical item in the path towards wide-scale ATM networking. In the context of this book, ATM network management spans both private enterprise networks and shared public ATM networks. While a detailed discussion of ATM network management could be a book in its own right, this chapter presents information that private network managers can use to better understand how to make use of the capabilities provided by public networks in their own network management systems.

10.1.1 Telecommunications Management Network Model

In the past, telecommunications network management was based upon a model whereby nearly all of the network management intelligence was centrally located, in so-called operations support systems (OSSs). Advances in computing and network element technology have led to a new management architecture, called the Telecommunications Management Network (TMN) Model.[1] In this model, operations functions are partitioned across multiple layers, including the Element Layer, Element Management Layer, Network Management Layer, and higher layers (e.g., Service Management Layer). These layers are illustrated in Fig. 10.1.

The underlying philosophy behind this multilayer model of operations is that each layer views the network at a different level of abstraction

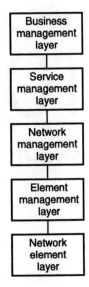

Figure 10.1 TMN Architecture Layers.

and thus manages it accordingly. The Element Layer's view of the network is the most detailed of all the layers. The Element Layer has visibility of the vendor-specific intricacies of the various elements in the network. The Element Management Layer contains functions that may be used to manage resources individually and in aggregation as a subnetwork. Higher levels of abstraction are provided at the Network Management, Service Management, and Business Management Layers. The Network Management Layer, on the other hand, deals with an aggregated view of network resources as presented by the Element Management Layer. More specifically, the Network Management Layer is responsible for providing management functions that require coordination across multiple subnetworks. The Service Management Layer maintains a view of the services being provided and supported by the network. The Business Management Layer provides the functions necessary to operating a network as a going business concern, e.g., billing and collection functions.

10.1.2 Network management functional areas

Modern network management has been subdivided into five functional areas:

- *Configuration management* comprises network management functions which are designed to identify, exercise control over, collect data from, and provide data to network elements.

- *Fault management* comprises network management functions which are designed to detect, verify, and isolate troubles within communications networks.

- *Security management* comprises network management functions which are designed to protect the integrity of networks from unauthorized intrusion.

- *Performance management* comprises network management functions which are designed to monitor and assess a system's ability to carry out its assigned functions, through the collection and analysis of appropriate performance data.

- *Accounting management* comprises network management functions which are designed to provide a network operator with usage information which can be used to charge customers for their use of network resources.

A brief set of example functions which are performed in each of these functional areas is given below.

1. Configuration management functions
   - Manage assignable inventory
   - Select and assign resources
   - Schedule and sequence the activation/deactivation of an assignment
   - Update and query data
   - Back up data for purposes of future restoral

2. Fault management functions
   - Correlate multiple alarms
   - Analyze alarms and report findings
   - Log alarms
   - Select, run, and abort generic testing routines and diagnostics
   - Analyze test/diagnostic results and report findings

3. Security management functions
   - Authenticate
   - Control access
   - Provide and manage audit trials
   - Report security alarms
   - Monitor data and system integrity
   - Recover from intrusions

4. Accounting management functions
   - Aggregate usage measurements
   - Format and transmit usage measurements

5. Performance management functions

- Accumulate performance monitoring and traffic management data
- Analyze alerts/alarms and report findings
- Update and/or query performance management data and control information

Each of these functional areas is treated in more detail in this chapter, after a brief discussion of operations communications. Readers desiring a more in-depth discussion than is provided in this chapter are encouraged to consult Ref. 2.

10.1.3 Operations communications

Efficient network management depends on effective communications among network elements and network management systems. Typically, private networks use network management systems which are based upon the use of the Simple Network Management Protocol (SNMP), while public networks have been moving towards the use of OSI network management protocols, namely the OSI Common Management Information Protocol (CMIP). This section describes operations communications in an ATM network.

The Simple Network Management Protocol.   The SNMP protocol[3] consists of five types of operations which are used to retrieve and manipulate management information. These are:

- *Get.* Used by the SNMP manager to retrieve specific management information
- *Get-Next.* Used by the SNMP manager to retrieve management information via traversal of the management information base (MIB)
- *Set.* Used by the SNMP manager to modify specific management information
- *Trap.* Used by the SNMP agent for unsolicited event notification
- *Get-Response.* Used by the SNMP agent to respond to Get, Get-Next, and Set messages

SNMP is widely used in IP networks, and SNMP messages are typically carried via the UDP/IP protocol stack.

The OSI Common Management Information Service.   The Common Management Information Service (CMIS)[4] comprises the following functions:

- *M-GET.* An operation which allows a CMISE service user to retrieve attributes from managed objects. M-GET is used for active control by network management processes.

- *M-SET.* An operation which allows a CMISE service user to modify attributes of managed objects. M-SET is used for active control and intervention by network management processes.

- *M-ACTION.* An operation which allows a CMISE service user to request an action on a managed object (or objects).

- *M-CREATE.* An operation which allows a CMISE service user to create an instance of a managed object.

- *M-DELETE.* An operation which allows a CMISE service user to delete an instance of a managed object.

- *M-CANCEL-GET.* An operation which provides a form of flow control mechanism for linked replies to CMISE commands.

- *M-EVENT-REPORT.* A notification service which is used by most system management functions. M-EVENT-REPORT is used for passive monitoring by network management processes.

CMIP messages are carried over an OSI protocol stack, using the Remote Operations Service Element (ROSE) protocol. Figure 10-2 illustrates the protocol stack used for carriage of CMIP messages. Figure 10-3 illustrates some of the ways in which network elements may communicate with management systems. These methods range from dedicated VCCs to dial-up lines. In some cases, a management system may not have direct communications access to a network element. In this case, the NE can use the SONET Section Data Communications Channel (DCC) to form an embedded operations channel to a device which has connectivity to the management system, such as an ATM switching system.

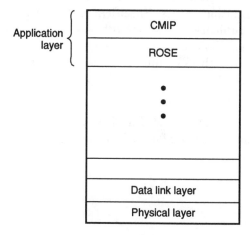

Figure 10.2   OSI protocol stack.

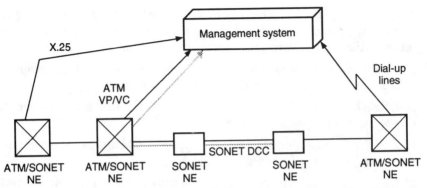

Figure 10.3 Communications among network elements and management systems.

10.1.4 Physical Layer and ATM Layer operations flows

Operations and maintenance procedures often require the exchange of operations information among various nodes in the network. At the Physical Layer, endpoints of each facility exchange operations information via well-defined overhead fields built into the signal framing structure.

When operations information is tightly coupled with the binary stream of user data across a physical or logical connection, as is the case with error detection codes or when timing is critical (e.g., in reporting failure/congestion indications), a simpler encoding technique (i.e., one that uses a bit-oriented protocol) must be employed. This section identifies mechanisms required at the Physical and ATM Layers to support the flow of bit-oriented operations information between peer-to-peer Physical and ATM Layer termination points. Specifically, this section identifies mechanisms to communicate operations information across DS1, DS3, and SONET facilities; Physical Layer convergence protocol (PLCP) paths; and ATM virtual path (VP) and virtual channel (VC) connections.

Physical Layer operations flows. In support of Physical Layer operations, bit-oriented operations flows are used for each of the following:[5–7]

- DS1 transport systems
- DS3 transport systems
- PLCP paths
- SONET transport systems

The mechanisms for such communications are discussed in the subsections that follow.

DS1 level operations flows.   DS1 rate facilities that support ATM use the extended superframe format (ESF). Bit-oriented operations information is communicated between the entities terminating a DS1 path via a 4-kbits/s data link channel and a 2-kbits/s cyclic redundancy check (CRC) channel. The extended superframe format makes these overhead channels available by making efficient use of the DS1 framing bits. Specifically, 18 of the 24 DS1 framing bits in the ESF are used for bit-oriented operations communications: 6 for error detection (CRC-6) and 12 for a 4-kbits/s data link channel. The 4-kbits/s data link channel is used to report far-end performance monitoring results, to activate and deactivate a line-level loopback, and to notify downstream equipment about failures that have occurred upstream.

DS3 level operations flows.   A DS3 M frame is divided into 7 subframes, each of which is subdivided into 8 blocks of 85 bits each. The first bit of each block is a DS3 overhead bit, thus making available a total of 7×8 = 56 overhead bits in a DS3 M frame. The overhead bits are categorized into 5 classes: F bits, M bits, P bits, X bits, and C bits. The F bits and M bits are used for M subframe and M frame alignment, respectively. The P bits, X bits, and C bits are used for the communication of operations information between peer DS3 termination entities. The P bits are used for parity checking and to gather performance monitoring data. The X bits are used by terminating equipment to signal a failure condition (yellow alarm) to the other end of the DS3 facility. The C bits have application-specific uses by DS3 transport systems.[5]

PLCP level operations flows.   The ATM Physical Layer Convergence Protocol (PLCP) defines the mapping of ATM cells onto the existing DS3 and DS1 facilities. PLCP overhead consists of the following: framing octets (A1 and A2), path overhead identifier octets (P11–P0), growth octets (Z6–Z1), Bit Interleaved Parity (BIP)—8 octet (B1), PLCP path status octet (G1), and the cycle/stuff counter octet (C1). Of these overhead fields, the B1 and G1 octets of each PLCP frame are used to communicate operations information between peer PLCP level management entities. The BIP-8 error detection code in the B1 field supports PLCP path error monitoring and the collection of PLCP path level performance data. The first 4 bits of the G1 byte are used to report far-end performance information to the near end [e.g., a far end bit error (FEBE) indication]. The fifth bit in the G1 byte is used to convey (to the downstream PLCP path-terminating entity) the detection of a yellow alarm condition upstream. The remaining 3 bits in the G1 byte are not used for ATM PLCP-based interfaces.

SONET level operations flows. SONET overhead fields exist at three distinct levels: the section level, line level, and path level. ATM switching systems terminate all three of these levels and process the three corresponding overhead fields. The bit-oriented operations information encoded in the SONET section, line, and path overhead fields is used to (1) report SONET-level alarm, failure, status, and error indications (such as the FEBE indication) and (2) provide forward error detection information (e.g., BIP-8 error detection codes) for the detection of transmission errors and the collection of SONET-level performance data.

ATM Layer operations flows. Two types of connections have been defined at the ATM Layer: virtual path connections (VPCs) and virtual channel connections (VCCs). For some VPCs or VCCs, in-band connection-specific operations information is communicated between the various VPC or VCC nodes (currently defined as any node accessing or terminating a VPC or VCC). Examples include failure indications, performance monitoring data, and test requests. The required mechanisms for transmitting such information at the VP and VC levels are discussed below.

VPC operations flows (F4 flows). VPC operations flows are made possible via specially marked ATM cells. These cells are referred to as operations and maintenance (OAM) cells and are distinguishable from user-data cells by an indicator in the ATM cell header. Specifically, VPC OAM cells are identified by a unique set of VCI values. There are two kinds of F4 flows which can simultaneously exist in a VPC.

- *End-to-End F4 flow.* This flow is used for communicating end-to-end VPC operations information. VCI value 4 is used for identifying OAM cells that make up F4 flows.
- *Segment F4 flow.* VCI value 3 is used for identifying OAM cells communicated within the bounds of a single virtual path link (VPL) or group of interconnected VPLs in the purview of a single provider's network. A VPL or group of VPLs that is independently managed using such OAM cells is referred to in I.610 as a VPC segment.

VCC operations flows (F5 flows). VCC operations (F5) flows also make use of OAM cells. These OAM cells have the same VCI/VPI values as the user cells of the VCC and are distinguished from other cells transported over a particular connection by the payload type indicator (PTI) value. There are two types of F5 flows which can simultaneously exist in a VCC:

- *End-to-End F5 flow*. PTI value 5 is used to identify OAM cells used for communicating end-to-end VCC operations information.

- *Segment F5 flow*. PTI value 4 is used to identify OAM cells communicated within the bounds of a single VCC link or group of interconnected VCC links in the purview of a single provider's network. A VCC link or group of VCC links that is managed using such OAM cells is referred to in I.610 as a VCC segment.

Endpoints of a connection or connection segment terminate and process all incoming OAM cells that belong to the connection. Such endpoints may also generate and insert OAM cells for downstream processing. Intermediate points along a connection or connection segment may monitor OAM cells passing through them and insert new OAM cells, but they do not terminate the OAM flow.

A number of VPC/VCC management functions exist. In order to accommodate these functions, three OAM cell types have been defined. These three OAM cell types are as follows:

1. *Fault Management OAM Cells*. These OAM cells are transmitted to indicate failure conditions, such as a failed facility or discontinuity at the virtual path or channel level. These cells may also be used to perform various test functions on a virtual connection or connection segment (e.g., as part of a reactive trouble isolation procedure).

2. *Activation/deactivation OAM cells*. This cell type is used for purposes of activating and deactivating the OAM cell generation and processing functions associated with certain VPC/VCC management capabilities.

3. *Performance Management OAM cells*. These OAM cells are transmitted regularly between endpoints of selected virtual connections or connection segments and are used to monitor parameters such as errored cell block ratio, cell loss ratio, and misinserted cells for performance monitoring.

While the OAM cell payload format for each OAM cell type is different, there are some fields that are common to all of them.[7] These fields are as follows:

- *OAM cell type*. This 4-bit field indicates the type of management function performed by the OAM cell (e.g., performance management, fault management, or activation/deactivation). Valid values for this field are shown in Table 10.1.

TABLE 10.1 OAM Type/Function Identifiers

OAM cell type	Value	OAM function type	Value
Fault management	0001	AIS	0000
		FERF	0001
		OAM cell loopback	0010
		Continuity check	0100
Performance management	0010	Forward monitoring	0000
		Backward reporting	0001
		Monitoring/reporting	0010
Activation/deactivation	1000	Performance monitoring	0000
		Continuity check	0001

- *OAM function type.* This 4-bit field indicates the actual function performed by the OAM cell. Standardized values of this field for each OAM cell type value are shown in Table 10.1.

- *Reserved field.* This 6-bit field has been reserved for future specification. It is encoded with a default value of all zeros.

- *CRC-10 error detection code.* This field carries a CRC-10 error detection code that is calculated over the entire OAM cell payload. It is used by ATM Layer entities to detect errored OAM cells and thus avoid processing any corrupted operations information. The generator polynomial for this error detection code is $x^{10} + x^9 + x^5 + x^4 + x + 1$.

The manner in which unused octets and unused bits (i.e., incomplete octets) are coded is also common across all OAM cell types. The term "unused" refers either to part of a cell that is not assigned to any field, or to any field that is not used in a particular application. All unused OAM cell information octets are coded as binary 01101010. All unused OAM cell information field bits are coded all zero.

The common part of the OAM cell is illustrated in Fig. 10.4.

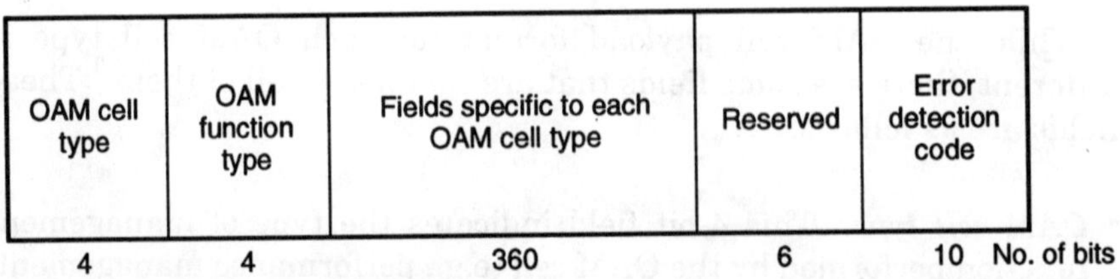

OAM cell type	OAM function type	Fields specific to each OAM cell type	Reserved	Error detection code
4	4	360	6	10 No. of bits

Figure 10.4 OAM cell common part.

10.2   Configuration Management

Configuration management refers to functions which identify, collect data from, exercise control over, and provide data to network elements. Configuration management can be either management-system-driven or NE driven. An example of management-system-driven configuration management is a management system communicating a cross-connection request to a switch. An example of NE-driven configuration management is an NE reporting to a management system upon the physical installation of an interface card. The main configuration management functions are described below.

Manage assignable inventory. This function involves maintaining data that describe the current state of the network. Systems responsible for this function maintain data representing the NEs, the facilities that terminate on the NEs, and the VPI/VCI translations.

Assign resources. This refers to the ability to select and assign previously installed network resources in response to requests initiated by higher-layer management application entities. For example, this would entail determining and ultimately assigning the most appropriate physical and logical resources to use in configuring a permanent virtual connection.

Activation/deactivation of an assignment. Associated with every assignable resource is a service state indicating whether the resource is in service (activated) or out of service (deactivated). The activation or deactivation of a resource may be based on pending/future activity or may involve multiple entities where sequencing of state changes is required.

Back up data. This function refers to the ability to maintain memory backups and restore memory upon recovery from a memory-affecting outage.

10.3   Security Management

Corporate MIS executives have been quoted as making statements such as, "Our network is the key to our competitiveness." Given that networks are literally flowing with enterprise-critical data, security of these networks is a high priority. Indeed, these networks can be the intended targets of industrial espionage, sabotage, or simply thrill-seeking "hackers." Security management deals with methods for protecting the network from unwanted or unauthorized intrusion.

In the past, securing a network was mainly a matter of restricting physical access to network facilities and devices. However, as network elements have become more "intelligent," the network now resembles a large distributed computing system. Thus, each element must not only be physically secured against security threats, but logically secured as well. The major known security threats include

- An entity gaining greater privileges by masquerading as another entity.
- Disclosure of data without authorization
- Alteration of data
- Access of system resources by unauthorized users
- Degradation of a system's performance or incapacitation of the system

Security features fall into the following categories:

- Identification of users (e.g., use of a user-ID)
- Authentication of users (e.g., smart card verification)
- Session control (e.g., session establishment procedures)
- Resource access control (e.g., restriction on user's access to certain data)
- Data and system integrity (e.g., consistency of intelligent network node data)
- Security logging (e.g., ability to establish an audit trail)
- Security administration (e.g., overriding vendor defaults)

Each category is discussed below.

The first security step an intelligent network node needs to take is the identification of a user as being valid or not. The user's ID must be stored in the intelligent network node in order for the user to gain access to the node.

After identification of the user, the authentication process is performed. This consists of verifying user attributes such as private identifier (e.g., password) and calling address (for remote dial access) to verify that users are, in fact, who they say they are. Mechanisms can include dial-back mechanisms and "smart card" verification.

Session control features, such as session timeouts and limiting the number of password attempts, can be implemented. Once a user passes these tests, the user is granted access to the intelligent network node. An intelligent network node has the capability to store these security attributes and update them in response to messages from a management system.

Once a user is deemed to be a valid user, resource access control functionality is employed to make sure that users are authorized to perform the functions they request. Resource access control is based on the user's identity and, when applicable, the user's calling address. Users and calling addresses can be assigned privilege codes that restrict access to some functions and data.

In order for a user to access a subset of the database (e.g., an object class in a CMIS implementation), the user's authorization level must meet or exceed the access restrictions on those data.

Data and system integrity checking provides for a level of automated security monitoring, e.g., through detection of network management data corrupted by viruses.

Security logs provide the ability to examine an audit trail when a security problem is suspected.

Security administration deals with functions such as:

- Providing a mechanism for a security administrator to display all currently active users and review the actions of selected users

- Providing a mechanism for the security administrator to authorize or revoke users, reset user passwords, disable user IDs, and review a user's access privileges

10.4 Fault Management

This section addresses the fault management functions used to detect, verify, and isolate troubles in an ATM network. The fault management functions presented here may be grouped into two general categories: alarm surveillance functions, which include failure monitoring and failure notification capabilities, and failure localization and testing functions, which include capabilities that enable an appropriate management system to sectionalize a fault, analyze circuit and equipment characteristics, and enable an NE to diagnose its own internal status. These are discussed below, followed by a description of the fault management cell.

10.4.1 Alarm surveillance

Alarm surveillance functions are designed to aid in the detection and notification of network faults. Alarm surveillance measurements are made on a continuous basis by features within NEs and management systems. Alarm surveillance is concerned with monitoring for anomalies, defects, and failures, which are defined as follows:[8]

Anomaly. A discrepancy between the actual and desired characteristics of an item. The desired characteristic may be expressed in the form of a specification. An anomaly may or may not affect the ability of an item to perform a required function. Framing bit errors and frame format code violations such as CRC and BIP are examples of anomalies.

Defect. A limited interruption in the ability of an item to perform a required function. It may or may not lead to maintenance action depending on the results of additional analysis. Successive anomalies causing a decrease in the ability of an element to perform a required function are considered a defect. Short intervals of loss of signal, alarm indication signal, loss of pointer, and loss of frame are examples of defects.

Failure. The termination of the ability of an item to perform a required function. A failure is declared when a defect has been detected and that defect persists for some specified length of time. Both local and remote failures can be observed by NEs using maintenance signaling functions in transport overhead (e.g., alarm indication signals for upstream failures).

Anomalies are the first indication that there is trouble in the network. If enough anomalies occur in a short period of time (usually a small fraction of a second), a defect is declared, and the network element notifies other network elements using in-band alarms such as an alarm indication signal (AIS). Automatic actions are initiated within the network element to correct the problem. If the defect continues to persist (e.g., for a few seconds), a failure is declared, and the appropriate management system is notified.

There are three major aspects of the alarm surveillance process. The first involves the detection of faults in the Physical and ATM Layers, respectively, and the declaration of defect and failure states in the network element. The second major aspect involves the transmission of in-band alarm indications such as AIS and remote defect indicators (RDIs) among NEs affected by the defect.

The third major aspect of alarm surveillance involves failure reporting.

Physical Layer defect and failure detection.   DSn and SONET interfaces, although similar, have some important differences in their failure states. Each is discussed separately below.

Alarm surveillance for ATM over DS1 and DS3.   At the Physical Layer, the following faults exist for DS3 transmission systems that use the PLCP to carry ATM cell streams:

- Loss of signal (LOS)
- Loss of frame (LOF)
- PLCP LOF

The PLCP LOF state is defined as the persistence of a PLCP Out of Frame (OOF) for 1 ms.[9] The PLCP OOF is declared when an error in both the A1 and A2 PLCP framing octets, or two consecutive invalid path overhead identifier (POI) octets, occurs.

The following faults exist for DS1 and DS3 systems that use direct cell mapping instead of the PLCP:

- LOS
- LOF
- Loss of cell delineation (LCD)

DS1 and DS3 in-band alarms. DS1 and DS3 downstream alarms include the AIS, as defined in Ref. 10. Upstream alarms include the DS3 RDI and (when PLCP is used) the PLCP yellow alarm.[9]

Alarm surveillance for ATM over SONET. At the Physical Layer, the following faults exist for SONET transmission systems carrying ATM cell streams:

- LOS
- LOF
- Loss of pointer (LOP)
- LCD

The LCD state is an ATM-specific state, and applies to all transmission systems that do not use PLCP. In normal operation, cells are delineated (i.e., extracted) from a transmission payload after the starting position of the first cell is located. However, if seven consecutive cells have HEC violations, an out-of-cell-delineation (OCD) anomaly will occur. The OCD anomaly will continue until either cell delineation is reestablished or a transition is made into the LCD defect state.

ATM Layer defect and failure detection. Faults can be detected at the ATM Layer from notification of Physical Layer faults. This section describes the communication of VP/VC alarms at the ATM Layer.

VP/VC alarm indications. At the ATM level, two alarm indications have been defined:

Alarm indication signals (AIS). VP-AIS and VC-AIS alarms are generated by the node detecting a defect to alert the downstream nodes that a defect has been detected upstream. These alarms are communicated by using fault management OAM cells with the AIS function type.

Remote defect indications (RDI). VP-RDI and VC-RDI alarms are generated by the node terminating a defective connection to alert the upstream nodes that a defect has been detected downstream. These alarms are communicated by using fault management OAM cells with the RDI function type.

An illustration of the flow of VP/VC AIS and RDI alarms is provided in Fig. 10.5.

The fault management cell contains fields to note the failure type and failure location. However, encodings of these fields have not yet been standardized.

VP alarms.   A VPC fault can be detected at the ATM Layer either by receiving an indication from the Physical Layer or by receiving an indication from an ATM entity. The procedure for generating alarms varies slightly, depending on whether the fault is detected at a connecting point, an originating point, or a terminating point of the VPC. Each case is discussed below.

1. *Fault at a connecting point.*   When a defect is declared at the ATM Layer of a connecting point, AIS cells are generated and periodically sent downstream for each VPC affected by the failure. The first cell is sent between 50 and 500 ms after the defect indication. The lower

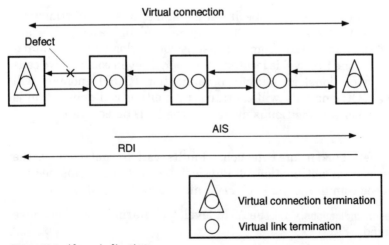

Figure 10.5 Alarm indications.

bound of 50 ms was chosen to allow for protection switching before generation of AIS cells. The upper bound of 500 ms is required to support signaling channels to provide defect detection times for signaling channels that are comparable to those obtained today. AIS cells continue to be generated until the defect state is exited.[2]

At the terminating endpoint, when one AIS cell is received on a VPC, the AIS defect state is declared, and the endpoint sends RDI cells upstream to alert upstream nodes that a defect has been detected downstream. This continues until either (1) a valid cell is received or (2) no AIS cell is received within a specified time period.

At the originating point, the RDI state is declared when one RDI is received, and the RDI state is exited when no RDI cell has been received for a specified period of time.

2. *Fault at the originating point.* When the defect is detected at the originating endpoint, the procedure is the same, except that RDIs received at the originating endpoint are ignored (as well as the RDI state).

3. *Fault at the terminating point.* When the defect is detected at the terminating endpoint, the procedure is the same as the connecting point case, except that no VP AIS cells are generated.

VC alarms. VCC faults can be detected at the ATM layer either by indications from the Physical Layer or by indications from a VPC terminating point. Unlike VP alarms, VC alarms are not generated for all VCCs, but rather only for preselected connections. This allows all VCCs to be alarmed if desired, but allows suppression of alarms where they are not desired. If a VC-AIS is generated, then the endpoint also generates a VC-RDI. The interaction between VP and VC alarms is shown in Fig. 10.6.

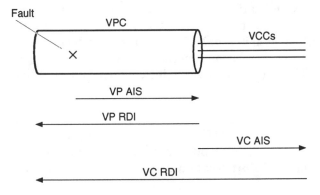

Figure 10.6 VP alarms and VC alarms.

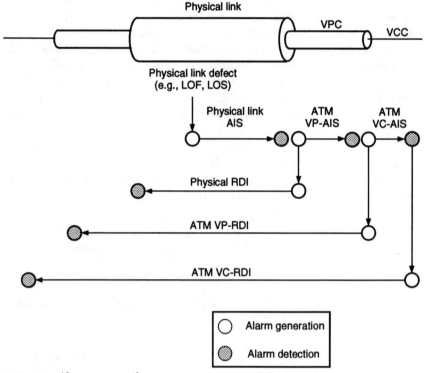

Figure 10.7 Alarm propagation.

The state transitions, flow of VC-AIS and VC-RDI cells, and timings for a VCC with a fault are the same as for VPCs, except that the generation of alarms for a VCC is optional.

Physical (DSn/SONET) Level alarm indications may result in the generation of VPC alarm indications, which in turn may result in the generation of VCC alarm indications. This interaction of SONET and ATM Level alarms is illustrated in Fig. 10.7. This propagation of alarms points to the need for alarm correlation functions in a network management system to identify cause-and-effect relationships and simplify rectification processes.

AIS/RDI cell payload structure. The AIS/RDI cell payload structure is shown in Fig. 10.8. Currently, both ITU and T1 have standardized the size of the failure type field as being 8 bits. At press time, ITU had not yet agreed on the size of the failure location field.

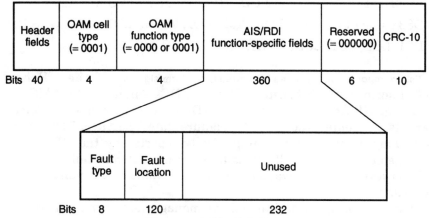

Figure 10.8 AIS/RDI fault management OAM cell format.

Each field is described below:

- *OAM function type.* This field identifies the function(s) of the fault management cell as being AIS (0000) or RDI (0001).

- *Failure type.* This field is used to identify the type of failure that has occurred.

- *Failure location.* This field is used to identify the location of a failure.

Failure reporting

Failure reporting when failure is detected locally. An entity may automatically recover from a defect in a short period of time. Thus, a transition into a defect state should not result in the generation of a report to a management system or the removal of the entity from service. To ensure this, a delay timing mechanism is used.

ATM-specific failures are declared only after the defect persists for a specified time interval. Once a failure is declared, a failure indication is set in the NE. When a NE detects a failure, it is reported to an appropriate management system as an alarm and thus requires immediate attention by the appropriate management system.

A low-level fault, such as a transmission system LOF, could cause multiple higher-level fault indications. When an entity detects a failure, it reports only the lowest-level failure. In increasing level, the relevant lower-level defects and failures for each interface type are

- SONET: LOS, LOF, LOP, LCD, VP AIS/RDI, and VC AIS/RDI
- DS3 using PLCP: LOS, LOF, PLCP LOF, VP AIS/RDI, and VC AIS/RD
- DS1: LOS, LOF, LCD, VP AIS/RDI, and VC AIS/RDI

Failure reporting when failure is inferred from alarm signals. If the NE has been informed of defects detected by other NEs, through VP/VC AISs or RDIs, the NE first enters the AIS or RDI defect state and, if the defect persists, then enters the AIS or RDI failure state. The AIS or RDI failure state may or may not be automatically reported by the NE to the management system. Indications that are not automatically reported will, however, be made available to and retrievable by the management system.[11]

In any network, it is desirable that a management system not receive redundant AIS and RDI defect notifications. This can be achieved by reporting AIS and RDI failures only at ingress to the network, i.e., at UNIs in the incoming direction.

10.4.2 Fault localization and testing

This section identifies testing functions that may be used to isolate internal network element failures down to the smallest repairable/replaceable unit of hardware or software. In addition, it identifies capabilities that enable a network provider to perform tests on individual VPCs and VCCs. Internal diagnostics relate to vendor-specific aspects of a NE, while VPC/VCC testing capabilities are generic.

OAM loopback capability

Indications of trouble on a particular VPC/VCC may come in the form of performance monitoring data, alarm surveillance procedures, and/or customer trouble reports that indicate that a particular VPC/VCC is experiencing trouble. Upon receipt of a trouble report, tests may be initiated to verify the existence of the reported trouble, identify the nature of the trouble, and isolate its cause.

The OAM loopback capability[2] can be used to

- Verify connectivity
- Isolate faults
- Perform preservice acceptance tests

OAM cell loopbacks are performed by inserting fault management loopback cells at one point along a connection, with instructions in the cell payload for the cell to be looped back at another point along the connection.

The format of the loopback fault management cell is shown in Fig. 10.9, and each field is described below.

- *OAM function type.* This field identifies the fault management cell as being a loopback cell (and therefore identifies the format of the function-specific fields).

- *Loopback indication.* The last bit of this field provides a boolean indication of whether the cell has been looped back or not. When the loopback point receives a loopback cell with the bit set to 1, it changes the loopback indication to 0, and initiates a loopback cell in the opposite direction containing the same information in the remaining loopback fields. When this indication is 0, the loopback cell is not to be looped back.

- *Correlation tag.* At any given time, multiple loopback cells could be inserted in the same connection. This field provides a means of correlating transmitted OAM cells with received OAM cells.

- *Loopback location ID (optional field).* This field identifies the point along the virtual connection or segment at which the loopback is to occur. The default coding is all 1s, and represents the endpoint of the connection or segment.

- *Source ID (optional field).* This field identifies the source originating the loopback cell. The default coding is all 1s.

Whenever an entity receives any loopback cell, it must determine the appropriate action. It must decide whether to

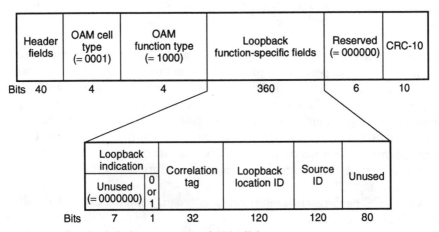

Figure 10.9 Loopback fault management OAM cell format.

1. Loop back the cell.

2. Copy the cell, if the entity initiated the cell which has completed its loopback.

3. Pass the cell without further action.

10.5 Performance Management

Performance management comprises network management functions which are designed to monitor and assess a system's ability to carry out its assigned functions, through the collection and analysis of appropriate performance data.

Performance monitoring refers to the periodic assessment of a system's ability to carry out its assigned function through the collection and analysis of appropriate performance data. The intent of performance monitoring procedures is to capture intermittent error conditions and troubles resulting from any gradual deterioration of network equipment. Performance monitoring is useful because it enables network providers to detect troubles early and correct them before they become more severe. Within the context of ATM networks, performance monitoring supports the following capabilities:

- Monitoring of physical transport facilities

- Monitoring of virtual path connections and virtual channel connections

- Protocol monitoring

Physical transport facility performance monitoring.   For public ATM facilities, DS1, DS3, and SONET transport systems may be used. These systems have a well-defined set of performance management functions,[5] and are not described here.

VPC/VCC performance monitoring.   VPCs and VCCs may extend across a number of independently monitored transport facilities, to connect service entities in ATM switching systems or to provide semipermanent logical connections for end-to-end customer services or customer-to-network signaling. In either case, it is expected that the network provider and/or users will, at times, want to monitor the performance of their semipermanent connections. A VPC/VCC performance monitoring function has been defined to meet this need. This function applies to VP/VC segments as well.

VPC/VCC performance monitoring is accomplished using OAM cells. This section discusses

- The mechanism for VPC/VCC PM cell generation
- The VPC/VCC performance monitoring parameters
- The activation/deactivation procedure for VPC/VCC monitoring

ATM Layer performance monitoring has two distinct aspects. The first is the generation of performance management cells that communicate forward monitoring and backward reporting information among nodes of a connection. The second concerns the storage of data for each parameter, and thresholding of selected parameters.

Performance management cells send forward monitoring information and backward report information. As is discussed, there is an option to send both types of information in the same cell.

Mechanism for VP/VC PM cell generation.   There are two classes of VP/VC monitored entities: end-to-end VPC/VCCs and VPC/VCC segments. End-to-end monitoring refers to monitoring the entire connection, which may span multiple networks. A VPC/VCC segment is a part of the connection, and is generally limited to one administration's network.

A performance management cell contains information about a block of user-information cells of one connection; performance management and other OAM cells such as fault management cells are not part of the block. Figure 10.10 illustrates the concept of a block. The allowable nominal block sizes[2] are 128, 256, 512, and 1024 cells. Note that the larger the block, the lower the transmission capacity overhead used for performance monitoring.

End-to-end VPC/VCC monitoring.   The steps for generating PM cells when performing end-to-end VPC/VCC performance monitoring are listed below.

1. The originating VPC/VCC endpoint generates a BIP-16 error detection code over the payloads of the user information cells in the block. Then the endpoint will place the following information in the payload of a performance management OAM cell: the monitoring sequence number of the PM cell, the total user cell count (modulo 65,536), the BIP-16, and

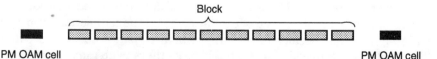

Block

PM OAM cell   PM OAM cell

Figure 10.10 Performance monitoring block.

an optional time stamp. This OAM cell is then the next cell transmitted on that VPC/VCC; i.e., it is transmitted before the next user-information cell of the VPC/VCC. Although the block size for a connection has a nominal value, the actual size of any given block may vary by as much as 50 percent from that nominal value. This variation allows PM cells to be inserted without delaying the flow of user cells in most cases.

2. The far-end VPC/VCC endpoint compares the number of the cells received in the block with the difference between the total user cell counts of the last two PM cells it received. A mismatch in this comparison indicates lost or misinserted cells. The endpoint compares the BIP-16 in the forward monitoring cell with the result of an identical BIP-16 calculation it has performed over the same number of user-information cells. A mismatch in this comparison indicates bit errors in the block. The results from this block count of lost/misinserted cells and the number of errored parity bits in the BIP-16 code are stored until the backward reporting cell is sent.

3. The far-end VPC/VCC endpoint reports the results (number of lost/misinserted cells and number of errored parity bits) back to the originating VPC/VCC endpoint using a Performance Management OAM cell to send a backward report.This procedure is performed symmetrically for both directions of VPC/VCC transmission if bidirectional PM has been activated. Figure 10.11 shows a connection, composed of connection segments, in which PM is active in both directions. Each VPC/VCC node has the capability to monitor the bidirectional VPC/VCC by accessing the backward reporting information.

In end-to-end performance monitoring, the insertion and extraction of OAM cells is performed only by the VPC/VCC endpoints, while the VPC/VCC monitor points need only monitor incoming OAM cells.

VP/VC segment PM cell generation.   Even if a VPC/VCC is already being monitored end to end, VPC/VCC segment monitoring can provide more accurate measures of the network provider's part of the connection. With VPC/VCC segment monitoring, performance problems outside the segment will not affect the results of segment monitoring.

The procedure for VPC/VCC segment performance monitoring is the same as the end-to-end procedure described earlier, except that performance management OAM cells are inserted and extracted at the endpoints of the segment instead of the endpoints of the connection. Another difference is that performance management cells are not forced when the block size is exceeded by 50 percent, so there is no maximum block size. However, it is desirable to enforce an average block size, because it improves the quality of the performance measures that are stored.

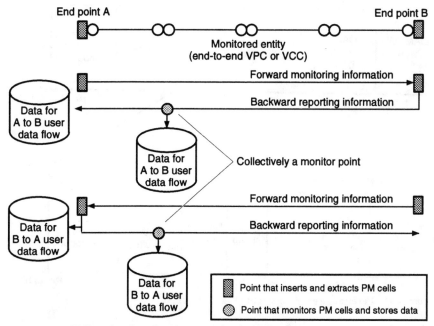

Figure 10.11 Bidirectional performance monitoring example.

An additional difference between end-to-end and segment monitoring is that the backward reporting flow is not always required.

Performance management cell payload structure. The performance management cell payload structure is shown in Fig. 10.12. The fields of the performance management cell are described below.

- *OAM type.* The OAM type is "performance management," encoded as 0010.

- *Function type.* The function type field specifies whether the cell is to be used for forward monitoring (0000), backward reporting (0001), or monitoring and reporting (0010). Note that although there are three function types, there are only two distinct functions of the PM cell: forward monitoring and backward reporting. For connections on which bidirectional performance monitoring is active, there exists the option of using all fields in a monitoring and reporting cell. In a monitoring and reporting cell, one PM cell is used to carry both the forward reporting information for one direction and the backward reporting information for the other.

- *Monitoring cell sequence number (MSN).* For PM cells containing forward monitoring information, this field contains the sequence

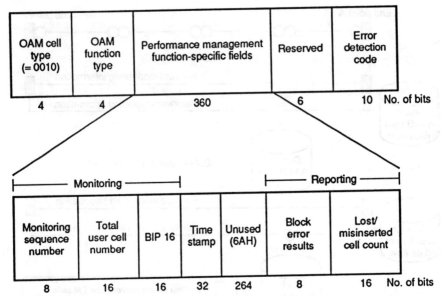

Figure 10.12 Performance management OAM cell format.

number, modulo 256. PM cells containing backward reporting information only (i.e., reporting cells) are not included in this sequence. This field allows for the detection of a lost or misinserted performance management OAM cell with forward monitoring information. For reporting cells, the MSN is encoded as 6A hexadecimal.

- *Total user cell (TUC) number.* This field indicates the total number (modulo 65,536) of user cells transmitted just before a monitoring cell is inserted.

- *Block error detection code.* This field contains the even-parity BIP-16 error detection code computed over the information fields of the block of user-data cells transmitted after the last monitoring cell.

- *Time stamp.* This optional field may be used to represent the time at which the OAM cell was inserted. If the field is not used, it is set to all 1s.

- *Unused.* Octets in this field are encoded as 6A hexadecimal (01101010).

- *Block error result.* This field carries the number of errored parity bits in the BIP-16 code of a received monitoring cell. The field is used for backward reporting.

- *Lost/misinserted cells.* This field carries the count of lost or misinserted cells computed over the received block. The value is calculated at the receiving ATM endpoint as the number of cells received minus the number of cells expected (i.e., actual – expected). This field is used for backward reporting.

When fields are not used (e.g., the monitoring fields are not used in the reporting PM cell), the fields are treated as unused fields, and encoded accordingly. Note, however, when a PM cell uses the monitoring fields but does not encode a time stamp into the time stamp field, it is not considered unused. In this case, the time stamp field is encoded to its default value of all 1s.

VP/VC Performance monitoring parameters. At press time there were no international standards agreements on specific parameters for performance monitoring using OAM cells. However, there are international agreements on fundamental principles of ATM Layer cell transfer performance as defined in I.356,[12] including

- Errored blocks
- Severely errored blocks
- Misinserted user information cells
- Lost user information cells
- Excessive cell transfer delay occurrences

It is expected that performance monitoring parameters will be defined to be consistent with those agreements, on a per-VP or per-VC basis.[2]

The block error result can be used to distinguish between errored and severely errored blocks. The BIP-16 error code was chosen for performance monitoring because, when using this type of error detection code, it is

1. Unlikely that a moderate level of background errors will result in more than four BIP columns being in error
2. Probable that a burst error event will affect more than four of the BIP columns.

Thus, the number of BIP columns in error can be used to distinguish between errored blocks and severely errored blocks.

1. *Errored blocks.* While acute failure conditions are generally detected by alarm surveillance methods, low-rate or intermittent error conditions in multiple equipment units may interact aggregately over a connection, resulting in poor service quality. The Errored Block parameter is designed to measure the overall qual-

ity of the connection to detect such deterioration. It may also be possible to detect characteristic patterns indicating an impending serious degradation before signal quality has dropped below an acceptable level.

2. *Severely errored blocks.* Whenever the number of errored columns is greater than a prespecified threshold, a block is counted as a severely errored block. When this threshold is set to a uniform value in a network, it allows a single interpretation of Severely Errored Block measurements by network managers. Thus, it may be desirable for all networks to adopt a uniform value.

3. *Lost user information cells.* This parameter measures cell loss, but cannot distinguish between cells lost because of header bit errors, ATM-level header errors, cell policing, or buffer overflows.

4. *Misinserted user information cells.* It is possible that a cell can be misrouted to an active VP/VC that is being monitored. This parameter is used to measure these occurrences.

5. *Excessive cell transfer delay occurrences.* Performance management OAM cells, each containing a time stamp, could be used to obtain an estimate of excessive cell transfer delay occurrences at the ATM switch that receives the time stamp information in the forward report. This count can be made and stored only at the connection/segment endpoint that receives the forward monitoring cell, as there is no field in the PM cell that allows backward reporting of Excessive Cell Transfer Delay Occurrences.

Activation/deactivation procedure for VP/VC monitoring. The activation/deactivation of VP/VC performance monitoring is a system management function, initiated by the appropriate management system or by the end user. Activation/deactivation cells are used in the network to provide "handshaking" between the two ends of the monitored entity. The performance monitoring activation/deactivation handshaking procedure serves the following purposes:

1. To coordinate and synchronize the beginning or end of the transmission and downstream reception of PM OAM cells

2. To establish agreement, based on the system management activation/deactivation request, on the block size and the direction(s) of transmission to start or stop monitoring

The activation/deactivation cell format is shown in Fig. 10.13, and each field is briefly described.

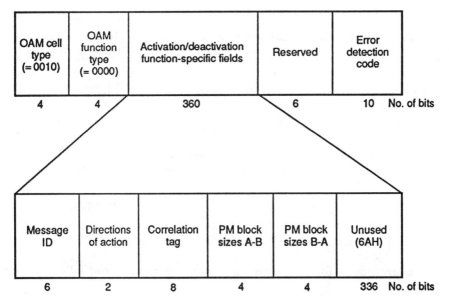

Figure 10.13 Activation/deactivation OAM cell format.

1. Message ID (6 bits). This field indicates the message ID for activating or deactivating VP/VC functions. Code values for this field are shown in Table 10.2.

2. Directions of action (2 bits). This field identifies the direction(s) of transmission to activate or deactivate the OAM function. The A-B and B-A notation is used to differentiate between the direction of user data transmission away from or towards the activator/deactivator, respectively. This field value is used as a parameter for the activate and deactivate messages. This field is encoded as 01 for B-A, 10 for A-B, 11 for two-way action, and 00 (default value) when not applicable.

TABLE 10.2 Message ID Codings

Message	Value
Activate	000001
Activation Confirmed	000010
Activation Request Denied	000011
Deactivate	000100
Deactivation Confirmed	000101
Deactivation Denied	000110

3. Correlation tag (8 bits). A correlation tag is generated for each message so that nodes can correlate commands with responses.

4. PM block sizes A-B (4 bits). This field specifies the A-to-B PM block size or block size choices supplied by the activator for performance monitoring. Each of the four bit positions in this field, from the most significant bit to the least significant bit, if set, indicates block sizes of 128, 256, 512, or 1024, respectively. For example, a value of 1010 would mean that block size 128 or 512 may be used, but not 256 and 1024. This field value is used as a parameter for the Activate and Activation Confirmed messages. The default value for this field is 0000.

5. PM block sizes B-A (4 bits). This field specifies the B-A block size or block size choices supplied by the activator. It is encoded and used in the same manner as the PM Block Sizes A-B field.

The procedure for activating performance monitoring (PM) is as follows:

- *Request for PM activation.* An end user or management system initiates a request at one end of the monitored entity. By definition, this endpoint is A and the other endpoint is B. The initiation includes a specification of the direction(s) of PM to activate and the requested block size(s) in the A-B direction (if appropriate) and the B-A direction (if appropriate). Endpoint A first determines whether it can support monitoring an additional monitored entity, and checks to make sure that PM cells are not already being generated in the requested direction(s). Then it determines which subset of the requested block size values in each direction it supports. If none of the value or values are supported by endpoint A, the request is denied, and the PM activation requester is informed.

- *Send Activate message.* If endpoint A can support the requested PM, it sends an Activate message, including the block size value(s) and monitored direction(s), to endpoint B.

- *Send Activation Confirmed message or Activation Request Denied message.* Endpoint B determines which of the requested block size value(s) it can support. If it can support multiple block sizes for a direction, it picks one. If there is at least one valid block size (one in each direction, in the case of a two-way monitoring request), then it sends an Activation Confirmed message to endpoint A. Each point along the segment/connection capable of monitoring the connection notes that PM is active.

If endpoint B does not support at least one block size in each direction of monitoring, if PM cells are already being generated in the requested direction(s), or if endpoint B is unable to support monitoring on any more monitored entities, then the request cannot be honored. In this case, endpoint B sends an Activation Request Denied message back to endpoint A. Endpoint A informs the PM activation requester of the denial.

- *Beginning of PM at endpoint B.* If endpoint B honors the PM activation request and sends an Activation Confirmed message, endpoint B begins the following processes: (1) it generates PM cells, if PM was activated in the B-A direction, and (2) it waits to receive PM cells, if PM was requested in the A-B direction. The first PM cell received is used only for initialization.

- *Beginning of PM at endpoint A.* When endpoint A receives the confirmation or if it receives a PM cell before the timer expires when PM was activated in the B-A direction, it begins the same two activities that endpoint B did, where appropriate, and notifies its management system that performance monitoring activities have begun.

The performance monitoring deactivation handshaking procedure is described below.

- *Request for PM deactivation.* An end user or management system initiates a request at one end of the monitored entity. By definition, this endpoint is A, and the other endpoint is B. There is no correlation between the point that activated PM and the point that deactivates PM; either end can request deactivation. The initiation includes a specification of the direction(s) of PM to deactivate. The two PM block sizes fields are not used, and hence are coded as 0000. Endpoint A first determines whether PM cells are being generated in the requested direction. If not, the request is denied, and the PM deactivation requester is informed.

It is possible that endpoint B is unable to respond (e.g., because of a power outage), and deactivation at A cannot use this handshaking procedure. Thus, the management system may deactivate its end only, but only after unsuccessfully trying deactivation with this procedure (i.e., by sending a Deactivate message).

It is possible that an endpoint will recover from a problem (e.g., power outage) and find that the other endpoint is no longer active because the other endpoint deactivated PM unilaterally during the problem. In such a case, the endpoint should initiate deactivation and reactivate if desired.

- *Send Deactivate message.* If endpoint A has no reason to deny the deactivation request, it relays a Deactivate message to endpoint B via an activation/deactivation cell.

- *Send Deactivation Confirmed message or Deactivation Request Denied message.* If endpoint B can honor the deactivation request, it sends a Deactivation Confirmed message to endpoint A.

If endpoint B has been set to ignore deactivation OAM cells, then the request cannot be honored. An endpoint may be set to ignore deactivation messages in order to prevent the other endpoint from deactivating PM. In this case, endpoint B sends a Deactivation Request Denied message back to endpoint A and informs its management system that a deactivation request was received and rejected. Endpoint A informs the PM deactivation requester of the denial.

If PM is not active in the requested directions, the request is considered to be honored.

- *Deactivation of PM at endpoint B.* If endpoint B honors the PM deactivation request and sends a Deactivation Confirmed message, endpoint B makes sure that PM cells are not being generated for the appropriate directions, if the deactivation request includes the B-A direction. Endpoint B notifies the management system that performance monitoring has ended. Any point along the connection that is storing data stops that activity and notifies its management system. No processing is performed on PM cells received after the deactivation request has been honored.

- *Deactivation of PM at endpoint A.* When endpoint A receives the confirmation, it ends the same two activities that endpoint B did, where appropriate, and notifies the appropriate management system that performance monitoring activities have ended. If a Deactivation Confirmed message is not received before the timer expires, the request is denied, and the PM deactivation requester is informed. If the confirmation is received after endpoint A's timer expires, endpoint A notifies the appropriate management system. The management system should then reinitiate a deactivation procedure.

An intermediate point that may wish to store PM history data needs to know when PM has been activated on a connection. It may do this by looking for Activation Confirmed messages and notifying the appropriate management system.

Protocol monitoring. Protocol monitoring is associated with every layer of the ATM protocol stack. Functions used for monitoring ATM cell header processing (i.e., the Physical and ATM Layers) and the AAL are given below.

Protocol monitoring of ATM cell header processing. ATM cells are processed at various levels internal to an ATM entity. For example, at the Transmission Convergence Sublayer of the Physical Layer, ATM cells are delineated from the SONET payload envelope, and the ATM cell header is examined for bit errors as part of a header error control algorithm. At the ATM Layer, the cell header is processed to support functions such as cell routing and generic flow control. Deterioration or defects in ATM cell header processing equipment, software bugs, and corrupted VPI/VCI translation tables could compromise the ability of an ATM entity to perform these functions, resulting in cell discarding and the degradation of end-to-end service. By monitoring the ATM entity's ability to successfully process ATM cells, network operators can quickly detect ATM cell header processing malfunctions and initiate corrective actions. This will serve to minimize the overall impact on the network as well as the end users supported by it.

In order to facilitate protocol monitoring, the ATM entity maintains counts of the following performance parameters:

Cells discarded because of header bit errors. A count is kept of the number of cells discarded because of header bit errors. Counting is suppressed when a Physical Layer problem is detected. This measure gives an implicit indication of intermittent errors in the Physical Layer, because Physical Layer problems will generally result in the corruption of multiple cell headers.

Cells with detected header bit errors. A count of the number of cell headers in which one or more bit errors *are* detected provides an indication of the effect of bit errors on ATM cells. The counting of cells with detected header bit errors is suspended when a Physical Layer problem occurs.

Cells discarded because of ATM Layer header errors. At the Physical Layer, cells are checked for header bit errors and discarded if necessary, and unassigned cells and invalid cells are extracted. The remaining cells are submitted to the ATM Layer, where a series of checks are performed on the contents of the headers. Cells with preassigned traffic type indications that do not conform to the allowed combinations of VPI/VCI, PTI, and CLP are discarded. For example, a cell used for point-to-point signaling cannot have a 1 in the first bit of the PTI. Cells without preassigned traffic type indications may also be discarded; for example, the VPI/VCI value might not conform to an active address. Another source of errors is receipt of OAM cells that cannot be processed—for example, PM cells being received on a connection for which performance monitoring is not active. If a cell has ATM Layer errors, then the cell will not be processed further. The number of cells discarded because of ATM Layer header errors is counted on a per-interface basis.

Protocol monitoring for the ATM Adaptation Layer.   This section discusses protocol monitoring for the Common Parts of AAL3/4 and AAL5.

AAL Type 3/4 supports the transport of connection-oriented and connectionless packet service. AAL3/4 processing is performed wherever the AAL3/4 is terminated.

Protocol monitoring for AAL Type 3/4 is based on maintaining counts of errors in received PDUs. The methods employed for storing, thresholding, and reporting AAL errors are the same as those employed for the ATM Layer. The occurrence of any one of a particular group of errors or abnormalities at a sublayer is recorded in a single, thresholded counter. Because multiple error types are captured in a common performance counter, this algorithm is referred to as the sum-of-errors algorithm, and any such counter is known as a sum of errors counter. Below is the description of the sum-of-errors algorithm.[2]

The purpose of the sum-of-errors algorithm is to detect nonbursty errors (moderate error rates) over an aggregation period. There is one sum-of-errors algorithm per connection (VPC or VCC) terminating AAL Type 3/4 per sublayer (SAR or CS). Whenever an error is detected, the current counter is incremented. If the counter's value exceeds a predetermined threshold value, a Threshold Crossing Alert message is generated and sent to the appropriate management system. If further errors are detected, the counter continues incrementing even after the Threshold Crossing Alert message is generated. If the counter reaches its maximum value, it does not "roll" but remains at that value for the duration of the aggregation period. A query of this counter may aid in determining the severity of the trouble. Only one threshold crossing alert message per sum-of-errors algorithm is generated during an aggregation period. After the aggregation period expires, the queue is advanced and the current counter is reset.

SAR Layer performance monitoring is performed by collecting and thresholding counts at each point where incoming SAR-PDUs are processed. Two error detection mechanisms may be employed for each connection termination where incoming SAR-PDUs are processed. One detects invalid fields, and the other detects incorrect fields. An invalid field is a field whose value falls outside of the range permitted by the protocol. For example, if a SAR-PDU User Information Length field is not equal to 44 for a SAR-PDU having a SAR type of beginning of message (BOM) or continuation of message (COM), then it is an invalid field, because only a length of 44 is permitted for BOMs and COMs.[2]

An incorrect field is a field whose value falls within the range permitted by the protocol, but that indicates the occurrence of a transmission or procedural error. For instance, a SAR-PDU CRC field that does not match the locally calculated CRC value is an incorrect field.

The principal difference between the two error types is that invalid fields indicate improper or incorrect implementations of the protocol, whereas incorrect field values indicate that a procedural or transmission error has occurred.

CS Layer performance monitoring.   CS Layer performance monitoring is accomplished by collecting and thresholding counts at each point where incoming CS-PDUs are processed. Outgoing CS-PDUs are not monitored.

As with the protocol monitoring for the SAR Layer, errors are divided into invalid fields and incorrect fields.

Protocol monitoring for AAL Type 5 (Common Part).   AAL Type 5 supports the transport of variable-length frames up to 65,535 octets long, with error detection extending over the entire frame. The frame is padded to align the resulting protocol data unit to fill an integral number of ATM cells.

Protocol monitoring for the AAL5 Common Part is accomplished by monitoring the following error conditions at the receiving point.

1. Invalid format of Control field

2. Length violations

3. Oversized SDU received

4. CRC violations

10.6   Accounting Management

Accounting management capabilities provide network operators with usage information that can be used to bill customers for their use of network resources and services. This usage information is also valuable for many other applications. As there are no standards for ATM accounting management per se, it is expected that these functions will be performed on a network-specific basis.

10.7   Management Information Exchange

A typical "network," as seen by end users, enterprise network managers, and public network providers, often consists of a complex interrelationship of individual networks, each owned and operated by a distinct entity. For efficient and complete network management, it is essential that management information be exchanged among these entities. This exchange of information can take place via a number of interfaces and procedures. This section describes one specific information exchange method, the ATM Forum–defined interim local management interface,[13] as well as a general architecture for the exchange of management information.

10.7.1 Interim local management interface

The interim local management interface (ILMI) provides bidirectional exchange of management information across a UNI between two adjacent UNI management entities (UMEs). SNMP has been chosen as the language for ILMI communications. A standard ILMI management information base (MIB) has been defined as well. This MIB contains configuration and status information related to the physical link and associated VPC/VCCs.

A UME can access the MIB information associated with its adjacent UME via the ILMI communication protocol. Figure 10.14 illustrates the ILMI communications protocol stack. Adjacent UMEs supporting ILMI act as peers, and each UME contains both an agent application and a management application. The adjacent UMEs contain the same MIB; however, semantics of some MIB objects may be interpreted differently.

The ILMI management information base. Management information related to the operation of the ATM UNI is organized into a MIB in a hierarchical fashion as follows:

- Physical Layer management information
- ATM Cell Layer management information
- VPC level management information
- VCC level management information

The UNI management information corresponds to configuration and status information. In addition, optionally, the ATM Layer performance

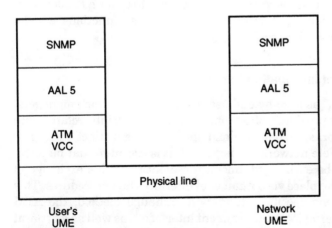

Figure 10.14 ILMI protocol stack.

and traffic statistics may be provided. The tree structure of the MIB is shown in Fig. 10.15.

MIB objects are defined using a subset of Abstract Syntax Notation One (ASN.1)[14] following the conventions specified in Ref. 15. All MIB objects are by default read-only across the ILMI, unless otherwise specified as readable and writable across the ILMI for a specific UNI MIB object. Tables 10.3 and 10.4 list the objects contained in the physical port and virtual path object groups, respectively.

10.7.2   Customer network management

This section describes what are commonly referred to as customer network management (CNM) service capabilities that will be supported for ATM PVC end users. CNM refers to a set of activities supported by public networks to facilitate planning, operations, administration, reconfiguration, and maintenance of an end user's communications network. CNM provides end users with the capability to manage their access to and use of the public ATM transport network and services.

To perform CNM functions, a public network CNM agent communicates with the end user's network management system. By accessing and controlling the CNM information, the end user's network management system manages the public network portion of the end user's communications network. The Simple Network Management Protocol (SNMP) is employed as the management protocol for communications between the NMS and the ATM PVC CNM agent. Alternative access configurations supporting SNMP exchange could be supported.

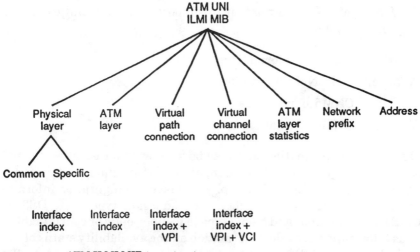

Figure 10.15 ATM ILMI MIB tree structure.

TABLE 10.3 Physical Port Object Group[13]

Objects	Type	Definition	Remarks
Interface index	Integer	Implicitly defines the physical interface over which the ILMI messages are received	Provides the UME with the identifier to retrieve UNI management information from its adjacent UME
Interface address	Integer	Public UNI address	Encoding is based upon ITU-T E.164 address and is currently defined as a number or a number plus subaddress
Transmission type	Object ID	Identifies the physical interface, which is currently defined as either STS-3c or DS3	Uniquely determines the transmission speed of the physical interface
Media type	Object ID	Defines the physical media type supported at a UNI	Currently public UNI types are coaxial cable, single-mode fiber, and multimode fiber
Operational status	Integer	Identifies the operational state of the physical interface (in service, out of service, or loopback)	Out of service and loopback indicate that the UNI is unavailable for cell transmission
Transmission type specific information	Object ID	Points to additional transmission and/or media specific information about a UNI	Points to other Physical Layer MIBs

UNI-specific CNM information to support ATM capabilities can be categorized as follows:

- Physical level CNM information
- ATM cell level CNM information
- VPC level CNM information
- VCC level CNM information

The types of information that may be supported for each level listed above are *configuration information*, *status information*, and *performance and traffic statistics*. At the physical level, configuration information provides information such as transmission type (e.g., DS3 or SONET transmission) and media type (e.g., fiber-optic or coaxial cable), status information provides information on the availability status of the physical link (e.g., DS3 alarm state), and performance and traffic

TABLE 10.4 Virtual Path Objects

Objects	Type	Definition	
Interface index	Integer	Implicitly defines the physical interface over which the ILMI messages are received	
VPI	Integer	Assigned VPI value for a VPC	
Operational status	Integer	Specifies the current operational state of the VPC (up, down, or unknown)	This information may be provided for the end-to-end VPC
Shaping traffic descriptor	Object ID	Points to the shaping parameters for cells transmitted on a VPC across a public UNI	
Policing traffic descriptor	Object ID	Points to the UPC parameters for policing cells received on this VPC	
QOS category	Integer	Defines the QOS category of the VPC	

statistics provides counts such as DS3 or SONET path severely errored seconds and unavailable seconds. At the ATM cell level, configuration information provides information such as number of configured VPCs, maximum number of VPCs, maximum number of active VPI bits, and amount of unused bandwidth available at a UNI; and performance and traffic statistics provides counts of ATM cells transmitted or received across a UNI, counts of errored cells, and counts of cells with unrecognized VPI and VPI/VCI values. At the VPC or VCC level, configuration information provides information such as VPI value or VPI/VCI values and usage parameter control (UPC) traffic parameters (e.g., the VPC peak rate and QOS parameter), status information provides information such as the operational state of a VPC or a VCC at a UNI (e.g., up, down, or testing state of a VPC or a VCC); and performance and traffic statistics provides counts such as the number of cells transmitted or received across a VPC or a VCC, the number of discarded cells due to UPC peak rate violation, and the number of times the cell rate exceeds the traffic peak rate on a VPC or a VCC.[2]

Potential ATM PVC CNM service capabilities. ATM PVC CNM service capabilities enable end users to

- Retrieve UNI configuration profile information
- Modify UNI configuration profile information
- Retrieve VPC/VCC subscription profile information
- Modify VPC/VCC subscription profile information
- Receive event notifications
- Request event notifications
- Request network intervention
- Initiate tests
- Retrieve general CNM information
- Modify general CNM information
- Retrieve performance information
- Retrieve usage information
- Request trouble reports

These are described briefly below.

Retrieve UNI configuration profile information.   This capability provides end users with the ability to retrieve UNI configuration information such as descriptions of how a UNI is currently provisioned or configured (e.g., number of VPCs configured at a UNI, transmission speed of a UNI, number of higher-level services supported at a UNI). In addition, this service capability also provides end users with the ability to retrieve information on the amount of unused bandwidth available at a UNI.

Modify UNI configuration profile information.   This capability provides end users with the ability to modify UNI configuration information such as the amount of unused bandwidth available at a UNI.

Retrieve VPC/VCC subscription profile information.   This capability provides end users with the ability to retrieve subscription related information such as descriptions of how a VPC is currently provisioned or configured.

Modify VPC/VCC subscription profile information.   This capability provides end users with the ability to modify parts of the VPC/VCC configuration, such as how a VPC or VCC is to be provisioned or configured.

Receive event notifications.   This CNM service capability provides an end user with the ability to receive unsolicited event notifications upon the occurrence of events that can affect the end user's use of the ATM network and services. An example of an unsolicited event notification could be the indication of a failure condition generated on occurrence of a VP-AIS (alarm indication signal). Event notifications can help end users isolate problems in their networks. Examples of events that could trigger event notifications are given below.[2,16]

- Restart/reset CNM service
- Failure/restoration of a UNI
- Failure/restoration of a PVC connection
- Failure/restoration of a specific higher-layer network service
- Changes to UNI configuration information
- Changes to ATM cell level configuration information
- Changes to VPC or VCC subscription information
- Changes to SVC service subscription information
- Authentication failure and authentication failure threshold exceeded

Request event notifications. This capability provides the end user with the ability to request notification of predefined and possibly end-user-defined events. An example is the ability to activate notification when there is a change in the end user's PVC configuration information (e.g., the UPC parameters of a VPC).

Request network intervention. This capability provides end users with the ability to request network intervention on their behalf. There could be situations in which the end user may not have immediate access to the malfunctioning equipment and thus cannot take care of the problem (e.g., reset or turn off the equipment) immediately. Therefore, the end user could request temporary suspension of a specific UNI or a PVC until the problem is fixed.

Initiate tests. This capability provides end users with the ability to initiate tests in isolating problems in their networks which span the public ATM network and services. For example, end users can activate an ATM-level loopback (e.g., activating OAM cell loopback capability using CNM service), which could help in fault isolation. Similarly, end users can activate VCC or VPC performance monitoring using this service.

Retrieve general CNM information. This capability provides end users with the ability to retrieve information related to the general characterization and status of a given UNI and the ATM PVC CNM system. Examples could include UNI operational status, CNM contact, and CNM system uptime.

Modify general CNM information. This capability provides end users with the ability to modify information related to the general administrative status of a given UNI. For example, this service might be used by an end user to turn off a UNI or to indicate that the UNI be subjected to a test by the network.

Retrieve performance information. This capability provides end users with the ability to retrieve information that will assist in the characterization of the performance of the network as well as network and service utilization. For example, an end user may want to determine the number of cells submitted and delivered over a VPC by the network, counts of errored cells, or other performance information, such as loss of cell delineation events per access link.

Retrieve usage information. This capability provides end users with the ability to retrieve usage information related to UNI. This information may be used by end users in determining how to allocate costs associated with the use of cell relay service within the end user's organization, and may also be used to support traffic analysis.

Request trouble reports. This capability provides end users with the ability to create a new trouble report (e.g., on detection of a problem) related to a UNI. In addition, end users can use this service capability to request the status of an existing trouble report (e.g., open or closed status), to remove an existing trouble report (e.g., in cases where the end user made an error in reporting the trouble), to add more information to an existing trouble report, and to retrieve information related to repair activity on reported troubles.

References

1. ITU-T Recommendation M.3010, *Principles of a Telecommunications Management Network*, Geneva, December 1991.
2. Bellcore Technical Advisory TA-NWT-001248, *Generic Requirements for Operations of Broadband Switching Systems*, October 1993.
3. RFC 1157, *Simple Network Management Protocol*, SRI International, May 1990.
4. ISO/IEC IS 9595, *Information Processing Systems—Open Systems Interconnection—Management Information Service Definition, Common Management Information Service Definition*, 1991.
5. Bellcore Technical Advisory TA-NWT-001112, *Broadband ISDN User to Network and Network Node Interface Physical Layer Generic Criteria*, August 1992.
6. ANSI T1.624–1993, *B-ISDN User-Network Interfaces: Rates and Formats Specifications*, 1993.
7. ITU-T Recommendation I.610, *B-ISDN Operations and Maintenance Principles and Functions*, Geneva, June 1992.

8. ANSI T1S1.5/93-004, *B-ISDN Operations and Maintenance Principles and Functions*, August 1993.

9. Bellcore Technical Reference TR-TSV-000773, *Local Access System Generic Requirements, Objectives and Interfaces in Support of Switched Multi-Megabit Data Service*, June 1991.

10. Bellcore Technical Reference TR-NWT-000191, *Alarm Indication Signal Requirements and Objectives*, May 1986.

11. Bellcore Technical Reference TR-TSY-000474, *OTGR: Network Maintenance: Network Element*, July 1991.

12. ITU-T Recommendation I.356, *B-ISDN ATM Layer Cell Transfer Performance*, Geneva, July 1993.

13. The ATM Forum, *ATM User-Network Interface Specification*, Version 3.0, 1993.

14. ISO/IEC IS 8824, *Information Processing Systems—Open Systems Interconnection—Specification of Abstract Syntax Notation One (ASN.1)*, December 1987.

15. RFC 1155, *Structure and Identification of Management Information for TCP/IP-based Internets*, SRI International, March 1991.

16. Bellcore Technical Advisory TA-TSV-001117, *Generic Requirements for Exchange PVC CRS Customer Network Management Service*, September 1993.

11

A Snapshot of Industry Activity

11.1 Introduction

The fate of a new technology, such as ATM, in the telecommunications marketplace depends on at least three factors:

1. Is equipment available which makes use of this new technology?
2. Are networks and network services being built which make use of this technology?
3. Will users accept this technology into their business?

This chapter examines the status of ATM, as of press time, with respect to the first and second factors. The organization of this chapter is as follows. First, a brief discussion of North American public network carrier activities associated with ATM deployment is given. Second, a brief listing of currently identified ATM equipment is given, along with a brief discussion of ATM switching technology. Finally, a description of several major leading-edge ATM trial activities is provided. Although the information contained in this chapter is time-dependent, it illustrates the level of early (and continued) interest in ATM on the part of the major telecommunications and equipment suppliers.

11.2   ATM Carrier Trials and Deployment Status

This section summarizes activities and plans publicly announced by telecommunications carriers as of early 1994 regarding ATM technology trials and deployment, as well as services to be offered on ATM technology platforms. ATM plans for local exchange carriers (LECs), interexchange carriers (ICs), competitive access providers (CAPs), and other carriers (e.g., CATV companies) are included.

11.2.1   BellSouth

Trial activity.   BellSouth is actively participating in the Vistanet gigabit testbed initiative (see Sec. 11.4.5 for a complete discussion of Vistanet).

Commercial deployment plans.   In May 1993 BellSouth announced plans to deploy a state-wide ATM network in support of the state of North Carolina's Information Highway Project.[1] The North Carolina Information Highway Project is expected to include over 3000 access lines by the late 1990s. This network is intended to provide dramatic improvements in health-care services, education, the state criminal justice system, and the efficiency of state government (e.g., consolidation of multiple state communications networks). Key applications to be supported on this network include distance learning, remote medical imaging for hospitals, and high-speed data transport (via SMDS, frame relay, and cell relay services). BellSouth's initial plans called for the deployment of 8 ATM switches in North Carolina, with up to 30 ATM switches throughout its territory during the 1993–1997 time period.

Vendors.   BellSouth had announced the choice of Fujitsu as the switch vendor for its North Carolina network. Fujitsu was also chosen to provide an ATM service multiplexer for use at the end user's premises.

11.2.2   Bell Atlantic

Trial activity.   Bell Atlantic is a participant in the Aurora, Blanca, and Nectar gigabit testbeds (see Sec. 11.4).

Commercial deployment plans.   Bell Atlantic offers a portfolio of high-speed data services which are available throughout the Bell Atlantic region. These services include SMDS, frame relay PVC, and three native-mode LAN interconnection services (FDDI network services, central office-based FDDI, and wire speed LAN interconnection).[2] At press time, Bell Atlantic's commercial ATM deployment plans had not been made public.

11.2.3 Ameritech

Trial activity. Ameritech is a participant in the Blanca gigabit testbed.

Commercial deployment plans. As of press time, Ameritech had not announced its commercial ATM deployment plans. Ameritech offers SMDS, LAN interconnection services, and frame relay PVC service in its major metropolitan areas.

Vendors. Ameritech issued an ATM Request for Proposal (RFP) for a number of ATM network equipment components. It had been reported afterward that the AT&T GCNS-2000 was Ameritech's chosen switching platform.

11.2.4 NYNEX

Trial activity. NYNEX announced its intention to build an ATM network to connect state universities and research laboratories in New York during 1993–1994. This ATM network testbed utilizes Fujitsu Fetex-150 host and remote ATM switches.[3] NYNEX is also a participant in the Aurora gigabit testbed project. NYNEX had also used an ATM switch as part of its Media Broadband Service (MBS) trial in Boston in 1992. This technology trial focused on multimedia applications which use ATM switching and transport. The applications scope of MBS has included health-care applications with Boston-area hospitals and publishing applications with *The Christian Science Monitor*.[4]

Commercial deployment plans. NYNEX offers a tariffed frame relay PVC service in the New York and Boston metropolitan areas. At press time, NYNEX's ATM deployment plans had not been made public.

11.2.5 Southwestern Bell Telephone

Trial activity. Southwestern Bell participated in a medical imaging trial with Washington University of St. Louis that used ATM switching and transport to support remote radiology applications. An RFI/RFP for ATM switches was issued in early 1994.

Commercial deployment plans. Southwestern Bell Telephone offers frame relay PVC service in the major metropolitan areas in its region. At press time, Southwestern Bell's ATM deployment plans had not been made public.

11.2.6 U S WEST

Trial activity.   U S WEST is a participant in the Blanca and Casa gigabit testbeds and the MAGIC (Multidimensional Applications and Gigabit Interworking Consortium) ATM trial in Minnesota. U S WEST conducted an ATM trial as part of its COMPASS (Computer Program for Advanced Switching Services) program.   This trial included ATM switches from AT&T, Fujitsu, and Siemens Stromber-Carlson. An important goal of the trial was to establish interworking among these three switches in support of multimedia distance learning applications at the University of Minnesota medical school.

Commercial deployment plans.   U S WEST offers SMDS, frame relay PVC service, transparent LAN services, and private line LAN interconnect services throughout the U S WEST region. U S WEST had also announced plans to upgrade its network infrastructure to be capable of supporting a range of broadband services and applications (e.g., access to movies, entertainment programs on demand, distance learning, telemedicine, and telecommuting) to residential and business customers. This plan will involve upgrading the access, switching, and interoffice network to support broadband services. The upgrade to support initial customers is expected to begin in 1994 with a half-million customers planned to be added to this network each year beginning in 1995.[5]

Vendors.   AT&T, Siemens, and Fujitsu supplied ATM switches for the COMPASS trials.

11.2.7 Pacific Bell

Trial activity.   Pacific Bell is a participant in the Casa and Blanca gigabit NREN testbeds.

Commercial deployment plans: Pacific Bell started building a communications superhighway connecting participating California universities, research labs, major hospitals, and high-tech firms in the San Francisco Bay area and Los Angeles in late 1993. This network will become part of CalREN (California Research and Education Network). CalREN will use ATM and SONET switching and transmission technologies in an advanced telecommunications network capable of transmitting voice, video, data, and images simultaneously. CalREN is targeted toward universities, research labs and hospitals, and high-tech companies, with the objective of speeding the development of applications which will run on broadband networks.[6]

11.2.8   GTE

Trial activity.   GTE was a participant in the Vistanet gigabit testbed. GTE also was planning an internal technology trial with the NEC NEAX 61E ATM switch and a customer trial with the AT&T GCNS-2000 ATM switch in early 1994. These trials were to take place in the Dallas/Forth Worth area.[7]

Commercial deployment plans.   GTE Telephone Operations has deployed ATM switches (in Research Triangle Park and Durham) as part of the North Carolina Information Highway Project.

11.2.9   AT&T

Trial activity.   AT&T is a participant in the Blanca gigabit testbed.

Commercial deployment plans.   AT&T is currently offering frame relay PVC as part of its InterSpan service. AT&T has announced plans for a controlled ATM service offering in the first half of 1994, with a generally available service offering in the second half of 1994.[8] AT&T has announced a partnership with Cisco and StrataCom. AT&T's proposed network architecture involves small ATM and frame relay switches (Stratacom BPX and IPX) at the edges of the network. These switches will gather frame relay, X.25, and ATM traffic and route it to a high-capacity backbone ATM network composed of AT&T GCNS-2000 switches. Cisco routers will be located on the customer's premises and at the interface to the AT&T network. A key part of AT&T's approach for ATM is to provide transparent service interworking between customers with frame relay service and ATM cell relay service. In articulating this approach AT&T is assuring customers that they can start with frame relay services today and upgrade to ATM when they have requirements for ATM, but in any event AT&T will allow them to communicate with either other AT&T frame relay users or ATM cell relay users.

11.2.10   Sprint

Trial activity.   Sprint is a participant in the MAGIC testbed.

Commercial deployment plans.   Sprint is currently offering frame relay and ATM cell relay PVC services. Sprint's basic approach is to use ATM as a multiservice technology platform which can support non-ATM interfaces (e.g., frame relay) as well as native ATM interfaces.
Sprint has communicated a three-phase strategy for ATM.[9,10]

1. Sprint considers its 1993 deployment of frame relay to be the first phase in its network transition to ATM.

2. In 1994–1995 Sprint may phase ATM into its network as a backbone transport and switching technology. ATM will transport the following types of services: frame relay, X.25, IP, SMDS, and native ATM cell relay. In this phase some of Sprint's private-line and circuit-switched services may be carried on ATM.

3. During 1994–1996 Sprint may upgrade its fiber transport facilities to become SONET-based. This phase will also see the introduction of additional broadband services including ATM SVC services.

Vendors. Sprint had reportedly chosen TRW as its initial ATM switch vendor.

11.2.11 Wiltel

Commercial deployment plans. Wiltel is currently offering frame relay PVC services. Wiltel has deployed NEC ATM switches in Los Angeles, Phoenix, Denver, Dallas, Chicago, Atlanta, Washington, D.C. and New York City.[11,12]

Wiltel's future plans call for expanding this network to cover 20 metropolitan areas. The initial ATM switches can be used as part of a high-speed backbone for Wiltel's frame relay service (which is currently based upon StrataCom IPXs).

The first ATM application Wiltel announced was a Channel Networking Service (Fig. 11.1) to support mainframe channel extension. This service is targeted at helping users with data center consolidations, data vaulting, central archiving, high-speed graphics, and remote printing.

Wiltel has also described the importance of ATM network management capabilities as a crucial feature which can enhance the attractiveness of its ATM offerings. It has stated that the flexibility of ATM will have significant positive impacts on users' ability to manage their service across the wide area and that these management capabilities enhance the value of these services to the users.

Vendors. Wiltel has initially deployed NEC ATM switches. Wiltel is also collaborating with Computer Network Technology Corporation and Network Systems Corporation on their channel extension service.

11.2.12 MCI

Trial activity. MCI is a participant in the Casa and Aurora gigabit testbeds.

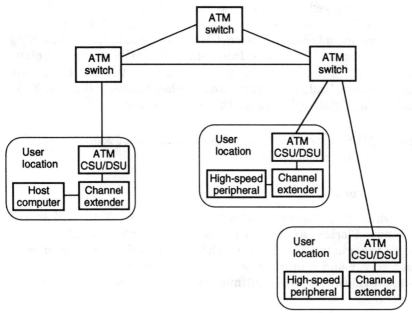

Figure 11.1   Wiltel's Channel Networking Service.

Commercial deployment plans.   MCI was currently offering frame relay PVC services and had announced plans to deploy SMDS. MCI had outlined plans to deploy services using ATM technology in 1994. In public talks MCI had stated that there were still a number of issues (e.g., service definitions) which needed to be addressed before the potential benefits of ATM technology could be translated into supporting useful applications for customers. To this end, MCI created an ATM users group to study end-user needs for wide area broadband connectivity.[13]

Vendors.   In 1992 MCI deployed Siemens EWSM switches. It had been reported at the time that MCI would select two types of ATM switches for deployment, one of these switches to be deployed on the perimeter of the network as a service node and the second set of switches to provide a high-capacity backbone network.

11.2.13   Metropolitan Fiber Systems (MFS)

Commercial deployment plans.   MFS expanded its metropolitan area LAN interconnect services to a national service availability through its MFS Datanet subsidiary. These services are called MFS Datanet High-Speed LAN Interconnection (HLI) services.[14]

MFS has deployed ATM switches in 14 cities with interconnection provided by Wiltel facilities (initially DS3 facilities). The initial set of HLI services included HLI Ethernet Interconnection, HLI Token Ring Interconnection, and HLI FDDI Interconnection. MFS announced plans to deploy ATM switches in the following areas: Atlanta, Baltimore, Boston, Chicago, Dallas, Houston, Los Angeles, Minneapolis, New York, Philadelphia, Pittsburgh, and northern New Jersey.

Vendors.   MFS reportedly deployed Newbridge 36150 *Main Street* ATM switches for this initial network.

11.2.14   Time Warner

Trial activity.   Time Warner is using an AT&T GCNS-2000 ATM switch in Orlando, Florida, as part of a video-on-demand trial. The trial is expected to begin in 1994. This switch is being used in conjunction with a video server and a number of access technologies including coaxial cable to provide interactive multimedia services to residential end users.

11.3   ATM Equipment

A myriad of vendors have developed or are developing ATM products, including

- Large switching systems targeted towards shared public networks
- Enterprise network switches, targeted towards high-end private networks
- LAN switches targeted towards high-end client server users
- LAN switches targeted towards use as campus backbone hubs
- Digital service units (DSUs) which, through the DXI, allow existing internetworking equipment (e.g., routers) to access ATM networks
- Interface cards, which allow high-end workstations to access ATM LANs
- Chipsets, which are marketed to manufacturers of all of the above

This section gives a brief snapshot of equipment that was either available or in development in the mid-1993 time frame. The primary focus of this section is on ATM switching equipment. This is not due to any *a priori* bias favoring switching over any of these other product types, but is instead based upon the observation that with ATM technology, the core switching technology can be used in many products, including multiplexers, interface cards, and DSUs.

A quick scan of product literature provided by the manufacturers of ATM equipment shows that there are actually a number of distinct switching technologies being used for ATM. Indeed, there are arguably a confusing number of terms manufacturers use to describe their core switching technology, including

- Crosspoint switch fabric
- Output buffered fabric
- Self-routing switch fabric
- Time-memory switch fabric
- Time-space-time switch fabric
- Etc.

Before listing the available products, we will briefly discuss the different switching architectures using a framework developed by Daddis and Torng.[15]

11.3.1   Broadband switching architectures

There are several basic choices a switch designer can make in designing a broadband switching fabric, including architecture, control, and physical topology. Daddis and Torng developed a tree-based taxonomy of broadband switching systems design (Fig. 11.2). Their goal in classifying switch designs in this way was to group together switches with fundamentally similar designs and to separate those based on radically different philosophies in architecture. In their tree structure, the end nodes represent particular switch designs, and each inner node specifies a design decision. This collection of design points classifies broadband switches through their fundamental properties. Five design points were chosen. In order of descending levels on the classification tree, they are

1. Dedicated versus shared links: A link is dedicated if at most one switch element may transmit onto it; otherwise the link is shared.

2. The transport mode is the discipline governing the transmission of data units onto links. It may be statistical or assignment-based (this corresponds roughly to circuit versus packet switching).

3. Centralized versus decentralized routing control: Routing decisions can be made at one point in the switch or distributed throughout the switch.

4. Buffered versus nonbuffered switch elements: A buffered switch element stores data units within the element to resolve output link

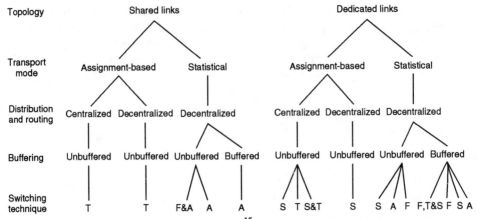

Figure 11.2 Taxonomy of broadband switches.[15] T = time; A = address filtration; S = space; F = frequency.

contention. Unbuffered switch elements incur a constant delay on data units relative to congestion in the system.

5. The switching technique: the method of directing the data units from one switch element to another. The four techniques are space switching, time switching, frequency switching, and address filtration.

11.3.2 Dedicated versus shared links

A look at Fig. 11.2 indicates that we are mainly interested in the right-hand side of the tree, namely, dedicated links. The majority of ATM products on the market or in development today use dedicated links, although a few products employ a shared-link (e.g., bus) switching approach.

11.3.3 Transport mode

A transport mode is the method the switch uses to transmit data over links in the interconnection fabric. This mode can be divided into links whose capacities may be dedicated to each call or made statistically available to all calls through a need-based scheme. Dedicated links form the basis of circuit switching, which has dominated the telecommunications business to the present day.

11.3.4 Distribution of routing intelligence

With centralized routing, a single logical entity controls the routing of data over the switch elements and interconnection fabric at a given level. In distributed (decentralized) routing, data routing is executed via processing that is localized to each switch element, possibly with the aid of global state information replicated at each of the elements. A "self-routing" switch fabric would be considered to have distributed control. An example of distributed routing is a Batcher/Banyan switch fabric, where the routing control is decided on an element-by-element basis as the data unit traverses the switch. Distributed routing is in general more complex than centralized routing. This complexity includes routing control for multiple services, deciding between the arbitration of access of cells to a link, and the switching of data. Output link contention occurs when data from one or more switch elements contend for the transmission capacity of a link.

11.3.5 Buffering in switch elements

A buffered switch element stores cells within the element to resolve output link contention. Data may be buffered before switching (input buffering), after switching (output buffering), within the switch elements (shared buffering), or not at all (no buffers). The choice of buffering method can have a dramatic effect on the characteristics of a switch (e.g., performance under heavy traffic loads).

11.3.6 Switching techniques

The switching technique influences or determines the physical structure, distribution, and execution of the switch intelligence. There are four primary switching techniques:

- Space switching refers to the technique whereby a transmitting switch element chooses among multiple physical routes to send data. An example of space switching is a simple crossbar switch, in which a crosspoint either routes a data unit along a vertical output bus or ignores it and allows it to continue along the horizontal input bus.

- Time switching refers to a technique whereby the transmitting switch element delays a data unit for an amount of time dependent on the routing.

- Frequency switching refers to when the transmitting switch element chooses among two or more carrier frequencies upon which to route data units.

- Address filtration refers to a technique whereby the receiving switch element selects labeled data units from among multidestination traffic. Fujitsu's FETEX 150[*] ATM switch architecture[16] is an example of such an arrangement. In the FETEX 150, buffered intelligent crosspoints select cells through addressing, and cells are injected onto horizontal input buses which later transmit the cells onto the attached

---

*FETEX is a registered trademark of Fujitsu.

vertical output buses. The switch elements do not route data units among physical links, but instead select cells from the broadcast input bus and retransmit them on a single output bus.

These four switching techniques may be used alone or, more commonly, in combinations.

11.3.7 Summary of available ATM products

Tables 11.1 through 11.3 give a list of some of the vendors which had, at press time, announced the availability of ATM-based products.[*]

11.4 Gigabit Testbeds

In 1991, the U.S. government introduced the High Performance Computing Act to foster the creation of information highways linking com-

---

[*]The products and descriptions listed herein are based upon publicly available information, including published reports and manufacturers' product literature. Product specifications and product names have been known to change. The authors make no representations as to the completeness or accuracy of this information.

TABLE 11.1 Network and WAN Equipment Vendors

ADC Telecommunications

AT&T Network Systems

Alcatel Network Systems

Ascom Timeplex

BBN Communications

Cascade Communications

DSC Communications

Fujitsu Network Switching

General DataComm

Hitachi

Loral Data Systems

NEC America

Newbridge Networks

Northern Telecom

Siemens Stromberg-Carlson

StrataCom

Telco Systems, Inc.

Thomson-CSF

TRW Space Communications

TABLE 11.2   Semiconductor Vendors

Applied Micro Circuits Corp.

Base 2 Systems

National Semiconductor

PMC Sierra

QPSX, Inc.

Texas Instruments

Toshiba

TranSwitch Corporation

puters at industrial organizations, universities, and national research laboratories. One objective of the resulting High Performance Computing Program is the establishment of a high-speed National Research and Engineering Network (NREN). NREN is intended to provide high-speed, real-time interconnection among institutions involved in general

TABLE 11.3   ATM LAN, Hub, Router, and DSU Vendors

Adaptive Corporation

ADC Fibermux Corporation

ADC Kentrox

AT&T/NCR Products Division

Cabletron Systems

Cisco Systems

Digital Link Corporation

FiberCom, Inc.

FORE Systems

GTE Government Systems

Hughes LAN Systems

IBM

Retix

Synernetics

SynOptics

3Com Corporation

TRW Space Communications Division

Ungermann-Bass

Wellfleet Communications

research activities.[17] Some members of Congress and various other proponents of NREN envision it as an upgrade or offshoot of the National Science Foundation Network (NSFNET).[18]

To this end, the Corporation for National Research Initiatives (CNRI) received an award of approximately $15.8 million from the National Science Foundation and the Defense Advanced Research Projects Agency for research on high-speed networking. CNRI now sponsors five gigabit testbeds throughout the United States.[17,19] These networks were selected to provide a solid foundation of research experience in the development, design, and operation of networks operating at data rates approaching 1 Gbit/s and beyond.

The gigabit testbed project has two goals:

- To examine and develop architecture alternatives suitable for use in the coming NREN

- To better understand the applications and uses of ultra-high-speed networks

The approach taken to address these goals was hands-on experimentation with actual transport and switching networks.

Table 11.4[18] gives a brief summary of the five CNRI-sponsored gigabit testbeds. Figure 11.3 shows the approximate layout of the testbeds.

TABLE 11.4 Gigabit Testbed Summary[18]

Project	Sites	Carriers	Applications
Aurora	Morristown, NJ Hawthorne, NY Cambridge, MA Philadelphia, PA	Bell Atlantic, MCI, NYNEX	Business and scientific applications, virtual laboratory
Blanca	Madison, WI Murray Hill, NJ Minneapolis, MN Champaign-Urbana, IL Berkeley, CA	AT&T, Norlight, several LECs	Medical imaging, multimedia digital libraries, multiple remote visualization and control of simulations, radio astronomy imaging
Casa	Pasadena, CA Los Alamos, NM San Diego, CA Los Angeles, CA	MCI, Pacific Bell, U S WEST	Chemical reaction dynamics, climate modeling, interactive data analysis, and visualization of geologic models
Nectar	Pittsburgh, PA	Bell Atlantic	Large combinatorial optimizations, process flow-sheeting
Vistanet	Research Triangle Park, NC Chapel Hill, NC Durham, NC	BellSouth, GTE Telephone Operations	Radiation treatment therapy planning, dispersed collaboration

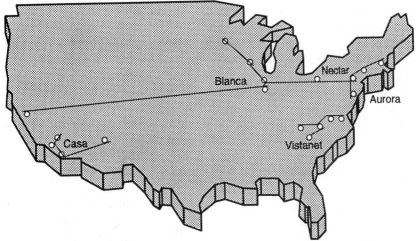

Figure 11.3 Gigabit testbeds.

11.4.1 Aurora

Aurora links several major laboratories and universities in Philadelphia, New Jersey, New York, and Massachusetts.[20] Aurora is an experimental platform for studying business and scientific applications of gigabit networks. The interconnected sites in Aurora are

- The University of Pennsylvania's Distributed System Laboratory, Philadelphia, Pennsylvania
- Bellcore's Morristown Research and Engineering Laboratory, Morristown, New Jersey
- MIT's Laboratory for Computer Science, Cambridge, Massachusetts
- IBM's Thomas J. Watson Research Center, Hawthorne, New York

The carriers providing interconnection facilities are MCI, Bell Atlantic, and NYNEX. All interconnection facilities are SONET OC-12 fiber links supporting 622-Mbits/s data rates.

One focus of Aurora's research is to discover any bottlenecks that will make implementations of existing protocols difficult to adapt to existing networks.[18] The goal of this effort is to ensure the maximum network throughput for any level of networked CPU utilization.

11.4.2 Blanca

Blanca links several sites across the continental United States. The principal participants in the Blanca testbed are Lawrence Berkeley Laboratory, the National Center for Supercomputing Applications

(NCSA), the University of California at Berkeley, the University of Illinois at Urbana-Champaign, and the University of Wisconsin at Madison. The companies providing switching and interconnection facilities for Blanca include Ameritech, Bell Atlantic, Pacific Bell, and AT&T.

The network research in Blanca is a collaborative effort between the computer science departments at the three universities and Lawrence Berkeley Laboratory. This includes work on switch control and design, fast call setup, development of traffic models, multiplexing strategies for different types of traffic, burst handling and congestion control, real-time communication, high-speed channel interfaces for supercomputers, and network virtual memory.[17]

The applications include multiple remote visualization and control of simulations (NCSA, Wisconsin); radio astronomy imaging (NCSA, Berkeley); multimedia digital library (NCSA); and medical imaging (NCSA, LBL). Supercomputers for the applications experiments are provided by Cray Research, the National Center for Supercomputing Applications, and the Astronautics Corporation.

11.4.3 Casa

Casa links several sites in New Mexico and California to study high-performance distributed computing for scientific applications. The overall emphasis of the CASA testbed is the demonstration of leading-edge distributed applications that run on multiple computer systems linked by a gigabit fabric.[21] The interconnected research sites in Casa are

- Los Alamos National Laboratory, Los Alamos, New Mexico, where a Cray YMP 264, a Thinking Machines CM-2, a Thinking Machines CM-5, and an IBM 3090 are located

- The San Diego Supercomputing Center, San Diego, California, where a Cray YMP 864 and an Intel iPSC/860 are connected to an NSC PS32

- California Institute of Technology, Pasadena, California, where an Intel Delta is located

- Jet Propulsion Laboratory, Pasadena, California, where a Cray YMP 116 is located.

At each site, the computers are connected to a Network Systems Corporation PS32 HPPI Crossbar Switch. Figure 11.4 shows the Casa distributed computing environment.

A primary objective of Casa is to examine the role that high-speed wide area networks can play in solving large-scale scientific applications.

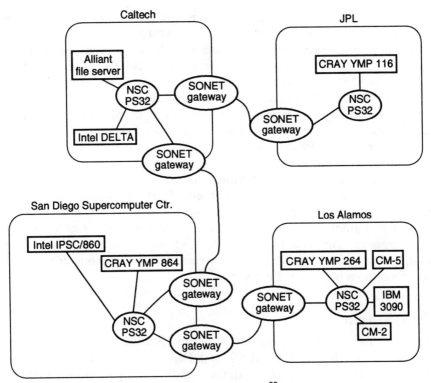

Figure 11.4 Casa distributed computing environment.[23]

11.4.4 Nectar

The Nectar testbed collaborators are Carnegie Mellon University (CMU), the Pittsburgh Supercomputing Center (PSC), Bellcore, and Bell Atlantic. Two sites are connected in this testbed, CMU and PSC. The CMU testbed site is located on the CMU campus in the Oakland section of Pittsburgh, while the PSC Cray supercomputer facilities are located approximately 30 kilometers away.

The research conducted in this testbed is based on several ongoing projects at CMU, in particular the Nectar project, out of which the gigabit Nectar testbed has been built. Nectar is a system for interconnecting heterogeneous computing resources via fiber-optic links, large crossbar switches, and dedicated network coprocessors. The original Nectar prototype used 100-Mbits/s links; the next version of Nectar will use 1 Gbit/s or higher-speed links.[17]

Researchers at CMU used to access the PSC Cray Y-MP/832 using a T1 link that was connected to the on-campus local area networks. This 1.544-Mbits/s link severely limited the use of interactive graphics and the distribution of computing between the Cray and the campus resources. The Nectar gigabit network is used to connect the Cray to various campus resources, such as CMU's iWarp parallel machine, and thus provide an extremely powerful, distributed computing environment. This new computing environment, illustrated in Fig. 11.5, will enable the simultaneous use of different computer architectures over the network to fit different needs of an application.

The Nectar testbed applications are large distributed computing applications that can benefit from a high-speed network. One of the applications is a process flowsheeting problem that models the control, design, and economic performance of large-scale chemical plants. A second application involves solving large combinatorial optimizations, such as the traveling salesman problem. These problems represent a class of important optimization problems whose solutions are essential to many engineering designs.[19] The Nectar researchers hope to use these applications as a vehicle to devise new computational methods that are capable of making effective use of heterogeneous computing resources on a high-speed network.

11.4.5 Vistanet

The Vistanet testbed participants include BellSouth, GTE, the University of North Carolina at Chapel Hill (UNC), and MCNC (The Microelectronics Center of North Carolina) in conjunction with North Carolina State University (NCSU). The MCNC site is located in

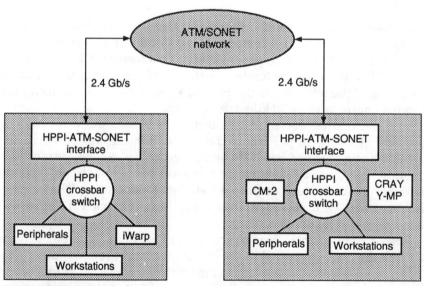

Figure 11.5 Nectar testbed.

Research Triangle Park, near the GTE Central Office in Durham, North Carolina. The UNC campus and BellSouth Central Office sites are all located in Chapel Hill, at a distance of approximately 18 miles apart (see Fig. 11.6).

Collaborative research is being undertaken in this testbed to demonstrate the achievements that can be realized when geographically dispersed research teams and their specialized resources are networked together at gigabit speeds. The resulting interactive computation system will be used to make important advances in communications research, computer visualization, and medical treatment planning.

The applications focus of Vistanet is research concerning radiation therapy treatment planning for cancer patients. Direct high-speed connections to the networked resources will allow new dose distributions to be calculated from modified treatment plans, enabling clinical oncologists to customize radiation treatment and obtain immediate feedback on the results of changes in treatment plans.

This radiation therapy application is also used to test the initial assumptions as to how such distributed networks will perform. The process of networking the application and analyzing the results will provide a point of departure for the next generation of networking research and development. The network will provide a testbed for new

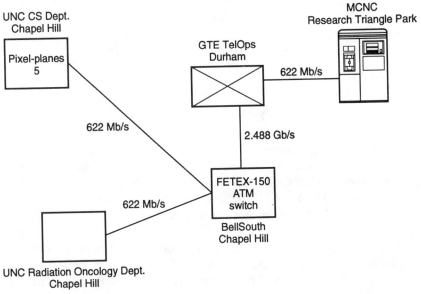

Figure 11.6 Vistanet testbed.

concepts and deployment of network architectures, network services, remote graphics processing and medical imaging.

The Vistanet testbed includes a supercomputing facility, networking technology, communications research infrastructure, and medical image processing research facilities. A network capability will be developed facilitating the high-speed image transfer needed by the applications research team. Once deployed, the network will link the North Carolina Supercomputing Center at MCNC with the centers for computer graphics and medical imaging research at UNC. Network capabilities will be made available in a staged process, providing a minimum of 622-Mbits/s access, with 2.488-Gbits/s trunks used between switches. Hardware and software designs will be completed to provide a Cray Y-MP, a Pixel-Planes 5 graphics processor, and a medical image workstation access to the network. The end network design will be based on the high-speed communications standards SONET, ATM, and HPPI.

From a networking technology perspective, the facility will be used to study and resolve several critical issues. The focus will be on the issues of protocols, performance analysis, and switching technologies needed to support multiple-service-class gigabit networks. For a network of this type, methods must be developed to measure and quantify the usage of critical network resources and to identify the problem areas, such as network bottlenecks. Techniques will be defined and implemented to measure traffic on the network under conditions of real use. The resulting data will be analyzed off-line and compared to statistical models developed for traffic on the existing 45-Mbits/s MCNC statewide data network, CONCERT. From these results recommendations will be made regarding the parameters which best reflect network and switch loading as well as contention.[17]

11.4.6 Other trials and testbeds

MAGIC test bed. The MAGIC (Multidimensional Applications and Gigabit Interworking Consortium) high-speed network testbed is a three-year multimedia research project which is based on a high-speed ATM network. Members of the consortium include Sprint, ARPA, Minnesota Supercomputer Center, U.S. Army High Performance Computing Research Center, U.S. Geological Survey Earth Resources Observation Systems Data Center, Future Battle Laboratory of the U.S. Army's Combined Arms Command, SRI International, Lawrence Berkeley Laboratory, University of Kansas, DEC, Southwestern Bell Telephone Company, Split Rock Telephone Company, Northern Telecom, Inc., and U S WEST.

The network technology goals of the MAGIC Test Bed are to study:

- Survivable routing for ATM
- Network management interfaces
- Network provisioning rules for an ATM network
- Local distribution systems for ATM networks
- B-ISDN service characteristics
- Large-scale ATM networking models
- Call management for B-ISDN services
- Multivendor ATM interoperability
- Multicarrier ATM interoperability
- Dynamic network management using artificial intelligence
- B-ISDN performance

The applications research that will take place on the MAGIC testbed is mainly concerned with high-performance (i.e., gigabit speed) multimedia applications distributed across a vast distance (approximately 600 miles) in the presence of multiple users (see Fig. 11.7).

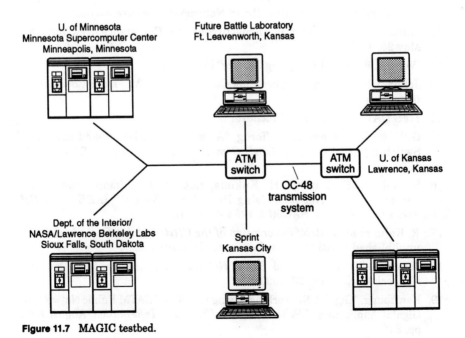

Figure 11.7 MAGIC testbed.

Nynet. New York Telephone has initiated an ATM testbed in order to stimulate development of commercial applications for high-speed business services. The network, dubbed Nynet, is constructed from backbone and remote switches supplied by Fujitsu Network Switching of America.[3] Nynet's initial sites are to be Syracuse and Cornell universities, with other university and research sites to be added in the future.

References

1. BellSouth press release, May 10, 1993.
2. "Fast Packet Services," Supplement to *Communications Week* sponsored by Bell Atlantic.
3. Anne Lindstrom, "N.Y. Tel to Launch ATM Network Project," *Communications Week*, July 1993.
4. "MBS Media Broadband Service," NYNEX brochure.
5. *U.S. WEST TODAY*, March 8, 1993.
6. Pacific Bell press release announcing CalREN, March 30, 1993.
7. "The ATM Movement Is Growing," *Communications Week*, Public Network Update, May 10, 1993, pp. PNU-1 ff.
8. "Asynchronous Transfer Mode," AT&T presentation at Yankee Group Demystifying ATM Conference, New York, May 25, 1993.
9. "Perspectives on Asynchronous Transfer Mode," Sprint presentation at Yankee Group Demystifying ATM Conference, New York, May 25, 1993.
10. Sprint "Perspectives on Broadband Networks" brochure.
11. Wiltel talk at Yankee Group Demystifying ATM Conference, New York City, May 25, 1993.
12. Wiltel "Channel Networking Service" brochure.
13. Johna Till Johnson, "Applications Catch Up to ATM" *Data Communications*, July 1983.
14. MFS DATANET product brochure.
15. G. E. Daddis Jr. and H. C. Torng, "A Taxonomy of Broadband Integrated Switching Architectures," *IEEE Communications Magazine* 27(s): 32–42, 1989.
16. S. Nojima, E. Tsutsui, H. Kukuda, and M. Hashimoto, "Integrated Services Packet Network Using Bus Matrix Switch," *IEEE J. on Sel. Areas in Commun.*, SAC5(8): 1284–1292, 1987.
17. R. Kahn et al., *A Brief Description of the CNRI Gigabit Testbed Initiative*, unpublished CNRI working document, January 1992.
18. James Kobielus, "Planned Super Networks Foreshadow 21st Century," *Network World*, Aug. 26, 1991.
19. Ken Young, "Gigabit Networking: Using the SONET/ATM Public Network for Gigabit Applications," *Bellcore Digest of Technical Information*, August 1992, pp. 3 ff.

20. "Nation's Most Extensive Gigabit Research Network Bridges Four States, Links Labs and Universities," Bellcore Press Release, June 24, 1993.

21. *CASA Gigabit Test 1993 Annual Report*, Caltech Concurrent Supercomputing Facilities Report #CCSF-33, California Institute of Technology, Pasadena, May 1993.

Chapter

12

Migrating a Pre-ATM Network to ATM

12.1 Introduction

The previous 11 chapters in this book attempted to explain the basics of ATM technology, the network services available through the use of ATM, and the status of ATM equipment and deployment. This chapter attempts to integrate the previous 11 into a brief discussion of how a pre-ATM enterprise network can evolve to take advantage of ATM technology.

12.1.1 Enterprise network evolution goals

In general, organizations undertake to evolve their networks in an effort to improve the way they do business. Organizations may attempt to attain one or more of the following goals in their evolution plans.

- *Reduce costs.* There are numerous ways in which an enterprise can save money through an upgrade of its network. Among these are the cost savings which can be achieved through the elimination of redundant parallel application-specific networks. These cost savings can be achieved through
  1. More efficient network engineering
  2. Enabling volume purchasing contracts with network suppliers
  3. Decreased management and maintenance expenditures

- *Enable new network applications and services.* New networking applications, such as videoconferencing or innovative uses of image storage and retrieval applications, can play a key role in a corporation's process reengineering strategy. Often these new applications simply cannot be accommodated on existing enterprise networks.

- *Facilitate interdepartmental information exchange through the integration of multiple departmental networks into one enterprisewide network.* In many organizations in the 1980s and early 1990s, the availability of low-cost PCs and LAN equipment led to a proliferation of independently owned and operated computer networks within the organization. While this explosion of low-cost computing power enabled increased productivity at the departmental level, it may have actually stifled the sharing of corporatewide information, as data on one LAN were not reachable by departments on another. Corporations now have recognized the need to integrate networks in an attempt to gain the maximum interdepartmental use of corporate data. This need drives many network evolution plans.

- *Maximum reuse of existing facilities.* One common goal of network evolution is the maximum reuse of existing networking equipment (e.g. wiring, routers, and hubs). Part of the popularity of multiprotocol IP routers can be traced to the fact that they allow upgrading without discarding existing network equipment. The appeal of new technologies such as "fast Ethernet" and ATM over UTP is partly because their use may allow the upgrading of LANs to multimegabit speeds without labor-intensive rewiring.

- *Enable multivendor distributed computing.* Often, achieving a true multi-vendor distributed computing environment is a key objective of enterprise network evolution. In these cases, network operators are often keenly interested in open, standards-based network environments.

- *Simplify network management into enterprisewide management.* In a multiple-network environment, network management is not a centralized, integrated function but an independently distributed function. This hampers interorganizational communications, and results in a high cost of network management and maintenance. A commonly found goal of network evolution is to evolve to one enterprisewide network management environment.

- *Enable survivable, fault-tolerant networking.* Modern enterprise networks transport information that is critical to the operations of the firm. If the network fails, the firm may lose millions of dollars, through idle factories, missed securities transactions, or business lost to competitors. A common goal of enterprise network evolution is to enable a closely engineered degree of network survivability and fault tolerance.

This chapter was written with the idea that readers would have one or more of these goals in mind as they undertake to upgrade their networks to include ATM technology and services. The remainder of this chapter is organized as follows. First, a brief discussion is given of the drivers toward the inclusion of ATM technology in enterprise networks. These drivers include new networking applications as well as technology and cost trends. Second, a brief set of examples is given which illustrate the evolution from specific networking scenarios to the inclusion of ATM networking.

12.1.2 Application drivers

To a corporation, an enterprise network has been likened to a transportation system. Just as an efficient, modern transportation system is essential to keep raw materials and finished products flowing from supplier to customer, so is a corporation's network critical in keeping information flowing among and within organizations. Enterprise networks are now considered crucial in an organization's fight to maintain competitiveness, meet ever-shorter time-to-market goals, and exploit interdepartmental linkages (e.g., sales to marketing to engineering to production).

Other changes are taking place in corporations throughout the world as well. A decreased emphasis on the use of mainframe computers has led to the evolution of computing applications to a client/server architecture in an attempt to exploit the availability of cost-effective low-end systems. This new emphasis on distributed computing has led to an increased corporate dependence on the communications network.

In addition to improvements in the cost-effectiveness of computing environments, new networking applications are emerging which create new networking challenges. Distributed database applications create the need for high-speed networking to ensure that the "user" perceives no performance difference whether the data are stored locally or remotely. New visual networking applications are emerging (e.g., graphics, still image, 3-D CAD, and video) which increase capacity requirements on the network, implying the need for network scalability.

12.1.3 Technology drivers

In addition to the "pull" of new applications, there is a technology "push" leading corporations to upgrade their enterprise networks. Several of the leading technological changes leading this push are described below.

LAN proliferation and evolution.   Before the advent of the PC, most corporate computing environments were

1. Mainframe-based
2. Centrally located
3. Centrally controlled by the corporate MIS department

In the 1980s, there began a general trend away from the use of centrally controlled mainframe computers. The relatively low cost of PCs led to the proliferation of desktop computing environments. Local area networks were introduced, initially as a means to share expensive peripherals (e.g., printers and plotters). Ultimately, the low cost and high performance of PCs, workstations, and LANs has led users towards the implementation of distributed client/server computing environments. In many organizations, this evolution has placed control of the network not in the hands of the MIS organization, but distributed throughout the corporation. Many corporations have discovered that there are numerous hidden costs associated with this type of distributed control. These costs may include

- Hardware costs associated with building parallel, redundant networks
- Personnel costs associated with running multiple networks
- Software costs associated with not taking advantage of coordinated volume purchases
- Other hidden costs

As a result, many corporations have by now recognized the need to regain control of their computing network. Part of this effort may include replacing multiple networks with a single enterprisewide network infrastructure.

LAN microsegmentation. As a rough rule of thumb, available CPU power in PCs and workstations has doubled every two years.[*] This rapid increase in computing power has enabled the development of applications that require large and ever-increasing amounts of data transfer. However, the throughput available on LANs has not kept pace with this increasing need for bandwidth; indeed, there has been explosive growth in the number of networked stations, yet typical LAN speeds have remained in the 4- to 16-Mbits/s range. The result of this increased need for bandwidth has been a noticeable reduction in the average number of workstations per LAN segment (this is referred to as "microsegmentation").[1] This is conceptually illustrated in Fig. 12.1. Still, decreasing

---

[*]This relationship is sometimes referred to as Joy's law, named after Bill Joy of Sun Microsystems.

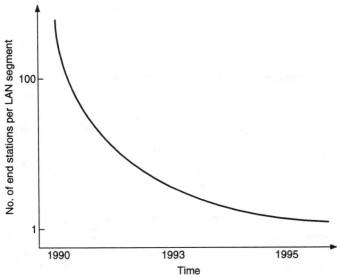

Figure 12.1 Microsegmentation trend.[1]

the number of stations can increase available bandwidth only up to a point; with Ethernet (802.3), one can at best get to the situation where one workstation gets 10 Mbits/s of instantaneous throughput. This increasing need for bandwidth has led many corporations to consider the use of new LAN architectures (e.g., star-based LANs) and higher speeds (e.g. ATM LANs, FDDI, and fast Ethernet) for their high-end work groups.

Public network broadband services.   In the 1980s, the only broadband services available from public network carriers were point-to-point DS-1 (1.544-Mbits/s) and, later, DS-3 (44.736-Mbits/s) private lines. Wide area broadband networking could only be accomplished through a company establishing its own WAN multiplexing, switching, and management platform interconnected through these leased high-speed digital lines. This was in general an expensive proposition (considering the equipment, staff, and management expenses) which generally limited the reach of broadband networking to corporate locations of a relatively large size. The emergence of broadband public data services, including SMDS, frame relay, ATM cell relay service, and LAN bridging services, is changing this interconnection paradigm. As public data services extend their reach from metropolitan areas to regional, national, and international interconnectivity, a number of key benefits to corporate users have emerged:

- The potential for lowering interlocation communications costs through the shared use of bandwidth. The public network can achieve economies of scale through sharing resources among a large number of users in multiple enterprises.

- The potential for reducing staff and management costs through outsourcing communications activities that in the past had to be performed in house.

- Full interconnection of all sites on the network, enabling a higher degree of fault tolerance and simplifying routing decisions.

- A higher degree of management and control capabilities compared to those available with point-to-point private lines.

Video/Imaging/DSP technologies.   Advances in digital signal processing technology have been as striking as those in computer CPUs. This has enabled great advances in image compression technology, which in turn has enabled the economical digital storage and transmission of images, both still and motion. This is evidenced by the evolution of digital videoconferencing equipment. Several years ago acceptable videoconferencing could be accomplished at transmission rates above 1.5 Mbits/s using equipment that cost upwards of $50,000 per endpoint; today, videoconferencing is often accomplished at transmission rates of under 256 kbits/s, and low-cost videoconferencing boards are available as add-ons to PCs.

Standard management systems/platforms.   Network management is evolving from hardware-vendor-specific monitoring systems to enterprise-wide network management platforms based upon standard protocols (e.g., SNMP) and information structures. This has allowed the separation of management software from network hardware, which has enabled management in a multivendor environment.

Internetworking standards.   The emergence of open, accepted internetworking standards, such as TCP/IP, frame relay, and now ATM, has fostered an environment of multivendor compatibility. This has helped to lower the effective costs of networking, which has in turn stimulated demand. Also, internetworking standards have enabled *inter*enterprise networking, for example in supplier-producer relationships.

12.2   Network Evolution Examples

This section describes several examples of evolution paths towards the inclusion of ATM in enterprise networks. This section is not meant to be all-inclusive; it is merely meant to illustrate some of the ways in which this network evolution may take place.

12.2.1   The ATM LAN: ATM to the desktop

When Ethernet was invented, a 100-MIPS computer would be almost considered a supercomputer, and 64K RAM chips were not yet commercially available. Today, a 100-MIPS workstation can be purchased in the under-$10,000 range, multiprocessor servers extend into the hundreds of MIPS, and even laptop computers can be configured with 32 MBytes of memory (or more). As end-user computing power has grown, so have the networking requirements for networked computers, especially for high-end workstation applications (e.g., computer-aided design stations). In general, this has led to a decrease in the number of end stations per LAN segment (see Fig. 12.2a and 12.2b). So-called smart hubs have become popular, in part because they allow the creation of "virtual LANs" extending across multiple LAN segments, thereby increasing the total effective throughput per end station without creating undue management and administrative headaches (Fig. 12.2c). For high-end users, a solution that has been available has been FDDI (Fig. 12.2d). However, even with FDDI, the total throughput of the LAN is limited to 100 Mbits/s, and ultimately the same cycle of microsegmentation may take place. A solution to this ever-growing need for bandwidth is a star-based LAN, such as an ATM LAN.* Figure 12.3 illustrates a switched ATM LAN. In this particular example, workstation interfaces can be at speeds of up to 155 Mbits/s, over single-mode fiber, multimode fiber, or twisted-pair copper. The server interface is illustrated at a bit rate of 622 Mbits/s; this will allow high-throughput client/server transactions.

12.2.2   ATM as a LAN backbone

The previous section illustrated an example evolution path for the power-hungry user, with high-MIPS workstations and dedicated 100-Mbits/s paths to a high-end server. For the bulk of corporate applications in the near future, this amount of dedicated power is not required, or is required only for a select few users. However, many of these corporations have other evolution goals in mind, including

- Managing the growth of networked stations
- Keeping existing LAN interfaces whenever possible
- Maintaining or improving throughput
- Enabling location-wide access to distributed data

---

*Other alternatives exist, such as "switched Ethernet" and hub architectures based on 100-Mbits/s "fast Ethernet."

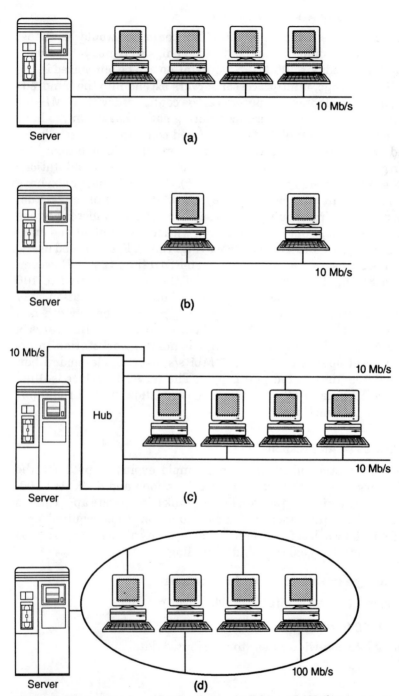

Figure 12.2 Stages of high-end LAN evolution. (*a*) Ethernet LAN; (*b*) microsegmentation; (*c*) hub arrangement; (*d*) FDDI LAN.

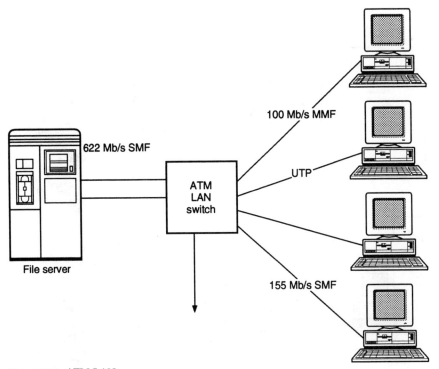

Figure 12.3 ATM LAN.

In general, the answer to this evolution question is to put in place a high-speed LAN backbone. Before ATM, the only reasonable LAN backbone alternative was to build an FDDI-based backbone. Now, ATM interfaces are being integrated into LAN hubs and routers, which enable users to maintain their existing LAN topologies while creating a scalable, high-speed premises backbone.[2] Figure 12.4 illustrates an example of the use of ATM as a LAN backbone network. Several concepts are illustrated in this example:

1. ATM interfaces can be built into existing hub and router products (see Chap. 11) which allow high-speed transport to and from the ATM backbone hub.

2. Survivability can be engineered into the architecture by using a dual-homing arrangement, whereby select routers or LAN hubs can have interfaces to multiple backbone hubs.

3. In some cases the backbone hub can perform as an ATM LAN hub as well.

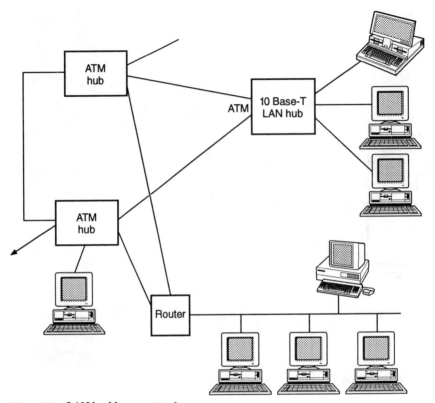

Figure 12.4 LAN backbone network.

12.2.3 ATM as a campus backbone network

The concepts of the previous section can be extended beyond in-trabuilding networking to a campus network environment. Figure 12.5 illustrates an ATM-based campus backbone network. Here, in-trabuilding backbones can be interconnected via fiber-optic facilities, providing a scalable, fault-tolerant backbone. The scalability of ATM interfaces and switches allows this network to grow through card swaps at the building hubs, without costly replacement of the hubs themselves.

12.2.4 Use of ATM in a wide area enterprise network

The previous two sections illustrated two possible backbone network evolution paths based upon the concepts of integration, scalability, and reuse of existing equipment. This section extends the discussion into wide area networking. Figure 12.6 illustrates a wide area corporate

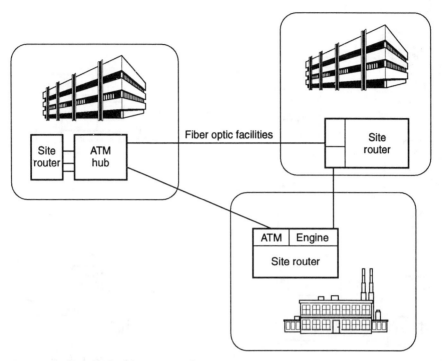

Fiber optic facilities

Site router — ATM hub

Site router

ATM | Engine

Site router

Figure 12.5 Campus backbone network.

network made up of parallel networks for LAN interconnection, voice traffic, videoconferencing, and data center connection. This network is based upon the use of leased lines connecting each site. The LAN interconnection network is T1-based. The corporate voice network uses a combination of leased lines and the public voice network for interconnection. The video traffic is limited to the two main sites with hub switches (although in practice many corporations use satellite-based transmission to achieve one-way video to several sites). The data center communications, illustrated here as a single host connected to two high-speed peripherals (these could be, for example, printers or high-speed storage devices[3]), is accomplished via dedicated facilities. Some integration is achieved by using T1/T3 multiplexers which use proprietary multiplexing schemes to consolidate the LAN interconnection and voice traffic on the same leased lines between locations 2 and 5.

Figure 12.7 illustrates the same network in an integrated fashion using premises-based ATM switching and multiplexing connected via leased lines. This scenario can improve upon the nonintegrated solution through either

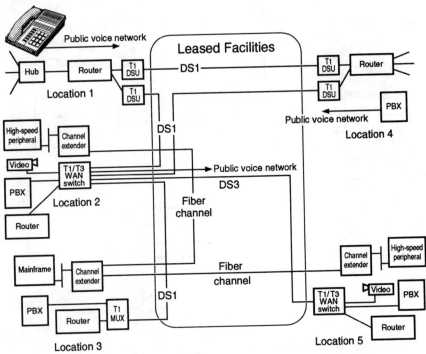

Figure 12.6 Wide area corporate network.

- Improving intersite throughput
- Increasing the availability of applications (e.g., videoconferencing) available at smaller locations
- Reducing the number of leased lines required

In this example, at least the first and third of these have been achieved. The data center channel extension traffic is not integrated with the other traffic, reducing the number of leased lines. Two-way videoconferencing has been added to locations 3 and 4.

Figure 12.8 illustrates an integrated corporate network achieved through using public network services. In this scenario, the number of access lines is further reduced from the leased-line scenario. In addition, the ATM hub switch at location 5 is not needed, and can be replaced by a much simpler multiplexer. This figure also shows the use of public frame relay service to interconnect the data traffic from location 1. Finally, this figure also illustrates the use of SMDS to enable interenterprise data networking.

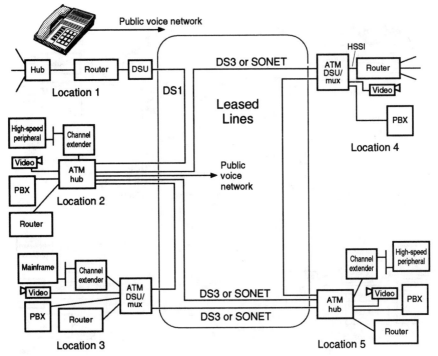

Figure 12.7 Integrated wide area network.

12.2.5 Medical imaging example

As an example of how these concepts can apply in a specific industry, this section discusses the use of ATM networking in a medical imaging context. Figure 12.9 illustrates

1. A medical center

2. An affiliated hospital located across town

3. A doctor's office

4. A remote site used for storage of x-rays

Before the availability of high-speed networking and PACS devices for digital storage and retrieval of images, several common activities that would take place at this hypothetical medical center are described below.

- X-rays were stored as film off-site, presumably in cheaper office space. When archived x-rays were required, they would be retrieved via

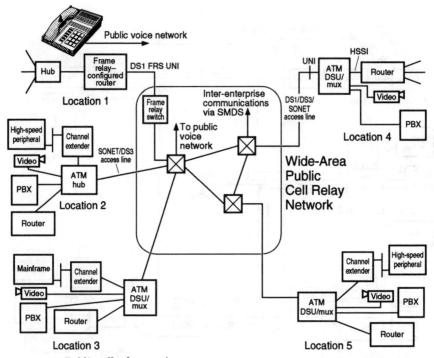

Figure 12.8 Public cell relay service.

courier (typically there are a number—say two—of scheduled "runs" each day between the hospital and the archive). Depending on the time of day, this could introduce a lengthy delay between when the doctor needed to consult the x-ray and when it was available.

- The affiliate hospital depended upon the medical center for training and consultation. Training required medical personnel to travel across town, resulting in an average of several hours of travel time per doctor or nurse each month. Remote consultation was also carried out via travel; either the personnel traveled or the medical records traveled (again, via scheduled courier service).

- Often, insurance companies require detailed documentation (e.g., copies of a patient's x-rays) before they make payment to the hospital. Again, requests would arrive via U.S. mail, and the records would be retrieved from the archives, copied, and mailed to the insurance company.

- Doctors had to be at the hospital to retrieve and view their admitted patients' records. If a complication developed when a doctor was not on-site, another physician had to handle it, or the doctor had to travel back to the hospital.

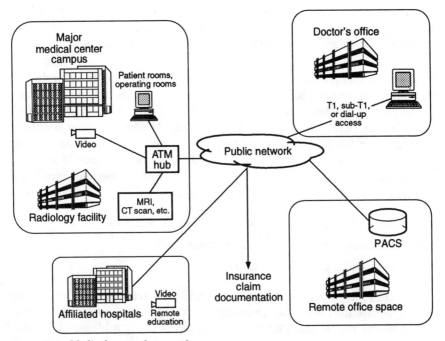

Figure 12.9 Medical network example.

Figure 12.9 illustrates how imaging and networking technologies can be applied to each of these activities. The use of digital storage of x-ray images coupled with high-speed networking can enable the near-instantaneous retrieval of archived images, thus reducing the amount of waiting time required for consultation. Videoconferencing can enable remote education between the medical center and the affiliate hospitals, reducing the amount of travel time previously required. Documentation can be quickly exchanged with insurance companies, resulting in shorter processing intervals. Finally, using inexpensive dial-up lines and SVGA graphics, doctors' offices can be equipped with the capability to remotely access patient records and x-rays. The reader may wish to refer to Ref. 4 for additional information of how ATM can be used in the imaging field.

12.3 Potential Pitfalls along the Evolution Path

Thus far, this chapter has described ways in which ATM cell relay may be employed as a key technology in the evolution of LANs, backbone networks, and WANs. However, there are a number of potential hurdles and roadblocks that can delay or deter the success of cell relay. The following are examples of potential roadblocks, all of which have occurred in the telecommunications industry in the recent past.

Lack of interoperability.   History has shown that in spite of industry standards, interoperability problems can exist if different manufacturers implement subsets (or supersets) of the required networking features. This has occurred, for example, when standards bodies included too many (or too few) features within their standards, without proper regard for the tradeoffs between desired features and time to market. To prevent lack of interoperability from becoming a serious roadblock requires that the standards bodies produce standards that fairly represent

1. The near-term capabilities of equipment developers

2. The abilities of public network carriers

3. The needs and desires of end users

For ATM standards, the first two conditions are being addressed by having equipment manufacturers and carriers participate in the standards-making processes. The third condition is being addressed by having users participate in the standards-setting process, mainly through the Enterprise Network Users Roundtable affiliated with The ATM Forum.

Lack of applications.   In many cases, networking technologies have been invented and available prior to the existence of any end-user application that truly required the new technology. This can result in slow acceptance of a new technology, which in turn results in manufacturers never being able to "ride the experience curve" to bring costs down. It is not clear that there is any one "killer application" that absolutely requires ATM technology; rather, ATM is envisioned for use as an integrating technology.

Rejuvenation of existing network technologies.   Advances in existing technologies may extend the life cycle of existing product lines and slow the acceptance of new technologies. An appropriate example for ATM is the introduction of "fast Ethernet" at 100-Mbits/s speeds and Ethernet switching. Wide acceptance, low cost, or ease of transition to these new technologies could hamper the acceptance of ATM as a high-end LAN technology.

Development of new technologies.   Technological innovation has been referred to in the strategic management literature as the "gale force of creative destruction,"[5] reflecting its potential for making an entire industry or, in this case, technology obsolete. An example of a possible new technology that could make ATM obsolete is photonic switching. However, photonic switching today in research laboratories is not yet at the level of progress that ATM was in *1986*, which could be an indication that it is a long way from viable commercial implementation on a large scale.

References

1. J. Herman and C. Serjak, "ATM Switches and Hubs Lead the Way to a New Era of Switched Internetworks," *Data Communications*, March 1993.
2. Johna Till Johnson, "ATM Comes Out of the Ether," *Data Communications*, March 1993.
3. G. Misukanis and J. Morin, "Channel Extenders: The Link to Long-Distance DASD," *Data Communications*, September 21, 1993.
4. D. Minoli, *Imaging in Corporate Environments: Technology and Communication*, McGraw-Hill, New York, 1994.
5. Jeffrey R. Williams, "How Sustainable Is Your Competitive Advantage?" *California Management Review*, Spring 1990.

Acronyms

AAL	ATM Adaptation Layer
AAL5 CPCS	ATM Adaptation Layer Type 5 Common Part Convergence Sublayer
AAL5 SAR	AAL5 Segmentation and Reassembly
AALCP	AAL Common Part
AALM	AAL Management
AIS	Alarm indication signal
API	Application programming interface
ARP	Address resolution protocol
ASN.1	Abstract syntax notation one
ATM DXI	ATM data exchange interface
ATM	Asynchronous transfer mode
B-ICI	Broadband intercarrier interface
B-ISDN	Broadband Integrated Services Digital Network
B-ISSI	Broadband interswitching system interface
B-LMI	Broadband local management interface
B-LT/ET	Broadband line terminator/exchange terminator
B-NT2	Broadband Network Termination 2
B-TE	Broadband terminal equipment
BAMM	Bi-directional asymmetric multipoint-to-multipoint
BAPM	Bidirectional asymmetric point-to-multipoint
BAPP	Bidirectional asymmetric point-to-point
BECN	Backward explicit congestion notification
BIP	Bit-interleaved parity
BISUP	Broadband ISDN User Part
BNI	Broadband-to-narrowband interface
BOM	Beginning of message
BSMM	Bidirectional symmetric multipoint-to-multipoint
BSPM	Bidirectional symmetric point-to-multipoint

BSPP	Bidirectional Symmetric Point-to-Point
BSS	Broadband switching system
BT	Broadband terminal
BT	Burst tolerance
CAC	Connection admission control
CAD	Computer-aided design
CalREN	California Research and Education Network
CAPs	Competitive access providers
CBR	Constant bit rate
CBRS	CBR service
CDV	Cell delay variation
CIR	Committed Information Rate
CLP	Cell loss priority
CMIP	Common Management Information Protocol
CMIS	Common Management Information Service
CNM	Customer network management
CNRI	Corporation for National Research Initiatives
COM	Continuation of message
COMPASS	Computer Program for Advanced Switching Services
CP	Common Part
CPAAL3/4	ATM Adaptation Layer Type 3/4 Common Part
CPCS	Common Part of Convergence Sublayer
CP	Control Plane
CPE	Customer premises equipment
CPI	Common part indicator
CRC	Cyclic redundancy check
CRS	Cell relay service
CS	Convergence Sublayer
DCC	Data communications channel
DFA	DXI frame address
DLCI	Data link connection identifier
DSU	Digital service unit
ESF	Extended superframe format
FDDI	Fiber Distributed Data Interface
FEBE	Far-end bit error
FECN	Forward explicit congestion notification
FERF	Far-end receive failure

FRBS	Frame relaying bearer service
GCRA	Generic cell rate algorithm
GFC	Generic flow control
HEC	Header error control
HPPI	High-performance parallel interface
IC	Interexchange carrier
IE	Information element
ILMI	Interim local management interface
ISDN	Integrated Services Digital Network
ISUP	ISDN User Part
IWF	Interworking function
IWU	Interworking unit
LATM	Local ATM
LCD	Loss of cell delineation
LEC	Local exchange carrier
LIS	Logical IP subnetwork
LMI	Local management interface
LOF	Loss of frame
LOP	Loss of pointer
LOS	Loss of signal
MBS	Maximum burst size
MIB	Management information base
MID	Message identification
MPEG II	Motion Picture Expert Group II
MSN	Monitoring cell sequence number
MTP	Message transfer part
N-BC	Narrowband bearer capability
N-IWU	N-ISDN interworking unit
NE	Network element
NNI	Network node interface
NREN	National Research and Engineering Network
NSFNET	National Science Foundation Network
OAM	Operations, administration, and maintenance
OCD	Out-of-cell delineation
OOF	Out of frame
OSIRM	Open Systems Interconnection Reference Model
OSS	Operations support system

PCI	Protocol control information
PCR	Peak cell rate
PDU	Protocol data unit
PLCP	Physical Layer convergence protocol
PMD	Physical medium–dependent
POI	Path overhead identifier
POTS	Plain old telephone service
PTI	Payload type indicator
PVC	Permanent virtual connection
QOS	Quality of service
RDI	Remote defect indicator
RMN	Remote multiplexer node
ROSE	Remote operations service element
SAP	Service access point
SAR	Segmentation and Reassembly Sublayer
SCR	Sustainable cell rate
SDT	Structured data transfer
SDU	Service data unit
SEAL	Simple and Efficient Adaptation Layer
SiVC	Signaling virtual channel
SMDS	Switched multimegabit data service
SNMP	Simple Network Management Protocol
SRTS	Synchronous residual time stamp
SSCF	Service-Specific Coordination Function
SSCOP	Service-specific Connection-Oriented Protocol
SSCS	Service-Specific Part of Convergence Sublayer
SSP	Service-Specific Part
STS-12c	Synchronous transport signal level 12, concatenated
STS-3c	Synchronous transport signal level 3, concatenated
SVC	Switched virtual connection
TCP/IP	Transmission Control Protocol/Internet Protocol
TMN	Telecommunications management network
TUC	Total user cell
UDT	Unstructured data transfer
UME	UNI management entity
UMM	Unidirectional multipoint-to-multipoint
UNI	User-network interface

UP	User Plane
UPC	Usage parameter control
UPM	Unidirectional point-to-multipoint
UPP	Unidirectional point-to-point
VBR	Variable bit rate
VC	Virtual channel
VCC	Virtual channel connection
VCI	Virtual channel identifier
VCL	Virtual channel link
VP	Virtual path
VPC	Virtual path connection
VPI	Virtual path identifier
VPL	Virtual path link
WAN	Wide area network

Index

ABOUT THE AUTHORS

DANIEL MINOLI is an expert in the data communications and telecommunications fields. He is the principal consultant at DVI Communications, Inc., an advisor to DataPro, and the author of numerous professional references, including *1st, 2nd, and Next Generation LANs*, published by McGraw-Hill.

MICHAEL VITELLA is a consultant at Bellcore specializing in the engineering and design of high-speed networks, services, and applications.